THE
JAZZ BOOK

**From New Orleans to Rock
and Free Jazz**

Development, Elements
Definition of Jazz
Musicians, Vocalists
Combos, Big Bands
Electric Jazz
Jazz-Rock of the Seventies
With an extensive Discography
and Index

THE
JAZZ BOOK

From NEW ORLEANS to ROCK and FREE JAZZ

By JOACHIM BERENDT
translated by DAN MORGENSTERN
and Helmut and Barbara Bredigkeit

Westport
LAWRENCE HILL & COMPANY, Publishers

Library of Congress Cataloging in Publication Data
Berendt, Joachim Ernst.
The jazz book.
1. Jazz music. I. Title.
ML3561.J3B4122   785.4'2'09   73-81750
ISBN *0-88208-027-X*
ISBN *0-88208-028-8 (pbk.)*

Copyright © Fischer Taschenbuch Verlag,
Frankfurt am Main, 1953, 1959, 1968, 1973.
English language translation and discography copyright © 1975
Lawrence Hill & Co. Inc., Publishers   New York • Westport
ISBN: 027-X (cloth); 028-8 (paper)
Library of Congress Catalog Card Number: 73-81750
First English Language edition 1975
Manufactured in the United States of America
4 5 6 7 8 9 10
Designed by Ray Freiman

One understands nothing
except through love.

GOETHE

You've got to love
to be able to play.

LOUIS ARMSTRONG

Jazz from Louis Armstrong
to Albert Ayler is new
music. The reality hasn't
really changed, only the
spectacle . . .

ANTHONY BRAXTON

For VERA

Table of Contents

Musical Examples and Tables

xi

Preface

IT HAS BEEN the aim in all editions of this book to show the whole range of what is jazz—from ragtime and New Orleans to the dominant styles and playing techniques of today. In this way, the span covering everything to be presented had to be stretched wider and wider—perhaps near the breaking point. How many young people today can appreciate the music of Scott Joplin and King Oliver as well as the music of the Mahavishnu Orchestra?

It is our goal to give an impression of the totality of jazz—free from the fanaticism and sectarianism which have been employed by partisans of older jazz styles against the new, and vice versa. This fanaticism has been a heavy burden from which jazz should be freed. Jazz has always been an eclectic music, but never more than today. Eclecticism is incompatible with sectarianism.

Because our primary concern is the total development, musicians dear to this or that reader may not get the coverage they deserve. This book would grow to gigantic proportions if we granted each musician space in exact ratio to his importance. This is also true of European jazz. Never before has it been as independent as today. Thus, a chapter dealing with it has been added to the book. But this chapter is not only the last in this book; it should be the beginning of a yet-to-be-written volume about European jazz. For this reason, we decided not to use the systematic approach in "European Jazz Today" that we apply in the other chapters.

The aim was to present only facts in accordance with the present internationally accepted position of jazz criticism and scholarship. The many "side theories" were not dealt with, and my own theories are expressly identified as such. Essentially, this applies to the swing phenomenon, and also to some thoughts on improvisation, blues, the shift of sound production toward phrasing, the problem of tension in jazz, the development of the drums, and to the definition of jazz. An attempt has been made to measure jazz by its own scale, i.e., to avoid yardsticks taken from other musical cultures—Europe or Africa, for example. Technical terms from European music are to be understood not as external measuring devices, but rather as a vocabulary shared with the reader which can help to clarify facts.

Generally speaking, there are as few record references as possible within the body of the text. There is too much fluctuation on the jazz record market; even most important records, which should be constantly available, frequently are not. For this reason, there is a discography at the end of the book, compiled by Achim Hebgen as follows: Every musician of importance mentioned in the book is represented by at least one record; the outstanding figures by their most important works, provided these are currently available.

Various editions of this book have been published in 11 languages, and altogether almost one million copies have been printed. There have been suggestions and critiques from all sides. Much of it has found its way into this edition. I am especially grateful to Shoichi Yui, who translated the two Japanese editions, and to Dan Morgenstern, who translated the American edition of 1962 and checked over the present one. Both are more than translators; both stimulate the author.

The first book in this series was published in Germany in 1953, the second in 1958, the third in 1968. This is the fourth. Partial revisions and additions were made for a Mexican translation in 1961, for an American edition (*The New Jazz Book,* Hill & Wang, New York) in 1962, and for the two Japanese editions (1965 and 1971.)

It is no exaggeration, then, to say that 20 years of jazz history have left their mark on this book. Each of the four main editions was written in direct contact with the dominant style of its time: the first with bebop, the second with cool jazz, the third with free jazz, and the present one with the jazz of the seventies.

In 1968, we planned to publish the next revised edition in ten years—1978. But the American publisher, Lawrence Hill & Co. Publishers, Inc., expressed an immediate desire for an edition updated to the latest point of development—an initiative for which I am grateful. Only while I was working on this new edition did the necessity for a new version of the book become clear. In the five years between 1968 and 1972, nearly twice as many additions and new sec-

xiv

tions had to be written as in the ten years from 1958 to 1967. I can only interpret this as proof of an especially intense vitality of jazz in this period. The devoted jazz fan will surely realize what was written in 1953, in 1958, in 1968, and in 1972. I do, however, want to oblige the readers who on the occasion of the 1968 edition said it should be noted what has been added.

Added, for one thing, were the new chapters: 1970, Soprano Saxophone, Flute, Keyboards, Violin, Male and Female Jazz Singers (though parts of these two chapters appeared in earlier editions), "European Jazz Today;" as well as the sections from "Gil Evans and George Russell" to the end of "The Big Bands of Jazz;" and, in "The Jazz Combos," the sections from "Ornette and After" to "Electric Jazz."

Extensive additions which cast light on the jazz of the seventies were made to the chapters on John Coltrane (Alice Coltrane) and Miles Davis, and to the blues chapter, in which the influence of the blues on the development of popular music required new treatment.

All chapters on the elements and instruments of jazz were brought up to date, especially the sections dealing with the central instruments: tenor saxophone, piano, guitar, and drums. The chapters on Bessie Smith, Louis Armstrong, and Duke Ellington were rewritten and/or expanded.

But even chapters and sections retained from earlier editions have been changed, shortened, expanded, revised, etc. Only 60 pages could remain unchanged from the 1968 edition.

More than 150 new musicians and groups are introduced in this edition.

In two of the earlier editions, predictions were made about the future of jazz. It is instructive to read them today. Nearly all the predictions have come true. Long passages that—in 1953 and 1958—were put in the future tense, as possibilities, could now be rephrased almost word for word in the past tense, about free jazz.

Necessarily, a book like this draws on works which preceded it. I am especially indebted to Leonard Feather's *Encyclopedia of Jazz* to André Hodeir's *Jazz—Its Evolution and Essence;* to the two anthologies edited by Nat Shapiro and Nat Hentoff, *Hear Me Talkin' to Ya* and *The Jazz Makers* and to Charles Keil's *Urban Blues*. Information not taken from these works for which a source is not specifically mentioned comes from articles in the jazz magazines *down beat* (U.S.A.), *Melody Maker* (England), *Jazz Hot* and *Jazz Magazine*

(France) and, first and foremost, from the source which remains the most important for a jazz critic: personal contact with musicians. It is my conviction that creative musicians know more about the nature of jazz than all the theoreticians.

It was, naturally, our intention to use all quotations in their original English version for the American edition. Only when a quotation was from German or French sources and the original unknown were quotations originally in English translated back into that language.

I am thankful to Achim Hebgen, who not only compiled the discography, but also was a helpful contributor to all phases of the development of this book; to Gerhard and Rosemarie Kühn and to my wife, who has been of great help both editorially and secretarially.

I cannot claim to have avoided all errors. Nor can I expect that my personal interpretations will be accepted by everyone. But this book, in its three German and many foreign editions and versions, has served so many jazz fans—and readers outside the field—that I felt it a challenge and duty to carry on.

Baden-Baden, Summer 1973   J.E.B.

THE
JAZZ BOOK

**From New Orleans to Rock
and Free Jazz**

THE STYLES OF JAZZ

The Styles of Jazz

JAZZ HAS always been the concern of a minority—always. Even in the twenties and thirties, the jazz of creative black musicians was—except for very few recordings—recognized by only a few. Still, taking an active interest in jazz means working for a majority, because the popular music of our times feeds on jazz: All the music we hear in TV series and on top-40 radio, in hotel lobbies and on elevators, in commercials and in movies; all the music to which we dance, from Charleston to rock; all those sounds that daily engulf us—all that music comes from jazz.

Taking an active interest in jazz means improving the quality of the "sounds around us"—the level of musical quality, which implies, if there is any justification in talking about musical quality, the spiritual, intellectual, human quality—the level of our consciousness. In these times, when musical sounds accompany the take-off of a plane as well as a detergent sales pitch, the "sounds around us" directly influence our way of life, our life styles. That is why we can say that taking an active interest in jazz means carrying some of the power, warmth, and intensity of jazz into our lives.

Because of this, there is a direct and sometimes demonstrable connection between the different kinds, forms, and styles of jazz on the one hand and the periods and spaces of time of their creation on the other hand.

The most impressive thing about jazz—aside from its musical value—is in my opinion its stylistic development. The evolution of jazz shows the continuity, logic, unity, and inner necessity which characterize all true art. This development constitutes a whole—and those who single out one phase and view it as either uniquely valid or

3

as an aberration, destroy this wholeness of conception. They distort that unity of large-scale evolution without which one can speak of fashions, but not of styles. It is my conviction that the styles of jazz are genuine, and reflect their own particular times in the same sense that classicism, baroque, romanticism, and impessionism reflect their respective periods in European concert music.

Almost all great jazz musicians have felt the connection between their playing styles and the times in which they live. The untroubled joy of Dixieland corresponds to the days just prior to World War I. The restlessness of the "roaring twenties" comes to life in Chicago style. Swing embodies the massive standardization of life before World War II; perhaps, to quote Marshall Stearns, Swing "was the answer to the American—and very human—love of bigness." Bebop captures the nervous restlessness of the forties. Cool jazz often reflects the resignation of men who live well, yet know that H-bombs are being stockpiled. Hard bop is full of protest, soon turned into conformity by the fashion for funk and soul music. This protest gains an uncompromising, often angry urgency in free jazz. After this, in the jazz of the seventies, there is a new phase of consolidation—not in the sense of resignation, but rather in the sense of painfully acquired wisdom, of wanting to accomplish the possible short of chaos and self-destruction. What has been said in such a generalized and simplified way here is even more applicable to the many different styles of individual musicians and bands.

This is why so many jazz musicians have viewed attempts at reconstructing past jazz styles with scepticism. They know that historicism runs counter to the nature of jazz. Jazz stands and falls on being alive, and whatever lives, changes. When Count Basie's music became a world-wide success in the fifties, Lester Young, who had been one of the leading soloists of the old Basie band, was asked to participate in a recording with his old teammates for the purpose of reconstructing the Basie style of the thirties. "I can't do it," Lester said. "I don't play that way any more. I play different; I live different. This is later. That was then. We change, move on."

Around 1890—Ragtime

Jazz originated in New Orleans; a truism, with all that is true and false about such statements. It is true that New Orleans was the most

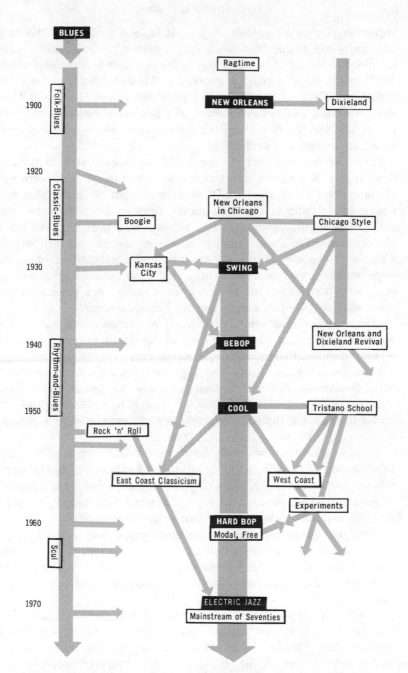

Table 1: The development of jazz (with the blues as the backbone).

important city in the genesis of jazz. It is false that it was the only one. Jazz—the music of a continent, a century, a civilization—was too much in the air to be reducible to the patented product of a single city. Similar ways of playing evolved in Memphis and St. Louis, in Dallas and Kansas City, in many other cities of the South and Midwest. And this, too, is the hallmark of a genuine style: different people in different places making the same—or similar—artistic discoveries independently of each other.

It has become customary to speak of New Orleans style as the first style in jazz. But before New Orleans style had developed, there was ragtime. Its capital was not New Orleans but Sedalia, Missouri, where Scott Joplin had settled. Joplin, born in Texas in 1868, was the leading ragtime composer and pianist—and thus we have made the decisive point about ragtime: It was composed, pianistic music. Since it was composed, it lacks one essential characteristic of jazz—improvisation. Yet, ragtime swings, and so it is considered part of jazz. And the practice of not only interpreting rags but also using them as themes for jazz improvisations began quite early.

Ragtime was written in the tradition of nineteenth-century piano music. It may adhere to the trio form of the classic minuet, or consist of several musical strophes in succession, connected in the fashion of a Strauss waltz. Pianistically, too, ragtime reflects the nineteenth century. Everything relevant to that time can be found in it—from Schubert, Chopin and, most of all, Liszt, to marches and polkas—all recast in the black rhythmic conception and dynamic way of playing. Ragtime is, as the name suggests, ragged time.

Ragtime found an especially fertile field in the camps of the migrant laborers engaged in building railroads. Ragtime was heard everywhere—in Sedalia and Kansas City, in St. Louis and Texas, Joplin's home state. The composers of rags hammered their pieces into player-piano rolls, which were distributed by the thousands.

That was before the time of the phonograph and, for a long period, little was known about all this. Only in the fifties—sometimes quite accidentally in places like antique stores and junk shops—were substantial numbers of old piano rolls rediscovered and transferred to records.

Aside from Joplin, there were many other ragtime creators: Tom Turpin, a St. Louis bar owner; James Scott, a theater organist in Kansas City; Charles L. Johnson, Louis Chauvin, and especially Eubie Blake. Even at 90, Blake was a spectacular success at the great 1973 "Newport in New York" festival, and in this decade, Blake has made thousands of young people "rag-conscious" once again.

There were several whites among the great rag pianists around the turn of the century, and it is significant that even experts were not able to detect differences in playing style between blacks and whites. Ragtime, as Orrin Keepnews once put it, is "on the cool side."

Scott Joplin was a master of melodic invention. He was amazingly productive, and his many rags include such melodies as "Maple Leaf Rag," which are still alive. In Joplin—as in ragtime per se—the old European tradition merged with the black rhythmic feeling. Ragtime, more than any other form of jazz, may be described as "white music —played black."

Among the first musicians to liberate themselves from the strictures of the composer-imposed interpretation of rags and take a freer and more jazzlike approach to melodic material was Jelly Roll Morton, one of the important musicians with whom the New Orleans tradition begins. "I invented jazz in 1902," he once claimed, and on his business card he described himself as "creator of ragtime." Both statements are hyperbole, but Morton's importance can hardly be overestimated.

In Morton, we recognize for the first time the decisive fact that the personality of the performing musician is more important in jazz than the material contributed by the composer.

Jelly Roll carried the ragtime tradition to the Chicago of the roaring twenties; even to California. Other pianists—James P. Johnson, Willie "The Lion" Smith, and young Fats Waller—kept ragtime, or at least the ragtime tradition, alive in New York during the twenties. At that time there was scarcely a pianist—aside from the boogie-woogie players—whose origins could not be traced, in one way or another, to ragtime. Even some boogie pianists (more about them later) used ragtime themes or elements.

1900—New Orleans

At the turn of the century, New Orleans was a witches' cauldron of peoples and races. The city had been under Spanish and French rule prior to the Louisiana Purchase. Frenchmen and Spaniards, followed by Englishmen and Italians, and lastly joined by Germans and

Slavs, faced the descendants of the countless Africans brought here as slaves. And among the black population as well there were differences of nationality and culture no less significant than those, say, between the whites from England and from Spain.

All these voluntary and involuntary immigrants loved first of all their own music: what they wanted to keep alive as sounds of home. In New Orleans, people sang British folk songs, danced Spanish dances, played French dance and ballet music, and marched to the strains of brass bands based on Prussian or French models. In the many churches could be heard the hymns and chorales of Puritans and Catholics, Baptists and Methodists—and mingled with all these sounds were the "shouts" of the black street vendors, and the black dances and rhythms. Deep into the eighties, blacks congregated periodically in Congo Square to perform Voodoo rites—thus preserving a cult with origins in ancient, half-forgotten African traditions. Recent converts to Christianity, they celebrated the new God in song and dance much as they had honored the deities of their native land.

All this created an atmosphere which made the New Orleans of those days a symbol of strange, exotic romanticism for travellers from all parts of the earth. It is certainly a "myth" that this city in the Mississippi delta was the sole birthplace of jazz, but New Orleans was indeed a point where many important aspects of the music first crystallized. New Orleans was a watershed—for the music of the countryside, such as the work songs of the black plantation laborers; for the spirituals which were sung during the religious services for which they gathered under open skies; and for the old "primitive" blues-folk songs. All these things merged in the earliest forms of jazz.

W. C. Handy, the composer of blues, relates that the music played in Memphis around 1905 was not very different from that of New Orleans. "But we didn't discover until 1917 that New Orleans had such music too," Handy says. "Any and every circus band played this way." The entire Mississippi delta was full of the new sounds— all rising independent of each other. "The River and the City were equally important to jazz."

New Orleans, in spite of this, held a special place. Well into the thirties about half the important jazz musicians came from there. Four reasons may have been decisive:

First, the old French-Spanish urban culture of the Delta city.

Second, the tensions and challenges arising from the fact that, as we shall see, two decidedly different black populations confronted each other here.

Third, the lively musical life of the city, in terms of European serious and popular music, with which the blacks constantly came in touch.

And finally, the fact that all these varied elements came together in Storyville, the city's red-light district, without prejudice or class consciousness.

The two black populations of New Orleans were the Creoles and the American Negroes. The Creoles—in the geographical sense—were just as "American" as other Negroes—perhaps even more so. The Creoles of Louisiana emerged from the old French Colonial culture. They were not—like the other blacks—descendants of slaves who gained freedom at the end of the Civil War. Their ancestors had been free much longer. They had been freed by rich French planters or merchants for reasons of distinguished service. The term "Free Negro" was an important one in old New Orleans.

The Creole Negroes had made French culture their own. Many were wealthy businessmen. Their main language was not English but "Creole": a French patois with admixtures of Spanish and African words. Their names were French: Alphonse Picou, Sidney Bechet, Barney Bigard, Albert Nicholas, Buddy Petit, Freddie Keppard, Papa and Louis deLisle Nelson, Kid Ory, etc. It was an honor to be a Creole. Jelly Roll Morton takes great pains in his autobiography to make clear that he is a Creole and that his real name is Ferdinand Joseph La Menthe.

Compared to the Creoles, the American Negroes were more "African." Their masters were of Anglo-Saxon origin, and thus they were not exposed to the more liberal social attitudes of the French-Spanish orbit. The "American" Negroes constituted the black proletariat of New Orleans. The Creoles looked down on them with a particular class- and color-consciousness which "at that time was even more prejudiced to other Negroes than the attitude of white people to the colored generally was," as guitarist Johnny St. Cyr put it.

Consequently, there are two very different groups of New Orleans musicians, and the difference finds expression in the music. The Creole group was more cultured, the American had more vitality. The main instrument of the French group was the clarinet, which has a great tradition in France. This old French woodwind tradition remained alive well into the thirties in the playing of the leading Swing clarinetists.

In New Orleans itself, the French influence can hardly be overestimated. Almost everything which gave the city the fascinating atmosphere without which its jazz life would have been inconceivable stems from France. Thus, there is the famous "Mardi gras," which has become the expression of the city's lust for life. Even the funerals, during which a band escorts the deceased to the cemetery with sad music, and then leads the procession back home with joyful sounds, derive from a French custom; it prevails to this day in rural districts of Southern France.

In the mingling of the many ethnic and musical strains in New Orleans, which occurred almost automatically in the laissez-faire climate of Storyville, New Orleans style was born. It is characterized by a "free counterpoint" played by the three melody instruments: cornet (or trumpet), trombone, and clarinet. The lead is taken by the brilliant sound of the cornet, effectively contrasted by the heavy, weighty trombone. The clarinet entwines the two brasses in an intricate pattern of melodic lines. This front line is supported by the rhythm section: string or brass, bass, drums, banjo or guitar, and occasionally, piano.

The early New Orleans rhythm is still very close to European march rhythm: The peculiar "floating" effect of jazz rhythm, stemming from the fact that 1 and 3 remain the strong beats, but 2 and 4 are accented, is as yet absent. The stress is still on 1 and 3, just as in a march.

The early New Orleans jazz bands resembled the marching and circus bands of the day in other respects, too, such as instrumentation and social function.

New Orleans style is the first example of "hot" playing. *Hot* connotes the emotional warmth and intensity of the music, and has come to stand for the peculiar sound, phrasing, "attack," and vibrato which characterize this style. From that point on, all this becomes individualized. The instrument is not so much played as made to "talk"— to express the individual feelings of the musician.

1910—Dixieland

In New Orleans, playing jazz was not exclusively a privilege of the black man. There seem to have been white bands almost from the start. "Papa" Jack Laine led bands in New Orleans from 1891. He is known as the "father" of white jazz. Bands traveled through the city on carts—known as band wagons—or marched along the streets. When two bands met, a contest or "battle" ensued. It sometimes happened that Negro and white bands became engaged in such contests, and when the white band was led by Papa Laine, it often "blew out" its opponent.

From the earliest time, there was a white style of playing jazz: less expressive, but sometimes better versed technically. The melodies were smoother, the harmony "purer," the sonorities not so unorthodox. There were fewer sliding notes, less expressive vibrato, less glissandi. Whenever these effects were used, there was an element of self-consciousness involved, and the music approached the eccentric, even the downright comic. In white jazz, the ability to play "legitimate" is always implicit, whereas the black style, whether joyful or blue, is integral.

All the successful early white bands stem from Papa Laine. And there is no doubt that the first successful groups in jazz were white: first and foremost the Original Dixieland Jazz Band, and then the New Orleans Rhythm Kings. The ODJB, as it has come to be known, with its punchy, collective style (there were almost no solos), made famous many early jazz standards. Among them were "Tiger Rag" and "Original Dixieland One-Step" (recorded in 1917) and "At the Jazz Band Ball" (recorded in 1919). The New Orleans Rhythm Kings, with their two outstanding soloists, Leon Rappolo, clarinet, and Georg Brunis, trombone, devoted more room to solo improvisation. They first recorded in 1922, and became famous in the early twenties.

In 1917, the ODJB played at Reisenweber's Restaurant on Columbus Circle in New York and made a tremendous hit. From that time on, the word "jazz"—first usually spelled "jass"—became known to the general public. Tom Brown, leader of a white band in Chicago in 1915, claims to have used the word publicly for the first time. But it appears as early as 1913 in a San Francisco newspaper, in reference to music. Prior to that, "jass" (and the earlier "jasm" and "gism") were in use as slang expressions for speed and energy in athletic pursuits—and probably in sexual contexts as well.

It has become customary to label all New Orleans white jazz "Dixieland," thus separating it from essential New Orleans style, but the borderlines remain fluid. Especially in later years, with black musicians playing in white bands or vice versa, it seldom makes sense to argue about which style is being played.

With ragtime, New Orleans and Dixieland, the history of jazz begins. What was earlier belongs to what Marshall Stearns has called "jazz prehistory." In Germany, Alfons M. Dauer has researched large amounts of material concerning this prehistory. The pricelessness of his work becomes clear if one sees it as material essentially pertaining to the African roots of and the rudimentary developing stages toward jazz, not as actually characteristic of jazz.

Jazz does not belong to Africa, where it was unknown at its time of origin, and where until this day it is little understood, albeit appreciated. As late as 1957, the American clarinetist Tony Scott was forced to conclude: "The musical level of the African jazz musician is not high, but they do all they can to improve themselves, in spite of a lack of opportunity to hear and learn about jazz." The most often cited statement in this context is Barry Ulanov's: "There is more of the sound of jazz in mid-European Gypsy fiddling than in a whole corps of African drummers." To which Leonard Feather adds: "In melodic and harmonic construction, the early jazz bears considerably more resemblance to such tunes of the 1850's as 'Arkansas Traveler' and 'Turkey in the Straw' than to any known African music."

Jazz was born in the encounter between black and white. That is why it originated where this meeting took place in the most intensive fashion: in the United States' South. Until this day, jazz is conceivable only in terms of this interaction. It loses its fundamental rationale when one or the other element is overemphasized, or even given a status of exclusiveness, as has been done.

The contact between the races, which has been so important in the evolution and development of jazz, symbolizes that spirit of "togetherness" per se which characterizes jazz in musical, national, international, social, sociological, political, expressive, aesthetic, ethical and ethnological terms.

1920—Chicago

We have chosen to divide the evolution of jazz into decades for the purpose of over-all perspective. To be sure, ragtime and New Orleans were alive at the beginning of our century, but both styles were still being played later. On the other hand, what is decisive is not how long a style was cultivated, but when it originated and when it unfolded its greatest vitality and musical power. From this point of view, it is a fact that a new style has come into being roughly every ten years—and most frequently at the beginning of each decade.

The essential things about jazz in the twenties are three: the great days of New Orleans musicians in Chicago, classic blues, and Chicago style.

The development of New Orleans jazz in Chicago is generally connected with the entry of the United States into World War I. This connection appears somewhat dubious, but may, along with other factors, have played a certain role. New Orleans became a war port. The Secretary of the Navy viewed the goings on in Storyville as a danger to the morale of his troops. Storyville was closed by official decree.

This decree deprived not only the ladies of Storyville but also many musicians of their daily bread. Many left town. Most of them went to Chicago. The "Windy City" on Lake Michigan had previously been a source of fascination for many New Orleans musicians. Now came the great exodus of New Orleans musicians to Chicago, and it is clear that this was only a part of the general exodus of blacks from South to North. It developed that the first jazz style, though called New Orleans, actually had its really great period in the Chicago of the twenties. It was in Chicago that the most famous New Orleans jazz recordings were made, as the phonograph became increasingly popular after World War I.

King Oliver was the leader of the most important New Orleans Band in Chicago. It was here that Louis Armstrong formed his Hot Five and Hot Seven, Jelly Roll Morton his Red Hot Peppers, Johnny Dodds his New Orleans Wanderers, etc. What is known as New Orleans style today is not the archaic and barely recorded jazz which existed in New Orleans in the first two decades of this century, but the music made by New Orleans musicians in Chicago during the third decade.

The blues also had its great period in the Chicago of the twenties. Certainly blues songs existed long before there was jazz—at least from the middle of the 19th century. In those days, they were heard in the rural districts of the South, probably without a steady jazz beat and not yet in the standard 12-bar pattern which characterizes the blues today. Itinerant blues singers traveled—as they still do today

—from town to town, from plantation to plantation, with a banjo (or guitar) and a bundle containing all their worldly possessions, singing those songs with the drawn-out "blue" notes known today as country or "primitive" blues.

When the first marching bands began to play in New Orleans, there was a difference between their budding "jazz" and the blues. But soon the rural blues began to flow into the mainstream of jazz, and from then on jazz and blues become so interwoven that, as Ernest Borneman has written, all of jazz is "nothing but the application of the blues to European music, or vice versa." Even the most modern and free jazz musician of today is indebted to the blues.

The twenties are considered the period of "classic" blues. Bessie Smith was its greatest singer. In later chapters, Bessie Smith herself and the harmony, melody, and form of the blues will be discussed. It is with good reason that the blues is treated in a special chapter as an "element of jazz." It was not only a certain style of jazz in the early times, but has left its mark on all forms of jazz and on the whole history of the music. The intention here is to give a summary of the development of jazz in its entirety for easier orientation in the following chapters.

Around the great jazz instrumentalists and blues singers from New Orleans there developed in Chicago a jazz life hardly less active than that of New Orleans in the Golden Age. Centered around the South Side, Chicago's black district, it lacked the happy exuberance of the old New Orleans days but reflected the hectic pace of the metropolis and, increasingly, the problems of racial discrimination.

Stimulated by the jazz life of the South Side, young white high school and college students, amateurs and professional musicians, began to develop what has been called Chicago style. They had become so enthused by the greats of New Orleans jazz that they wanted to emulate their style. As imitation their music was unsuccessful; instead they came up with something new: Chicago style. In it, the profusion of melodic lines, so typical of New Orleans style, is more or less absent. The voicings, if there is more than one line, are neatly parallel. The individual has become the ruler. From this point on, the solo becomes increasingly important in jazz. Many Chicago-style recordings consist of hardly more than a sequence of solos.

Only now the saxophone, which to many laymen represents jazz incarnate, begins to gain importance. Chicago may be considered the second "cool" style of jazz (the first being piano ragtime). Bix Beiderbecke is the foremost representative of this style. In the chapter about him, it will be discussed at greater length.

1930—Swing

The older styles of jazz are grouped together under the heading "two-beat jazz." Toward the end of the twenties the two-beat styles seemed all but exhausted. In Harlem, and even more in Kansas City, a new way of playing developed around 1928-29. With the second great exodus of jazz history—the journey from Chicago to New York —Swing begins. Swing may be characterized as "four-beat jazz," since it puts stress on all four beats of the bar. This is true in general, but as is so often the case in jazz, there are confusing exceptions. Louis Armstrong (and some Chicago-style players) were already conversant with four-beat style in the twenties. On the other hand, Jimmie Lunceford's big band at the height of the Swing era employed a beat that was simultaneously 2/4 and 4/4.

The word "swing" is a key term in jazz, used in two different senses. This may lead to a certain amount of confusion. First swing connotes a rhythmic element from which jazz derives the tension classical music gets from its formal structure. This swing is present in all styles, phases, and periods of jazz. It is so essential that it has been said that if music does not swing, it is not jazz.

The other use of the term refers to the dominant jazz style of the thirties—the style through which jazz won its greatest commercial success. Thus Benny Goodman became "the King of Swing." In order to avoid confusion, the *style* Swing will be capitalized throughout, while lower-case swing will connote the rhythmic element.

One feature of the Swing era was the development of big bands. In the Kansas City band of Bennie Moten (and later Count Basie), the "riff" style developed. This was an application of the old, important call-and-response pattern (originating from Africa) to the sections of a large jazz band. These sections are trumpets, trombones, and saxes. Another contribution to big-band jazz was made by the white Chicago style: a more "European" approach to the music. In Benny Goodman's band, the most diversified styles flowed together: some New Orleans tradition, through Fletcher Henderson, who arranged for the band; the riff technique of Kansas City; and that white precision and training through which this brand of jazz lost much in vitality.

On the other hand, the easy melodic quality and clean intonation of Goodman's band made it possible to "sell" jazz to a mass audience. It only seems to be a contradiction that the individual soloist gained in importance alongside of the development of big bands. Jazz has always been simultaneously collective and individualistic. That jazz, more than any other music, can be both at one and the same time, clarifies much about its nature. This is due to the "sociological phenomenon" of jazz, which mirrors the social situation of modern man.

Thus, the thirties also became the era of great soloists: the tenor saxists Coleman Hawkins and Chu Berry; the clarinetist Benny Goodman; the drummers Gene Krupa, Cozy Cole and Sid Catlett; the pianists Fats Waller and Teddy Wilson; the alto saxists Benny Carter and Johnny Hodges; the trumpeters Roy Eldridge, Bunny Berigan, and Rex Stewart; and many, many more . . .

Often these two tendencies—the orchestral and the soloistic—merged. Benny Goodman's clarinet seemed all the more glamorous against the backdrop of his big band. Louis Armstrong's trumpet stood out in bold relief when accompanied by his big ensemble. And the voluminous tone of Coleman Hawkins' or Chu Berry's tenor sax seemed to gain from contrast to the "hard" sound of Fletcher Henderson's big band.

1940—Bebop

Toward the end of the thirties, Swing had become a gigantic business enterprise. It has been called the "greatest music business of all-time" (which was true then, but the record sales of the thirties and forties are minimal compared to the dimensions of today's music business). The word "swing" became a marketing device for all sorts of goods, from cigarettes to articles of female clothing, while the music, conforming to general commercial demands, often became a matter of endlessly repeated clichés.

As is so often the case in jazz when a style or way of playing becomes too commercialized, the evolution turned in the opposite direction. A group of musicians who had something new to say—something radically new—found each other in a healthy reaction against the general Swing fashion.

This new music developed—at first in spurts—originally in Kansas City and then, most of all, in the musicians' hangouts in Harlem (particularly Minton's Playhouse) and once again at the beginning of a decade. Contrary to what has been claimed, this new music did *not* develop when a group of musicians banded together to create something new, at whatever cost, because the old was no longer a draw. The old style drew very well—it was still the "greatest music business of all time." Nor is it true that the new jazz style was shaped as a conscious effort by an interrelated group of musicians. The new style was formed in the minds and instruments of different musicians in different places, independent of each other. But Minton's became a focal point—as New Orleans had been 40 years earlier.

The new style was eventually named bebop, a word which mirrored, onomatopoetically, the vocalization of the then best-loved interval of the music: the flatted fifth. The term "bebop" came into being spontaneously when someone attempted to "sing" these melodic leaps. There are as many theories about the origin of the word as there are about most jazz expressions. Most of them seem dubious.

The flatted fifth became the most important interval of bebop—or, as it was soon called, bop. Until then, this device would have been felt to be erroneous, or at least wrong-sounding, although it might have been used in passing chords, or for the special harmonic effects which Duke Ellington or Willie "The Lion" Smith liked to use as early as in the twenties. But now it characterized an entire style, as the narrow harmonic base of earlier jazz forms was constantly broadened. Within ten or 12 years (as we shall see) the flatted fifth had become a "blue note," as common as the open thirds and sevenths familiar to the blues.

The most important musicians who gathered at Minton's were Thelonious Monk, piano; Kenny Clarke, drums; Charlie Christian, guitar; trumpeter Dizzy Gillespie and altosaxist Charlie Parker. The latter was to become the real genius of modern jazz, as Louis Armstrong was the genius of traditional jazz.

One of these musicians—Christian—not only belongs among the founders of modern jazz but also among those who fashioned from Swing the foundations for its development. There is a whole group of such "pioneers"; at once the last generation of Swing and the pathbreakers for bop. Among trumpeters, it is Roy Eldridge; among pianists, Clyde Hart; among tenors, Lester Young; among bassists, Jimmy Blanton; among drummers, Jo Jones and Dave Tough; among guitarists, Charlie Christian.

To the listener of that time, the sounds characteristic of bebop seemed to be racing, nervous phrases which occasionally appeared as melodic fragments. Every unnecessary note was excluded. Everything was highly concentrated. As a bop musician once said: "Everything that is obvious is excluded." It is a kind of musical shorthand, and one must listen as one would read a stenographic transcript, establishing ordered relationships from a few hasty signs. To be sure, one had to listen to a good deal of bop to develop this facility, and due to this bop in its early years encountered a good deal of misunderstanding. But this holds true for all art music—only music without artistic merit is immediately comprehensible.

Under the influence of the then avant-garde bop sound, many friends of jazz were led astray in their approach to the evolution of the music. With great determination, they oriented themselves backwards, towards the basic forms of jazz. "Simple" music was demanded. There was a New Orleans renaissance—or, as it was called, "revival"—which spread all over the world.

This development began as a sound reconsideration of the roots of jazz—the tradition which to this day nourishes jazz in all its forms and phases. But soon the revival led to a simplified and cliché-ridden "traditional" jazz from which black musicians turned away. (With the exception of the surviving New Orleans jazzmen, for whom traditional jazz was the logical form of expression, no important black musicians participated in the Dixieland revival—strange as this may sound to some.) Amateurs often worked against the commercialization of Dixieland, but regularly themselves fell victims to it as they attained professional status. In the fifties, the Dixieland revival more and more became the domain of white amateurs.

After World War II, the "jazz boîtes" in Saint-German-des-Prés became the bulwarks of the traditional movement, fortified with existentialist philosophy. But soon the young existentialists discovered that their philosophy was better suited to a music which did not reflect the happy, carefree attitudes of the early years of the century, but rather the unrest of their own times. They gravitated toward more contemporary jazz forms, and the center of the movement shifted to England. In that country, Dixieland concerts in the fifties were organized with the same commercial effort and success as presentations of rock and roll singers.

In this section, bebop and the Dixieland revival have been contrasted in the same way that they appeared to be in contrast to each other to jazz fans at that time: as extremes of antagonistic opposition. Today—and actually since the genesis of free jazz in the sixties —these poles have approached each other, for today's young listener can no longer appreciate this contrast. To him, Charlie Parker is almost as much part of the jazz tradition as Louis Armstrong.

In describing bebop, we have used terms like "racing," "nervous," "melodic fragments," "cypher," "hasty." But in the face of what is "racing," "nervous," "fragmented," and "hasty" in today's scene, most of the jazz of the forties seems of almost classic completeness to the young listener of our times. One can only hope that listeners and critics of today's jazz learn from this development and use greater caution in the application of extreme words and concepts. The critics who foresaw the "end of jazz" or even the "end of music" in reaction to the "nervousness" of bop seem a bit ridiculous today, but there were a lot of them once. They are here today, too, in reaction to what today seems "nervous" and loud.

1950—Cool; Hard Bop

Toward the end of the forties, the unrest and excitement of bop were more and more replaced by a tendency toward calm and smoothness. This trend first became apparent in the playing of trumpeter Miles Davis. As an 18-year-old, he had played in Charlie Parker's Quintet of 1945 in the "nervous" style of Dizzy Gillespie; not much later, however, he began to blow in a relaxed and "cool" manner. It also showed up in the piano improvisations of John Lewis, an anthropology student from New Mexico who traveled with Dizzy Gillespie's big band to Paris in 1948 and only then decided to remain in music; and in the arrangements Tadd Dameron wrote in the second half of the forties for the same Gillespie big band and for various small combinations. Miles Davis' trumpet solos of 1947 with Charlie Parker, such as "Chasin' the Bird," or John Lewis' piano solo in Dizzy Gillespie's "Round Midnight," recorded at a concert in Paris in 1948—these are among the first "cool" solos in jazz history . . . excepting Lester Young's tenor sax solos with Count Basie from the late thirties, in which he paved the way for the "cool" conception even before the bebop era had begun.

With these three musicians—Miles Davis, John Lewis, and Tadd Dameron—the style known as "cool jazz" begins.

The cool conception dominates all the jazz of the first half of the fifties, but it is notable that it found its most valid and representative expression at a moment almost coincidental with its origin: in the famed recordings of the Miles Davis Orchestra, which was formed for a brief engagement at New York's Royal Roost in 1948, and was recorded by the Capitol label in 1949 and 1950. In the chapter dealing with Davis, this group—of decisive importance to the ensemble sound and musical conception of the decade—will be discussed in detail.

Lennie Tristano—a blind pianist from Chicago, who came to New York in 1946 and founded his "New School of Music" there in 1951 —gave a theoretical foundation to cool jazz through his music and thinking. The musicians of the Tristano school (notably altoist Lee Konitz, tenorman Warne Marsh, and guitarist Billy Bauer) were to a large extent responsible for the layman's idea of cool jazz as cold, intellectual, and emotionless music. However, there can be no doubt that Tristano and his musicians improvised with remarkable freedom, and that linear improvisation stood at the center of their interests. Thus Tristano let himself be advertised as "Lennie Tristano and his Intuitive Music"; he wanted to emphasize the intuitive character of his conception and ward off the lay opinion that his was an intellectually calculated music. Still Tristano's music held for many listeners a coolness which often bordered on a chill. The evolution of modern jazz soon found less abstract, more sensuous and vital forms.

The problem was, as Stearns has said, "to play cool without being cold."

The influence of the Tristano school has remained traceable in all of modern jazz, however far removed from the "tristanoite" mode of coolness. This is true harmonically, but most of all in a distinct preference for long, linear melodic lines.

After Tristano, the center moved initially to the West Coast. Here evolved, directly connected to the Miles Davis Capitol Band, a "West Coast" jazz, often played by musicians who made their living in the Hollywood studio orchestras. Trumpeter Shorty Rogers, drummer Shelly Manne, and clarinetist-saxophonist Jimmy Giuffre became the style-setting musicians of the West Coast. Their music contained elements of the academic European musical tradition; direct and vital jazz content was often pushed into the background. The experts frequently pointed out that New York remained the true capital of jazz. This was where real and vital jazz was made: modern, yet rooted in jazz tradition. West Coast jazz was confronted with "East Coast jazz."

In the meantime, it has become apparent that both "coasts" were not so much stylistic entities as advertising slogans promoted by record companies. The real tension in the evolution of the jazz of the fifties was not between two coasts, but between a classicist direction and a group of young musicians, mostly black, who played a modern version of bebop, so-called hard bop.

The new jazz-classicism—as French critic André Hodeir has called it—finds its "classics" in the music Lester Young and Count Basie played in the thirties, first in Kansas City and later in New York. Many musicians from either coast, white or black, were oriented toward this music: Al Cohn, Joe Newman, Ernie Wilkins, Manny Albam, Johnny Mandel, Chico Hamilton, Buddy Collette, Gerry Mulligan, Bob Brookmeyer, Shorty Rogers, Quincy Jones, Jimmy Giuffre. In the fifties, a massive number of "Count Basie tributes" were recorded. Basie's name stands for clarity, melodiousness, swing, and certainly that "noble simplicity" of which Winckelmann spoke in his famous definition of classicism. (It is amazing how often it is possible to employ, almost literally, the words of the German classicists of the Goethe period when speaking of modern jazz classicism. One needs only to substitute for the names and concepts from Greek art and mythology Count Basie and Lester Young, swing, beat, and blues.)

Confronting this classicism stood a generation of young musicians whose foremost representatives lived in New York, though few of them were born there. Most were from Detroit or Philadelphia. Their music was the purest bop, enriched by a greater knowledge of harmonic fundamentals and a greater degree of instrumental-technical perfection. This hard bop was the most dynamic jazz played in the second half of the fifties—by groups under the leadership of, among others, drummers Max Roach and Art Blakey and pianist Horace Silver; by musicians like trumpeters Clifford Brown, Lee Morgan and Donald Byrd, and tenor men Sonny Rollins, Hank Mobley, and others—among them initially John Coltrane.

In hard bop, something new was created without sacrifice of vitality. All too often, the new in jazz can only be attained at the expense of vitality. But while, for example, drummer Shelly Manne had to pay for the amazing musical refinement of his playing with some reduction in directness and vitality, Elvin Jones managed to discover rhythms which simultaneously possess a complexity of structure *and* a vitality the likes of which, in such a relationship, was previously unheard of in jazz. Horace Silver found new ways of combining the 32-bar song structure, which is the foundation for most jazz improvising, with other forms—combing them into "groups" or "blocks" of forms (as had been done in similar fashion by the ragtime pianists, Jelly Roll Morton and other musicians of the early jazz period under the influence of the serial form of the Viennese Waltz). Tenor saxophonist Sonny Rollins created through his improvisations grandiose polymetric structures, while striding across the given harmonic materials with a freedom and ease which not even the Tristano school could match.

Marshall Stearns has said: "Indeed, modern jazz as played in New York by Art Blakey and his Messengers, Jay and Kai, Max Roach and Clifford Brown, Art Farmer and Gigi Gryce, Gillespie, Davis, and others . . . has never lost its fire. The harmonies of cool jazz—and bop—were taken over, the posture of resignation disappeared, the light sound remained, but the music always has a biting sharpness. In a word: It has changed, but fundamentally it remained 'hot' and 'swinging'. . . . The word 'cool' has lost its meaning—unless it is taken in a general sense of 'sensitive' and 'flexible.' " The last sentence applies to both directions of the jazz of the fifties: classicism and new bop.

It is also true of both movements that they had found a new relationship to the blues. Pianist-composer Horace Silver—and with him a few others—broke through with a manner of playing known as "funky": slow or medium blues, played hard, on the beat, with all the feeling and expression characteristic of the old blues. Jazz musicians of all persuasions on both coasts threw themselves into "funk" with notable enthusiasm. They did so in a manner which, since musical reasons are not readily apparent, leads one to conclude that extramusical influences were present. In a letter to the editor of *down beat* magazine (spring, 1958), a reader suggested that "the cool musician, in his use of the funky-blues framework, may be thinking about the content which is hidden behind this framework. . . . This content expresses a 'warm'—as opposed to 'cool'—relationship to life. . . . Though the content of the real blues may be sad, it is not a hopeless sadness." The letter continues with talk of a "spiritual transformation" of the cool jazz musician. Novelist Jack Kerouac, who had a genuine relationship to jazz, suggests there might even be religious or quasi-religious tendencies behind this phenomenon.

The spiritual orientation found in many aspects of jazz seems strange—maybe even artificial—to the European observer. This reaction seems superficial, as it remains unaffected by the unavoidable interpretation of drug addiction among jazz musicians as an escape from meaninglessness; or even by the telling conversion of many jazz musicians to Islam.

As for the tendency toward "funk"; it may well express the wish to belong, and the desire for something offering a semblance of security in a world of cool realism. That is why, since the sixties, the word "soul" has come into such general use—especially in connection with funky playing—that one can say it has almost become a touchstone of jazz criticism. As Horace Silver puts it: "Everybody has the kind of soul I mean here; only there are some people who have more of it than others . . . some have so much that it reaches out and touches you." The whole point behind this becomes clear if one would imagine such use of the term "soul" around the turn of the forties. Lennie Tristano didn't talk about "soul." He talked about "neurosis."

Pianist-blues singer Mose Allison spoke of Charlie Parker as a "blues-player trapped in the age of anxiety." Surely Parker was that, but particularly from the point of view of funky jazz, from which Southerner Allison had to speak, if only as a typical representative of the modern jazzman's return to the origins of jazz: "Down South, they look at me as a progressive bebop type. In New York they see me as a country-blues folk type. In reality, I think, I'm neither one nor the other. Maybe I'm a little bit of both." The use by Jimmy Giuffre and others of old folk songs and their musical atmosphere may also have been caused by this wish to belong. The musical and technical material is so simple and slight that it is hard to discover a musical reason—from the point of view of the complexity of modern jazz.

This trend becomes even clearer a decade later, in free jazz. Albert Ayler, for example, transplanted circus and country music—clearly motifs from the safe and sane "good old days"—into his free, atonal, ecstatic improvisations. Other free jazz musicians overemphasize their hate for the white world and find a substitute realm of group acceptance and security in communion with those who share this hate—a psychological reaction familiar to any specialist in psychoanalysis.

During the cool jazz period, the contrapuntal and linear music of Johann Sebastian Bach fulfilled this need to belong in the Modern Jazz Quartet of pianist John Lewis. A whole tide of jazz fugues rose in the first half of the fifties; it subsided as funk increased in importance.

It is significant that only the truly superior musicians were in a position to escape such tides—trumpeter Miles Davis, who achieved the synthesis of bop and classicism, or tenor saxophonist Sonny Rollins, one of the most important exponents of hard bop.

1960—Free Jazz

These are the innovations of the jazz of the sixties—of free jazz:

1. A break-through into the free space of atonality.
2. A new rhythmic conception, characterized by the disintegration of meter, beat, and symmetry.
3. The flow of 'world music' into jazz, which is suddenly confronted by all the great musical cultures—from India to Africa, from Japan to Arabia.
4. An emphasis on intensity unknown to earlier styles of jazz. Jazz had always been superior in intensity to other musical forms of the Western world, but never before had the accent been on intensity in such an ecstatic, orgiastic—sometimes even religious—sense as in free jazz. Many free jazz musicians are involved in a "cult of intensity."
5. A wider application and interpretation of musical sound into the realm of noise.

Around the early sixties, jazz music broke through into the free realm of atonality, as concert music had done 50 or 60 years earlier. Jazz specialists had expected this development for some 15 years; it was anticipated in Lennie Tristano's "Intuition" of 1949, to name one; and particularly George Russell and Charles Mingus paved the way for it. A "new music," a "new jazz" was born—as many innovations in the arts, initially relying on shock value. The power and hardness of the new jazz, along with a revolutionary, partially extramusical pathos, affected the jazz scene of the sixties vehemently. This vehemence was even stronger because so many things had been bottled up in the fifties, when the break-through was imminent but was avoided with almost pathological anxiety. All these bottled-up things came down like an avalanche on a contented jazz public, which had accommodated itself to Oscar Peterson and the Modern Jazz Quartet.

For the young generation of free jazz musicians, the music preceding them had been depleted in terms of playing and procedural possibilities, harmonic structure and metric symmetry. It had become rigid in its clichés and predictable formulas, similar to the situation 20 years earlier, when bebop was created. Everything seemed to run according to the same, unchangeable pattern in the same, unchanging way. All possibilties of traditional forms and conventional tonality seemed exhausted. That is why the young musicians searched for new ways of playing—and in the process, jazz again became what it had been in the twenties when the white public discovered it: a great, crazy, exciting, precarious adventure. At last, there was collective improvisation again, with lines rubbing against and crossing each other wildly and freely. That, too, is reminiscent of New Orleans—with modifications to be discussed later.

Don Heckmann, the critic and musician, once said: "I think there's been a natural tendency toward this freeing of the improvisatory mind from harmonic restrictions throughout the history of jazz."

In jazz, atonality is understood in a basically different way from European concert music. A new ordering principle in the mainstream of twentieth century concert music, dodecaphonic and serial in nature, has taken the place of the old principle of functional harmonics. Even when modern concert music became aleatory—that is, when it made room for certain elements of chance and improvisation—it usually remained committed to a serial order or was sooner or later forced back into it. In the free jazz of the New York avant garde around 1965, this aspect of commitment and relationship existed only in the sense of so-called "tonal centers" (cf. the chapter dealing with harmonics). Here, the music loosely partakes in the general gravitation from the dominant to the tonic, but has a wide range of freedom in all other aspects—a freedom which in its intensity made the tonic-dominant relationship increasingly irrelevant during the course of the sixties.

This development was so spontaneous and non-academic that the term 'atonality' cannot be used in an exclusively academic sense. Small wonder that many free jazz musicians have expressed their explicit contempt for academic music and its vocabulary (Archie Shepp: "Where my own dreams sufficed, I disregarded the western musical tradition altogether."). In the new jazz, 'atonality' has a wide range of meaning: It includes all steps, from the intimated 'tonal centers' to complete harmonic freedom. However, in the face of radical atonality, the tendency to realize that the harmonic system cannot simply be replaced by 'nothing'—by no system at all—has become stronger. In spite of the brevity of its history, jazz has a longer 'atonal tradition' than European music. The "shouts" and "field hollers," the archaic blues of the southern plantations, indeed nearly all musical forerunners of jazz—which also survived as elements of jazz—were atonal. This atonality may have resulted from the singers' ignorance of European tonality. In the old days of New Orleans, too, there were musicians unconcerned with harmonic laws. Certain Louis Armstrong records from the twenties—"Two Deuces" with Earl Hines, for example—are among his most beautiful, though they contain notes that are "wrong" in terms of European academic harmonic theory.

Marshall Stearns, who pointed out all these things when they first surfaced during the hard bop era, foresaw: "The knack for harmonic liberties, which jazz musicians well knew how to take within the system of perfect intonation of European music, moves steadily toward a predictable goal: the freedom of the street cry and the field holler."

In other words, there is a tradition of atonality in the whole history of jazz, while atonality in European music was first introduced by an avant-garde—the "classical avant-garde" beginning with Schönberg, Webern, and Berg. Thus, jazz atonality has become the meeting ground for tradition and avant-garde—a truly healthy and advantageous point of departure rarely encountered in an art in flux!

There is no doubt: musicians like Ornette Coleman, Archie Shepp, Pharaoh Sanders, and Albert Ayler are closer to the "concrete," folk music-like atonality of the "field cry" and of the archaic folk blues than to "abstract," intellectual European atonality.

In the middle of the sixties we come to a point where the freedom of free jazz was often understood as freedom from any musical system formed in Europe—with the emphasis on "formed in Europe." The formal and harmonic emancipation from the music of the "white continent" is part of a greater racial, social, cultural, and political emancipation. "Black music," as it was interpreted by many of these musicians and by LeRoi Jones, one of their most eloquent spokesmen, became "blacker" than ever before in this process of breaking its strongest link with the European tradition, the harmonic laws.

There is a parallel between jazz and modern European concert music, but only insofar as both displayed a growing disgust with the mechanistic, machine-like character of the traditional system of functional harmonics. This system had become a road-block in the development of the musics by increasingly substituting for individual decisions its own functional mechanics, and its abolition is a legitimate development familiar from many other arts, cultures, and traditions: When a structuring principle has been worn out and the creative artists become convinced that within its limits everything possible has been said, the principle must be abandoned.

The claim of exclusive validity for European harmonics is contradicted not only by artistic and physical considerations, but also by the many different principles and systems which have proven their value in other musical cultures of the world. Especially in view of today's political and cultural developments, the contention has become irrelevant that one system could have all the answers. On the other hand, it remains to be seen to what extent the free harmonic conception is the answer. It is not correct, however, to simply invalidate this conception as "incomprehensible," since it is a fact that it was immediately understood without prior discussion by a minority of listeners and a majority of young jazz musicians all over the world.

Jazz should be seen as a spiritual and cultural phenomenon within the spiritual and cultural movements of this century. Parallels of a more than accidental nature can be found between the liberation of jazz from functional harmonics and similar developments in other contemporary arts. We have discussed concert music. The parallel with modern literature is even more obvious: The anti-grammatical and anti-syntactic tendencies of so many modern writers—Raymond Queneau, Arno Schmidt, Helmut Heissenbüttel, Butor, William Burroughs, and of course, James Joyce plus many others in all important languages—correspond to the anti-harmonic tendencies of the free jazz musicians, even down to details. Increasingly, the gravitation of syntax and grammar draws language into the same functional and causal tunnel into which music moved under the influence of functional harmonics. Each step derives directly and necessarily from the preceding one, so that the creative artist finally could do little more than choose from a catalogue whose limits were syntax, grammar, and harmonics.

All new jazz styles have created new rhythmic concepts. Free jazz is no exception. Two basic facts determine the different rhythmic concepts in the history of jazz from New Orleans to hard bop: A fixed meter, generally 2/4 or 4/4 (until the emergence of the waltz and other uneven meters in the fifties), is carried out constantly. Further, the jazz beat produces accents which do not necessarily correspond to those a classically trained musician would place within that same meter. Free jazz demolished the two pillars of conventional jazz rhythm—meter and beat. The beat was replaced by the "pulse" and the meter, which is passed over by the free jazz drummers as if it did not exist, was replaced by wide circles of rhythmic tension, built up with an incredible intensity. (More about this in the chapters on rhythm and the drums.)

Just as important to free jazz as harmonic and rhythmic innovation was gaining access to world music. Jazz developed within a dialectic —the meeting of black and white. In the first 60 years of jazz history, the counterpart of jazz was European music. Interaction with the European musical tradition was not a marginal activity. Nearly all styles of jazz came into being in and through this dialectical interaction.

In this process, the realm of what was meant by "European music" grew continually larger. To the ragtime pianists of the turn of the century it meant the piano compositions of the nineteenth century. To the New Orleans musicians it meant French opera, Spanish circus music, and German marches. Bix Beiderbecke and his Chicago colleagues of the twenties discovered Debussy. The Swing arrangers learned orchestration skills from the late romantic symphonic period. . . . Finally, when the development had gone beyond cool jazz, jazz musicians had incorporated almost all elements of European music they could possibly use, from Baroque to Stockhausen.

Thus, the role of European music as the stimulating counterpart of jazz—at least as its only conterpart—had run out. Aside from this musical reason, there were extra-musical ones—racial, social, and political—as we have already mentioned. This is why jazz musicians discovered new partners with growing fervor: the great non-European musical cultures.

The Arabic and Indian cultures and musics have held a special fascination. There have been Islamic tendencies among Afro-Americans since the mid-forties; since the time, in other words, when modern jazz originated. Dozens of jazz musicians converted to Islam, and occasionally took Arabic names: Drummer Art Blakey is known to his Muslim friends as Abdullah Ibn Buhaina; in the forties, saxophonist Ed Gregory had already become Sahib Shihab.

It was only a small step from religious conversion to Islam to a growing interest in Islamic music. Musicians like Yusef Lateef, Ornette Coleman, John Coltrane, Randy Weston, Herbie Mann, Art Blakey, Roland Kirk, Sahib Shihab, and Don Cherry in the U.S.; and, among others, George Gruntz and Jean Luc Ponty in Europe —many of them not Muslims by faith—have expressed their fascination with Arabic music in compositions and improvisations.

What fascinates jazz musicians most about Indian music is, above all, its rhythmic wealth. The great classical music of India is based on talas and ragas.

Talas are rhythmic series and cycles of immense variety—from three to 108 beats. It must be understood that Indian musicians and sophisticated listeners are able to appreciate even the longest tala— 108 beats—as a series and as a pre-determined musical structure and to recall it as such.

Talas usually have a great wealth of rhythmical structuring possibilities. A tala consisting of ten beats, for example, can be conceived as a series of "2-3-2-3" or "3-3-4" or "3-4-3" beats.

Within the series, there is ample room for free improvisation; the improvising musicians can wander far away from each other. But the tension characteristic of Indian music is to a large extent founded on the fact that the individual lines of improvisation must meet again on the first beat, "one"—the so-called "sam." After the widely diverging melodic movements, this meeting very often is felt like an almost orgiastic relief.

It is this rhythmic wealth of Indian music that particularly fascinates modern jazz musicians. They want to liberate themselves from the 4/4 uniformity of the metrically conventional, constant jazz beat, while at the same time searching for rhythmic and metric structures which create a jazz-like intensity.

In contrast to the rhythmically well defined tala, the raga is a melodic series in which many elements which have been categorized in numerous ways in European music come together, theme, key, mood, phrase, and the form determined by the melodic flow. A particular raga may require, for example, that a certain note can be used only after all other notes of the raga have been played. In this respect, there is a certain similarity to twelve-tone music. There are ragas which can be played only in the morning, at night, at full moon, or only with religious thoughts in mind.

The chief instruments of Indian music are the sitar and the tabla. Developed about 700 years ago, the sitar generally has six or seven main strings and 19 others for resonance. Usually, the tabla consists of two small drums, of which the one on the right is tuned in the tonic or the dominant. It can be re-tuned with a tuning hammer during the playing. The drum on the left, called "banya," has the function of a bass drum. It can be made to produce sounds of different pitch by pressing the ball of the left thumb against the rim or the center of the drumhead.

In this way, with two simple, small drums the tabla player accomplishes what the contemporary jazz drummer tries to do with his large, involved battery: to be rhythm and melody instruments at the same time. Several modern drummers have studied with tabla drummers from the music schools of Ravi Shankar, India's most important musician.

The openness with which dozens of jazz musicians of the fifties and sixties have approached the great exotic musical cultures goes far beyond comparable developments in modern European concert music. Overwhelming intensity and complexity are generated when Don Ellis derives big band compositions, such as "3-3-2-2-2-1-2-2-2" and "New Nine," from Indian talas; when Miles Davis and Gil Evans transform Joaquin Rodrigo's "Concierto de Aranjuez" into Flamenco jazz; when Yusef Lateef converts Japanese, Chinese, and Egyptian elements into blues on his record "A flat, G flat and C"; and when Sahib Shihab, Jean Luc Ponty, and George Gruntz play with Arab bedouins on the album "Noon in Tunisia." Compared to that, Debussy's, Messiaen's and Roussell's use of Indian and Balinese sounds and the influence of Chinese rhythms on the contemporary German composer Boris Blacher seem timid and marginal.

Today's jazz musicians transform world music into swinging sounds. They do this with the liberating joy of the adventurer and discoverer, and with a fervor whose messianic, all-embracing gesture of love is manifest in many of their record album titles: in Albert Ayler's "Spiritual Unity" and "Holy Ghost;" Don Cherry's "Complete Communion;" Carla Bley's "Communication;" Schlippenbach's "Global Unity;" Yusef Lateef's "Try Love;" Ornette Coleman's "Peace;" John Coltrane's "Love," "Love Supreme," "Elation," and "Ascension;" or in tunes such as "Sun Song," "Sun Myth," and "Nebulae" from "Heliocentric Worlds" by Sun Ra and his Solar Arkestra. The message of these titles can be felt when they are seen in a single context: ". . . from spiritual unity to complete communion and communication with the globe as a unity—and, through that, love and peace for everybody and salvation in pan-religious ecstasy . . . cosmic ascension and elation to mythological suns and nebulae and heliocentric worlds."

It is important to note that the jazz musicians merely emphasize artistically and musically what the more aware members of the black community have been realizing extra-musically. In March of 1967, for instance, teachers and students of a predominantly black New York High School boycotted all concerts of classical European music, not because they were not interested in European concert music—quite the contrary: musical activity at this school was above average—but because they felt it was wrong to be offered only concerts of European music, not jazz or Indian, Arabian, African, etc. music.

The opening of musical sounds into the realm of noise has to do with both world music and increased intensity. For centuries, there have been sounds in different exotic musical cultures, which may not necessarily seem "musical" to a classically trained ear. Their explosive intensity has literally burst open the conventional sound barriers of the instruments of many free jazz musicians: Saxophones sound like the intensified "white noise" of electronic music, trombones like the noises of conveyor belts, trumpets like steel vessels bursting from atmospheric pressure, pianos like crackling wires, vibraphones like winds haunting metal branches; collectively improvising groups roar like mythical, howling primeval creatures.

Indeed, the border between musical sound and noise, which seems so clear and natural to the average listener, is not physically definable; it is founded on traditional, tacit conventions. Fundamentally, music can use anything audible. In fact, this is its goal: the artistic utilization of what is audible. This goal cannot be reached when only some sounds are deemed suitable for music while all others are branded inappropriate.

Stockhausen says: "Sounds previously classified as noise are now being incorporated into the vocabulary of our music. . . . All sounds are music . . . music using all sounds is the music of today, not tomorrow, in our space age where the movement, direction, and speed of sounds are calculated elements of a composition. The object is to refresh and renew our known world of sounds with the available means of our time, just as every period of history has done."

To be sure, Stockhausen says this essentially as a result of his experiences with electronic music. But it is true about every acoustic process generated by man: Pianos can be played not only on the keys, but also inside, on the strings; violins can be beaten; trumpets can be used (without mouthpiece) as blowpipes. People ridiculing these ways of playing instruments simply prove that to them, music is nothing but fulfilling conventional rules. An instrument exists to produce sounds. There are no laws governing the procedure of this production. On the contrary, it is the job of the musician to continually find new sounds. In doing so, he can use conventional instruments in new ways, or invent new instruments, or further develop conventional instruments. This job has become a major challenge for many musicians. For an edition of the avant-garde magazine *Microphone,* many modern British drummers wrote detailed, page-long statements, but Tony Oxley simply wrote one sentence: "The most important activity for me is the enlargement of my vocabulary." This opinion is characteristic of many contemporary musicians.

We are living in an age which has created new sounds of unimaginable variety: jet planes and atomic explosions, the noises of oscillation and the ghostly crackling in the assembly buildings of the precision industry. Big city dwellers are subject to a barrage of decibels which men of former times not only would have been unable to withstand physically, but which would have cast them into paroxysms of psychological confusion. Scientists have amplified the sounds of plant growth by millions of strengths so that they become a deafening roar. We now know that fish, deemed to be the quietest of all creatures by the romantics of the last century, exist in an environment of continual sounds. Every human being alive today is affected by this expansion of the realm of the audible. Are musicians supposed to be unaffected?

Within a few years, free jazz became a richly varied means of expression, mastering the gamut of human emotions. We should free ourselves from the misconception that this music only voices anger, hate, and protest. This impression was created mainly by a small group of New York critics and musicians far from representative of all of free jazz. Besides the protest of the Archie Shepp of the sixties to name one, there are the hymn-like religious fervor of John Coltrane, the joyous air of the folk musician in Albert Ayler, the intellectual coolness of Bob James, the cosmic amplitude of Sun Ra, the tender sensibility of Carla Bley.

Here are the most important dates of the period from 1955 to

1967, during which the new jazz developed and established itself—as far as it is possible to describe an artistic development by simply giving a few especially important dates. (The musicians named below will be discussed in detail later):

1954   Sun Ra introduces a big band in Chicago.

1955   Miles Davis hires tenor saxophonist John Coltrane for his quintet.

1957   Ornette Coleman forms a quartet with trumpeter Don Cherry in Los Angeles. Cecil Taylor appears at the Newport Jazz Festival.

1959/60 The Coleman Quartet (with Cherry, Charlie Haden, and Billy Higgins) successfully appears at the "Five Spot" in New York for several months.

1960   Coltrane plays with Miles Davis for the last time and with a "free" jazz musician, Cherry, for the first time. First appearance of the expression "free jazz" on Coleman's record for double quartet, "Free Jazz." On this record; a musical meeting of Coleman and Eric Dolphy. "Rival festival" of the "rebels" in protest against producer George Wein's established Newport Jazz Festival. Coleman plays with Charles Mingus, Kenny Dorham, and Max Roach. The first European group directly influenced by Coleman: Muniak Stanko Quartet from Cracow, Poland.

1961   Coltrane's tribute to Arabic and African music: "Olé Coltrane" and "Africa Brass."

1962   Coleman gives a concert with his trio (David Izenzon, bass; Charles Moffett, drums) at New York's Town Hall, then retires from public appearances for two years. Cecil Taylor and Albert Ayler, as well as Ayler and Sunny Murray, meet for the first time in the club "Montmartre" in Copenhagen. Beginning this year, almost all important free jazz musicians visit Europe. Free jazz is the first jazz style whose history cannot be written without mention of a host of happenings in Europe.

1963   Sonny Rollins appears—after long seclusion—with Don Cherry. Thus, the most outstanding exponent of the preceding jazz style—of hard bop—embraces the new jazz. The "New York Contemporary Five" (with Archie Shepp, John

Tchicai, and Cherry) is formed and appears in Scandinavia.
Coltrane's tribute to India: "India," with Eric Dolphy on
bass clarinet.

1964   Dolphy dies in Berlin. George Russell appears at the Berlin Jazz Days, then in Scândinavia, where a Russell Septet
is formed (later a big band). Don Cherry moves to Europe.
A "Jazz Composers Guild" is founded. Free Jazz Festival
(December 28 to 31) with Cecil Taylor, Archie Shepp, the
New York Art Quartet, the Jazz Composers Orchestra, Bill
Dixon, and many others in New York. (It is the first
festival devoted exclusively to the new jazz; many others
will follow, almost all of them in Europe.)

1965   Ornette Coleman in concert again. Triumph at the Berlin
Jazz Days. In Harlem, LeRoi Jones (later to call himself
Imamu Amiri Baraka) starts the "Black Arts Theater" to
promote all "black arts"—among them the new jazz.

Coltrane furthers the career of Archie Shepp and en-
larges his group with saxophonist Pharaoh Sanders and
drummer Rashied Ali. He records "Ascension;" Coleman
records several albums in London and Stockholm.

1966   Coltrane and Coleman dominate the jazz polls of the
world. Coleman is voted "Musician of the Year" by the
readers of *down beat* magazine.

With unprecedented success, Don Ellis introduces his
new big band at the Monterey Jazz Festival. The 1966
Berlin Jazz Days present more free jazz than any previous
European festival. Cecil Taylor appears with his "Unit" in
Germany and Paris.

1967   John Coltrane dies in Huntington, New York on July 17.
"Jazz Meets the World," an MPS record series, documents
for the first time the encounter of jazz and other musical
cultures—Arabia, India, Java, Bali, Japan, Brazil, Spanish
Flamenco music, etc.

Ornette Coleman and John Coltrane became the central figures of
the new jazz. Increasingly, young musicians and jazz fans all over the
world were finding their way to the new sounds. While critics and unappreciative fans were still saying "chaos," the new jazz was finding
its audience.

One hears time and again in the frequently pointed criticisms of this music that the new freedom will ultimately end in chaos—or that it has reached that point. However, after the understandable initial elation over the new freedom, the musicians began to emphasize that freedom was not the only point. Sunny Murray, one of the "freest" drummers of the new jazz, said: "Complete freedom you could get from anyone who walks down the street. Give them $20, and they'll probably do something pretty free."

But there is another reason why "chaos" is an inappropriate concept. Let's take a look at the history of European music.

Three times in that history, a "new music" appeared. First, there was *Ars Nova,* appearing around 1350; its most important composer was Guillaume de Machaut. Two and a half centuries later, around 1600, *Le Nuove Musiche* came into existence with the monodical music of the *Stilo Rappresentativo,* centering around composers like Orazio Vecchi and Monteverdi. Both times, secular and religious musical authorities agreed that the new music meant the beginning of chaos in music. From this point on, that fear never vanished: Johann A. Hiller spoke "with disgust" of Bach's "crudities." Copies of the first edition of Mozart's quartets were returned to him because the engraving was "quite imperfect." "Many chords and dissonances were thought to be engraving faults." (Franz Roh)

The reactions of critics contemporaneous with Beethoven are applicable to today: "All neutral music specialists were in full accord that something as shrill, incoherent, and revolting to the ear was utterly without parallel in the history of music." (This about the overture to "Fidelio"!) Brahms, Bruckner, Wagner—at one time or another, they were all in the "guild of chaotics." Then came the third "new music"—with all the well-documented scandals, misinterpretations, and misunderstandings. One need only recall the turbulence at the premiére of Stravinsky's "Sacre du printemps" in Paris in 1913; the various Schönberg scandals; or the premiére of Debussy's "Pelléas et Mélisande" in 1902 (it was labeled "brain music" and an example of "nihilistic tendencies"). Today, all this music is considered "classical," and the young avant-garde finds it "old-fashioned."

It was similar in jazz. At first, the "new music" from New Orleans sounded "chaotic" to the European ear: a wild, free departure to a confusing new land. However, by the turn of the fifties, New Orleans jazz had become party music for the young European bourgeois.

When bebop appeared in 1943, the nearly universal opinion was that chaos had finally taken over, that jazz was nearing the end. To-day, Dizzy Gillespie's trumpet and vocals sound as gay and familiar to us as "When the Saints Go Marching In."

The conclusion to be drawn from all this is that the word "chaos" is merely a refrain that rhymes with "history of music"—as simply as "fun" and "sun". Free jazz also rhymes with it very well.

A bourgeois world which agrees on nothing as readily as the need for security is first of all in need of awareness of the chaos surround-ing it, so that it may avoid the fatal plunge into despair. By bringing order to chaos, by giving it artistic expression, free jazz is an avenue for this consciousness. One thing should be clear, however: Ordering chaos is possible only by getting close to it. This is where the "sound of chaos" enters, first in classical European music; then, during the sixties, in jazz.

This is how music falls prey to the comforts of the establishment: Others have already done the job of ordering the chaos—the "chaos" which 20 or 30 years earlier was chaotic, and which now has nothing left in it of the chaotic; chaos has been ordered, there is nothing to worry about. Meanwhile, however, the chaos has grown again—it grows continually. This is where the challenge of the artist lies—not only of the musical artist: to give order to the growing chaos around us, again and again; to always continue giving it a new artistic form, again and again. If the artist fails, chaos will also overpower those—especially those—who neither suspect nor understand what is going on.

Because the unsuspecting are so numerous, there will be more and more possibilities for ordering chaos—each coming chaos being more threatening, more "chaotic" than the previous, of necessity. It is our unsuspecting attitude, our indolence, which eliminates the culinary aspect from the arts and places them on the conveyor belts of mass production.

Free jazz wants to force us to cease understanding music as a means to self-affirmation. Man, who builds computers and sends sat-ellites to Venus, has better means for self-affirmation. And the person whose racial problems and power politics are still in the style of the nineteenth century does not deserve self-affirmation.

By self-affirmation in music I mean the way all of us have been listening to music: always anticipating a few bars ahead—and when it comes out exactly (or at least nearly) as expected one felt con-firmed, one noted with pride how right one had been. Music had no other function but to cause such self-esteem. Everything worked out perfectly—and the few places where things deviated simply increased the fascination.

Free jazz must be listened to without this need for self-affirmation. The music does not follow the listener anymore; the listener must follow the music—unconditionally—wherever it may lead. The members of a German avant-garde group, the Manfred Schoof Quintet, have spoken of the absolute "emptiness," the "tabula rasa" indispensible to that kind of musical experience. It was observed in the U. S. that children could be enraptured by free jazz. They simply listened to what was happening—and a lot was! Wherever the sounds go, children follow. There is no place in their minds or sensory systems which, in the middle of each musical phrase, demands: This is the way it must continue; that is where it has to go; if it does anything else, it is "wrong." They demand nothing, and so get everything. The adults, however, for whom a piece of music—or a poem or picture—has almost no other function but to fulfill their demands, should not fool themselves: Except for guaranteed self-affirmation, they get nothing.

1970

As usual at the beginning of a decade, the seventies have brought a new jazz style. This new style is not a revolutionary one—as bebop was in its time, or free jazz was in the early sixties. The new style of the seventies grew organically from the preceding style, much in the way cool jazz grew from bebop or Chicago style from New Orleans jazz. In fact, cool jazz had a relationship to bebop similar to that the jazz of the seventies has to its predecessor: Both are "cool" styles. Just as cool jazz had a "cooling" effect on the nervousness of bop, just as Chicago style displays a "classical"—or better, classicist —relationship to New Orleans so is the new jazz of the seventies a cooling-off of free jazz. In a sweeping and classicistically grand manner it utilizes nearly everything that preceded it.

This new style developed so inevitably, so "tacitly" that, at the turn of the decade, the majority of the jazz audience was totally unaware that it stood at the dawn of a new era in the history of jazz styles. Still, the music of the seventies is different from the jazz played in the sixties. It is developing through the interaction of free jazz with conventional tonality and musical structure, traditional jazz elements, modern European concert music, elements of exotic musical cultures—especially Indian culture—with European romanticism, blues, and rock. "There's no longer just a free style of playing, it's all together," says clarinetist Perry Robinson. Of course, the fundamentally new aspect is that the categorical character of all those elements is dissolving. The elements no longer noticeably exist independently, as they did in earlier amalgams; they are losing their singular nature, are becoming pure music. In this context, it is a positive note that the new style doesn't have a name—at least not yet (although the term "electric jazz" is used occasionally). Names imply categorization, and categorizing should be avoided—because of its musical as well as extra-musical implications. Kant's "Categorical Imperative" is a tautology. The imperative cannot essentially be separated from the categorical. Both, "imperative" and "imperialism," come from the Latin *imperare* = to rule.

Some critics have claimed that certain contemporary musicians use elements of, for example, Indian music or the blues without actually knowing much about them. That sort of statement only shows that some of the critics simply have not realized what is happening in music today. Similarly uninformed were the critics who, even as late as 1972, renounced free jazz—as if they were making topical statements on the position of jazz—and spoke about the death of jazz, in a negative sense. The positive aspect of this music was exactly that free jazz was so strong as to be able to generate a new style and go beyond its own limitations.

After all that has been said in the preceding sections of this book (and in those to follow dealing with the elements of jazz), almost all the aspects mentioned above are self-explanatory. Only two points deserve some explication. The first is what we shall call melodizing and structuring of freedom. The second is rock.

The freedom of free jazz did not simply mean caprice and chaos. Free jazz musicians knew and emphasized this from the beginning— and by the first years of the seventies, even outsiders recognize it. The question what goal the freedom of free jazz had finds its answer today. We understand why the freedom of free jazz was necessary: not so everybody could do what he wanted, but rather to enable the jazz musician to freely utilize all those elements whose mechanistic and automatic characteristics had been eliminated.

In harmonics, for example, jazz musicians have not abandoned all harmony by learning to play atonally. They merely liberated themselves from the automatic, machine-like functioning of conventional school harmony which, once a certain harmonic structure had been established, determined all harmonic progressions. The free jazz musicians have broken through this "authoritarian," machine-like circularity of the harmonic process—and by doing so, are now that much better equipped to play aesthetically "beautiful" harmonies.

Another example may be found in rhythm: It has become clear that the regular meter of conventional jazz was not dissolved in order to destroy it, as it appeared to some in the initial phase of free jazz. Rather, it was dissolved because the automatic, mechanistic nature of the constant beat was in question. Indeed, an even, constant meter had become so taken for granted during the first 60 years of jazz history that personal artistic decisions in this realm were more or less impossible. Since the first half of the sixties, nothing in rhythm any longer is taken for granted. All kinds of rhythms and meters, constant or not, can now be used, with that much more freedom and independence.

Free jazz was a process of liberation. Only now can the jazz musician be really free, free to play all the things that were taboo for many creative musicians of the free jazz period: thirds and triads, functional harmonic progressions, waltzes, songs and four-beat meters, discernible forms and structures, and romantic sounds. And of course, he can also play "free" in the most extreme sense of the sixties.

In the liner notes to a record by the German-Dutch group Associaton P.C., which represents the new freedom exemplarily, Achim Hebgen writes: "After the term 'free' meant mainly 'beyond tonality, melodies, and meter' in the sixties—again, a new kind of categorization—the music of most of the important groups of the seventies represents a totally new quality of musical freedom: No more mere lip-service to the concept of freedom; but a truly independent mastery of all musical elements. There is no more co-existence of different styles, no more vacillation from one category to the other: Styles and categories have themselves become means of expression."

The jazz of the seventies melodizes and structuralizes the freedom of the jazz of the sixties.

At the beginning of the chapter, we compared this development to what happened in the forties, on the road from bebop to cool jazz—and West Coast jazz. At that time, too, a music which seemed chaotic to the mass audience was subdued and structuralized. However, it was a different motivation that led to the subduing and structuralization. In the early fifties, it was fear: "Music is getting more and more complicated—where will it all end?" "It can't go on like this!" "We're destroying the music, nobody can understand us anymore." Or simply: "Musicians have to eat, too." Consciously or unconsciously—often enough both—those were the motivations that caused the liberation of bebop to wither away into pedantic drills, glum counterpoint, and the conceited professionalism of West Coast jazz and its New York appendage.

Today, none of that is left. Subduing, melodization, and structuralization are not caused by such fears. This time, the road Charlie Parker mapped out was really followed to the end—with all the consequences. Those who went down that road were not afraid enough, if anything. They plumbed the depths of atonality unchained more persistently than anybody would ever have done in modern concert music, where traces of "series," "structure," and "aleatoriness" brought in through the back door persisted. Anyone who found his way back from these depths has no more fear. He has wisdom and maturity, and will never again give up the freedom he has gained. But he has also learned the limits and goals of freedom; and he has learned that aimless freedom is nothing but the inconsistent, misunderstood freedom of the fashionable emancipation movements— in politics, society, and the arts.

That is the novel aspect of melodics and structure in the jazz of the seventies: The freedom of free jazz remains audibly present in them.

Musicians such as Herbie Hancock, Keith Jarrett, Chick Corea, Pharaoh Sanders, Leon Thomas, Wayne Shorter, Joe Zawinul, Joe Henderson, McCoy Tyner, Garry Bartz, Alice Coltrane, and many others—and, above all, Miles Davis—are representative of this development.

The other new element in the jazz of the seventies is rock. Certainly, the influence of rock on jazz—preceded by a much stronger reverse flow from jazz to rock—began long before the end of the sixties. Initially, this influence produced essentially artificial, musically unsatisfying combinations—particularly of rock rhythm sections with jazz horns, the horns mainly playing in the bebop manner, while the rhythm sections played like those of popular rock groups. Bands like Blood, Sweat & Tears, Chicago, The Flock, Dream, Chase, and others were formed according to this principle. Quite often, the goals of producers and record companies were more influential in their formation and development than a spontaneous creative impetus from the musicians.

In this context, the group Chase was exemplary. The leader, trumpeter Bill Chase, came from Woody Herman's big band. Listening to Chase's music, one can clearly appreciate the conditions under which the group must have been founded: Bill Chase was a brilliant trumpeter who loved the bravura of big band trumpet sections. But this kind of playing, within the framework of conventional big bands, had not really "made it" with a youthful audience since the sixties. So Chase lifted the four-piece trumpet section from the big band and combined it with a rock rhythm section. Such combinations can have many fascinating aspects and may be commercially promising because of their attraction for both jazz and rock audiences. However, few sophisticated listeners find such groups artistically successful. It should be granted though, that there are some—above all Blood, Sweat & Tears—who put together this combination more skillfully than did Chase. Granted, too, that in this whole development there is that one exceptional musician—Frank Zappa, who has been integrating jazz and rock since the mid-sixties. But he is an exceptional figure in both rock and jazz. Zappa comes from modern concert music, particularly Varese. (See chapter on big bands.) Beyond that, however, it was only toward the late fifties that a significant number of records showed an authentic tendency, an organic development—promised a true integration, a new convincing union of rock and jazz. The key figure in this development is Miles Davis; the decisive record is his "Bitches Brew," released in 1970.

International critical reaction to "Bitches Brew" was immensely enthusiastic. For years, convincing musical results had been expected from rock-jazz in vain. There was almost something like a rock neurosis in the jazz world. It was obvious that an integration of rock by contemporary jazz musicians was the challenge—but it had not been met. After John Coltrane's death in 1967, jazz had been idling, to a large extent—there was even despair.

Many jazz musicians died young—from Bix Beiderbecke, the great trumpeter of the twenties, to Fats Navarro in 1950, or Albert Ayler in 1971. It almost seems as if the intensity demanded of the creative musician in jazz, the direct transformation of life as it unfolds into musical sounds, raises the death toll among active jazz musicians above the level found in other arts. Still, it has always been considered that a jazz musician left behind him a completed life-work. Even the most glowing admirers of Bix Beiderbecke or Bunny Berigan never assumed that their idols would have created anything totally new had they lived longer. Coltrane's case is different. Here, a musician was taken from us at the apex of his creative life and of the development he had generated. Unlike anyone else—with the exception of Ornette Coleman—he had towered above his contemporaries and had left his mark upon them; and unlike anyone else—even Coleman —his work had set a guiding example. This development was abruptly halted. The jazz world had lost its "leader," and it took years to make up for the loss. Even today, the wound is not fully healed. In this situation, many felt Miles Davis' "Bitches Brew" to be a solution.

Meanwhile a whole generation of young musicians was growing up which had gained fame in various Miles Davis groups during these years, and had been molded by the music of Davis. One is Dave Holland, the British bass player. After Holland left the Davis Quintet, he expressed feelings probably shared by most of these young musicians (in an interview with British critic Richard Williams), saying that Davis was still following the line of the old bebop tradition. "The premise on which Miles' music is built is still largely the old-fashioned one of a soloist and a rhythm section . . . I feel that the most positive direction for him to take now would be to get into the concept of playing a supporting role, as well as a supported one, and into more interaction between the players on a somewhat subtler level." This is exactly what Davis, meanwhile, does in his new music of around 1973/4.

Musicians originating within the Davis groups of those years, or directly influenced by Miles, have taken to creating a still tighter, closer integration of jazz and rock. The most important musicians in this field are discussed at the end of the chapter on the jazz combos in the section "Electric Jazz."

The point in time when all this occurred is noteworthy. As we mentioned, "Bitches Brew" was released in 1970, the *Götterdämmerung* of the rock age: Jimi Hendrix, Janis Joplin, Brian Jones, Jim Morrison and Duane Allman died; the Beatles broke up. The worst catastrophe of the rock age occurred in Altamont, California, at a Rolling Stones concert: Four persons died, hundreds were wounded; all the wonderful good will of Woodstock was destroyed; and Woodstock—the miracle of the "Woodstock Nation," of a new, young society full of love, tolerance, and solidarity—showed its real business face. In New York and San Francisco, "Fillmore East" and "Fillmore West," centers of rock music, closed their doors for the last time. Suddenly, the rock age had lost its drive, the age had lost its rock. No new groups or individual artists were appearing on the scene to tower above it. Toward the end of this period, Don McLean sang the sad, resigned refrain about the "day when the music died," in his song "American Pie," the closing hymn of the rock age. It was interpreted that way by the whole world. For weeks, the song was on the hit lists.

All that has been enumerated here happened between 1969 and 1972. The new jazz developed in exact parallel to these events, integrating rock and jazz. The year 1969 marked the release of Miles Davis' "In a Silent Way," the album which paved the way for "Bitches Brew." In 1971, Weather Report and the Mahavishnu Orchestra were formed. From 1972 on, the new jazz is here, full-fledged, with all the groups to be introduced in the section "Electric Jazz." Anybody who "integrates," who does not always focus on the one, rock *or* jazz, cannot help but conclude that this chronological parallel is not totally accidental. The rock age—or at least the best elements of it—flowed into the new jazz. The new jazz sensitized the rock music of the sixties, as the latter had similarly sensitized the rock 'n' roll of the fifties.

This point becomes clearer when one notes that there is a rock influence on jazz in three essential aspects: in the electronization of instruments, in rhythm, and in a new attitude toward the solo. In each of these aspects, the new jazz makes more sophisticated a characteristic of rock which rock musicians were unable to develop further.

In the area of electronics, the following instruments and accessories were added to the store of jazz instrumentation: electric pianos, organs, and other electronic keyboards; electronically amplified guitars and other instruments (among them saxophones, trumpets, and even drums), often used in connection with wah-wah and fuzz pedals, echolettes, phase shifters, ring modulators, and feedback units; varitones, multividers, etc. (for octave duplication and automatic harmonization of melodic lines); two-board guitars (combining the possibilities of both six-string and twelve-string guitar); and synthesizers of various kinds.

The musicians of John McLaughlin's Mahavishnu Orchestra, for example, stand in front of a mountain of equipment that fills the stage: dozens of different speaker enclosures, amplifiers, and other electronic gear which beams several thousand watts at the audience.

At a superficial first glance, the tempting impression is that the jazz musicians simply took over all this equipment from rock and pop music; but on closer inspection, one discovers that the electric guitar, for example, was first featured by Charlie Christian in 1939 in Benny Goodman's sextet. And the electric organ first became popular in black rhythm and blues music, played by such musicians as Will Bill Davis; it found its way into mass consciousness through the great success of jazz organist Jimmy Smith after 1956. The music world first became aware of the sparkling sound of the electric piano through Ray Charles' hit "What'd I Say" in 1959. White rock music did not incorporate the instrument until, in 1968, Miles Davis recorded "Filles de Kilimanjaro" with Herbie Hancock and Chick Corea on electric piano. The first experimentation with electronically amplified horns, varitones, and multividers was done by jazz musicians Sonny Stitt (1966) and Lee Konitz (1968). The synthesizer comes from concert music, where it had been developed and tested since 1957 by R. A. Moog in cooperation with Walter Carlos. Ring modulators, phase shifters, and feedback techniques were also first developed in the electronic studios of concert music.

The impression that all these sounds are sounds of rock is essentially the result of the gigantic publicity machine of the rock media and the record industry. Thus these sounds reached general mass consciousness. It must be seen, on the other hand, that the electronization of instrumental sounds is the work of black musicians, while the production of "purely" electronic sounds first came from avantgarde concert music.

In this connection, it might be interesting to remember that it was a black singer in the thirties, Billie Holiday, who was among the first to realize the potential of the microphone for a completely new use of the human singing voice. It has been said that Billie Holiday's style, which at the time was felt to be new and "revolutionary," consisted mainly in "microphonizing" the voice—in a way of singing unthinkable without the microphone. This "microphonic" style has become so commonplace for all kinds of popular music that hardly anyone mentions it.

Charles Keil and Marshal McLuhan point to the special talent of the Afro-American for making audible the new possibilities of electronics. Keil supposes that "if McLuhan's thesis is correct, the electronic or post-literate age and its high-powered auditory forces that are now upon us ought to give Negro culture a big technological boost."

In summary, we have shown that the electronization of the instruments was prepared by black musicians and that "purely" electronic sounds were first developed in the studios of electronic concert music. The rock scene popularized these sounds: Jazz, rhythm and blues, electronic concert music, rock and pop all worked together. Such wide-spread cooperation, covering so many different areas of music, allows the conclusion that the introduction of electronics to music was a demand of the times. Not only the instruments but also the auditory needs of modern man are "electronized"—of modern man from all social strata and classes, from the slums and ghettos to the music festivals of the intellectual world.

The question of loudness also belongs in this context. This point causes the outsider as many problems as did the constant beat of the basic meter 30 years ago. So many things have been said about loud volume. I have heard them all: that it is physiologically wrong, incommensurate with the potential of the human ear; that it therefore endangers the auditory faculties or eventually destroys them. There is always an otologist who can confirm this "from daily experience" and the bourgeois press loves to print things like that. However, increased volume can also create new sensibilities: Just a few years ago, nobody would have been able to discover as many subtleties as we can hear today in the gale-force range of sound waves generated by the Mahavishnu Orchestra or the British group Soft Machine, to name two. The new volume is a new challenge: He who meets that challenge will be capable of working with acoustic maxima that just yesterday seemed impossible for the ear to differentiate. In other words, loud volume widens human capacity and, thus, human consciousness —and therein lies its challenge. At a time when the sounds of our daily lives have reached decibels of unimagined demensions, music cannot and must not remain fixed to the volume of yesterday or the day before. That would mean relinquishing the artistic break-through into the auditory ranges in which we live.

So much for electronics. Let us consider rhythm next. The inadequacies of the jazz-rock combinations of the sixties were due mainly to the fact that the conventional rock rhythms were much too undifferentiated to be of jazz interest. Already in the early sixties, drummers like Elvin Jones, Tony Williams, or Sunny Murray were beating out rhythms without equal in Western music in their highly stratified complexity. In the face of this, the work of even the best rock drummers seems regressive. Interestingly, only jazz drummers have generally been successful in dealing with the extroverted, aggressive attitude of rock rhythms in such a way that structures corresponding to the high standards of jazz were produced. In the early seventies, the leading drummer in this field, Billy Cobham (of the Mahavishnu Orchestra), was modest enough to say: "I want my playing to be simple enough for the audience to understand, but intricate enough for them to be awed by what I'm doing."

The third aspect of the rock influence on jazz is the new approach to the solo. In all its periods, jazz always had its true culmination in the solo improvisations of outstanding individual artists. However, in the sixties—first in the U.S., then even more in Europe—an increasing number of free jazz collectives came into being. These began to doubt the validity of the conventional solo principle. There had been a feeling among jazz musicians that the practice of individual improvisation, in which only the top individual performance counts, reflects all too faithfully the performance principle of the capitalist system. Parallel to the growing social and political criticism of this principle—in fact, even a few years before its rise—a questioning of the value of the principle of individual improvisation had begun. The tendency to improvise collectively became stronger and stronger. The way for this was paved by bassist Charles Mingus, in whose groups there was free collective improvising already in the late fifties. At the time it could not be foreseen that just a few years later such "collectives" would be the hallmark of an entire musical development. Bands of the caliber of the Mahavishnu Orchestra show such a high degree of complex interplay when improvising that one can barely tell which of the five musicians is leading at any given moment. Here, solos in the traditional sense have virtually been abolished. Pianist Joe Zawinul said about his band, Weather Report: "In this group, either nobody plays solo, or we all solo at the same time."

As is almost always the case in jazz, the movement toward the collective solo has its counter-movement toward the solo unaccompanied by a conventional rhythm section. Initiated by vibraharpist Gary Burton, there have been many such unaccompanied solo or duo performances since the late sixties, from such musicians as guitarist John

McLaughlin, pianists McCoy Tyner, Chick Corea, Keith Jarrett, Cecil Taylor, and even traditionalist Oscar Peterson, saxophonists Archie Shepp, Anthony Braxton and Roland Kirk; and vibraharpist Karl Berger—and in Europe by Gunter Hampel, Martial Solal, Derek Bailey, Terje Rypdal, Albert Mangelsdorff, Alexander von Schlippenbach and John Surman; in Japan, by Masahiko Sato and others.

Certainly, there had been earlier unaccompanied jazz solos. Coleman Hawkins recorded the first *a cappella* horn solo in 1947, "Picasso." Above all, unaccompanied playing was favored by the great pianists—and, of course, as in almost all areas of jazz, Louis Armstrong was a forerunner in the field of the unaccompanied solo, too: in his duet with Earl Hines in 1928, "Weather Bird," and in dozens of solo cadenzas and solo breaks.

However, these musicians merely paved the way for what today clearly is a tendency reflecting the isolation of the jazz musician, the opposite of the collective spirit described above.

The development toward the unaccompanied solo performance in the seventies is a romantic tendency, away from the loudness of electronic amplification toward an intimate, extremely personalized and sensitized form of expression: the symptom of a growing trend toward a new, objective, clear romanticism. (In this connection, we could perhaps mention the concerts "Solo Now!" and "The Art of the Solo!" which the author arranged for the jazz festival on the occasion of the Munich Olympic Games and for the Berlin Jazz Days in 1972—the first jazz concerts where all the artists played without accompaniment, among them Gary Burton, Chick Corea, Albert Mangelsdorff, Jean Luc Ponty, John McLaughlin, Pierre Favre, Gunter Hampel, and ragtime pianist Eubie Blake.)

Only a few years ago, rock and jazz musicians represented two rather irreconcilable poles. Rock musicians found free jazz esoteric and hard to understand. On the other hand, free jazz musicians thought rock primitive and simple-minded, produced with an eye on financial success. To be sure, this polarity continues to exist. Since the start of our decade, however, there have been more and more groups that integrate the elements of jazz and rock and free-playing —and all the other elements mentioned at the beginning of this chapter—into a new union.

One of the main reasons why rock elements were integrated into jazz with relative ease is that, conversely, rock has drawn nearly all its elements from jazz—and especially from blues, the spirituals, gospel songs and the popular music of the black ghetto, rhythm and blues. Here, the symmetrical, steady rock beat, the gospel and soul phrases, the blues form and blues sound, the penetrating sound of the electric guitar, etc. had all been in existence long before the appearance of rock. Shelly Manne, the drummer, once said: "If jazz borrows from rock, it only borrows from itself."

The key figure in this development is blues guitarist B. B. King, who created almost every element in the music of today's young rock and top-forty guitarists. Among these, one of the most successful is Eric Clapton, who was honest enough to admit: "Some people talk about me like a revolutionary. That's nonsense—alll I did was copy B. B. King. . . ."

It is one of the internal contradictions of the rock business that today's young guitarists idolize and imitate Eric Clapton, a white musician, without realizing that their music does not come from him, but from black bluesman B. B. King.

In this sense—and in this sense only—can one understand Gary Burton when he says: "There is no rock influence on us. We only have the same roots. . . ." This does not contradict what has been said above. It merely shows the complexity of the situation, especially since Burton's music is often cited when the subject is the influence of rock on jazz.

THE MUSICIANS OF JAZZ

The Musicians of Jazz

"I PLAY what I live," said Sidney Bechet, one of the great men of old New Orleans. And Charlie Parker stated: "Music is your own experience, your thoughts, your wisdom. If you don't live it, it won't come out on your horn."

We shall see how the unmistakable sounds of the great jazz soloists, right down to technical elements, depend on their personalities. The jazz musician's life is constantly transformed into music—without regard for "beauty," "form," and the many other concepts which mediate between music and life in the European tradition. That is why it is important to speak of the lives of the jazzmen. That is why the jazz enthusiast's desire to know the details of the lives of great musicians is legitimate. And it is also legitimate that such details make up a great part of the literature of jazz. They help us understand the music itself, and thus are quite a different story from the details fan magazines report about the lives of Hollywood stars.

"A person has to have lived to play great jazz, or else he'll be a copy," says Milt Hinton, the bassist. Only a few musicians who exemplify this dictum could be selected for this book. But they are musicians in whose histories the history of a style is involved, and each one of them stands for a specific period. Buddy Bolden represents the transition from folk music to the earliest form of jazz; Louis Armstrong stands for the great New Orleans period; Bessie Smith for the blues and jazz singing; Bix Beiderbecke for Chicago style; Duke Ellington for orchestral Swing; Coleman Hawkins and Lester Young for combo Swing; Charlie Parker for bebop, and modern jazz itself; Miles Davis for the whole development from cool jazz to the music

51

of the seventies; and Ornette Coleman and John Coltrane for the jazz revolution of the sixties.

Buddy Bolden

"Since his career predated the making of commercial records of his kind of music, there is nothing left of him but legend," writes Leonard Feather in his *Encyclopedia of Jazz*. "When you come right down to it," said the late trumpeter Mutt Carey, "the man who started the big noise in jazz was Buddy Bolden."

Certainly there is a difference between Feather's and Carey's statements. Perhaps we can conclude that if a phenomenon such as jazz could possibly have started with a single personality, then Bolden is it. In any case, he is the first important jazz musician whose name crops up in the recollections of the New Orleans jazz pioneers. Of course, a way of playing music, which jazz is, does not begin with one individual.

It is part of the legend of Buddy Bolden that much that is told of him is contradictory. Most if it was related by men who, being questioned by jazz experts and researchers 40 or 50 years after the fact, noticed that the name Buddy Bolden had something like "historical significance." After such a long time, much becomes blurred, and one tends to hold that to be true which one has wished to be so all through life.

Buddy Bolden was born in the early seventies of the last century. He was a barber. In a junk shop he acquired an old accordion. He could read no notes, but soon played with ease any melody he had ever heard—Negro blues as well as the operatic arias sung at the famous "French Opera" of New Orleans.

Music was in the air of the lively city on the Mississippi delta. Nothing happened without music. The band wagons drove through the streets, accompanying almost every occasion in life—from birth to death—with their music. Young Buddy Bolden heard it all, and he wanted to play. He soon discovered that the accordion wasn't appropriate and switched to cornet. That he found a cornet lying in the street is a legend, but in the sense that applies to authentic legends, quite "true."

In the nineties, Bolden led a band which had unmatched success. When they heard his horn, people would say: "Buddy Bolden is calling his children home." The "children" were people in New Orleans who liked to dance and have fun.

Around 1895 or 1896, Bolden hired a second cornet for his band —much as King Oliver 25 years later would get Louis Armstrong to join him. This second cornet was Bunk Johnson, a musician who was rediscovered after a long search in the late 1930's; he was outfitted with new teeth so he could play once more. He finally played a considerable role in the later New Orleans Revival.

Almost all who speak of Bolden praise the loudness and power of his playing. Alphonse Picou said: "He was the loudest there ever was, because you could hear Buddy's cornet as loud as what Louis Armstrong played through the mike." It is always reiterated that Bolden's cornet was audible all over New Orleans—a statement that sounds dubious, for New Orleans was a large city even then. Yet it gains in credibility when one considers that it has been made by so many different people and in such thoroughly consistent fashion. Guitarist Danny Barker explains this, and the fact that the air of New Orleans was literally "filled with music," by noting that "the city of New Orleans has a different kind of acoustics from other cities. There is water all around the city. There is also water under the city . . . adding to this dampness there was the heat and humidity of the swamps, of the bayous all around New Orleans . . . and because of all this, because sound travels better across water . . . when you blew your horn in New Orleans—especially on a clear night—when guys like Bolden would blow their beautiful brass trumpets, the sound carried."

All in all, there were close to 30 known orchestras in New Orleans during the first decade of this century. Let us consider for a moment what this means. The Mississippi delta town then had less than 200,000 inhabitants. That is approximately the size of Hartford, Connecticut. In a town of this size there were 30 bands, playing a living, spontaneously improvised music—and growing and evolving along with it!

The greatest time for these bands was the yearly Mardi gras. People in the know regard this New Orleans specialty as the most free-wheeling carnival in the world. The bands moved through the streets, marching or on wagons, from one dawn to the next and on to the one after that, transforming the city into a cauldron bubbling over with joyous spirits.

It is worth noting that we know more about many of Bolden's contemporaries than about the man himself. Perhaps the aura of fascination which surrounds his name is due to the shadowiness of his appearance. Maybe it is also due to his fate. And surely it is due to the women. They spoke less of "King Bolden" than they did of "Kid Bolden." "He was," Bunk Johnson said, "a good-looking brown-skinned man, tall and slim and a terror with the ladies." Others too, have mentioned his considerable effect on women.

Toward the year 1906, Bolden's decline began. At the time, he was living with a girl named Nora Bess, his mother, and his sister Cora. He often complained to them about intense headaches. Soon the pains became so strong that he began to play wrong notes. During a street parade in 1906, he ran amok. He was arrested. Soon he lost all ability to play. He didn't recognize his closest friends. After many complaints from neighbors, he was committed to a mental hospital in April 1907.

Toward the end of World War I, Bolden was temporarily released. He stayed with his mother and sister in New Orleans. But no one knew him any more. He had been forgotten—the man who ten years earlier had been the hero of the city. Buddy, on the other hand, failed to recognize the few who did remember him. He did not even recall having been a musician.

Soon he had to be taken back to the hospital. There he lived—or vegetated—until November 4, 1931. For 24 years—briefly interrupted by the few days at home—he looked out of the window of his cell upon the endless fields which his ancestors had worked for centuries as slaves. Once a year he was examined. The examination reports of the many years sometimes correspond literally. Thus from 1921: "Approachable, answers fairly well, paranoid delusions, also of grandeur, acoustic hallucinations, also optic, talks to himself. Very reactive. Takes things down from wall. Able to undress himself. Feeling and judgment lacking. Health good. Blood negative. Getting worse. Speaks sequences of words without connection. Hears voices of people who annoyed him before he came here. Diagnosis: Dementia praecox, paranoid type."

These reports—they bear a strong resemblance to the ones describing the illness of Vincent van Gogh—remain to this day in East Louisiana State Hospital. There, too, rest the letters written once or twice a year by his mother or sister to inquire about his condition—haltingly written, one or two lines only, no punctuation. Like the one dated February, 1927: "Dr. please let me know about the health of my son Charley Bolden please let me know if he got the Christmas package from his mother Mrs. Alice Bolden 2338 Phillip Street New Orleans." Two years prior to his death there is the notation: "Lost his mother."

There are 40 or 50 documents in the hospital files about Buddy Bolden. Twenty of these deal with the five dollars required for his burial. There is not one word in any of them stating that Buddy Bolden was a musician: a creative musician in a branch of music chosen and in part created by him.

Louis Armstrong

What remains legend about Buddy Bolden is fact about Louis Armstrong. About no other musician in the history of jazz is there so much agreement. . . . Until the rise of Dizzy Gillespie in the forties, no jazz trumpeter did not stem from Louis Armstrong—or "Satchmo," as he was called—and even after that, every player has been at least indirectly indebted to him.

The immense size of this debt became clear when impressario George Wein made the 1970 Newport Jazz Festival into one big birthday celebration for 70-year-old Armstrong. World-famous jazz trumpeters competed for the most appropriate homage to Louis. Bobby Hackett called himself "Louis Armstrong's Number One admirer;" Joe Newman took exception: Not Hackett, but he himself, should be called Louis' "A-number one fan;" Jimmy Owens said that if he could not claim to be Armstrong's "number one fan" or even "A-one fan," he was at least his "youngest fan;" and Dizzy Gillespie said: "Louis Armstrong's station in the history of jazz . . . all I can say is UNIMPEACHABLE. If it weren't for him, there wouldn't be any of us. So I would like to take this moment to thank Louis Armstrong for my livelihood."

Musicians other than trumpeters have also expressed their great debt to Armstrong. Frank Sinatra has pointed out that Armstrong made an art of singing popular music.

When Louis Armstrong died two days after his 71st birthday, on July 6, 1971, Duke Ellington said: "If anyone was Mr. Jazz, it was Louis Armstrong. He was the epitome of jazz and always will be. Every trumpet player who decided he wanted to lean towards the

American idiom was influenced by him. . . . He is what I call an American standard, an American original. . . . I love him. God bless him."

He spent his youth in the turmoil of the great port on the Mississippi—in the old Creole quarter of New Orleans. The symbolic borders of this quarter were a jail, a church, a school for the poor, and a ballroom. His parents—his father was a factory worker, his mother a domestic—were separated when Louis barely had been born. Nobody paid much attention to him. Once or twice the authorities considered putting him in a reformatory, but nothing was done untill, one New Year's Eve, Louis fired a pistol loaded with blanks in the streets. Now they put him in the reformatory. He became a member of the school chorus. He received his first musical instruction on a battered old cornet from the leader of the reform school band.

One of the first bands in which Louis played was that of trombonist Kid Ory. Little Louis happened to be passing by with his cornet as Ory's band was playing in the street. Somebody asked for whom he was carrying the instrument. "Nobody. It's mine," said Louis. Nobody would believe him. So Louis started to blow. . . .

When during World War I the red light district of Storyville was closed down by the secretary of the Navy and the great exodus of musicians began, Louis was among those who remained. He did not go to Chicago until, in 1922, King Oliver sent for him to join his band, then playing at the Lincoln Gardens. Oliver's band—with the King himself and Louis on cornets, Honoré Dutrey on trombone, Johnny Dodds on clarinet, his brother Baby Dodds on drums, Bill Johnson on banjo, and Lil Hardin on piano—was then the most important jazz band. When Armstrong left it in 1924, it began to decline. To be sure, Oliver made several good recordings in later years —such as the 1926/27 series with his Savannah Syncopators—but by then other bands had become more important (Jelly Roll Morton's Red Hot Peppers, Fletcher Henderson, young Duke Ellington); and the end of Oliver's career presents the tragic spectacle of an impoverished man, without teeth, unable to play and earn money to live, a man who hides from his friends because he is ashamed and yet was once "King of Jazz." Here is an example of the tragedy of artistic existence—and there are many such tragedies in the annals of jazz. Louis Armstrong escaped this fate in an almost supernatural way. The ups and downs that characterize the lives of so many jazz musicians hardly ever affected him. For him there was only one direction: up.

It is a mark of Louis Armstrong's superiority that throughout his long career he had only two ensembles worthy of him . . . actually only one. The first of these was a group organized for recording purposes only: Louis Armstrong's Hot Five (and later, Hot Seven) from 1925 to 1928. The other was the Louis Armstrong All Stars of the late forties—with trombonist Jack Teagarden, clarinetist Barney Bigard, and drummer Sid Catlett. With these All Stars—and they really were—Armstrong won tremendous acclaim all over the world. With them in Boston in 1947, he gave one of the most famous concerts of his career; it was later released on record.

The musicians who surrounded Satchmo in his Hot Five and Hot Seven are among the great personalities in jazz. Johnny Dodds, the clarinetist, was there, as was trombonist Kid Ory, who many years earlier had given Louis a job in New Orleans. Later, pianist Earl Hines was added. He created a style of piano playing based on Louis' trumpet which became—and still is—a model for many pianists throughout the world.

There are few artists whose work and personality are as closely joined as Armstrong's. It is almost as if they had become interchangeable—and thus even the musically flawed Armstrong was made effective through his personality. In the liner notes to a record taken from Edward R. Murrow's film, *Satchmo the Great,* Armstrong says: "When I pick up that horn . . . the world's behind me, and I don't concentrate on nothing but that horn. . . . I mean I don't feel no different about the horn now than I did when I was playing in New Orleans. No, that's my living and my life. I love them notes. That's why I try to make them right. . . . That's why I married four times. The chicks didn't live with that horn. . . . I mean, if I have an argument with my wife, that couldn't stop me from enjoying the show that I'm playing, I realize I could blow a horn after they pull away. . . . I've expressed myself in the horn. I fell in love with it and it fell in love with me. . . . What we play is life and a natural thing. . . . If it's for laughs, for showmanship, it would be the same as if we were in a backyard practicing or something. Everything that happens there is real. . . . Yeah, I'm happy. Doing the right thing, playing for the highest people to the lowest. . . . They come in Germany with them lorgnettes, and looking at you and everything, and by the time they get on the music, they done dropped the lorgnettes, and they're swinging, man! . . . When we played in Milano; after I finished my concert . . . I had to rush over to the La Scala and stand by those big cats like Verdi and Wagner . . . and take pictures, cause they figure our music's the same. We play them both from the heart."

In such passages more is revealed about Armstrong's nature and music than from all the words one can say about them. The musical findings are, anyhow, as simple and immediate as the music itself: Louis Armstrong made jazz "right." He brought together emotional expression and musical technique. After Armstrong, it is no longer possible to make excuses for wrong notes with claims of vitality or authenticity. Since Armstrong, jazz has to be just as right as other music.

A brilliant article written on the occasion of Armstrong's death by critic Ralph Gleason has this to say: "He took the tools of European musical organization—chords, notation, bars and the rest—and added to them the rhythms of the church and of New Orleans and (by definition) Africa, brought into the music the blue notes, the tricks of bending and twisting notes, and played it all with his unexcelled technique. He went as far with it as he could by using the blues and popular songs of the time as skeletons for his structural improvisations."

Many of the young people who love to operate with the term "revolution" have forgotten that Armstrong was the greatest of all jazz revolutionaries. They may be thinking of Charlie Parker or of Cecil Taylor and John Coltrane when they talk of musical revolutions. But the difference between the music before Armstrong and what he made of it is greater than the difference between the music before Parker or Taylor or Coltrane and what they made of it. The jazz revolution started by Armstrong is certainly the greater one.

A young jazz-rock drummer, Bob Melton, was right when after Armstrong's death he wrote in a letter to the editor of *down beat* magazine: "We've lost some great ones in the last five years . . . Today we lost the most daring innovator of all . . . I'm young, a 'long-hair,' a 'jazz-rock' drummer. . . . I've just played over and over about 20 times a 1947 Town Hall concert track of 'Ain't Misbehavin' ' with Pops. . . . I've played it over that many times because in the last three years I've been filling my head with 'free' tenor men and rock guitarists, and I've forgotten how audacious . . . is that the word? . . . I've forgotten how *outrageous* it *really was* . . . I mourn especially that so many of my generation . . . never heard Pops' message, and might not have listened if they had. You know that line of bull about not trusting anybody over 30? Pops is one of the few people in this century I trusted!"

Between the Armstrong of the Hot Five and Hot Seven and the Armstrong of the All Stars of the forties and fifties stands the Armstrong of the big bands. This period began when Armstrong became a member of Fletcher Henderson's orchestra for a year, starting in 1924 and immediately following his departure from King Oliver. Armstrong brought to the heretofore rather mediocre Henderson aggregation so much stimulation that one could say that the year 1924 marks the real beginning of big-band jazz. There is much meaning and logic in the fact that Armstrong, the most important personality of the New Orleans jazz tradition, was co-founder of the jazz phase which years later replaced the great era of New Orleans: the Swing era of the thirties, with its big bands. Even with the recordings of his Hot Five and Hot Seven, however, Armstrong soon placed himself beyond the New Orleans form, with its three-voiced interweaving of trumpet, trombone, and clarinet. Armstrong is the man who, precisely with the most significant records of the Hot Five and Seven, dissolved this fabric . . . an achievement characteristic of many stylistic developments in jazz: Again and again, the important personalities within a style have paved the way for the next style when at the zenith of their own. Only the "fans" demanded a standstill in one particular style. The musicians never wanted it.

Armstrong's playing in Fletcher Henderson's band at the Roseland Ballroom in New York was a sensation among musicians. Armstrong himself found much inspiration in the—for that time—compact section sounds of the big band. Later he became convinced that his trumpet could unfold better against the backdrop of a big band than with a small ensemble—a feeling not shared by many jazz fans.

This feeling may be related to the fact that from the start Armstrong wanted to reach a larger audience—a wish which perhaps was the prime mover of his musical career. It might also account for the records through which the Armstrong of later years so often entered the realm of popular music. In fact, what is lost in simply saying that essentially all of Armstrong's music was meant to be "popular" music —no matter how this might clash with the romanticism of many a jazz fan?

"There is a definite implication that Louis has a primary interest in pleasing his audiences," George Avakian has stated. Many jazz fans ignored Armstrong's success in the hit charts with "Hello Dolly" with a determination that could give the impression that they were somewhat discomforted by this success. For Armstrong, however—and maybe even more so for his wife, Lucille—the real climax of his career came in 1964, when he took the top spot on the charts—the listings of the world's most popular records—away from the reigning Beatles, and held this spot for weeks with "Hello Dolly."

To Armstrong, singing was at least as important as trumpet playing—not just during his final years when, if sometimes hardly able to blow his horn because of failing health, he remained a brilliant singer. During all phases of his career, he knew he could reach a larger audience as a singer than as an instrumentalist.

Rex Stewart, himself a trumpeter—in fact, one of the best—had to admit: "Louis has bestowed so many gifts upon the world that it is almost impossible to assess in which area his definitive impact has been most felt. My vote would be for his tremendous talent of communication. As profoundly creative as his trumpet ability is, I would place this in a secondary position. He was revered mostly by other professionals, whereas his gravel-voiced singing has carried his message far and wide, to regions and places where not only was the music little known, the language foreign, but where there also was the further barrier of a political system having labeled jazz as decadent. But when Satchmo sang, the entire picture changed. People saw the truth."

In a television program produced on the occasion of the 1970 Newport Jazz Festival, Louis said: "Well, people love me and my music and, you know, I love them and I have no problems at all with people. The minute I walk on the bandstand they know they're going to get something good and no jive and they know what they're there for and that's why they come. . . . I'm the audience myself. I'm my own audience and I don't like to hear myself play bad or something, so I know it ain't no good for you."

During all of Armstrong's life, again and again, there was talk of the impending "end of jazz music" or "death of jazz" in papers and magazines, from the twenties right on up to the seventies. The communicative genius in Armstrong never believed such talk: "I'd get me a record company and record nothing but what people said was finished—and we'd make a million dollars. You get those boys blowing out there—waitin' for that one gig, that one recording session, and we'd get together and set up, you know—we wouldn't go wrong. Everybody's looking for that top banana, but they're asleep on the good music that started all this," he told Dan Morgenstern.

Louis Armstrong's success is, in a very important sense, the success of his personality. Anybody who knew him or worked with him can tell of an experience that illuminates the warmth and sincerity of Armstrong's personality. In 1962, I produced a television show in New York with the Armstrong All Stars. Only a few minues before, Satchmo had been on camera sending regards to his German fans, asking them to have his *sauerkraut* and *wurst* ready for his upcoming tour. Then we were done; in a few minutes the studio had become dark and empty. I was next door, discussing the editing of the film. Satchmo, surrounded by a throng of fans, had left. . . . About 45 minutes later, the elevator door opens and out comes Louis Armstrong, to tell me that he had already been sitting in a taxi when he realized he had not said goodbye to me. Somewhat in doubt, I suspected he had forgotten something. No, said Satchmo, he had just come back up to say goodbye. Which he did—and then he left. Jack Bradley, the jazz photographer, commented, "Yes, that's the way he is."

In the sixties, it became fashionable to call Armstrong an "Uncle Tom" who had not shown any involvement in the black liberation struggle. However, in 1957 Satchmo said to a reporter of the Grand Forks (North Dakota) *Herald*: "The way they are treating my people in the South—the Government can go to hell!" And then he cancelled a tour of the Soviet Union organized by the State Department, refusing to go abroad for a government led by such a President: "The people over there ask me what's wrong with my country. What am I supposed to say? I have had a beautiful life in music, but I feel the situation the same as any other Negro. . . ." His words resounded throughout the globe.

On a Scandinavian tour in 1965, as he was watching television coverage of the black protest in Selma, Alabama, he told a reporter: "They would beat Jesus if he was black and marched."

Louis Armstrong had human solidarity and human compassion, but he was not a political man. "He loves people so much, he would even find some good in a criminal. He is not capable of hate," a British critic once wrote.

"Of how many American artists can it be said that they formed our century?" asks Martin Williams, and answers: "I am not sure about our writers, painters, our concert composers. But I am certain: Louis Armstrong has formed it."

In a television program on the occasion of Louis Armstrong's death in 1972, I said: "There is no sound today on radio, television, or record which could not somehow be traced back to Armstrong. He must be compared with the other great innovators in the arts of this century—Stravinsky, Picasso, Schönberg, James Joyce . . . He was the only native American among them. Without Armstrong, there would be no jazz—without jazz, there would be no modern popular music. All the sounds that surround us daily would be different without Satchmo; they would not exist without him. If it had not been for Armstrong, jazz would have remained the local folk music of New Orleans—as obscure as dozens of other bodies of folk music."

"Folk music?" he once asked. "Why daddy, I don't know no other kind of music *but* folk music. I ain't never heard a horse sing a song."

Soviet poet Yevgeny Yevtushenko wrote this poem in the days when the news of Louis Armstrong's death went around the world:

> Do as you did in the past
> And play.
> Cheer up the state of the angels,
> And so the sinners won't get too
> unhappy in Hell
> Make their lives a bit more hopeful
> Give to Armstrong a trumpet
> Angel Gabriel.

Bessie Smith

> Papa, Papa, you're in a good man's way
> Papa, Papa, you're in a good man's way
> I can find one better than you any time of day.
> You ain't no good, so you'd better haul your freight
> You ain't no good, so you'd better haul your freight
> Mama wants a live wire, Papa, you can take the gate.
> I'm a red hot woman, just full of flamin' youth
> I'm a red hot woman an' I'm full of flamin' youth
> You can't cool me, daddy, you're no good, that's the truth.

"There was no pretense. It was the real thing: a woman cutting her heart open with a knife until it was exposed for all to see . . . ," as Carl Van Vechten wrote.

Bessie Smith is the greatest of the many singers from the "classical" period of the blues, the twenties. She made 160 records, was featured in a movie short and was so successful at the peak of her career during the early and mid-twenties that her record sales saved the old Columbia Record Company from bankruptcy. Nearly ten million Bessie Smith records were sold. Bessie is "The Empress of the blues."

Her personality had an awesome effect. She often elicited responses from her listeners similar to religious experiences. They would shout "amen" when she finished a blues—as they did after the spirituals or gospel songs in the churches. At this time, nowhere else could one see as clearly the relationship between spirituals and the blues.

Mahalia Jackson, the great singer of the modern spirituals, the gospel songs, has said: "Anybody that sings the blues is in a deep pit yelling for help." The blues tells of many things that have been lost: lost love and lost happiness, lost freedom and lost human dignity. Often the blues tells its story through a veil of irony. The coexistence of sorrow and humor is characteristic of the blues. It is as if what one is singing about becomes more bearable because it is not taken quite seriously; even the most desperate situation may reveal something amusing. At times, the comic element arises because one's misfortune is so limitless that it cannot be presented in adequate words. And always there is hope in the blues. As in "Trouble in Mind": ". . . I won't be blue always 'cause the sun will shine in my back door some day."

Bessie Smith sang like someone who hopes that the sun one day will shine in her back door. And the sun did shine. Bessie earned a great deal of money. But she lost it all. She spent it on drink, and on whatever else she wanted; she gave it away to relatives and people who seemed needy, or lost it to the men she was in love with.

Bessie Smith was born during the last decade of the nineteenth century, in Tennessee. Nobody took care of her, but she started to sing early. One day, blues singer Ma Rainey—"the mother of the blues"—came to town. Ma heard Bessie and took her in tow as a member of her troupe.

Bessie sang in the circus and tent shows in the cities and towns of the South. Frank Walker heard her, and signed her to a contract. In 1923 she made her first record: "Downhearted Blues." It was a sensation. It sold 800,000 copies—almost all bought by blacks.

Aside from Bessie, there were many divas of the classic blues: Ma Rainey; Mamie Smith, who in 1920 made the first recording of a blues; Trixie Smith and Clara Smith, like Mamie, not related to Bessie; Ida Cox, who made "Hard Times Blues" and was rediscovered and recorded in 1961, when she was past 70; or Bertha "Chippie" Hill, who recorded "Trouble in Mind" with Louis Armstrong in 1926 and again with Lovie Austin's Blues Serenaders in 1946. But Bessie towers above them all.

It is hard to describe the magic of her voice. Maybe it is that its hardness and roughness seem to be edged with deep sorrow—even in the most frisky and humorous songs. Bessie sang as a representative of a people that had lived through centuries of slavery and, after Emancipation, often had to live through human situations that seemed worse than the darkest days of slavery. The fact that her sorrow found expression, without a trace of sentimentality, precisely in the rough hardness of her voice—this may be her secret.

On her recordings Bessie Smith often had first-rate accompanists —musicians like Louis Armstrong or James P. Johnson, Jack Teagarden, Chu Berry, Benny Goodman, Tommy Ladnier, Eddie Lang, Frankie Newton, Clarence Williams, and more of the best jazz musicians of the day. Fletcher Henderson—director of the then leading jazz orchestra—was responsible for her supporting combos for several years and placed his best men at her service.

No female singer in jazz is not influenced to some degree—directly or indirectly—by Bessie Smith. Louis Armstrong has said of her: "She used to thrill me at all times, the way she would phrase a note with a certain something in her voice no other blues singer could get. She had music in her soul and felt everything she did. Her sincerity with her music was an inspiration."

Her decline began in the later twenties. By 1930, Bessie Smith, who five years earlier had been the most successful artist of her race (and one of the most successful in America), was in such dire straits that she had to accept bookings no longer in the great theaters of the North, but back where she had started from: rural traveling shows in the Deep South.

On September 26, 1937, Bessie Smith died after a highway collision near Clarksdale, Mississippi.

In an earlier edition of this book, a story of Bessie Smith's death was retold which reflected a belief still widespread in jazz circles: The singer died because the white hospital to which she was taken after the accident refused to treat a black patient; she bled to death "on the steps" of this hospital.

While it must be granted that this story reflects the situation of the American Deep South at that time, it seems to have been proven (B. J. Skelton of the Clarksdale *Press Register* in the magazine "The Second Line" Vol. 9, Nos. 9&10, 1959) that the jazz world was misinformed in the case of Bessie Smith. She died in an ambulance en route to a black hospital in Clarksdale. It has also been ascertained that the wrong story originated in reports by members of the Chick Webb Band, which played Memphis shortly after the tragedy.

But the story of Bessie Smith's life and work does not end here. In 1971, Columbia Records rereleased the complete life work of Bessie Smith on five double albums. The "Empress of the Blues" thus received an honor unprecedented in popular music: Thirty-four years after her death, she gained world-wide fame for the second time. Marketing analyses have shown that mainly young people bought the results of this "most important and biggest single reissue project in history." This shows that the words of Bessie Smith's great fan and rediscoverer, John Hammond, were understood: "What Bessie sang in the twenties and thirties *is* the blues of today."

This renaissance of the music and name of Bessie Smith was also the cause for the fact that her grave—a hardly identifiable hill in range 12, lot 20, section 10 of the Mount Lawn Cemetery in Sharon Hill, Pennsylvania—finally received a headstone. Black Philadelphia citizens and Janis Joplin, the white popular singer from Texas who had learned so much from Bessie, contributed toward the 500-dollar bill for the tombstone. The inscription reads: *The Greatest Blues Singer in the World Will Never Stop Singing—Bessie Smith—1895-1937.*

Bix Beiderbecke

Bix Beiderbecke is among those musicians so well hidden by the myth which has evolved about them that it is difficult to discover the reality of the man. He was an inhibited person who never seemed satisfied with his achievements and always set unattainable goals for himself: "I think one of the reasons he drank so much was that he was a perfectionist and wanted to do more with music than any man possibly could. The frustration that resulted was a big factor," says trumpeter Jimmy McPartland, who came particularly close to him musically.

And Paul Whiteman relates: "Bix Beiderbecke, bless his soul, was crazy about the modern composers—Schönberg, Stravinsky and Ravel—but he had no time for the classics. One evening I took him to the opera. It happened to be *Siegfried*. When he heard the bird calls in the third act, with those intervals that are modern today, when he began to realize that the *leitmotifs* of the opera were dressed, undressed, disguised, broken down, and built up again in every conceivable fashion, he decided that old man Wagner wasn't so corny after all and that Swing musicians didn't know such a helluva lot."

Why Bix played in the dance orchestras of Whiteman and Jean Goldkette has often been misunderstood. The fans usually say he had to, because he could not make a living from jazz. But Bix was one of the most successful jazz musicians during the second half of the twenties. He was in a position to play where he wanted, and always earn money enough. George Avakian has said: "No one put a pistol in his back to make him join these bands." Actually Bix joined Whiteman—the epitome of commercial music of the day—because he was fascinated by the fancy arrangements written for the band. Here he could at least hang on to a reflection of the colorful orchestral palettes of Ravel, Delius, Stravinsky, and Debussy.

And thus it was—later in the thirties and forties—that record collectors all over the world bought the old records of Paul Whiteman to listen over and over again to eight or sixteen bars of solo blown by Bix—and these recordings have repeatedly been reissued up to this day. (Indeed, no other musical form from the first quarter of the century has remained so alive on records as jazz. In opera, reissues of Caruso and a few other great stars are still an exception, for example. In jazz, on the other hand, the rerelease of many of the recordings of every important musician from the first 25 years of jazz on records has become the rule.)

When Beiderbecke's work in Whiteman's orchestra is viewed from a contemporary perspective, the difference between it and the jazz records made by Bix with his friends is really not too great. Few of the musicians with Bix on his own recording dates could shine his shoes. Not much lasts on them aside from Bix's cornet: the ensemble passages he leads and the solos he improvises.

Bix Beiderbecke is—more than any other musician—the essence of Chicago style. The following musicians—although some only stem from it and gained real importance in other styles—were part of Chicago style: Saxophonist Frankie Trumbauer; trumpeters Muggsy Spanier and Jimmy McPartland; drummers Gene Krupa, George Wettling, and Dave Tough; the Dorsey Brothers (Jimmy on alto and clarinet, Tommy on trombone); tenor man Bud Freeman; violinist Joe Venuti, one of the few jazz violinists of those times; guitarists Eddie Lang and Eddie Condon; trombonists Glenn Miller and Jack Teagarden; clarinetists Pee Wee Russell, Frank Teschemacher, Benny Goodman, and Mezz Mezzrow; pianist Joe Sullivan; and a dozen or so others.

Their history is tragic in more ways than one. Rarely was so much enthusiasm for jazz concentrated in any single place as among them. Even so, most of their records from the period are unsatisfactory. The chief reason may be that there was no single band which, on a higher level, represented Chicago style per se. There is no ensemble like the Hot Seven or Jelly Roll Morton's Red Hot Peppers, which immediately come to mind when New Orleans style is mentioned; or like the bands of Count Basie or Benny Goodman and the Teddy Wilson combos in Swing; or the Charlie Parker Quintet in bop. From an ensemble point of view—in the sense explicated in the combo chapter of this book—Chicago style failed to produce a single satisfying recording. Almost always, only solo passages are remarkable: the unmistakable sound of Frank Teschemacher, the improvisations of Bud Freeman, the "cool" lines of Frankie Trumbauer, and—most of all—Bix Beiderbecke's cornet.

It has been argued that Chicago style is not really a "style." Its best recordings, indeed, come so close to Dixieland or New Orleans that what is most typical of Chicago style seems to be only the unfinished quality of its few fine records. And yet, there are a few musical signposts—mainly the rather novel emphasis on solo contributions—which differentiate Chicago from New Orleans and Dixieland. Most of all, the *human* unity and rapprochement among the Chicagoans was so strong and was reflected in their music with such immediacy that one hesitates—even now—to tear them apart on theoretical and academic grounds.

Bix Beiderbecke came from Davenport, Iowa. He was born there in 1903, the son of a family of German immigrants. His ancestors had been clergymen and organists in Pomerania and Mecklenburg for generations. One of his father's first names was Bismarck and this name—shortened to Bix—was inherited by the son. As a boy,

Bix sang in the chorus of the Lutheran church in Davenport. His grandfather led a male German glee club.

Bix was a musical prodigy. It is said that he first became acquainted with jazz through the riverboats which docked on the Mississippi; some of them had bands from New Orleans, and the music carried across the water.

Soon Bix became so absorbed in music that people began to think him a bit strange. He was expelled from school because he was interested only in music. The image of young Beiderbecke wandering the streets like a dreamer, his beat-up cornet wrapped in newspaper, became proverbial to all who knew him.

With Beiderbecke German romanticism—and the whole spectrum of feelings that belongs to it—entered jazz. Perhaps it was this romantic heritage, fraught with yearning and moodiness, which created in Bix a state of mind similar to that which had come to black people through their American experience. What to the great New Orleans musician was the musical heritage of Africa, if preserved only subconsciously, was to Beiderbecke the "Blue Flower" of German romanticism. He was a Novalis (a lyric poet of German romanticism [1772 to 1801]) of jazz, transported into the "jazz age" of the roaring twenties along with all the life-hungry characters of F. Scott Fitzgerald.

Beiderbecke was—aside from the old ragtime pianists—the first great "cool" soloist of jazz history. From him a line leads straight to Miles Davis.

At 18, he began to play in public. In 1923, he was with the first real Chicago style band, the Wolverines. In 1924, he met saxist Frank Trumbauer, with whom he made many of his finest records. There followed jobs with a variety of groups—with Jean Goldkette, Hoagy Carmichael, and other bands, until, by the late twenties, Bix was among the select musicians who gave the music of Paul Whiteman its jazz spice.

Around 1927 a lung complaint became noticeable. Bix paid no attention. He played and played, and when he wasn't playing, he drank or went to symphony concerts. He experimented in the harmonic world of Debussy. He did this primarily at the piano. He wrote a few pieces in which—in astonishingly simple, naïve fashion—Impressionism was captured. The titles are revealing: "In a Mist," "In the Dark," "Flashes."

As a trumpeter he was mainly a jazz musician: at the piano he was rather more indebted to the European tradition.

Finally, Whiteman sent him to Davenport for a rest. (He kept him on salary.) But it was too late. Bix could not stay home long. A girl —one of the few in his life—persuaded him to move to Queens and got him an apartment.

Bix spent the last weeks of his life in the apartment of bassist George Kraslow. Here something occurred which is characteristic of the love which Bix inspired in everyone. He was in the habit of getting up around three or four in the morning to play his cornet. It is hard to imagine a jazz musician doing such a thing without bringing down upon himself the wrath of all the neighbors. Nothing of the sort happened. The neighbors told Kraslow: "Please don't mention we said anything . . . we would hate for him to stop."

In August, 1931, Beiderbecke died of pneumonia in Kraslow's apartment. In Germany—on the "Lüneburger Heide" south of Hamburg—there are still Beiderbeckes. I asked them about Bix once. They had never heard of him.

Duke Ellington

Duke Ellington's Orchestra is a complex configuration of many spiritual and musical elements. To be sure, it was Duke Ellington's music which was created here; but it was just as much the music of each individual member of the band. Many Ellington pieces were genuine collective achievements, but it was Ellington who headed the collective. Attempts have been made to describe how Ellington recordings came into being—but the process is so subtle that verbalization appears crude. Duke, or his alter ego, the late Billy Strayhorn, arranger and jazz composer, or one of the members of the band, may come to the studio with a theme. Ellington plays it on the piano. The rhythm section falls in. One or another of the horn men picks it up. Baritone saxophonist Harry Carney may improvise a solo on it. The brass make up a suitable background for him. And Ellington sits at the piano and listens, gently accenting the harmonies—and suddenly he knows: This is how the piece should sound and no other way . . . later, when it is transcribed, the note paper only happens to retain what was—in the real meaning of the word—improvised into being.

The dynamic willpower with which Ellington stamped his ideas on his musicians, yet giving them the impression that he was only helping them to unfold and develop their hidden powers, was one of his many great gifts. Owing to this relationship between Duke and his musicians, which can barely be put into words, everything he had written seemed to be created for him and his orchestra—to such a degree that hardly anyone can copy it.

Duke Ellington has written countless popular melodies—melodies in the genre of Jerome Kern, Richard Rodgers, Cole Porter, or Irving Berlin. But even the most popular among them—"Sophisticated Lady," "Mood Indigo," "Creole Love Call," "Solitude," "Caravan" —have seldom become big hits. No matter how memorable and melodic, they seem to lose too much of their essence when not played by Ellington himself.

When Ellington was 18, he wanted to become a painter. By becoming a musician he only seemed to have abandoned painting. He painted not in colors but in sounds. His compositions—with their many colors of timbre and harmony—are musical paintings. Sometimes this is revealed by the titles: "The Flaming Sword," "Beautiful Indians," "Portrait of Bert Williams," "Sepia Panorama," "Country Girl," "Dusk in the Desert," "Mood Indigo," and so forth. Even as a conductor, Ellington remained the painter: in the grand manner in which he confronted the orchestra and, with a few sure movements of the hand, placed spots of color on a canvas made of sounds.

It may be due to this that he perceived his music as "the transformation of memories into sounds." The memories are pictures. Ellington said: "The memory of things gone is important to a jazz musician. I remember I once wrote a sixty-four-bar piece about a memory of when I was a little boy in bed and heard a man whistling on the street outside, his footsteps echoing away."

Again and again Ellington has expressed his pride in the color of his skin. Many of his larger works take their themes from black history: "Black, Brown, and Beige," the tone-painting of the American Negro who was "black" when he came to the New World, became "brown" in the days of slavery, and today is "beige"—not only in his color, but in his being as well; "Liberian Suite"—a work in six movements commissioned by the small republic on the west coast of Africa for its centennial; "Harlem," the work in which the atmosphere of New York's black city has been captured; "Deep South Suite," which reminds us of the locale of the origins of jazz, or "New World a-comin'," the work about a better world without racial discrimination.

"I want to create the music of the American Negro," Ellington once said, placing the accent on "American." He was conscious of the fact that the American Negro had more in common with the world of the white man than with that of black Africa. To a man who once wrote him that he should take his jungle music and go back to Africa as soon as possible, he replied with extreme courtesy that this unfortunately was impossible, inasmuch as the blood of the American Negro in the course of generations had become so mixed with that of the letterwriter that he would hardly be accepted there. But if it were all right with the writer, he would go to Europe. "There we are accepted."

Many critics have said that Ellington often comes too close to European music. They point to his concern with larger forms. But in this very concern is revealed an insufficiency in the molding of these forms which is certainly not European: An astonishing, amiable naïveté. This naïveté is also present in those medleys—long series of his many hits—with which the Duke again and again upset many of his more sophisticated fans at his concerts. Ellington simply failed to see why the idea of the hit medley should be alien to an artistic music.

In 1923 he joined a five-piece combo, which already included three of his later-to-be-famous instrumentalists: Otto Hardwicke, alto sax; Sonny Greer, drums; Arthur Whetsol, trumpet. The combo took the name "The Washingtonians"—from the capital, where Ellington was born in 1899, and where he spent a sheltered, carefree youth.

The Washingtonians went to New York where—as Duke tells—they sometimes had to split a hot dog five ways to keep from starving. After six months they gave up.

Three years later, Ellington tried again. This time it worked. Soon he was playing in Harlem's most expensive night spot, the "Cotton Club," located in Harlem but nevertheless catering to white tourists —to give them the feeling that they had "really been to Harlem." Ellington's first famous records were made: "East St. Louis Toodle-oo," "Jubilee Stomp," "Birmingham Breakdown," and "Black and Tan Fantasy."

The germ cell of his Cotton Club orchestra was preserved by Ellington well into the fifties. No other band leader has known so well how to keep an orchestra together. While other successful bands had personnel changes every few months, Ellington in 20 years only had six or seven significant alterations. Among the important soloists with Ellington at the Cotton Club were trumpeter Bubber Miley, trombonist Joe "Tricky Sam" Nanton, and baritone saxophonist Harry Carney. Ellington created his "jungle style" with Miley and Nanton. The expressive growl sounds of trumpet and trombone reminded of voices moaning in a jungle night.

The "jungle style" is one of the four styles identified with Duke Ellington. The other three are "mood style," "concerto style," and a "standard style" which came rather directly from Fletcher Henderson, the most important band leader of the twenties, and initially did not contribute much that was new. What it did have to offer, though, was clothed in typically Ellingtonian colors and sounds. In addition, of course, there is every imaginable mixture of these "styles."

The "mood style" partakes of blues-feeling—even in pieces which are not really blues. "Solitude," which says more in three minutes about the feeling its title describes than many a bulky book, is the most famous example of "mood style."

As far as the "concerto style" is concerned, there are really two: real small concerti for different soloists in the Ellington orchestra—such as the famous "Concerto for Cootie" for trumpeter Cootie Williams; and the aforementioned attempts to write jazz in larger forms.

The history of Duke Ellington is the history of the orchestra in jazz. No significant big band—and this includes commercial dance bands—has not been directly or indirectly influenced by the Duke. The list of innovations and techniques introduced by Ellington and subsequently picked up by other orchestras or players is unrivaled.

In 1927, he was the first to use the human voice as an instrument. The voice was Adelaide Hall's; the tune, "Creole Love Call." Later, he was to create similar effects with Kay Davis' coloratura soprano. Today, the expression "voice as instrument" has become a household phrase.

With his 1937 recording, "Caravan," a tune written by his Puerto Rican trombonist Juan Tizol, he paved the way for what has been called "Cuban jazz" since the forties—and what is today called "Latin jazz": The combination of Afro-Cuban, or rather Latin American, rhythms with the melodies and harmonies of North American jazz.

Duke Ellington was first to use so-called echo chambers in recording. Today, echo chambers are taken for granted. In 1938, Johnny Hodges' solo on "Empty Ballroom Blues" was the first solo ever to be recorded with echo chamber.

Toward the end of the twenties there is evidence of the "flatted fifth," the interval so characteristic of bop, in more than one Ellington piece.

With his baritone saxophonist, Harry Carney, Ellington created a place for the baritone in jazz.

For years, the history of the jazz bass was so closely tied to the Ellington orchestra that it might be as appropriate to discuss it here as in the later chapter about the bass. There is a straight-line development from the first recording with amplified bass—"Hot and Bothered" with bassist Wellman Braud in 1928—to the playing of Oscar Pettiford and especially Jimmy Blanton, who as a member of the Ellington band around 1940 made the bass the instrument it is in jazz today.

Everything we mean when we speak of sound and instrumentation in jazz can almost without exception be traced to Duke Ellington—at least until the mid-forties.

And most significantly: Duke Ellington anticipated by decades that strange and paradoxical something called the "jazz composer." He was the only one from 1925 to 1945 composing on the level on which jazz compositions are written today. Only then came all the others: John Lewis, Ralph Burns, Jimmy Giuffre, Bill Russo, George Russell, Gerry Mulligan, Charles Mingus, Carla Bley, Gil Evans. . . .

Incomparable, too, is the way in which Ellington dealt with the problem of the piano in jazz—about which we will hear later. The piano became an extension of his conducting hands. He plays only what is most necessary, indicates harmonies, bridges gaps, and leaves everything else to his musicians. His piano breaks are like a drummer's. Duke often executes them without using the piano stool, but they are filled with admirable tension, and when he plays one of his rare solos, one feels his roots in the old, genuine ragtime.

Many of these elements—Duke Ellington's origins in the Harlem and ragtime piano traditions of the twenties, his dominating interest in sound, instrumentation, composition, and jazz in larger forms— have overshadowed the rhythmical component which is so important to jazz. Critics have said that during lengthy periods of Ellington's career the drummer was "the weakest man in the band." When, in the early fifties, as excellent a drummer as Louis Bellson joined the Ellington orchestra he seemed to be a foreign element in the band. Only as recently as in the sixties, with drummers like Sam Woodyard and Rufus "Speedy" Jones, did Ellington seem to have solved the drummer problem in his band. The other big Swing bands—Count Basie, for example, or Chick Webb—were rhythmically superior—a statement which does not destroy Ellington's greatness. In fact, it is exactly Ellington's greatness which demands that the critic use criteria of only the highest level.

This is an impression which has been gained again and again, especially in Europe: When 60 or 70 year-old Ellington, on one of his round-the-world tours, brought his musicians, often a bit tired and worn out, to a European city, we found that even a weak Ellington orchestra is more impressive than many other famous jazz orchestras in top shape.

Ellington's two most famous orchestras were that of the late twenties, with Bubber Miley and "Tricky Sam" Nanton, and that of the early forties, with bassist Jimmy Blanton and tenor man Ben Webster. Modern big band jazz begins with the latter; "Ko Ko" is its best-known piece. After that, there was occasional talk about the decline of Ellington. Some people advised him to disband his orchestra, or to keep it together for only a few months of the year and spend the rest of his time composing. But Duke needed his musicians: "I want to have them around me," Leonard Feather quoted him, "to play my music. I'm not worried about creating music for posterity, I just want it to sound good right now!"

Besides, Duke Ellington himself put an end to the "decline" of which hasty critics had spoken. This occurred at the Newport Festival in 1956. Duke Ellington was billed as just another of the many attractions. Nobody expected anything out of the ordinary, but his appearance proved to be the climax of the whole festival. Duke played his old (1937) "Diminuendo and Crescendo in Blue," one of his first extended compositions; Paul Gonsalves blew 27 choruses of stimulating tenor sax on it, and the band generated a vitality and drive the likes of which had not been heard from Ellington in a long time.

It was one of the great jazz nights of the fifties. And what had been forgotten for a few years again became apparent: Duke Ellington was still the "grand old man" of big band jazz. A string of new masterpieces came into being: First and foremost the Shakespeare suite "Such Sweet Thunder," dedicated to the Shakespeare Festival at

Stratford, Ontario. With its spirited glosses, persiflages, and caricatures of great Shakespearean characters, it is one of the most beautiful of larger Ellington works.

In 1967, Billy Strayhorn died; in 1970, altoist Johnny Hodges. Since the death in 1932 of trumpeter Bubber Miley, who together with Ellington had formed the "jungle style" with his "growl play" between 1925 and 1929 (and who was replaced by another outstanding soloist, Cootie Williams), Ellington had not taken any personal loss so hard as the death of these two great musicians. The rich, sensuous solos of Johnny Hodges had reflected almost uninterruptedly since 1928—for 42 years!—the romantic, sensuous, impressionistic side of Ellington's character. Composer and arranger Billy Strayhorn had contributed many important pieces to the band's repertoire, such as "Lush Life," "Chelsea Bridge," and "Take the A Train," the theme song of the Ellington orchestra. As an orchestrator, he "tuned in" to Duke so perfectly that even specialists often were hard put to differentiate between what was written by Ellington and what by Billy "Sweet Pea" Strayhorn.

But Strayhorn's loss unearthed once again unforeseeable changes in Ellington. During the sixties, he had increasingly left the main composing and arranging work to Strayhorn. Now he began—alone again—to take the initiative himself. A large number of important new great works were created: The "Sacred Concert" and, following that, "Second Sacred Concert;" Duke Ellington's "70th Birthday Concert" (chosen as "Jazz Record of the Year" 1969 all over the world); the "Far East Suite" (in which Ellington reflects on a tour of Asia, sponsored by the Department of State, in a highly personal manner); and—above all—the "New Orleans Suite," which became the 1970 "Record of the Year." In the latter recording, Ellington salutes the New Orleans heritage of the jazz tradition, and transforms it into Ellingtonian music.

Jazz specialists have said that these years after Strayhorn's death comprise one of the richest and most fruitful periods in Ellington's fifty-year life work—in terms of composition, as well as in terms of the number of concerts and tours by the Ellington orchestra.

In 1970, the Ellington band went on the longest tour ever made by a jazz orchestra: The Soviet Union, Europe, Latin America—all without a break, for three months. And again and again, one had the impression that 70-year-old Ellington was the youngest, most active, most dynamic man in this orchestra of his juniors.

In 1969, we turned the Berlin Jazz Days into a grand birthday celebration for 70-year-old Ellington, and dozens of famous musicians
—not only the older generation, but also personalities like Miles
Davis or Cecil Taylor—payed tribute to the Duke. And a critic wrote
that Ellington had been "the youngest musician at the whole festival."

Four years later, on May 25, 1974, Duke Ellington—the Great
Orchestrator of Jazz—died of pneumonia in a New York hospital.
Just a couple of weeks before, *down beat,* on the occasion of his
75th birthday, had dedicated to him a whole issue full of congratula-
tions. The music world from Leonard Bernstein to Miles Davis paid
homage to him. Drummer Louis Bellson, possibly, found the most
moving words: "You, the MAESTRO, have given me a beautiful
education musically and have guided me to be a good human being.
Your valued knowledge and friendship will be with me forever. You
are the model citizen of the world. Your music is Peace, Love and
Happiness."

Coleman Hawkins and Lester Young

The sound of modern jazz is—to use a favorite term of arranger
Bill Russo—"tenorized." The man who tenorized it was Lester
Young.

More important musicians play tenor saxophone than any other instrument. The sound of Miles Davis' "Capitol" band has been described as the orchestration of Lester Young's tenor sound, and this
band was one of the shaping factors of modern jazz sound. The other
important jazz sound of the fifties—the "Four Brothers" sound of the
Woody Herman band—is tenorized, too. The tenor men who played
it, almost all other important tenorists, and even trumpeters, trombonists, pianists, alto and baritone saxists of the cool jazz of the fifties
—all were influenced by Lester Young.

With Lester "Pres" (from President) Young cool jazz, the jazz of
the fifties, began long before there was bebop, the jazz of the forties.
It began with the solos played by Lester in the old Count Basie band:
"Song of the Islands" and "Clap Hands, Here Comes Charlie," recorded in 1939—or "Lady Be Good," recorded by a Count Basie
combo in 1936—or even earlier, when Lester Young became a
member of Fletcher Henderson's band in 1934. "The whole band was
buzzing on me," Lester reminisced, "because I had taken Hawk's

place. I didn't have the same kind of sound he had. I was rooming at the Henderson's house, and Leora Henderson would wake me early in the morning and play Hawkins' records for me so I could play like he did. I wanted to play my own way, but I just listened. I didn't want to hurt her feelings."

Coleman Hawkins and Lester Young—these two names designate two great eras of jazz. Since "Bean" and "Pres" both play tenor, and since each of them holds approximately the same position in the phase of jazz he represents, no two other personalities could show more clearly how wide the scale of being and meaning in jazz really is. At one end stands Coleman Hawkins—the extroverted rhapsodist with the voluminous tone. Hard and gripping on fast pieces, erotically expressive on slow numbers, always vitally communicative, never shying away from quantity in utterances or notes, he is a Rubens of jazz. . . . And opposite him stands Lester Young—the introverted lyricist with the cautious tone, friendly and obliging on fast pieces, full of tender abandon on slow numbers, reserved in utterance, never stating a nuance more than absolutely necessary. He is a Cézanne of jazz, as Marshall Stearns has called him—which not only indicates his artistic but also his historical position: As Cézanne paved the way for modern painting, so Young paved the way for modern jazz.

It would be oversimplification, however, to assign one man to the jazz tradition and the other to modern jazz. Both stem from the tradition; both were "modern." Coleman Hawkins emerged from the "Jazz Hounds," the group accompanying blues singer Mamie Smith; Lester Young was born near New Orleans and in his youth received the same impressions which affected the old, famous New Orleans musicians: Street parades, Mardi gras, and New Orleans funerals. When the modern jazz of the forties sprang up, Coleman Hawkins was the first noted "traditional" jazz musician to play with the young bebop revolutionaries. And in the second half of the fifties, the period just preceding the death of Young (who after years of indulgence in alcohol and marijuana was only a shadow of his former self), the man who preceded him—Coleman Hawkins—retained his old, indestructible vitality and power.

Hawkins is "the father of the tenor saxophone." To be sure, there were some tenor players before him, but the instrument was not an acknowledged jazz horn. It fell into the category of strange noise makers—like the euphonium, the sousaphone, or the bass sax.

Coleman Hawkins was 21 when he came to New York with

Mamie Smith in 1923. He was playing blues and jazz in the style of that time—similar possibly to King Oliver and Louis Armstrong. That same year, he joined the first important big band—Fletcher Henderson's—and remained until 1934. He was one of the first real soloists, in the sense of the great virtuosos of the Swing period. He was one of the first to make records with the young European musicians who were just then beginning to hear the jazz message: in 1934 England, in 1935 with The Ramblers in Holland and with Django Reinhardt in Paris. And as modern jazz began—as we have mentioned—he was again one of the first to participate. Hawkins could always be found where alive and original jazz was being created.

His first famous solo on record was "Stampede," in 1926 with Fletcher Henderson. In 1929 came "One Hour" with the Mound City Blue Blowers, who included some of the Chicago style practitioners. And then—in 1934, again with Henderson, "Talk of the Town"—probably the first great ballad interpretation in jazz history, the foundation for everything now meant by ballad playing in modern jazz. (Miles Davis said: "When I heard Hawk, I learned to play ballads.") Then came the European recordings, such as "I Wanna Go Back to Harlem" with the Dutch Ramblers, or "Stardust" with Django Reinhardt. When Hawkins returned to the United States in 1939, he almost immediately scored the greatest success of his career: "Body and Soul," a jazz record which became a world-wide hit. Hawkins could not understand it: "I've been playing like that all my life . . . it wasn't anything special." In 1943 he blew a breathtaking solo on "The Man I Love" with Oscar Pettiford's bass and Shelly Manne's drums, and then, in 1947, came "Picasso"—a long improvisation for unaccompanied tenor saxophone, based on the harmonies of the piece identified with Hawkins—"Body and Soul." It is reminiscent in structure and delineation of Johann Sebastian Bach's Chaconne from the D-minor Partita for solo violin, and full of the same baroque vitality and linearity.

On all these records, and in almost everything he has ever played, Hawkins is the master of the chorus. A Hawkins solo, it has been said, is the classic example of how to develop a solo statement from a phrase. And almost every phrase Hawkins has blown could itself be used again as the theme for a jazz improvisation. There is only one musician who can be compared to him in this respect—the one who in almost every other respect is his opposite: Lester Young.

While everything about Hawkins, the human being, is simple and comprehensible, everything about Lester is strange and incomprehensible. A booking agent, Nat Hentoff relates, was alienated from Lester because he couldn't talk to him. "I'd talk to him," the agent said, "and all he'd say was 'Bells!' or 'Ding Dong!' I finally decided I'd go to Bellevue if I wanted to talk to crazy people. . . ."

He left the Count Basie band, from which he emerged and with which he was connected as Hawkins had been with Fletcher Henderson's band, because Basie had set a recording date for a Friday the 13th—and Lester refused to play on that day.

His jargon was almost a language in itself, which made it hard for people to understand him in conversation. No one has coined as many jazz expressions as he—right down to the word "cool"—so that not only the style but also the expression stems from him. He called his colleagues "lady" and addressed club owners as "Pres"; he asked pianist Bobby Scott about his "left people" when he wanted to tease Scott about the habit (shared by most modern pianists) of running hornlike lines with his right hand while the left hardly came into play. Norman Granz says that Lester for a time pretended to be speaking a foreign language: "It was gibberish, but he did it with a straight face and with conviction."

Lester—or "Pres," as he was called—had the sensibility of a Baudelaire or James Joyce. "He lives in his own world," an agent said about him. What was outside of this world, was, according to Pres's convictions, not in the world at all. But this world of his was a wonderful world, a world that was mild and friendly and lovely. "Anything that hurts a human being hurts him," said drummer Jo Jones.

Jones relates: "Everyone playing an instrument in jazz expresses what's on his mind. Lester would play a lot of musical phrases that were actually words. He would literally talk on his horn. That's his conversation. I can tell what he's talking about in 85 percent of what he'll play in a night. I could write his thoughts down on paper from what I hear from his horn. Benny Goodman even made a tune out of a phrase Lester would play on his horn—'I want some money.' " Because Lester talked on his horn, he loved to listen to singers: "Most of the time I spend in listening to records is listening to singers and getting the lyrics to different songs."

When improvising on a melody, Lester Young attempted to convey the lyrics of this melody to the listener directly and without the aid of words. Thus, he recorded some of his most beautiful solos as accompanist to a singer: Billie Holiday, the greatest female singer between Bessie Smith and Ella Fitzgerald—perhaps simply the greatest, and in any case the personification of swing singing, as Bessie Smith was the personification of the classsic blues, and Ella is the personification of the modern jazz song. The way in which Pres backed "Lady Day"—the name he gave her—set the standard for accompaniments to singing in jazz, with such pieces as "Time on My Hands," "Without Your Love," or "Me, Myself and I."

What Lester tells us when he improvises freely on his tenor sax might sound something like this: "I was born near New Orleans, August 27, 1909. I stayed in New Orleans until I was ten. During the carnival season we all traveled with the minstrel show, through Kansas, Nebraska, South Dakota, all through there.

"I played drums from the time I was ten to about thirteen. Quit them because I got tired of packing them up. I'd take a look at the girls after the show, and before I'd get the drums packed, they'd be gone.

"For a good five or six years after that I played the alto, and then the baritone when I joined Art Bronson's band. Ran away from my father when I was about 18. . . . I joined Art Bronson and his Bostonians. Played with him for three or four years . . . anyway, I was playing the baritone and it was weighing me down. I'm real lazy, you know. So when the tenor man left, I took over his instrument. . . .

"Used to hear the Basie band all the time on the radio and figured they needed a tenor player. They were at the Reno Club in Kansas City. It was crazy, the whole band was gone, but just this tenor player. I figured it was about time, so I sent Basie a telegram. . . .

"But Basie was like school. I used to fall asleep in school, because I had my lesson, and there was nothing else to do. The teacher would be teaching those who hadn't studied at home, but I had, so I'd go to sleep . . . you had to sit there and play it over and over again. Just sit in that chair.

"I joined Fletcher Henderson in Detroit in 1934. Basie was in Little Rock then, and Henderson offered me more money. Basie said I could go . . . was with Henderson only about six months. The band wasn't working very much . . . then back to Basie until 1944 and the army."

The army broke Lester Young. Nat Hentoff has told of this. He was harassed, and his individuality and sensitivity were deadened, in the way armies all over the world deaden individuality and sensitivity. Through the army, hate came into his life. For a musician whose message was lyricism and tenderness and amiability there was not much left.

The other thing which oppressed him—subsconsciously and sometimes consciously—was the fact that almost every tenor player was playing *à la* Pres . . . until during the last years of his life Sonny Rollins and the musicians of his school came up. There was, for example, Paul Quinichette; Lester called him "Lady Q." Pres's manager tells of the time when both were playing at Birdland—the famous, now defunct jazz club in New York—and Lester came off the stand saying: "I don't know whether to play like me or like Lady Q, because he's playing so much like me."

It was a peculiar brand of irony: On the one hand, nothing underlined Lester's enormous artistic success more than that a generation of tenor men should play like him; on the other hand, an uncompromising individualist like he found it intolerable that they all should play like him—and he like them.

Most of the records Lester made in the fifties—such as the ones for Norman Granz's Verve label—are in this category. They were only a pale reflection of the great "President." But often there were sparks, and one could still feel something of the genius of this great musician—for instance, on the record "Jazz Giants of 1956," with Teddy Wilson, Roy Eldridge, Vic Dickenson, and other great Swing musicians.

For years Lester traveled with Norman Granz's concert unit, "Jazz at the Philharmonic," all over the world. Night after night, he witnessed how Flip Phillips or Illinois Jacquet brought audiences to their feet with the exhibitionism of their tenor solos. He disliked this exhibitionistic, ecstatic way of playing tenor, but it reached the point where he himself often utilized it—and from this, too, he must have suffered. For years, Lester Young lived almost uninterruptedly in a state of mild intoxication, until, in March of 1959, he died after a tragic engagement at the "Blue Note," a Paris jazz club. Ben Benjamin, the club owner, reports: "Lester was very sick when he worked for me. He was almost apathetic. He wanted to go home because, as he said, he couldn't talk to the French doctors. He had ulcers, and I think he drank a little too much. . . ."

Lester came back to New York in time to die. On the early morning of his arrival, he died in the Hotel Alvin, on the "musician's crossroad" at 52nd Street and Broadway, where he had lived during the last years of his life.

The only thing Lester retained throughout the crisis periods of his life, and down to his last days, was his sound—as Coleman Hawkins retained his. "The only thing nobody can steal from you is your sound. Sound alone is important," Hawkins once said.

Lester's sonority stems from Frankie Trumbauer and Bud Freeman, the Chicago-style musicians. "Trumbauer was my idol. . . . I imagine I can still play all those solos off the records. He played the C-melody saxophone. I tried to get the sound of a C-melody on a tenor. That's why I don't sound like other people. . . . I did like Bud Freeman very much. Nobody played like him." The line that leads from Chicago style via Lester Young to cool jazz is direct.

The name of Lester Young even stands at the beginning of bebop. Kenny Clarke tells about it: "They began to talk about Bird (Charlie Parker) because he was playing like Pres on alto. People became concerned about what he was doing. We thought that was something phenomenal because Lester Young was the pace setter, the style setter at that time. . . . We went to listen to Bird at Monroe's (a Harlem club) for no other reason except that he sounded like Pres . . . until we found out that he had something of his own to offer . . . something new." And Parker himself said: "I was crazy about Lester. He played so clean and beautiful, but I wasn't influenced by Lester. Our ideas ran on differently."

Indeed, these were two different directions. It would be possible to show that modern jazz as a whole—up to free jazz—has developed in the counterplay of the ideas of Lester Young and Charlie Parker. Lester came first; then, when Parker arrived, *his* influence became dominant—but then, in the fifties, Pres's hour struck again, with a host of musicians playing "cool" *à la* Lester Young . . . until finally, with the coming of hard-bop, Bird's influence again gained overwhelming importance. And with this Bird influence, with the sonority of Sonny Rollins' tenor sax, we return—and so the circle of this chapter closes—to Coleman Hawkins: His hard, dramatic style now was in the right place—after Lester Young's desire to make the world "nice and cozy" had proven vain, although it had been shared by all jazz musicians for so many years. Hawkins, whose career preceded that of Lester Young by almost ten years, also survived Lester by ten years. His health was as robust as his playing (with the exception of the last years of his life), and only weeks before his death—in June of 1969—he appeared in public and on television. The tenor saxophonists of free jazz who meanwhile had so radically changed jazz—Archie Shepp, Pharaoh Sanders, Albert Ayler, and others—all agreed who had been the first impulses for those expanding inflections of tenor sound that were their main focus: Coleman Hawkins. Archie Shepp said it clearly: "I play Hawk today."

For Coleman Hawkins, this whole rich era he had lived through —from Mamie Smith in 1922 to the post-Coltrane period in 1969— was not as varied as it seems to us today. It was *one* style and *one* era. The style was jazz, and from the beginning until today and beyond, it was the era of jazz. Progress was a foreign word to Hawkins. He once said to the critic Stanley Dance: "What Charlie Parker and Dizzy were doing was 'far out' to a lot of people, but it was just music to me." And he made recordings with the young bebop people only because "they needed help." When Dance talked to him about Mamie Smith and Fletcher Henderson and the good old days, Hawkins said: "I don't think I ever was a child."

Charlie Parker and Dizzy Gillespie

"Just a week before his death," Leonard Feather tells, "Parker ran into Gillespie at Basin Street. He was desperate, pitiful, pleading. 'Let's get together again,' he urged Dizzy. 'I want to play with you again before it is too late.' "

"Dizzy can't get over Bird saying that to him," recalls Loraine, Dizzy's wife. "His eyes get full of water even now when he thinks about it. . . . He was downstairs a week later when I heard all this crying. I found out somebody had called and told him Charlie was dead. I didn't say anything; what could you say? I just let him sit there and cry it out."

Charley Parker and Dizzy Gillespie are the Dioscuri of bebop.

Charlie Parker comes from Kansas City. He was born on August 29, 1920, but when he died in 1955, the doctors who performed the autopsy said that he might as well have been 55 as 35.

Dizzy Gillespie comes from South Carolina. He was born on October 21, 1917. In all phases of his life he has appeared to be five to eight years younger than he is.

Both grew up in the world of racial discrimination and from early youth learned to know all this signifies in terms of indignity.

Nobody cared much about the growing Charlie. Throughout his youth, he lacked love and the warmth of the nest.

Dizzy had a sheltered youth and grew up in a well-ordered family environment.

No one was musical in Charlie Parker's family. At 13, he was playing baritone sax. A few years later, alto was added.

Dizzy Gillespie's father was an amateur musician. He taught his kids to play several instruments. At 14, Dizzy's chief horn was the trombone. A year later, trumpet was added.

To this day, no one has discovered why Charlie Parker became a musician. The alto-saxophonist Gigi Gryce—one of his best friends—says: "Parker was a natural genius. If he had become a plumber, I believe he would have been a great one."

It seemed decided from the start that Dizzy would become a musician. He studied theory and harmony.

At 15 years of age— Charlie Parker was forced to earn his own keep. "We had to play," he said, "from nine in the evening to five in the morning without a break. We usually got $1 or $1.25 a night."

At the age at which Dizzy completed the studies paid for by his father . . .

In 1937—at 17—Charlie became a member of Jay McShann's band, a typical Kansas City riff and blues orchestra. It is questionable whether Parker had a model. It is probable that Parker's style was wholly conceived from the start; that his colleagues at first considered it "terrible" was most likely because he played "different" from anybody else.

In the same year—1937—Dizzy took over Roy Eldridge's chair in Teddy Hill's band. Roy was Dizzy's great model. The Hill band had grown out of the Luis Russell orchestra, and Russell himself had taken over the King Oliver band in 1929. Thus, the jazz genealogy from Dizzy back to King Oliver is surprisingly short.

Parker's real schooling and tradition was the blues. He heard it constantly in Kansas City, and played it night after night with Jay McShann.

Dizzy Gillespie, too, has roots in the jazz tradition, but it is rather the gay tradition of New Orleans and Dixieland music.

The titles of the first records made by both men are symbolic:

Charlie Parker recorded "Confessin' the Blues" in 1941 with Jay McShann's band when they came to New York.

Dizzy Gillespie recorded, in mid-1937, just after becoming a member of Teddy Hill's band, Jelly Roll Morton's "King Porter Stomp."

Charlie Parker at first did not get far from Kansas City. He lived a deary, joyless life and became acquainted with narcotics almost simultaneously with music. It is believed that Parker had become a victim of "the habit" by the time he was 15.

Dizzy went to Europe with Teddy Hill's band in the summer of 1937. Teddy Hill writes: "Some of the guys threatened not to go if the frantic one went too. But it developed that youthful Dizzy, with all his eccentricities and practical jokes, was the most stable man of the group. He was able to save so much money that he encouraged the others to borrow from him so that he'd have an income in case things got rough back in the States."

The inhibitions and complexes of his life began the moment he became a musician.
Charlie Parker played with Jay McShann until 1941. There were a few interruptions. Once he landed in jail for twenty-two days when he refused to pay his cab fare. Then there was a fugitive journey to Chicago. He arrived there dirty and tattered as if he had "just got off a freight car." But he was playing "like you never heard. . . ."

Dizzy Gillespie was successful from the moment he began to play. In Paris it was first noticed that his playing was different. A French drummer wrote at the time: "There is in the band of Teddy Hill a very young trumpeter who promises much. It is a pity that he has no opportunity to make recordings here. He is—along with trombonist Dickie Wells—by far the most gifted musician in the band. His name is Dizzy Gillespie."

For three months he was a dishwasher for $9 a week in a second-rate Harlem restaurant. Sometimes he didn't even have a horn to play on. "I was always on a panic," is one of his best-known quotes. He slept in garages, became completely run down. "Worst of all was that nobody understood my music."

Upon his return from Europe, Dizzy Gillespie became a successful musician, playing in different bands. In 1939, he became a member of Cab Calloway's orchestra.

When Parker once played in a jam session in Kansas City with members of the Basie band, and nobody liked what he was blowing, drummer Jo Jones, "as an expression of his feelings took his cymbal off and threw it almost the entire distance of the room. Bird just packed up his horn and went out."

Cab Calloway didn't like the way Dizzy played. Nor did he care for Dizzy's penchant for practical jokes. During an engagement in Hartford, someone (not Dizzy) threw a spitball out on the stage. After the curtain, Cab blamed Diz, "and an argument ensued," bassist Milt Hinton relates. "Cab made a pass at Dizzy, and Dizzy came at him with a knife. I grabbed Diz's hand . . . but Cab was nicked in the scuffle. Cab hadn't realized he'd been cut until he was back in the dressing room. . . ."

Parker tells: "I'd been getting bored with the stereotyped changes that were being used all the time at the time, and I kept thinking there's bound it be something else. I could hear it sometimes, but I couldn't play it."

Dizzy tells: "When I was growing up, all I wanted to play was Swing. Eldridge was my boy. All I ever did was try to play like him; but I never quite made it. I'd get all messed up because I couldn't get it. So I tried something else. That has developed into what became known as bop."

"Well, that night I was working over 'Cherokee,' and, as I did, I found that by using the higher intervals of a chord as a melody line and backing them with appropriately related changes, I could play the thing I'd been hearing. I came alive."

Dizzy's first record with Cab Calloway's band had the odd title, "Chop, Chop, Charlie Chan"; that was March 8, 1940. Dizzy didn't yet know Charlie Parker. A dozen years later, Parker's name appeared on the last record made by Dizzy and Bird together under the pseudonym "Charlie Chan."

When he was not playing with Jay McShann, Charlie Parker pulled through with menial jobs. He participated in every jam session he could find.

Starting in 1939 Dizzy had begun to arrange. Successful bands like Woody Herman's, Jimmy Dorsey's and Ina Ray Hutton's bought his arrangements.

In 1941 he came to New York with the McShann band. They played at the Savoy Ballroom in Harlem.

Dizzy Gillespie came by to sit in.

Soon, the McShann band left New York. Parker went along to Detroit. Then he no longer could stand the routine arrangements and left the band, without saying anything. He never cared much for big bands.

Dizzy Gillespie evolved more and more into a big-band musician. After the row with Calloway he worked in the big bands of Benny Carter, Charlie Barnet, Lucky Millinder, Earl Hines (1943), Duke Ellington, and Billy Eckstine.

After he had left the McShann band, Charlie Parker went almost daily to Minton's in Harlem. There a band consisting of pianist Thelonious Monk, guitarist Charlie Christian, trumpeter Joe Guy, bassist Nick Fenton, and drummer Kenny Clarke was playing. "Nobody," Monk was to say later, "was sitting there trying to make up something new on purpose. The job at Minton's was a job we were playing, that's all." Yet, Minton's became the point of crystallization for bop. There Charlie Parker and Dizzy Gillespie met again.

Monk relates that Charlie Parker's ability and authority were immediately accepted when he began to show up at Minton's. All could feel his creative productive genius.

Billy Eckstine relates: "Now Diz is like a fox, you know. He's one of the smartest guys around. Musically, he knows what he is doing backwards and forwards. So what he hears—that you think maybe is going through—goes in and stays. Later, he'll go home and figure it all out just what it is."

Charlie Parker and Dizzy Gillespie became inseparable. In 1943 they played together in Earl Hines's band; in 1944 they were both with Billy Eckstine. In the same year they co-led a combo on 52nd Street, which became The Street of bop. In 1944 they also made their first joint recording.

Tony Scott relates: "And Bird came in one night and sat in with Don Byas. He blew 'Cherokee' and everybody just flipped. . . . When Bird and Diz hit The Street regularly a couple of years later, everybody was astounded and nobody could get near their way of playing music. Finally, Bird and Dizzy made records, and then guys could imitate and go from

In Leonard Feather's words: ". . . Dizzy's followers were aping his goatee, beret and glasses, even his gait." Dizzy created then what was to go around the world as "bebop-fashion." Fan magazines advertised "bebop ties."

there. Everybody was experimenting around 1942, but nobody had set a style yet. Bird provided the push. An odd thing about Bird's influence on The Street is that the style he was so influential in developing was played on all instruments but his own horn—the alto. The reason was that Bird was so supreme on the alto."

Charlie Parker had found, in the quintet format of bebop, the instrumentation most congenial to him: sax, trumpet, and three rhythm. The Charlie Parker Quintet became as significant to modern jazz as Louis Armstrong's Hot Five had been to traditional.

Deep inside, Dizzy is a big-band man. In 1945, he founded his first own big band. From 1946 to 1950 he had large bands almost steadily. In 1948 he took one to Europe. His Paris concert had long-lasting effects on European jazz.

It becomes clearer: Dizzy Gillespie in those days was the most frequently mentioned bebop musician. If he did not bring to this music the creative impulses that radiated from Charlie Parker, he gave it the glamor and power without which it could not have conquered the world.

Billy Eckstine says: "Bird was responsible for the actual playing of [bebop], more than anyone else. But for putting it down, Dizzy was responsible."

With his Charlie Parker Quintet, Bird made the most important combo recordings of bebop: "Koko," based on the changes to "Cherokee," the piece with which he first had attracted attention; "Now Is the Time," a blues; "Chasin' the Bird," with the fugato entry of trumpeter Miles Davis —commencing the fashion of fugues and fugati in modern jazz . . . and countless others. Accompanied by Erroll Garner he recorded "Cool Blues," relating coolness and the blues in the title itself.

"Things to Come" became the most important record of the Gillespie big band, an apocalyptic vision of the things that were to come: a broiling, twitching mass of lava, out of which for a few seconds arise ghostly figurations, to disappear again at once. But above it all the clear and triumphant sound of Dizzy's trumpet. Music of the chaos, but also music about man's victory over chaos!

Charlie Parker's alto sax became the most expressive voice of modern jazz—each note arising from the blues tradition, often imperfect, but always from the depths of a tortured soul. In a period when playing without vibrato was almost taken for granted, the most creative musician of the period played with a pronounced vibrato —the vibrato of the great blues instrumentalists.

Dizzy Gillespie's trumpet became the clearest, most clarionlike and yet most flexible trumpet voice in the history of jazz. Almost every phrase he played was perfect.

Bird became the basic improviser, the chorus-man par excellence, interested more than anything in the flow of the lines he played. Parker made the 18-year-old trumpeter Miles Davis a member of his quintet—the man who was to become the dominant improviser of the next phase in modern jazz. Parker encouraged Davis, who had begun à la Gillespie and Parker, to find a style of his own.

Dizzy Gillespie became more and more interested in the percussive aspects of the new jazz. In the words of Billy Eckstine: "If you ever listen to Diz humming something, he hums the drum and bass part and everything because it all fits in with what he's doing. Like 'Oop-Bop-Sh'Bam.' That's a drum thing. And 'Salt Peanuts' was another. It was a drum lick. . . ."

Years later, when Parker was under contract to Norman Granz, he recorded with Machito's orchestra. But the results were hardly representative Bird. Parker's formula remained the quintet: the smallest instrumentation in which it was possible to create "form" through the unison statement of theme at beginning and end, while retaining complete improvisatory freedom for the remainder.

Dizzy was interested in Afro-Cuban rhythms. He played with musicians from the Cuban orchestra of Machito. In 1947 he added the Cuban drummer Chano Pozo to his band and thus brought a wealth of ancient West African rhythms and drum-patterns into modern jazz.

In Charlie Parker's words: "I'd be happy if what I played would simply be called 'music.' "

To the question how the future of jazz would develop he answered: "Probably it will go back to where it all started from: a man beating a drum."

On another occasion, Charlie Parker said: "Life used to be so cruel to musicians, just the way it is today. They say that when Beethoven was on his deathbed he shook his fist at the world because they just didn't understand. Nobody in his own time ever really dug anything he wrote. But that's music."

According to Leonard Feather, Dizzy Gillespie never took himself, or the music he created, as seriously as did the countless music lovers and musicians who, for the last decade or more, have spent so much time investigating, discussing, and imitating everything.

In 1946 Charlie Parker had the first major breakdown of his life. It came during the recording of "Lover Man" at the Dial record studios. When Charlie came home after the session, he started a fire in his hotel room and ran—naked and screaming—into the hall.

"The other musicians who took part in the incubating process that evolved into bop today are dead, or struggling intermittently with the drug habit. Gillespie apparently has never suffered any major frustration or neurosis. . . ."

According to Orrin Keepnews: "There can be little doubt that he was a tortured man, and there are several who emphasize the loneliness." Often he would stay up all night, riding aimlessly around on the subway. As a musician, on stage, he never developed the ability to "sell" himself and his music. He just stood there and played.

The more it became apparent that Dizzy could not keep his big band together permanently, the more consciously he became the comedian of his music. As the "clown of bebop" he attempted to sell that which otherwise had proven itself unsaleable. He was not only the best trumpeter of bop but also one of its foremost vocalists. Always, he retained controlled superiority.

In the year 1950, both Dizzy and Bird made recordings with large string ensembles—Bird in New York, Dizzy in California. This was to become the only major financial success of Parker's career. The fanatics among the fans beat their breasts: Bird and Dizzy had gone "commercial." It was revealing how differently the two reacted:

Parker, for whom recording with strings was the fulfillment of a lifelong wish, and for whom the strings represented that aura of the symphony which he had always admired, suffered from the prejudiced judgment of the fans.

Gillespie, for whom the string recordings actually had meant not much more than another record date, made fun of the ignorance of those who talked about "commercialism."

Charlie Parker was never satisfied with himself. He never knew how to answer the question of what recordings he thought to be his best. In answer to the question about his favorite musicians, a jazz man only came in third place: Duke Ellington. Before him came Brahms and Schönberg, after him Hindemith and Stravinsky. But more than any musician he loved Omar Khayyám, the Persian poet.

Leonard Feather: "Charlie drank more and more in a desperate attempt to stay away from narcotics while still avoiding the terrors of sober reality."

At a time when there was hardly a musician playing anywhere in the world who was not in some degree or fashion under Bird's influence —when this influence had even penetrated into the world of dance and pop-music—Parker was only playing occasionally. According to Orrin Keepnews: "He had given up the fight towards the end . . . in 1954 he sent [his former wife] Doris a poem . . . in part it sets forth a credo that might easily have been his own: 'Hear the words! Not the doctrine. Hear the speech! Not the meaning . . . Death is an imminent thing . . . My fire is unquenchable.' "

On March 12, 1955, he died. He had been watching television, laughing about a joke on the Dorsey Brothers' Show.

The Parker myth began almost immediately. Among those who paid him tribute was disc jockey Al "Jazzbo" Collins: "I don't be-

In 1954, at a birthday party for his wife, somebody fell over Dizzy's trumpet and bent the horn so that the bell pointed upwards. "After his anger had subsided," according to Leonard Feather, "Dizzy tried to play the horn and found that the sound seemed to reach his ears better. . . . The next day he went to a trumpet manufacturer to ask whether he could put the idea into mass production. . . ." Dizzy wanted to take out a patent. But it was discovered that a similar instrument had been patented 150 years earlier.

Dizzy Gillespie became the first "world statesman" of the international jazz tours organized by the American Department of State. With the help of funds from Washington, he managed to put together a big band again. He went on world-wide tours first to Asia and southeastern Europe, later to Latin America. In Athens he gave the most triumphant concert of his career. It was during the height of the Cyprian crisis. The Greeks were furious at the Americans. The headlines in the newspapers asked why the Americans were sending a bunch of jazz musicians instead of guns to chase the British out of Cyprus. Dizzy's concert began in a very tense atmosphere. But when the four white and nine black musicians swung into Dizzy's "Tour de Force," written shortly before the tour, the audience broke into wild applause. All Athens was filled with enthusiasm over the Gillespie band, and the political climate

lieve that in the whole history of jazz there was a musician more recognized and less understood than he."

"Bird Lives!" This is still true to-day—and especially today again. At the beginning of the seventies, all the important altoists are shaped directly by Parker: Ornette Coleman, Phil Woods, Lee Konitz, Charlie Mariano, Sonny Stitt, Gary Bartz, Jackie McLean, Frank Stro-zier, Cannonball Adderley, Charles McPherson, Anthony Braxton, all the others. And Bird's greatness is shown in that this influence lives on in the playing of so many musi-cians who vary greatly from each other—and this influence will con-tinue to live.

changed so markedly that a news-paper stated: "Dizzy Gillespie is a better diplomat than all the diplo-mats the U.S.A. ever had in this part of the world."

More than anyone else, Dizzy has carried the bop idiom through all subsequent styles and ways of playing: cool and hard bop, free, and rock-influenced—and yet, he unmistakably remained Dizzy Gil-lespie.

For the young audience of the six-ties and seventies, he stands di-rectly beside Louis Armstrong. This audience does not realize any more—and justifiably—that John Birks Gillespie once had begun as Satchmo's antipode.

Miles Davis

"Don't we have to admit," asked André Hodeir as early as 1956, "that the only complete aesthetic achievements since the great period of Parker and Gillespie belong to Miles Davis?" And the British critic Michael James has stated: "It is no exaggeration to say that never before in jazz had the phenomenon of loneliness been exam-ined in so intransigent a manner [as by Miles Davis]."

Our first quotation establishes the historical situation of Davis' music, the second its aesthetic situation. Both are contained—at least up to the beginning of the seventies—in the sound with which he blows. His tone—one of great purity, full of softness, almost with-out vibrato or attack—represents an image of the world; in each sound of Miles this image is contained. . . .

The sound of Miles Davis is the sound of sadness and resignation. Sadness and resignation, paired with an unconditional, less musical than personal protest, exist independently of whatever else Miles has to say. He says many amusing, pleasant, and friendly things, but says it all in this tone of sadness and resignation.

Arranger Gil Evans said: "Miles couldn't play like Louis [Armstrong] because the sound would interfere with his thoughts. Miles had to start with almost no sound and then develop one as he went along, a sound suitable for the ideas he wanted to express. He couldn't afford to trust those thoughts to an old means of expression. If you remember, his sound now is much more highly developed than it was at first."

Gil Evans is the man who translated the Miles Davis sound into orchestral terms. Evans arranged for the Claude Thornhill band from 1946 to 1948, when Lee Konitz was in the band. He says: "At first, the sound of the band was almost a reduction to an inactivity of music, a stillness . . . everything was moving at a minimum speed . . . and was lowered to create a sound. The sound hung like a cloud."

When improviser Miles Davis and arranger Gil Evans met, it was one of the great moments in the history of jazz. The result was the Miles Davis Capitol Band, formed for a two-week engagement in September, 1948, at the Royal Roost, and actually in existence only for those two weeks. "The instrumentation," Evans recalled, "was caused by the fact that this was the smallest number of instruments that could get the sound and still express all the harmonies the Thornhill band used. Miles wanted to play his idiom with that kind of sound." This band consisted of Miles on trumpet, a trombone (J. J. Johnson or Kai Winding), two saxophones (Lee Konitz, alto; Gerry Mulligan, baritone), and, as sound factors, two instruments rarely used in jazz: French horn and tuba. In addition, there was a rhythm section of Al Haig or John Lewis on piano, Joe Shulman or Nelson Boyd on bass, and Max Roach or Kenny Clark on drums.

Mulligan and Lewis also arranged for this group but its sound was created by Evans, and he also arranged its two most significant pieces, "Boplicity" and "Moon Dreams." With these pieces, the texture of sound which became a model for the entire evolution of cool jazz was created. It was, of course, more than just the Thornhill sound with fewer instruments. It was a jazz sound, and if at all comparable to a cloud, the clouds were frequently pierced by rays of sunshine, which struck the listener through the gentle veil of a fog.

The most important and most "modern" piece recorded by this group was "Israel" by John Carisi, a trumpeter and student of the modern symphonic composer Stefan Wolpe, with whom many first-rate jazzmen have studied. "Israel" is a minor blues, and characteristically this piece, which with its harsh, brittle sounds opened new tonal horizons, remains indebted to the core of the jazz tradition: the blues.

This Davis Band, recorded by Capitol in 1949 and 1950, was of a size between combo and big band. Seven years later—1959—Miles Davis went a step further. He recorded with a large orchestra, and naturally he asked Gil Evans—of whom little had been heard in the interim—to do the arrangements. "Gil," says Gerry Mulligan, "is the one arranger I've ever played with who can really notate a thing the way the soloist would blow it." And Miles himself said: "I haven't heard anything that knocks me out as consistently as he does since Charlie Parker."

Gil put together a unique big band. There was no saxophone section, but in its place—alongside the conventional trumpets and trombones—there was a strange grouping of French horns, a tuba, alto saxophone, clarinet, bass clarinet, and flute. In some of the pieces—as "Miles Ahead," a theme by Miles Davis—Gil realizes a "continuation" of the Capitol band's sound and here it becomes apparent which big band sound the old Capitol band aimed at—not the sound of Claude Thornhill in the late forties, but rather the sound of this Gil Evans-Miles Davis big band of 1957. It has consciously been stripped of every trace of heated attack. It is calm, lyrical, static—each climax planned way in advance. Broad lines are always preferred, in terms of melody as well as dynamics. But it moves above the old, swinging, pulsating rhythm, laid down by Paul Chambers, bass and Art Taylor, drums.

Further climaxes in the Evans-Davis collaboration were reached with the album of Gershwin's music from "Porgy and Bess" and—above all—with the great "Sketches of Spain," incorporating Spanish, flamenco-conscious compositions. Here, too, Miles made a decisive contribution to a jazz tendency which since has steadily gained in importance: The opening up of jazz to world music.

There can be no doubt: Miles is an improviser. But he improvises out of a great feeling for arrangement and composition. Presumably Miles, when he asked Dizzy Gillespie and Charlie Parker at 18 how to play right, took Dizzy's advice literally: "Learn to play the piano, man, and then you can figure out crazy solos of your own." Marshall Stearns, who tells of this, concludes: "It was the turning point in the playing of Miles Davis." This fits in with Evans' story of the Royal Roost engagement: "There was a sign outside: 'Arrangements by Gerry Mulligan, Gil Evans, and John Lewis.' Miles had it

THE MUSICIANS OF JAZZ   95

put in front; no one before had ever done that, given credit in that way to arrangers."

Until the mid-fifties, Miles had made his most beautiful recordings in quartets, accompanied only by a rhythm section—often with John Lewis or Horace Silver on the piano. Up to that point, he had never had lasting success with audiences. Then, at the 1955 Newport Festival, the turn came.

All of a sudden, the name of Miles Davis—until then known only to informed fans and critics—could be heard everywhere. Since then success has never left. For the first time in jazz history, the best-paid and most successful musician of an era was not white, but black —Miles Davis. It is self-evident why Miles became the image-setter for a whole generation of black musicians, not only musically, but in terms of personality as well. Proud black parents began to name their sons "Miles," or even "Miles Davis."

The quintets Miles Davis has led since then are of crucial importance. The first—with John Coltrane (tenor), Paul Chambers (bass), Red Garland (piano), and Philly Joe Jones (drums)—probably was the most highly lauded. It set standards for all quintets that were to follow—in fact, for modern jazz quintets between 1956 and 1970 in general. In the chapter about the most important combos, there is an astounding list of all the musicians who gained fame after emerging from a Davis quintet.

An important factor in Miles' great popularity also is his way of playing the muted trumpet—almost as if he were "breathing" into the microphone. The solo he recorded in this manner on Thelonious Monk's "Round Midnight" was particularly successful; the muted solo on "All of You" has been praised, especially by musicians, as one of the most beautiful jazz solos of the fifties. Even more than his open-horn playing, Miles muted work makes it apparent that there is no definitive attack. No longer, as in traditional jazz, and as with most other trumpeters, does the sound begin in one definite, clearly stated moment. Miles' sound begins in a moment which cannot be grasped; it seems to come out of nowhere, and it ends equally undefined. Without the listener quite knowing when, it fades into nothingness.

Miles Davis is the most significant creative musician of a movement in jazz best defined as having applied the findings of bop to Lester Young. The basic difference between Young's music and that of Davis and his followers is that Miles plays with the knowledge that between himself and Lester there was bop. André Hodeir's remark, "Miles Davis is the only trumpeter who could give to Parker's music that intimate quality in which lies a considerable part of its charm," may be interpreted in this sense. The "intimate quality" is Lester Young.

This intimate quality is also found in the simplicity of Miles' playing. No other musician in jazz has developed simplicity with such refinement and sophistication. The basic contradiction between complexity and simplicity ceases to exist in Miles' playing. In his desire to play simply, Miles (since the second half of the fifties) tends to free his improvisations from the underlying structure of chord changes. He bases his solo work on "scales." About his big-band version of Gershwin's "Porgy and Bess," Miles says: "When Gil wrote the arrangement of 'I Love You, Porgy,' he only wrote a scale for me to play. No chords. This gives you a lot more freedom and space to hear things." One of Miles' most influential compositions, "So What," is based in its first 16 measures on a single scale; relieved in the bridge by another scale, it returns to the first scale for the final eight bars.

Miles, and with him John Coltrane, who then was in Davis' Quintet, made this method of improvisation based on "scales" standard practice for the whole jazz world, thus creating the last step required for the total freedom of free jazz. This is also referred to as "modal" improvisation. (See the chapter dealing with harmonics.)

The simple phrases, often consisting of only a few notes, which Miles makes up on such "scales" have not only an aesthetic but also a practical basis: From an instrumental point of view the possibilities of Miles Davis, the trumpeter, are limited, especially when he is compared to his chief competitor among modern trumpets, Dizzy Gillespie, a masterful trumpeter who seems able to execute anything conceivable on his horn. If Miles wanted to maintain himself alongside Dizzy, top him in popularity, he had to make a virtue of his instrumental limitations. Hence the cult of simplicity. Significantly, recording directors agree that Miles always selects for issue those "takes" from a record date which are instrumentally most perfect, though he might have played with more ideas and inspiration on others. Miles does not seem to want his record audience to know that there are frequent "clams" in his playing.

This "sophistication of simplicity" may be related to the fact that Miles—no matter how many avenues for new possibilities in jazz he may have opened—very often chose tradition when faced with a choice between it and avant-garde. He once complained that pianist Thelonious Monk was playing "wrong chords," though no doubt Monk's chords were not "wrong," but merely more abstract and modern than was suitable to Miles' conception at the time. Miles complained bitterly to the recording director who had hired Monk for the record date. The results, however—whether Miles likes it or not—were some of the most important and artistically successful recorded works of the fifties (Miles, Monk and Milt Jackson on Prestige).

A further example of Miles Davis' traditionalism is the sharp words with which for years he assessed one of the most important members of the new jazz avant-garde, the late Eric Dolphy—some of them insults which Davis had to retract in later years.

When an ultra-modern fanatic once called Art Blakey "old-fashioned," Miles said: "If Art Blakey is old-fashioned, then I'm white." About the avant-garde of the sixties, he said: "What's so avant-garde? Lennie Tristano and Lee Konitz were creating ideas 15 years ago that were stranger than any of these new things. But when they did it, it made sense."

Often Miles makes harsh judgements—not only about outsiders (which would be understandable), but also about his colleagues. In a "Blindfold Test" with critic Leonard Feather, Davis voiced such gross insults in connection with many well-known jazz musicians that *down beat* magazine hesitated to spell out all his four-letter words. Reputable musicians like Clark Terry, Ellington, Dolphy, Jaki Byard, Cecil Taylor, and others were insulted by Davis at that time.

On the other hand, it must be seen that—with the exception of Charles Mingus, George Russell, and Dolphy—no other musician led the "tonal" jazz of the fifties closer and closer to the "atonal" jazz of the sixties with such increasing consistency as Miles Davis. Justifiably, Dan Morgenstern calls Miles one of the "spiritual fathers" of the new jazz. In the mid-sixties, Davis had a quintet whose members played "free" or almost "free" on their own records (mostly on the Blue Note label): Tony Williams (drums), Herbie Hancock (piano), Ron Carter (bass), and Wayne Shorter (tenor)—musicians discussed in the instrument chapters. Only Miles himself avoided the final step across the border at that time. But the relevant fact remains that the "atonal" musicians also admired him greatly and looked up to him as an example. German free-jazz cornetist Manfred Schoof expressed this mood of the sixties: "If Miles would also play atonally, he'd be the greatest."

Not only his choice of musicians shows that for Davis the music does not stop at the borders of tonality, but also, for instance, his praise for Don Cherry, the leading trumpeter-cornetist of free jazz.

Davis' goal in this area of tension between traditionalsm and avant-garde is not license, but rather, controlled freedom. "Look, you don't need to think to play weird. That ain't no freedom. You need controlled freedom."

With this "controlled freedom," Miles Davis was diametrically opposed to many extreme avant-garde musicians of the sixties. But in the context of the new jazz of the seventies, "controlled freedom" is the actual cue word—no longer just for Miles' music, but for a whole generation of young musicians continuing where Davis' "electric jazz" only seems to leave off.

Japanese critic Shoichi Yui, in 1972, went so far as to think of Davis as the "absolute apex of the development up to this point." He believes Davis is superior even to Louis Armstrong and Charlie Parker, each of whom dominated the jazz scene for only a few years, while Davis "has been the dominating personality from the end of the forties until today—longer than anybody else." Armstrong's influence, for instance, essentially originates in his playing during the period between his first Fletcher Henderson engagement in 1924, and his first visit to Europe in 1932. The period during which Charlie Parker made his most important recordings is even shorter. (From the Dizzy Gillespie session with "Groovin' High" and Parker's first own session in 1945—when—among others—"Now's the Time" was created—to the Clef session of 1951 with Miles Davis, when "K. C. Blues" was recorded: six years!)

It is hard to say which is more admirable: the power with which a musician like Parker made a host of creative, new recordings within such a short time span in a concentrated, explosive eruption—or the permanence with which Miles Davis, for a quarter of a century, has continued to set new signposts relevant to the majority of jazz musicians.

In order to be able to gain a perspective on this period of a quarter-century, one should remember that Davis has basically gone through four different stylistic phases—including all the overlaps and interconnections which of course, have existed between these phases:

1. bebop: from playing with Charlie Parker from 1945 to 1948

2. cool jazz: from the launching of the Miles Davis Capitol Orchestra in 1948 to the big-band recordings with Gil Evans in 1957/58

3. neo-bop: from the success of the first Davis Quintet with John Coltrane at the 1955 Newport Festival, via the many subsequent Davis Quintets—such as the one with Bill Evans—to ca. 1968 (during this period, an increasingly clear tendency toward modal improvisation)

4. electric: from "In a Silent Way" in 1969 and "Bitches Brew" in 1970 until. . . .

The term "electric jazz," coined by an American disc jockey, aptly characterizes the music Davis has been making since "Bitches Brew" —incorporating electronic sounds. Records like "Jack Johnson" and "Live-Evil" also belong to this movement—with such musicians as saxophonist Wayne Shorter and British guitarist John McLaughlin, and, above all, with the collective sound of different pianists playing electric instruments. Among the latter are such players as Chick Corea, Larry Young, Herbie Hancock, Keith Jarrett, the Brazilian Hermeto Pascoal, and—mainly—the transplanted Viennese Joe Zawinul, who has played a special, perhaps even triggering role in this phase of Davis' work.

It can be expected that during this "electric" phase as well, Miles will go through as far-reaching a development as during his earlier phases. The solo continues to recede while collective playing increasingly gains in importance. "On the Corner," released in 1973, emphasizes the percussive aspect of the music to a degree hitherto unknown in Miles Davis. This percussiveness is in line with a general contemporary development, as shown in the early seventies in records by Herbie Hancock ("Crossings"), Santana, and others. On the other hand, it is a conscious concession by Miles to the black popular record market.

Miles now plays trumpet with a wah-wah pedal and through an amplifier. In most cases, the pure, clear, "lonely," always somewhat sad sound of the earlier Miles is hardly recognizable. But Miles is reaching a youthful mass audience—something no black jazz musician since Louis Armstrong has accomplished. He has given the decisive impulse to a development clarified in the chapter about the jazz of the seventies, which will again be discussed in the combo chapter.

The electrifying success of the "electronic Miles" led to a point when the world of rock and popular music wanted to seize upon

Miles Davis. In the summer of 1970, when he was supposed to play with rock musicians like Eric Clapton and Jack Bruce at the Randall's Island Festival in New York, Miles had music people all over the world holding their breath for several weeks, but then he said No; he wouldn't play except with his own group: "I don't want to be a white man. Rock is a white man's word."

Miles Davis has the same kind of "leadership" position in today's jazz scene as Louis Armstrong or Charlie Parker had earlier. But he does not play his role with Satchmo's natural ease. Miles—exactly like Armstrong—wans to "make it" with a large audience. But he reflects the pride, self-assurance, and determination to protest that is characteristic of today's black generation; he plays "black music," but he must also acknowledge the fact that his audience—the buyers of his records and the listeners at his concerts—is mainly white. In a revealing interview with Michael Watts of the London publication *Melody Maker,* Miles said: "I don't care who buys the records as long as they get to the black people so I will be remembered when I die. I'm not playing for any white people, man. I wanna hear a black guy say, 'Yeah, I dig Miles Davis.' "

The cover of Miles' album "On the Corner," for instance, consciously aims—according to the trumpeter's express wishes—at the black market: A comic strip style display of a group of dancing, "hip" street blacks, with slogans like "Vote Miles," and "Free me" on their shirts and hats.

Again and again, he has said to dozens of critics and reporters: "I just do what I feel like doing." If a man says something like that too often, he obviously has a reason for saying it—he does *not* simply do what he feels like. Miles asked the above-mentioned *Melody Maker* reporter Michael Watts how long he had waited before deciding to ring his doorbell. And then, Miles was noticeably eager for Watts to take a grand tour of his "rococo house" and enjoyed that his visitor was astonished and impressed by the luxury with which Davis surrounds himself.

Miles Davis mirrors himself in his surroundings and his audience —and he needs this mirror. This is his dilemma: The whites mirror him, but he wants to be heard by the blacks. He may curse at the whites, but he needs the mirror even more than the applause of the blacks.

This possibly has to do with the fact that Miles frequently plays

with his back to the audience. Miles says: "What should I do? Smile
at 'em?" And then comes the sentence which reappears so often: "I
just do what I feel like doing."

Any man with so many complexes, so split within himself, must
truly have charisma to be successful. Davis' charisma often takes astounding forms.

Twice, Miles has been involved in violent public encounters. Once,
gangsters shot at him when he was sitting with a girl in his parked car
in Brooklyn. Miles set a reward of $10,000 for the capture of the two
assailants. Nobody collected the reward, but a few weeks later the
two gangsters were mysteriously shot.

Several years earlier, Miles was standing in front of the "Birdland"
Club on Broadway, when a white policeman asked him to move on,
then hit him over the head with a club. "The cop was killed, too. In
a subway," Miles has claimed.

"You want me to tell you where I was born—that old story? It was
in good old Alton, Illinois, in 1926. I had to call my mother a week
before my last birthday and ask her how old I would be.

"There was a very good instructor in town. He was having some
dental work done by my father. . . . 'Play without any vibrato' he
used to tell us. 'You're going to get old anyway and start shaking.' . . .
That's how I tried to play—fast and light, and no vibrato.

"By the time I was 16 . . . Sonny Stitt came to town with a band
and heard me play. He told me: 'You look like a man named Charlie
Parker and you play like him, too. Come with us.'

"The fellows in his band had their hair slicked down, they wore
tuxedos and they offered me 60 whole dollars a week to play with
them. I went home and asked my mother if I could go with them.
She said no, I had to finish my last year of high school. I didn't talk
to her for two weeks. And I didn't go with the band, either.

"I knew about Charlie Parker in St. Louis—I even played with him
there, while I was still in high school. We always used to try to play
like Diz and Charlie Parker.

"When we heard that they were coming to town, my friend and I
were the first people in the hall, me with a trumpet under my arm.
Diz walked up to me and said: 'Kid, you have a union card?' I said:
'Sure.' So I sat in with the band that night. I couldn't read a thing
from listening to Diz and Bird.

"Then the third trumpet man got sick. I knew the book because I loved the music so much I knew the third part by heart. So I played with the band for a couple of weeks. I just *had* to go to New York then.

"A friend of mine was studying at Juilliard, so I decided to go there, too. I spent my first week in New York and my first month's allowance looking for Charlie Parker.

"I roomed with Charlie Parker for a year. I used to follow him around, down to 52nd Street where he used to play. Then he'd get me to play. 'Don't be afraid,' he'd tell me, 'Go ahead and play.' . .

"You know, if you can hear a note, you can play it. The note I hit that sounds high, that's the only one I can play right then—the only note I can think of to play that would fit. You don't learn to play the blues. You just play. . . .

"Would I rather compose or play? I can't answer that. There's a certain feeling you get from playing, but never from writing, and when you're playing it's like composing, anyway. . . ."

John Coltrane and Ornette Coleman

The jazz of the sixties—and certainly of the seventies as well—is dominated by two towering personalities: John Coltrane, who died quite unexpectedly in July 1967, and Ornette Coleman. One must appreciate the difference between these two in order to realize the extent of their influence and appreciate the scope of the expressive possibilities of the new jazz. Neither man is a revolutionary, and if the effect of their work nevertheless was such, this was not their wish. Both are from the South—Coleman was born in Texas in 1930; Coltrane in North Carolina in 1926. Both are solidly rooted in the blues tradition—Coleman more in the country tradition of the folk blues; Coltrane more in the urban rhythm-and-blues tradition.

Coltrane had a relatively solid musical education within the limits possible for a member of the black lower middle class—his father was a tailor. Coleman's parents were too poor to be able to afford music lessons for him; Ornette acquired his musical tools on his own. No one told him that a saxophone is notated differently than it is tuned. So, at the age of 14 to 15—a crucial phase of his development—he played everything written "wrong" in the academic sense. Critic Martin Williams takes this to be a decisive reason for the harmonic uniqueness Coleman displayed from the start.

Wherever young Ornette played, he made a kind of music whose harmonies, sound, and instrumental technique could be placed only with difficulty within the conventional framework of jazz, blues, and rhythm-and-blues—that is, within the musics to which he related most in terms of style, inclination, expression, and origins. He remembers: "Most musicians didn't take to me; they said I didn't know the changes and was out of tune." He says about one of his first leaders, singer-guitarist Pee Wee Crayton, to whose rhythm-and-blues band he belonged: "He didn't understand what I was trying to do, and it got so he was paying me not to play." Nightclub owner and bassist Howard Rumsey recalls: "Everybody—the musicians, I mean—would panic when you'd mention Ornette. People would laugh when his name was brought up." This is placed in correct perspective if we remember that Lester Young in the Fletcher Henderson band and young Charlie Parker in Kansas City triggered similar reactions.

In contrast, Coltrane—or, as he was called, "Trane"—was accepted from the start. His first professional job was in 1947 with the Joe Webb rhythm-and-blues band from Indianapolis, with singer Big Maybelle. After that, he played mainly in better-known groups, mostly for lengthy periods: Eddie "Cleanhead" Vinson (1947-48), Dizzy Gillespie (1949-51), Earl Bostic (1952-53), Johnny Hodges (1953-54) . . . until, in 1955, Miles Davis hired him in for his quintet and he gained immediate fame with his solo on "Round About Midnight." It must be clearly understood: He was accepted and successful within the jazz that was accepted and successful at the time.

Ornette Coleman's emergence, however, came as a shock. He had to take work as an elevator operator in Los Angeles because the musicians would not accept him. Since his elevator was seldom in demand, he would stop it on the top floor and study his harmony books. Then, in 1958/59, producer Lester Koenig recorded the two first Coleman albums for his Contemporary label: "Something Else: The Music of Ornette Coleman" and "Tomorrow is the Question." A few months later, Coleman attended the Lenox School of Jazz. Many famous musicians were teaching there: Milt Jackson, Max Roach, Bill Russo, Gunther Schuller, John Lewis. . . . Yet, after a few days of the summer courses, the unknown "student" Ornette Coleman had attracted more attention than all the famous teachers.

Right away, John Lewis decided that "Ornette Coleman is doing the only really new thing in jazz since the innovations of Dizzy Gil-

lespie and Charlie Parker in the forties and since Thelonious Monk."
The leader of the Modern Jazz Quartet described the way Coleman
played on his plastic alto with his friend Don Cherry, who used a
miniature trumpet, as follows: "They're almost like twins. . . . I can't
imagine how they manage to start together. Never before have I
heard that kind of ensemble playing."

Although Coleman was not at all trying to bring about a musical
revolution—he always only wanted to make his own music, and otherwise be left alone—there was suddenly the feeling in the jazz world
of 1959 that this was a turning point; that a new style begins with
Ornette Coleman—"He is the new Bird!"

The harmonic freedom marking all the music played and composed by Coleman has been particularly well described by George
Russell: "Ornette seems to depend mostly on the over-all tonality of
the song as a point of departure for melody. By this I don't mean the
key the music might be in. . . . I mean that the melody and the chords
of his compositions have an over-all sound which Ornette seems to
use as a point of departure. This approach liberates the improviser to
sing his own song, really, without having to meet the deadline of any
particular chord. . . ." Ornette himself feels that the rules of a music
must be based not in harmonic principles applied from the outside,
but rather within the instrument and the tune themselves. The music
he blows on his alto is like a permanent search for all the possibilities
within the instrument—untroubled by conventional rules of playing.

The harmonic freedom Coleman had achieved from the start in a
manner self-evident to him, John Coltrane had to struggle for in a
slow, laborious development spanning an entire decade: from the
first cautious attempts at "modality" with Miles Davis in 1956 to
"Ascension" in 1965.

It is a fascinating, exciting "adventure in jazz" to follow this development by way of records. In the beginning stands the encounter
with Miles Davis and modality. That means: No more improvisation
on constantly changing chords, but rather on a "scale" which, un-
changingly, underlies the whole melodic activity. It was a first step
into freedom. In spite of the tense, aware attention with which the
jazz world was observing this development in all its phases, it was
never made clear precisely whether Davis or Coltrane had taken the
first step. This is fitting because the step was not taken consciously. It
"happened"—as something does that is "in the air."

The second phase—beginning in 1957—was the collaboration

with Thelonious Monk (though Trane returned to Miles after that; only in 1960 did he permanently separate from him). Coltrane himself is best qualified to discuss Monk: "Sometimes he would be playing a different set of altered changes from those that I'd be playing and neither one of us would be playing the changes to the tune. We would reach a certain spot and if we got there together we'd be lucky. And then Monk would come back in to save everybody. A lot of people used to ask us how we remembered all that stuff but we weren't remembering so much. Just the basic changes and everybody tried anything they wanted to. . . ."

It was around this time that Coltrane developed what Ira Gitler named "sheets of sounds"—creating the impression of metallic, glassy, crashing, colliding "sheets" of sound. This was best described by LeRoi Jones (Imamu Amiri Baraka): "That is, the notes that Trane was playing in the solo became more than just one note following another. The notes came so fast, and with so many overtones and undertones, that they had the effect of a piano player striking chords rapidly but somehow articulating separately each note in the chord, and its vibrating sub-tones. . . ."

Many of the recordings Coltrane made in the second half of the fifties for Blue Note or Prestige are exemplary for this way of playing —on Prestige, f. ex., with the Red Garland Trio; on Blue Note, for instance, "Blue Train." The critic John S. Wilson, has written that "he often plays his tenor sax as if he were determined to blow it apart." In *Jazz Review*, Zita Carno coined that often-quoted sentence: "The only thing you can, and should expect from John Coltrane is the unexpected. . . ." It is one of the few statements about Coltrane which are equally true about all his stages.

The critics at that time overlooked a fact musicians probably felt instinctively—that the "sheets of sounds" had an immediate rhythmic effect which was at least as important as the harmonic effect: If the notes were no longer perceivable as eighths, sixteenths, thirty-seconds, or some other definable value, then the precision of the relationship to the underlying meter was gone, too. The "sheets of sounds," therefore, were a step toward substituting for the clarity of the conventional beat the flowing, vibrating quality of the pulse—a conclusion which Elvin Jones, starting in 1960, arrived at in the Coltrane Quartet, and young Tony Williams, beginning in 1963, in the Miles Davis Quintet.

When Coltrane signed exclusively with Atlantic Records in 1960, the "sheets of sounds" soon moved into the background—although, until his death, Trane on many occasions proved that he had not lost the technical ability necessary to play them. Instead of the "shreds of sounds" and "sheets of sounds," there was a strong concentration on melody: Long, widely curved lines that condensed and dissolved according to an immanent, non-apparent principle of tension and relaxation. One had the feeling that Coltrane first had to supply the harmonic and rhythmic prerequisites so that he could deal more exclusively with the musical dimension that interested him most—melody. It was Coltrane the melody man who for the first time had a real hit with a large audience—with "My Favorite Things," in its original version a somewhat simple-minded waltz from a Richard Rodgers musical. Coltrane played the piece on the soprano sax with the nasal sound of a zoukra (a kind of Arab oboe); and from the constant, always just slightly altered repetition of the notes of the theme, he built an accelerating monotony previously unknown in jazz, but akin to aspects of Indian and Arabic musics.

Around this time, he claimed that Eastern and Asiatic music interested him, and proved it a year later (1961) with "Olé Coltrane" (Atlantic). After he had moved to the Impulse label, on the momentum of his success with "My Favorite Things," he made further records of the same orientation: In "Africa Brass" (1961) he paid homage to Arab music, and in "Impressions" (1963)—with the late Eric Dolphy on bass clarinet—to Indian music.

It is certainly not presumptuous to believe that Coltrane—considering that conventional tonality, stemming from European music, had meanwhile been stretched almost to the breaking point—was searching for a kind of substitute (even emotional security) in the "modes" of Indian and Arab musics.

From 1960 on, Coltrane led a quartet including—with occasional substitutions or additions—Elvin Jones (drums) and McCoy Tyner (piano). The bass spot changed several times—a sign of Coltrane's continually developing conception of the basic harmonic (and rhythmic!) tasks of the bassist: From Steve Davis, he went first to Art Davis, then to Reggie Workman, and finally to Jimmy Garrison —the only musician whom Coltrane retained in his quartet until the end, even after the great change of 1965. Incidentally, Coltrane was fond of using two bassists.

This John Coltrane Quartet—with, above all, Jimmy Garrison—

was a perfect group. It followed the intentions of its leader with marvelous empathy—up to the crucial change in 1965. At that point, Coltrane needed a totally "free" drummer—Rashied Ali—and an equally "free" pianist—he chose his wife, Alice Coltrane.

Before that, in 1964, a record was created that for many was the apex of Coltrane's work: "A Love Supreme"—a singular, great prayer of hymnic intensity. Coltrane wrote the lyrics himself: "Let us sing all songs to God to whom all praise is due. . . . I will do all I can to be worthy of Thee o Lord. . . . I thank You God. . . . Words, sounds, speech, men, memory, thoughts, fear and emotions—time—all related. . . . they all go back to God. . . ." At the end of this prayer appear the three words which most aptly characterize the music the Quartet plays to these lyrics: "Elation, Elegance, Exaltation."

An outsider may not have expected such religious testimony from the most-discussed modern jazz musician. But Coltrane—not unlike Duke Ellington—has frequently dealt with religious matters during his varied career. He said that in 1957 he experienced, through the grace of God, "a spiritual awakening." And in 1962, he said: "I believe in all religions," to which LeRoi Jones comments that music for Trane was "a way into God."

Coltrane sees religion as a hymn of praise to the cosmos which is God, and to God who is the cosmos. The psalm-like monotony which builds whole movements of the four-part "Love Supreme" on a single chord, and in this manner seems to lead from nowhere to everywhere, is for him an expression of infinity as sound. In many records made after that, Coltrane again took up religious topics, for instance, in "Meditations." "Father, Son, and Holy Ghost" and "Love"—religious love—are two of the movements on this album.

In the meantime, the culmination of a process that had been going on for years—at first unnoticed by the jazz public—and was the real jazz surprise of the winter of 1964/65 had taken place: John Coltrane, personally and musically, had joined the New York avantgarde. In March 1965, he played at the New York Village Gate in a not just musically, but also socially and racially, revealing Free Jazz concert of "New Black Music," produced as a benefit performance for LeRoi Jones' short-lived Black Arts Repertory Theatre-School.

On several records, Coltrane allowed the star quality of his name to aid young, little known, uncompromising free jazz musicians reach a wider audience. And recordings made by tenor saxophonist Archie

Shepp at the Newport Jazz Festival of that year were coupled with a Coltrane performance on the Impulse label. This meant a decisive break-through for Shepp.

A few days before the Newport Festival, on June 28, 1965, "Ascension" was produced. This was Coltrane's first record to be not only tonally free, but uncompromisingly atonal. Coltrane gathered under his wings almost all the important musicians of the New York avant-garde: Three tenormen—beside "Trane" himself, Pharaoh Sanders and Archie Shepp; the two trumpeters, Freddie Hubbard and Dewey Johnson; two altoists, John Tchicai and Marion Brown; two bassists, Art Davis and Jimmy Garrison; and in addition, McCoy Tyner on piano and Elvin Jones on drums. Marion Brown, attempting to describe the mad intensity of "Ascension" which—at the time—seemed to strain the limits of the appreciable and physically tolerable, said: "You could use this record to heat up the apartment on those cold winter days." It is a hymnic-ecstatic music of the intensity of a 40-minute orgasm.

At this point, we are back with Ornette Coleman, because with "Ascension," Coltrane had reached a harmonic freedom Coleman had achieved many years before. However, how much more overpowering, gripping, aggressive is the freedom of "Ascension"! It is what the title implies: an ascension into heaven, from man to God, taking in both—the divine and mankind, the whole cosmos.

Compared to that, Ornette's freedom seems lyrical, quiet, melodious. It is illuminating that the structure of "Ascension"—consciously or unconsciously—follows a structural scheme Coleman had used five years earlier on his record "Free Jazz" (Atlantic). (This was where the term later applied to so much of the jazz of the sixties appeared for the first time: on a 1960 album by Ornette Coleman!) It was a collective improvisation by a double quartet, in which the Coleman Quartet (Don Cherry, trumpet; Scott La Faro, bass; Billy Higgins, drums) faced another quartet (Eric Dolphy, alto sax; Freddie Hubbard, trumpet; Charlie Haden, bass; Ed Blackwell, drums). From the dense complexity of collective parts rubbing against each other, a solo emerged that led to another set of collective playing, from which was born—in precisely that meaning: free solos born in painful labor—the next solo.

During the years when Coltrane underwent his dynamic development, breathlessly attended by the jazz world, it became relatively quiet around Ornette Coleman. For two years, he lived in nearly total seclusion in New York.

It has been said that he played so little then because he was unable to find work. But the opposite is true: he was showered with tempting offers, but did not want to play in public. He was developing his music; he composed, and learned to play two new instruments: trumpet and violin. He also worked on compositions for string quartet (which he gave Béla Bartók-like sounds) and for other chamber-music ensembles—among them the score for Conrad Rooks' film, "Chappaqua." The director found himself wondering if he should use music "in itself so beautiful." Rooks commissiond a new score—from Ravi Shankar—and Ornette's "Chappaqua"—scored for Coleman's trio, Pharaoh Sanders (tenor) and a chamber ensemble of 11 musicians—was released on record in Europe only.

In early 1965, Coleman re-entered public life at the "Village Vanguard." Only now was the album Coleman had recorded before his voluntary retirement (in 1962 at a concert at New York's Town Hall) released (on ESP). Further Coleman records were made in Europe. It was the year when "A Love Supreme," though not recorded then, was released; the year that also brought us "Ascension" —perhaps the richest jazz year since Charlie Parker and Dizzy Gillespie made their great recordings during the forties.

It was also in this year of 1965 that Coleman went on a European tour. It was a surprise to the jazz world that he, who had turned down all offers for years, now signed a contract—accepting the writer's invitation to appear at the Berlin Jazz Days. He arrived with the same trio he had made his last appearances with in New York more than two years before: bassist David Izenzon and drummer Charles Moffet. At the Berlin *Sportpalast* he scored such a terrific success that the man who had been expected to make the hit of the evening, Gerry Mulligan, had a fit of anger. In the Stockholm restaurant, "Gyllene Cirkeln," Ornette recorded two albums that soon appeared on Blue Note, and are comparable in lyrical beauty to Coltrane's "A Love Supreme." Swedish critic Ludwig Rasmusson wrote in the liner notes: "The content of his music is mostly pure beauty, a glittering, captivating, dizzying, sensual beauty. A couple of years ago nobody thought so, and everyone considered his music grotesque, filled with anguish and chaos. Now it is almost incomprehensible that one could have held such an opinion, as incomprehensible as the fact that one could object to Willem de Kooning's portraits of women or Samuel Beckett's absurd plays. Thus Ornette Coleman has been able to change our entire concept of what is beautiful merely through the power of his personal vision. It is most beautiful when Coleman's bass player, David Izenzon, plays bowed bass with him. Then, it is almost hauntingly beautiful. . . ."

If one compares Coleman's "At the Golden Circle" with Coltrane's "A Love Supreme," the difference between the two can, from this vantage point, be reduced to its common denominator. The quiet, naturally balanced static character of Coleman is opposed by Coltrane's dynamic nature. Both musicians play—in the simple, naïve sense of the word—beautiful music. The music of both is immensely intense. But in Coltrane's music, the dynamic nature of the intensity ranges above the static quality of beauty. In Ornette Coleman's music, the reverse is true.

That is also why it is not surprising that almost all of Coltrane's recordings are conceived from the improvisatory point of view—including his compositions!—while in Coleman's work, composition ranks above improvisation. Coleman is first and foremost a composer. There is an illuminating story—critic John Tynan tells it—that Coleman, in Los Angeles in 1958, was at a point where he simply no longer knew how to make ends meet. Full of despair, he went to record producer Lester Koenig and asked him to buy some of his compositions. Ornette did not ask for a recording date—he only wanted to sell his compositions. He believed that to be a more promising avenue; his first thought was that the compositions would be a way out. And Ornette's first recording on the Contemporary label was made only because Koenig asked him to play the compositions on the alto saxophone.

Later, when there were heated discussions in the jazz world about the pro and con of Ornette Coleman's music for years, it became apparent that even the critics who rejected Ornette as an improviser recognized the beauty and competence of his compositions. Coleman the composer was accepted faster than Coleman the improviser. One of the main reasons why Coleman managed to withdraw from the jazz scene for two years was that his creative genius can be satisfied for long periods by composing alone. More often than most other new musicians he speaks of "tunes" or "songs." He says: "If I play an F in a tune called 'Peace' I don't think it should sound the same as an F that is supposed to express sadness." The atmosphere of the composition, in other words, the way the composer felt it, determines the atmosphere of the improvisation—a way of thinking that had become rare in jazz after Lester Young.

The fact that Coleman taught himself to play trumpet and violin is also connected with the priority of the compositional element over the improvisational. His music is supposed to be a whole. He would prefer to play everything necessary to make his music into sound himself. In an interview, he once said that he wished he was able to record all the parts himself on multi-track.

In this light one should judge the way Ornette plays his self-taught instruments. Certainly he is a perfect instrumentalist only on the alto sax. But the crux of the matter is missed if one speaks of the "amateurish" nature of his violin and trumpet playing. The criteria for amateurishness refer back to the "professionalism" of academic music. Ornette, however, plays the violin left-handed and tunes it as if it were played right-handed; he does not bow it, but rather beats or fiddles it with "unorthodox" arm movements. He is not interested in the note he might generate by bowing on a single string, but rather in the sound he can gain from sounding as many strings as possible at once. What is left of the conventional violin when Coleman plays it is only its external shape. He plays it like an independent, newly discovered instrument. And he produces exactly those effects required for his compositions. There—and nowhere else—is where the criterion lies—and that criterion is met brilliantly by Ornette's violin playing. Ornette: "I can't talk about technique because it is everchanging. That's why for me the only method for playing any instrument is the range in which it is built. Learned technique is a law method. Natural technique is nature's method. And this is what makes music so beautiful to me. It has both, thank God."

Ornette Coleman is the master of an immense compactness. This became even clearer when he—finally!—found a horn partner with whom he really enjoyed playing: tenorman Dewey Redman. Through him, Coleman found his way back to quartet music. And two musicians who had already been connected with Ornette in his early days, bassist Charlie Haden and drummer Ed Blackwell, joined the new quartet. The latter comes from New Orleans, where Ornette so often played in his youth, and does with the rhythm-and-blues patterns of the South basically the same thing Ornette did with the Texas blues: he abstracts them.

Ornette has knowledge of the conscious structuring of a composition or an improvisation. But almost everything that he plays or composes seems to be cut from the same cloth. For that reason, Coleman's recorded pieces usually are significantly shorter than Coltrane's. Listening to Coltrane meant to bear witness to a laborious birth. Hearing Ornette means viewing the newborn creature.

Archie Shepp comments on this phenomenon: "One of the many things (Trane) accomplished was the breakthrough into the concept that a jazz musician need not—could not—be limited to a solo lasting a few minutes. Coltrane demonstrated that a man could play much longer, and that in fact it was an imperative of his conception to improvise at great length. I don't mean that he proved that a 30- or 40-minute solo necessarily is better than a three-minute one. He did prove, however, that it was possible to create 30 or 40 minutes of music, and in the process, he also showed the rest of us we had to have the stamina—in terms of imagination and physical preparedness —to sustain these long flights. . . ."

This indeed touches on one of the more superficial among critical opinions: that the great old musicians—King Oliver, Lester Young, Teddy Wilson—were able to express all they wanted in one or two choruses of 16 or 32 bars, and that it simply indicates lack of conciseness that such contemporary musicians as Coltrane (and many others of his generation) play such lengthy solos. In fact, the older musicians recorded short solos because records at that time usually only afforded some three minutes of music. But when they were able to play the way they really wanted—in jam sessions or clubs—they preferred, even back then, to play relatively long solos. Great music—from European symphonies to the ragas and talas of India— requires time.

But back to Ornette Coleman. I believe his origin in Texas and the world of country blues cannot be overemphasized. For good reason he made his first records—as a sideman, of course—in the early fifties with blues singer Clarence Samuels (who had been with the Jay McShann Band—the orchestra in which Charlie Parker got his start). Elsewhere, (in the free-jazz chapter) we have shown that Ornette's free harmonic conception is a direct result of the harmonic freedom Southern country and blues musicians have always had.

Tenorist Archie Shepp—one of the great musicians of the new jazz —says: "It was Coleman, who, in my opinion, revitalized and refurbished the blues idiom without destroying its simplistic milieu. Far from taking it beyond its original intentions, Coleman restored (the blues) to their free, classical (African) unharmonized beginnings. I have always felt that this early work of Ornette's was much closer to the 'old thing'—hoedowns—foot-tappin'—than the new. Certainly Blind Lemon Jefferson and Hudie Leadbetter must have played 13, 17, 25-bar blues. Regardless; no pundit would have been foolish enough to label them avant-garde. . . ."

And A. B. Spellman, the critic, says: "Ornette's music is nothing but the blues." Ornette is a total blues musician. And if conventional jazz includes only two—or rather, since the advent of bebop's flatted fifth, three—blue notes, it can be said that Coleman has turned the whole scale into blue notes. Almost all his notes are bent up or down, off-pitch, tied, flatted, or augmented—in short: vocalized in the blues sense. Remember his statement that an F in a tune called "Peace" should not sound the same as an F in a context that is supposed to express sadness? Precisely that is a blues musician's concept. And if after years of conventional jazz, this concept is found astonishing—because all F's, whether concerned with peace, sadness, or whatever, simply must have the identical pitch—this merely illustrates the influence of the European tradition—an influence that Ornette eliminated, at least in this realm.

The ease with which Ornette deals with atonality has been contrasted with Coltrane's immensely tense, complex relationship to it. This became clear when, right after "Ascension," the album "Coltrane —Live at the Village Vanguard Again" was released. At this point, Coltrane could no longer play just with the musicians who'd been with him for so many years. He founded—as we have mentioned—a new group—a quintet: with Pharaoh Sanders as a second tenor sax voice, wife Alice Coltrane on piano, drummer Rashied Ali and—as the only holdover from the old quartet—bassist Jimmy Garrison. When Coltrane plays on this record well-known themes from his earlier recordings—"Naima" or "My Favorite Things"—one feels that he loved these themes and would have preferred to continue playing them as they appeared to him as themes—if only he would have been able to express within them everything he so much wanted to express! If John Coltrane had seen a possibility to reach—by conventional means—the degree of ecstatic heat he was aiming for, he would have continued to play tonally to the end.

Coltrane hesitated for a long time. For good reason Martin Williams once called him "the man in the middle." Trane needed ten years to take the step he finally took in 1965, and which a whole generation of musicians in this era took in one day. Anybody who hears the sermon-like, sublimely swinging lines of "Naima" understands: this musician mourned for tonality. He knew how much he had lost with it. And he would have loved to return to it, had he not, during these ten years, again and again run into the limitations of conventional tonality before having been able to express all that seemed necessary to him.

It was only for the sake of increased intensity that Coltrane hired a second tenorist—and in terms of physical power and the ability to bring forth the wildest and most unbelievable sounds on his instrument, the man he chose was certainly the most amazing tenor player in the field: Pharaoh Sanders. In interaction with him Coltrane became greater, as the great gospel preacher Bishop Kelsey rose to the occasion in his Washington D. C. Temple of God in Christ in interaction with a younger preacher—Rev. Little—in the course of their ecstatic double sermons.

Coltrane totally exerted himself in this process. That was why he had to cancel a European tour in the fall of 1966. That is why he began to frequently need recuperation breaks. Repeatedly, during such shorter or longer breaks, friends would anticipate that this particular one would last several years. But just weeks later, Trane would be on the scene again, carrying on with the tearing, ecstatic power of his jazz and love hymns.

The liver ailment doctors determined was the cause of his death may merely have added the final blow to the complete exhaustion resulting from a life led continually at the edge of humanly possible intensity.

It was possible to observe that he seemed to be drained of his strength after a concert appearance. He was like a relay runner: At a certain point, he would hand the torch to Pharaoh Sanders, who then had to press forward—even *more* powerfully, intensely and ecstatically, yet without the hymnic power of love that radiated from Coltrane.

Another musician has this power of love. In 1967, when Trane died, she had not yet emerged clearly in the jazz world, but since then, she has probably become the purest and clearest successor and heir to the music of John Coltrane.   This is his wife, pianist, harpist, or-

ganist and composer Alice Coltrane—or, as she was named when vibraharpist Terry Gibbs introduced her in the early sixties, Alice
McLeod; or, as she now calls herself in accordance with her religious
conviction: Turiya Aparna.

Alice made a pilgrimage to India and studied Hinduism and
Buddhism; she took a Hindu name, and she believes that John Coltrane—had he lived longer—would also have gone this way: "I would
like to play music according to the ideals set forth by John and continue to let a cosmic principle of the aspect of spirituality be the underlying reality behind the music as he had. . . . I know how badly
John wanted to do this work."

Alice Coltrane—as years before her husband John—knows what
she is talking about. She does not merely flirt with ideas that are in
the air. For her—as in John's prayer "Love Supreme"—the great
universal Godhead, the "Universal Consciousness," is a fact that determines life and music; she knows that all those divine names
which people use are only transcriptions of the one, identical Great
Divine Power.

For her record, "Universal Consciousness," Alice enlisted—and
thus a circle closes—the cooperation of Ornette Coleman. Ornette
shaped—or at least essentially determined—a violin sound for Alice
without equal among the numerous violin experiments of the last few
years. The four violinists are from the most diverse schools: two
from concert music—Julius Brand and Joan Kalisch; one a free-jazz
man—LeRoy Jenkins; and the fourth a soul musician—John Blair.
These four, in pieces like "Oh Allah" and "Hare Krishna," play a
dense texture of sounds that combines the complexity of avant-garde
concert music with traditional jazz intensity, the spiritual power of
Alice Coltrane with the tradition of bebop and blues.

Ornette Coleman loves violins. He admires—as did Charlie Parker
20 years earlier—the great tradition of European concert music.
Again and again during recent years, he has presented compositions
for symphony orchestra, chamber ensembles, and string quartets—
most impressively in "Skies of America," recorded in 1972 by the
London Symphony Orchestra conducted by David Measham. At the
time of the refined string sounds of such composers as Ligeti and
Penderecki, Coleman writes simply, almost naïvely, for the symphony
orchestra—using parallel lines and a host of parallel and duplicated
voices. The more astonishing how rich and expressive the effects that

he produces! Ornette Coleman remains a jazz musician—even when composing for symphony orchestra. The symphony orchestra, to him, is an enlarged "horn" on which he improvises.

Ornette has become a classicist in his improvisations, too. At the 1971 Berlin Jazz Days, the audience, with no idea of the new Ornette Coleman, expected the musician who in the early sixties had revolutionized jazz with an immense, overpowering energy and was astonished to hear a man who was simply making "beautiful music": clear, singing, wonderfully balanced alto lines.

Jazz needs classicists of this kind. To demand permanent revolution means to demand the impossible—anyone who does only reveals his immaturity.

Coltrane's music has remained too alive during the years since his death—causing discomfort, triggering developments everywhere, from rock to jazz, in the most diverse of transitional stages—for us to be able to consider it 'classical' yet.

The hymn-like element prevalent on the entire contemporary jazz and rock scene comes from Coltrane—above all from "Love Supreme."

To his friends, Coltrane was a marked man, at least after "Love Supreme." He already knew back then that his sounds were shaping today's jazz, and he suffered from this responsibility. He saw himself too strongly as a ceaseless seeker to be able to enjoy the fact that the whole jazz world now praised each of his statements as "the last word." After 1962 or '63, I know of no photograph that shows him smiling.

In answer to the question if there would ever be an end to the development that had already led him through a half-dozen different ways of playing since the mid-fifties and the Miles Davis Quintet, Coltrane told Nat Hentoff: "You just keep going all the way, as deep as you can. You keep trying to get right down to the crux."

If Ornette Coleman is the Phoenix whose music from the start was revealed to us—if not in its mature form, then at least in its basic conception—as if it had sprung from the head of Zeus, then Coltrane was a Sisyphus, who again and again—from the very bottom up to the mountaintop—had to roll the hard, cumbersome rock of knowledge. And perhaps, whenever Coltrane got to the top, Coleman would already be standing there in a resplendent suit, playing his beautiful melodies. But the music John Coltrane would blow then, from the top of the mountain—standing next to Ornette—was imbued with the power of the pilgrim who had reached yet another station on the long, thorny road to knowledge (or might we better say—because it was Coltrane's conviction—to God), and knew there were many more stations to come—though in the months of exhaustion preceding his death he no longer knew how to go on.

THE ELEMENTS OF JAZZ

The Elements of Jazz

Sound and Phrasing

WHAT PARTICULARLY distinguishes jazz from traditional European music is sound. Crudely put, the difference is this: In a symphony orchestra, the members of, say, the string section, may wish to play their passages as homogeneously as possible. Thus it will be to their advantage for each member of the specific section to have the same ideal of sound and to know how to achieve it. This ideal corresponds to transmitted cultural standards or aesthetics: an instrument must have a "beautiful" sound.

For the jazz musician, on the other hand, it is of no particular importance to conform to a commonly accepted conception of sound. A jazz musician has his own sound. The criteria for this sound are based not aesthetically so much as emotionally and expressively. To be sure, the latter criteria are also found in European music. But in jazz, expression ranks above aesthetics, while in European music, aesthetics rank above expression.

Thus, one may find in jazz a tendency contradictory to the standards of aesthetics—and opposed to standardized aesthetics—but this tendency does not imply that jazz of necessity must be "unaesthetic." It does imply, however, that a music is conceivable which conforms to the highest standards of jazz, yet is contrary to certain conventions of aesthetics.

The self of the musician is clearly mirrored—in the most immediate and direct fashion—in the non-standardized sound of the great jazz improvisers. In jazz, there is no *bel canto,* no "schmaltzy" vio-

121

lins, but hard, clear sounds—the human voice, plaintive and com-
plaining, crying and screaming, sighing and moaning. The instruments are expressive and eruptive, not filtered through any regulations or rules of sound. The majority of the 100 or 120 musicians in
a large symphony orchestra probably do not feel the "titanic strug-
gles" which occur in Beethoven's music, nor do they fully sense the
secrets of form which are the basis of symphonic music. But a jazz
musician—even in a big band—senses and feels, knows and understands what he plays. The lack of understanding among the "civil
service" musicians in the symphony orchestras, of which so many
conductors have complained—especially where modern music is concerned—is unthinkable in jazz.

Because a jazz musician's playing is "true" in a direct, naïve, and
"primitive" way, it may possess beauty even when it contradicts aesthetic standards. One could say that the beauty of jazz is ethical
rather than aesthetic.

To be able to respond to jazz means first and foremost to be able
to feel this kind of beauty.

The first word the layman thinks of when jazz is mentioned—
"hot"—is not just a matter of rhythmic intensity. It is first of all a
matter of sound. One speaks of "hot intonation."

The personal, inimitable sound of a great jazz musician is the
reason for something that always astonishes the outsider: that the jazz
connoisseur is able to recognize, after relatively few notes of music,
who is playing. This certainty does not exist in classical music, where
it is only with difficulty, and seldom with complete assurance, that
one can guess who is conducting or playing certain parts in a symphonic orchestra.

Sound in jazz is—to give a few examples at random—the slow, expressive vibrato of Sidney Bechet's soprano sax; the voluminous,
erotic tenor sax sound of Coleman Hawkins; the earthy cornet of
King Oliver; the "jungle" sound of Bubber Miley; the elegant clarity
of Benny Goodman's clarinet; the sorrow and lostness of Miles Davis
or the victoriousness of Louis Armstrong; the lyrical sonority of Lester Young; the gripping, concentrated power of Roy Eldridge or the
clear glow of Dizzy Gillespie.

In the older forms of jazz the shaping of sound is more marked
than in the more recent ones. In the newer forms, an element that
often was absent in earlier times is added: jazz phrasing. Trombonist
Kid Ory, for example, played phrases that existed in circus and

marching music at the turn of the century and are not necessarily jazz phrases. Nevertheless, what he plays clearly is jazz—because of his sound. Stan Getz, on the other hand—especially the Getz of the fifties —has a sound which, when isolated from its surrounding elements, is not so far removed from classical saxophone sound. But he phrases with a concentrated jazz feeling no symphony player could emulate. There are modern jazz recordings—such as those by Jimmy Giuffre —which are very close to the chamber music of modern "classical" composers. Yet the phrasing is so definitely jazz that the music is felt to be jazz, even when a regular beat is not present.

Thus one notes a shift in emphasis from sound to phrasing in the history of jazz—in a sense that will be clarified at the end of this section, in connection with our attempt to define jazz.

Sound and phrasing can represent everything of importance in jazz to the extent that a jazz musician, were he to play a piece of European concert music, could transform it into "jazz"—even when playing his part note for note.

The sound of jazz and the jazz phrasing connected with it are the "blackest" elements in jazz. They lead back to the shouts of Southern plantation Negroes, and from there, back to the coast of West Africa and the jungles. Along with swing, they are the sole predominantly Negroid elements in jazz.

One might compare the sound which the blacks, in the formative years of jazz, coaxed from their European instruments with the situation in which the Africans deported as slaves to the New World were forced to speak European languages. It has been pointed out that the "singing" way of speaking peculiar to the Southern United States can be traced back to Negro influence, and it is ironic that even the Southerners who have no other word than "nigger" for a black person also speak in this manner. Originally, the word was nothing but the black way of saying "Negro." In the same sense, jazz sound and jazz phrasing are nothing but the black way of playing European melodies on European instruments. And this way—like Southern speech—has penetrated the white world so completely that it has conquered audiences in this white world, and that it is employed often enough by white musicians as legitimately—or usually, almost as legitimately—as by blacks.

From the vantage point of sound it becomes clear that the question of a musician's skin color remains superficial without due regard for the underlying complexities. From the inner conviction that most of the creative jazz musicians were black, Roy Eldridge once claimed that he could always distinguish a white musician from a black one. Critic Leonard Feather gave him a blind-fold test: Eldridge had to listen to a number of unfamiliar records, and judge from them. It turned out that he frequently erred about race. In spite of this, Feather did not—as he believed—disprove Eldridge's point and prove that black and white jazz musicians are equals. He only pointed up the many sides of the problem.

On the one hand: Fletcher Henderson, black, wrote the arrangements without which Benny Goodman, white, might not have become "King of Swing." On the other hand: Benny Goodman played these arrangements "better" with his white orchestra than Henderson did with his black orchestra—according to any standards, and even according to the standards of black musicians.

Furthermore—in reverse: Neal Hefti, white, has written some of the most brilliant arrangements for Count Basie's black band. But Basie's band played them better than Hefti's own band, which mainly consisted of white musicians.

Finally: As early as the fifties—i.e., before the time of today's avant-garde—Charles Mingus, black, was an exponent of an experimental, deliberately abstract tendency one would almost certainly ascribe to a white rather than to a black musician—if all the generalizations we carry to the race problem made any sense. On the other hand: Even before the hard-bop movement, white musicians such as Gerry Mulligan or Al Cohn again and again pointed to the importance of beat, swing, and blues—of originality, vitality, and simplicity—in other words, they did what the simplistic average judgment would sooner have expected of black musicians.

Always, there is this duality when the question of race arises in jazz—and not only in jazz. It is impossible, especially for a European critic, to do more than acknowledge both points of view.

Improvisation

"A hundred and fifty years ago our ancestors went to hear Beethoven and Hummel and Thalberg and Clementi improvise richly and splendidly; and before that to the great organists—to Bach, Buxtehude, Böhm, Pachelbel; not forgetting Samuel Wesley, though he came later. Today we have to go for the same sort of musical per-

formance to Lionel Hampton, Erroll Garner, Milt Jackson, Duke Ellington, and Louis Armstrong. I will leave you to digest the implications to be drawn from that curious circumstance." Thus Burnett
James in an article about improvisation in jazz.

Indeed, during the whole history of jazz, from New Orleans to the
avant-grade, jazz improvisation has been accomplished according to
the same techniques as employed in old European music—with the
aid of harmonic structures.

On the other hand, improvisation atrophied in European music
from the beginning of the last century, to such a degree that even leading soloists sometimes are unable to make up the cadenzas left open
to improvisation as late as in the great concertos of romantic music.
Concert performances today are judged according to "authenticity," i.e., as to whether a piece of music is played and/or sung
as the composer "meant it to be," but if, for example, we were to
perform a Vivaldi concerto or a Handel sonata as the composers
wrote them, we would simply be "interpreting" a bare, skeletal framework of notes. The entire improvisatory force and freedom of
Vivaldi's and Handel's music—and, in general, of all of baroque
and pre-baroque, soloistically conceived music—have been lost to
the ideal of "authenticity." Arnold Dolmetsch has said that the omis-
sion of ornamentation—the improvised embellishment of the notated
music—is as "barbaric" as would be removing the flamboyant Gothic
architectural ornamentation from a cathedral with the excuse that
one preferred a simpler style. The jazz musician improvises on a
given harmonic structure. That is exactly what Johann Sebastian
Bach and his sons did when playing a chaconne or an air: they
improvised on the harmonies on which the melody was based, or
embellished the given melody. The whole technique of ornamentation—the embellishment of melody—which flowered during the
Baroque period, still survives in jazz . . . for instance, when Coleman
Hawkins played his famous "Body and Soul." And the ground bass,
organ point, and *cantus firmus* of the old music came into being to
give structure to improvisation and to make it easier—in the same
sense that jazz musicians today use blue chords and the blues form
to give shape to their improvisations. Winthrop Sargeant speaks
about harmony in this sense as a "controlling structural principle
in jazz."

Of course it is not as if the early jazz musicians had consciously
taken over the improvisational techniques of the old music. They

knew nothing of Bach and all these matters, and the parallels which exist here are meaningful precisely because they developed unconsciously: the result not of the same but of a related basic musical conception. On the contrary, the parallels between jazz and old music become suspect when they are practiced deliberately, and when, because similarities in improvisational methods do exist, the two forms are thrown into one pot. Nor does the relationship in conception which stands behind all this stem from the old European music. It is a conception basic to *all* musical cultures in which it is "more important to make music yourself than to listen to the music of others," in which the naïveté of the relationship to music does not allow for any questions of interpretation or conception to arise, in which the music is judged not according to what it means but to what it is. There are such musical cultures and styles in Africa as well as in Europe, in America as well as in Asia—one might even say that almost all musical cultures anywhere in the world have this common basic conception, with the exception of the music which had its flowering in nineteenth-century Europe, and still rules the musical sensibilities of the white world.

Jazz, then, has improvisation. But the problem of improvisation is not exhausted with this conclusion. It begins with it. The statement "there is improvisation in jazz" is an old saw so widespread that many fans and laymen proceed to draw from it the conclusion that if there is no improvisation in a piece, it is not jazz. Humphrey Lyttleton, the most brilliant representative of traditional jazz in Europe, says: "In the full sense of 'composing extemporarily, that is, without preparation,' improvisation has proved to be not essential to, and practically nonexistent in, good jazz."

Every jazz improvisation is based on a theme. Usually, it is—excluding the free jazz of the sixties and the more complex song forms coming into use in the seventies—a standard song in 32-bar form—the "AABA" form of our popular tunes—in which the 8-bar main theme (A) is first presented, then repeated, then followed by a new 8-bar idea—the so-called bridge (B)—and in conclusion, the first 8 bars are sounded once more. Or it may be the 12-bar blues form, about which more in the section about blues. The jazz musician places new melodic lines over the given harmonies of the song or the blues. He can do this by embellishing or making slight alterations in the songs or blues—André Hodier calls this manner of improvising "paraphrasing." He can also accomplish this by creating entirely new melodic lines over the given harmonies—a manner of improvising which Hodeir calls the "chorus-phrase."

The decorative, embellishing "paraphrase" was the main improvisatory device of the older jazz forms. Clarinetist Buster Bailey relates: "At that time [1918] I wouldn't have known what they meant by improvisation. But embellishment was a phrase I understood. And that was what they were doing in New Orleans." The "chorus-phase," on the other hand, which creates entirely new melodic lines, is the main improvisatory manner of modern jazz. Its possibilities are vast. Example 1 shows, in the top row, the beginning of the song, "How High the Moon," the favored theme of the bop-era, with its related harmonies, and below it three different improvisations on it by three leading jazz musicians. One can see at a glance that three completely different melodic lines have come into being. There is no connection between these three lines as far as melody is concerned, but the connection is given through the harmonic structure of "How High the Moon": the same harmonies constitute the basis for three very different improvisations.

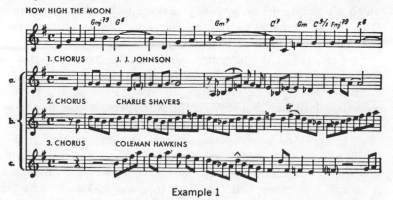

Example 1

This example was transcribed from a record which does not even give a clue to the original theme in its title. This RCA record is entitled "Indiana Winter." The three choruses—that is what improvisations on the harmonies of a theme in the number of bars corresponding to that theme are called—cited in the example were played by trombonist J. J. Johnson, trumpeter Charlie Shavers, and tenorman Coleman Hawkins.

The habits of jazz ensure that the most important jazz themes repeatedly become the foundations for the improvisations of jazz musicians. They are played day after day and night after night in hundreds of clubs and concert halls. After 100 or 200 choruses, a musician may arrive at certain phrases which then will crop up more and more frequently in his playing of the tune. After a while something like a "standard chorus" on the respective theme will have developed.

Many choruses have become so famous that the listener would be disappointed if the musician who made them up suddenly were to play something different. King Oliver's "Dippermouth Blues," Alphonse Picou's "High Society," Charlie Parker's "Parker's Mood," Ben Webster's "Cotton Tail," Stan Getz's "Early Autumn," Bix Beiderbecke's "Singing the Blues," Louis Armstrong's "West End Blues," Lester Young's "Song of the Islands," Chu Berry's or Coleman Hawkins' "Body and Soul," Miles Davis' "All of You," Coltrane's "My Favorite Things"—these (written down as they came to mind) are high points one would be loath to see transplanted to other peaks . . . especially as one cannot be sure they would be peaks. On the contrary, such a result would be unlikely. It would be foolish to claim that choruses which are among the greatest in jazz cease to be jazz when repeated. Thus, what is created by improvising, and, having proved to be of value, is repeated, also belongs to improvisation.

This concept of the once-improvised is important. It makes clear that what was once created by improvising is linked to the man who created it. It cannot be separated from him, notated, and given to a second or third musician to play. If this happens, it loses its character, and nothing remains but the naked formula of notes.

At this point we can differentiate between improvisation and composition. European music—insofar as it is composed—is capable of limitless reproduction by anyone who possesses the instrumental, technical, and conceptual capacities to grasp it. Jazz can be reproduced solely by the musician who produced it. The imitator may be technically better and intellectually superior—but he still cannot reproduce the music. A jazz improvisation is the personal expression of the improviser and of his musical, spiritual, and emotional situation.

In other words, the concept "improvisation" is actually inaccurate. A jazz musician who has created a chorus is at one and the same time improviser, composer, and interpreter. In jazz—even in arranged jazz, as will be shown later—these three aspects *must* be in evidence lest the music become questionable. In European music they *can* be separated without affecting the quality of the music. On the contrary: the quality may improve. Beethoven was considered a poor interpreter of his own music; others were able to play it better. Miles Davis in his formative years was, as far as technique is concerned, not an outstanding musician. Yet it is unthinkable that a technically better equipped trumpeter should have copied Miles' phrases and, playing them note for note, have played a "better Miles Davis" than Miles himself. To express it as a paradox: Miles might have been only a fair trumpet player, but he was the greatest interpreter of his own music one could wish for. Indeed, the spiritual power of his improvisations had impact and influence on trumpeters who were technically superior.

An improvised jazz chorus stands in danger of losing its authenticity and of becoming dishonest and untrue when it is copied by someone who did not create it. Given the multiplicity of human experience, it is inconceivable that the "other" could play from the identical situation from which the "one" improvised his chorus. The relationship between the music heard and the man who created it is more important to jazz improvising than complete lack of preparation. When copying and imitation occur without proper preparation jazz is in greater danger than when, after hour-long, systematic preparation, phrases are created which belong to the player as expressions of his artistic personality. This is the meaning of the passage from Humphrey Lyttleton quoted above. A musician as different from Lyttleton as Shorty Rogers means the identical thing when he says: "In my opinion all good jazz musicians are composers. I have utilized them as composers by having parts in which I merely wrote instructions and left the rest to the men to compose spontaneously, mutual instinct being the connecting link between us." (In other words, between arranger and improviser.) In the formulation "composing spontaneously" the identity of improviser, composer, and interpreter is expressed in a different way.

This identity of improviser, composer, and interpreter is what is meant when we speak of improvisation in jazz. Not a wild, head-on extemporization. The identity of improviser, composer, and interpreter also has to suffice for the arranger who—aside from relating what is to be improvised to what has been once-improvised—finds the real justification for his position in the fact that he can sometimes respond more satisfactorily to the demand for the identity of improviser, composer, and interpreter than the spontaneously improvising soloist can. Jack Montrose, one of the leading arrangers on the West

Coast, said: "The jazz writer forms a unique contrast to his colleagues in other fields of musical composition in that his ability to *write* jazz music is a direct extension of his having acquired the ability to play it first. He must have shared the experience of creating jazz music, the *jazz experience*. It is my contention that jazz music bearing the stamp of true authenticity has never been written except by composers who have first attained this prerequisite." Elsewhere, Montrose contended that as long as the music is the work of a jazz musician, jazz will be the result. We shall discuss this more extensively in the next chapter. But at this juncture we propose six points which may serve as a summary of the problem of improvisation in jazz.

1. The once-improvised is equal to improvisation.

2. The once-improvised can be reproduced by the one who produced it, but by no one else.

3. Both improvisation and the once-improvised are personal expressions of the situation of the musician who produced them.

4. The concurrence of improviser, composer, and interpreter belongs to jazz improvisation.

5. Insofar as the arranger corresponds to point 4, his function differs from that of the improvising-composing interpreter in terms of craftsmanship and technique: the arranger writes, even when writing for others, on the basis of his experience as an improvising-composing interpreter.

6. Improvisation—in the sense of points 1 through 5—is indispensable to jazz; improvisation in the sense of complete unpreparedness and unlimited spontaneity *may* occur, but is *not* a necessity.

The Arrangement

Many jazz lovers and almost all laymen believe there is a contradiction between improvisation and arrangement. Because, in their view, improvisation is decisive, the presence of an arrangement must automatically indicate a state of decadence, since "the more arrangement, the less improvisation."

The jazz musician—not just today, but from the start of jazz, or at least from the great days of New Orleans jazz in Chicago on—is of another opinion. He sees the arrangement not as an inhibition of the freedom to improvise but as an aid. For him, it is a matter of experience that the possibilities for free and unlimited improvised solo playing are particularly enlarged when the soloist knows what the musicians playing with him are doing. With an arrangement, he knows. Many of the greatest improvisers—first and foremost Louis Armstrong—have demanded arrangements. Only to a superficial observer does it appear contradictory that Fletcher Henderson on the one hand was the first jazz arranger with a precise conception, while on the other hand his orchestra offered greater freedom of improvisation than almost any other big band of its day.

In the relationship between arrangement and improvisation there is an inherent tension, which can be fertilized to an unimagined extent. Jelly Roll Morton told his musicians: "You'd please me if you'd just play those little black dots—just those little black dots that I put down there. If you play them, you'll please me. You don't have to make a lot of noise and ad-lib. All I want you to play is what's written. That's all I ask." And despite this, clarinetist Omer Simeon— long a member of Morton's bands—and guitarist Johnny St. Cyr said: "Reason his records are so full of tricks and changes is the liberty he gave his men. . . . He was always open for suggestions." This is the tension which has to be dealt with in art—and one cannot do much theorizing about it.

Arrangements came into being as early as during the formative years of jazz. Even the early jazz musicians—King Oliver, Jelly Roll Morton, Clarence Williams, Louis Armstrong—arrived through improvisation at set, repeatable turns of ensemble playing, and once their effectiveness had been tested, these turns remained. This shows how rapidly improvisation is transformed into arrangement. What was once-improvised yesterday has perhaps already become a permanent arrangement by tomorrow.

George Ball relates how the New Orleans Rhythm Kings—the most successful Dixieland band between 1921 and 1925—did this kind of thing: ". . . by predetermining definite parts for each man to play; by introduction of patterns, simple though they were, and a more even rhythmic background. Arrangements were, of course, impossible as we know them today, if only from the fact that the most important members of the melody section, Mares, Rappolo and Brunies, could not read music. (Elmer) Schoebel nevertheless spent numberless rehearsals drilling these men in their parts which we might call arranged, although not a note of music was set down for them, and which the performers had perforce to learn by sheer memory."

Many other great groups of New Orleans and early Dixieland jazz

—not to mention later ones—valued arrangements: the Hot Seven, the Memphis Five, the Original Dixieland Jazz Band, the California Ramblers—groups which have come to represent the incarnation of free, unfettered improvisation to traditional jazz fans.

Perhaps the misunderstanding arises from the fact that the term "arrangement" has not been precisely defined. There is a tendency to speak of arrangements only when something has been written down beforehand. But it is easy to see that it is actually only a question of procedure if a certain passage actually has been written down in advance or merely has been discussed. The arrangement begins the moment something is agreed upon in advance. It is immaterial whether this is done in writing or orally. Between the agreements among the New Orleans Rhythm Kings and the complex scores of the modern big-band arrangers, who may have studied with Milhaud, Stefan Wolpe, Ernst Toch, or other great modern composers and are conversant with the traditional European art of instrumentation, there is only a difference of degree.

Since the thirties, the expression "head arrangement" has gained currency among big bands. In the bands of Fletcher Henderson and Count Basie, or in the first Woody Herman "Herd" of the forties it was common practice to establish only the first 24 or 32 bars of a piece—the remainder was left to the improvisatory capacities of the musicians. This term also makes clear how logical and unforced the development from improvisation through the once-improvised to arrangement is.

Since there is no contradiction between arrangement and improvisation, the latter has not faded into the background by reason of the progressive development of the former in jazz history. Improvisation and arrangement have both developed equally. Charlie Parker, Miles Davis, and John Coltrane—and later even more so Albert Ayler or Marion Brown and the other free jazz musicians—command a freedom of improvisation which King Oliver, Louis Armstrong, or Bix Beiderbecke never possessed at the zenith of traditional jazz. This can be determined quite rigorously: often several "masters" of one title are recorded until recording director and musicians are satisfied. On several versions of a given piece available by Armstrong or Beiderbecke, for example, the solos vary but are by and large quite comparable; structure and line were only rarely changed. "Takes" by Charlie Parker, however, differ so markedly that one might say that a new piece was created each time. Of the four masters of Parker's

"Cool Blues," recorded in immediate succession on the same day (only the final one was approved by Parker), three were put on the market under different titles: "Cool Blues," "Blowtop Blues," and "Hot Blues."

Thus it is not contradictory for musicians who are members of groups dependent on arrangements to speak of improvisation as the "key word." Carson Smith, for instance (bass player of Chico Hamilton's Quintet during the successful years of West Coast jazz) coined the phrase about improvisation being the key word. And he added: "We find freedom in writing." Fred Katz, a cellist who played a significant role in the founding of the Hamilton Quintet, and had come to jazz from classical music, said: "It seems to me that the general principle of jazz is improvisation." John Lewis, the maestro of the Modern Jazz Quartet, where arrangements and composition are of decisive importance, has said: "Collective improvisation is what makes jazz singular." And clarinetist Tony Scott, who has undertaken many avant-grade experiments as arranger and jazz composer, said during a round-table discussion at Newport in 1956 that jazz was more likely to progress through improvisation than through writing.

Clearly, the arrangement can only fulfill its task when the arranger lives up to the demands expressed by Jack Montrose at the end of the last chapter: he must be a jazz musician and a jazz improviser. In the entire history of jazz there is no exception to this basic rule. It is significant that it is not possible to speak of the arrangement in jazz without mentioning improvisation.

Insofar as the arranger has to be an improvising jazz musician, it is only a small step from arranger to jazz composer. Without doubt, the actual contradiction is not between improvisation and arrangement, but between improvisation and arrangement on the one hand and composition on the other. Because improvisation is of importance in jazz, the music has arrangements but no compositions which are completely "composed through;" and since European music—at least since romanticism—is a composed and compositionally grounded music, it has practically no improvisation prior to modern "aleatorics" (but that is a different matter, which by the way casts further light on the strained relationship between concert music and improvisation with its theory-laden clumsiness!).

Thus, the "jazz composer" is a paradox. "Jazz" means improvisation, and "composer"—at least in Europe—means the exclusion of improvisation. But the paradox can be fruitful: the jazz composer can structure his music in the sense of the great European tradition and nonetheless leave room for jazz improvisation. Most of all, he can write what he structures in the sense of the European tradition in a jazz manner. There can be no doubt that jazz is subordinate to European music as far as formal structure is concerned, and that it might gain if mastery of form and structure becomes possible in jazz—provided nothing is lost in respect to the elements in which the singularity of jazz is contained: vitality, authenticity, immediacy of expression . . . in short, all that is jazzlike. From this point of view, Stravinsky's dictum that composition is "selective improvisation" acquires a much greater degree of importance for the jazz composer than it can have for the composer in the European tradition.

Musicians such as Jimmy Giuffre, John Lewis, Horace Silver, Bill Russo, Ralph Burns, Oliver Nelson, Charles Mingus, and Carla Bley have since the fifties given new meaning to the term "jazz composer," with credit to both elements of the term. But only Duke Ellington, who has been a jazz "composer" since the mid-twenties, stands on the level of the truly great jazz improvisers—the level of Charlie Parker, Louis Armstrong, Lester Young, Coleman Hawkins, John Coltrane, Miles Davis. . . .

Beyond all these considerations, of course, stands the kind of composer who could be found in jazz from the very start: the musician who simply writes 12-bar blues or 32-bar song themes, supplying himself and his players with materials for improvisation. This line leads straight from early musicians—Jelly Roll Morton, for example —through, say, Fats Waller in the twenties and thirties and Thelonious Monk from the forties on to the well-known improvisers of modern jazz who write much of their own material: Sonny Rollins, Miles Davis, John Coltrane, Herbie Hancock, Archie Shepp—in fact, practically everyone who plays improvised jazz. This sort of composing is directly related to the improvisatory process—without detouring through the arrangement. Of course, there are many stages—from simple sets of changes and themes merely setting up a blowing line to the complex jazz composition, formally structured and scored for many voices. Each successive step follows so logical a sequence that the erection of boundaries appears more or less arbitrary.

The relationship between arrangement and improvisation reflects the frequently asked question about the relationship between the collective and the individual in jazz. Jazz has been called "the music of the mass-collective" as well as "the music of boundless individualism." But the symphony orchestra, in which a hundred musicians subordinate themselves, almost in self-sacrifice, to a single will, is collective to a much greater degree. And a disdain for rules, regulations and laws would seem to be a prerequisite for "boundless individualism." Jazz—except for a few instances of extreme free jazz—shows no signs of such disdain.

What happened in free jazz only *seems* to follow different laws. Certainly, it has none—or only very few—of such exact written-down scores as those written by Oliver Nelson or Gerry Mulligan or Gary McFarland for the big bands. The concept of arranging actually returns to its position at the beginning of jazz history—to the orally predetermined arrangements of the King Oliver Band or of the New Orleans Rhythm Kings. And that same fruitful and inspiring tension between the freedom of the improvisatory principle and the order of the arrangement that existed in the other jazz styles is retained. Of course, there is aside from that, also the kind of improvisation that entails no predetermination, in which there is no trace of arrangement whatsoever; but the impression grows stronger that such total lack of restraint was only a passing stage within the process of liberation during the sixties.

At any rate, since the arrangement had been growing in scope and importance for so many years, it was logical that improvisation should do the same. With his usual cogency, Dave Brubeck summed it up: "Jazz is about the only form of art existing today in which there is freedom of the individual without the loss of group contact." This coexistence of collectivism and freedom expresses what we characterized as "the sociological situation of jazz" at the start of this book.

The Blues

Two jazz critics, a recording director, and a musician were discussing "if the blues is essential to the jazz idiom." Pianist Billy Taylor —the participating musician—said: ". . . I don't know of one giant —early, late, mid-thirties, or cool—who didn't have a tremendous respect and feeling for the blues, whether he played the blues or not. The spirit of it was in his playing or he wasn't really a giant as far as jazz was concerned. . . ." Nesuhi Ertegun, vice president of Atlantic Records followed up: "Let me ask you one question. Do you think a man like Lester Young would play a tune like 'Body and Soul' in the same way if he had never played the blues?" Billy Taylor's answer was "No." And Leonard Feather summarized: "I think what it all boils down to is that the blues is the essence of jazz, and merely having a feeling for blues means having a feeling for jazz. In other words, the chords or the notes of the chords which are essential for blues are the notes that are essential for jazz—the flat third, flat seventh, etc." To which Billy Taylor countered: "Well, I hesitate to oversimplify in that particular case because I tend to go back to the spirit. It's not the fact that a man on certain occasions would flat a certain note, bend a note or do something which is strictly a blues-type device. It's just that whatever this nebulous feeling is—the vitality they seem to get in the blues—whatever it is makes the difference between Coleman Hawkins' 'Body and Soul' and a society tenor player's 'Body and Soul' . . ."

It becomes clear from this discussion that the blues can be defined in several ways: emotionally, racially, sociologically, musically, and formally. Nearest at hand and most useful at this point is the emotional definition. Leadbelly, a singer from the olden days when the blues was wholly a folk art, set down the emotional definition in incomparable fashion: "Now this is the blues. No white man ever had the blues, 'cause nothin' to worry about. Now, you lay down at night and you roll from one side of the bed to the other all night long—you can't sleep . . . what's the matter? The blues has got you. You get up and sit on the side of your bed in the mornin'—may have your sister and brother, your mother and father around but you don't want no talk out of 'em . . . what's the matter? The blues has got you. Well you go and put your feet under the table and look down on your plate—got everything you want to eat—but you shake your head and get up and say 'Lord! I can't eat and I can't sleep! What's the matter with me?' Why, the blues has got you, wanna talk to you. . . ."

Bessie Smith sings: "Nobody knows you when you're down and out." And John Lee Hooker: "I've got the blues so bad, it's hard to keep from cryin'." In "Trouble in Mind Blues" it goes: "If you see me laughin,' I'm laughin' just to keep from cryin'. . . ."

This emotional definition also holds true for the blues when it is happy and full of humor—as it often is. The blues artists in whose

work there are as many happy as sad blues—such as Big Bill
Broonzy, B. B. King, or Ray Charles—have included themselves in
this emotional definition of the blues.

Next to the emotional stands the musical and formal definition. T-
Bone Walker, the blues singer, has said: "You know, there's only
one blues, though. That's the regular 12-bar pattern and then you interpret over that. Just write new words or improvise different and
you've got a new blues."

The blues strophe consists of twelve bars, based on the most fundamental of all chords: tonic, dominant, and subdominant.

Example 2

This 12-bar chord structure is consistent—from the earliest blues
(insofar as they already conform to the manifest blues pattern) down
to the most complex blues improvisations of the modern musicians,
who expand the harmonics in the most subtle way but of course
without disturbing their function.

The blues melodies and blues improvisations which rest on this
12-bar chord structure derive their peculiar fascination from the
"blue" notes. The music of the blacks brought from Africa to the
New World was largely pentatonic, i.e., their scale consisted not of
seven notes, like ours, but of five. When these blacks, confronted with
European music in America, began to make music of their own, they
adapted their pentatonic sensibilities to our tonal system with astonishing rapidity. Only the two steps which were absent from their
system remained problematic: the third and seventh steps. The Negro
found these unfamiliar and did not know what to do with them. And
so he sang and played—at first from insecurity—sometimes the minor
and sometimes the major third; sometimes the minor and sometimes
the major seventh. He sang and played without basic reference to
what we perceive as "major" and "minor," without relation to what,
in each musical piece, determines for us how the third and seventh
steps shall be executed. In this fashion there came into being a kind of
"contemporaneity" of the feelings which we associate with the major

and minor modes. And so the blues became emotionally ambiguous, without this clearly defined contrast between the extremes of joy and sadness to which we are accustomed.

Later, when the bebop musicians introduced the flatted fifth, this note, too, became a "blue" note—at first in the minor blues, then in all kinds of blues music—equal to the blue notes of the third and seventh steps.

In the blues it frequently happens that a conventionally tonic or dominant chord falls under a blue note, so that the major third may be played in the bass, and the minor third in the treble. This creates frictional sounds, which certainly can be interpreted as arising from a friction between two different harmonic systems: the chord structure, which corresponds to the European tradition, and the melodic line, with its blue notes originating in African music.

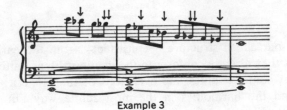

Example 3

Example 3 shows a very typical melodic line. Every other note is a blue note. The traditional blue notes at the third and seventh steps are marked by a single arrow; the double arrows indicate blue notes originating in the flatted fifth. The C-chord is the basis for the whole cadence—unharmed by the constant friction. Each blue note thus stands before a "normal" note, into which the blue note resolves—so that the cadence actually is nothing but a sequence of tension and relaxation, repeated six times. The tendency in jazz to create tension only to dissolve it immediately and then to create new tension which is again dissolved here becomes particularly clear. These tensions do not have the broad span they possess in European music.

Since the blue notes are always resolved by a note which lies one half tone lower, there is a strong tendency in the blues toward descending melodic lines—as Example 3 also shows. It is a melodic line which occurs, in this or similar form, in thousands of jazz improvisations—within and outside of blues.

The 12 blues bars consist of three 4-bar phrases, developed in such a way that a statement is made in the first four, repeated (over different harmonies) in the following four, and a "conclusion" drawn from it in the final four.

Sara Martin sings:

> *Blues, Blues, Blues why did you bring trouble to me?*
> *Yes, Blues, Blues, Blues why did you bring trouble to me?*
> *O Death, please sting me and take me out of my misery.*

This threefold form, with its double question and contrasted answer, creates a finite and compact mode of expression which is comparable to the important "minor forms" of art—from a literary standpoint as well. The causal interconnection of form and content fulfills the highest criteria of form. It is astonishing that the highest ideal of Western art—the unity of form and content—is approximated in the "proletarian" and "Negroid" world of the blues, and so tightly and clearly that the relationship between them becomes causal.

The finite blues form was of course not given from the start—neither musically nor textually. When looking at old folk blues, one must conclude that the threefold four-bar AAB-structure was present in the beginning merely as an "idea," which was approximated and deviated from. This "idea" of the blues form became increasingly crystallized over the years, and today it is so pure that nonconformity to it is generally felt to be an error. But in the great, "classical" period of the blues it was no error not to conform.

Harmonically as well there were many "errors" in the old, primitive blues. The singers floated with sovereign ease above certain basic chords, doing much as they pleased. Big Bill Broonzy often pointed out that to be emotionally right was much more important than to be formally and harmonically correct.

The blues singer generally fills the three 4-bar phrases only up to the beginning of the third, seventh, and eleventh bar. The remainder of each phrase is at the disposal of an improvisation called a "break"; a short, cadenzalike burst, which sets off the preceding from the following phrase. These one-and-a-half bars of the classic blues-break are the germ cell of jazz improvisation as a whole, with its fascinating interplay of forces between the unbonded freedom of the soloist and the obligation toward the collective of players.

The blues lyrics correspond in level to their form. According to Jean Cocteau, the poetry of the blues is the only substantial contribution to genuine folk poetry in our century. Everything of importance in the life of the blues singer is contained in these lyrics: love and racial discrimination; prison and the law; floods and railroad trains and the fortune told by the gypsy; the evening sun and the hospital. . . . Life itself flows into the lyrics of the blues with a surprising straightforwardness and directness to which nothing in Western poetry—and this goes for folk poetry as well—is comparable.

The majority of blues deal with love. Love is viewed, simply and clearly, as that toward which love aims . . . yet it is able to remain love. At a time when everyday love poetry has barely risen above the level of "Roses are red/violets are blue," the blues reflects that lofty, unsentimental stature and strength of the emotions and the passions which we know from great literature. Not a single blues is on the housemaid level of "Too Young" . . . and yet the blues belongs to the world of those who have supplied an entire continent with domestics, butlers and nursemaids!

There are funny blues and fast blues. But mainly blues are the music of a first rural, then urban proletariat whose life is filled with suffering. The social origins of the blues are at least as important as the racial ones. I do not know of a single genuine, authentic blues which does not make it obvious at once that the singer is of the pro-letariat. It would not make sense for members of the "aristocracy" to sing the blues. "They don't have the blues."

It is not without reason that references to "having" or "not having" the blues are made time and again in blues lyrics. You have to have the blues to be able to sing them. "The blues are a part of me," says singer Alberta Hunter.

From its mood and atmosphere the blues achieves continuity—something it seems to be lacking to a notable degree at first glance. It almost seems as if lack of coherence—in other words, diametrical op-position to all that stood for art in the Western sense until the end of the last century—is a mark of the blues. Lines and verses put together from the most varied blues and songs are linked up, unconcerned with what we call logic and context. Sometimes the singer himself seems to be the actor, and then a third person is acting. A moment ago the subject was a "he," and now it is a "she" . . . we were in the past, now we are in the future . . . suddenly, we switch from singular to plural.

Almost every blues furnishes examples of this "blues-discontinu-ity," while it seems quite difficult to find a blues in which each word follows logically from the foregoing. It would be wrong to conclude that this stems from an inability to create continuity. No, continuity is not the point. The lines and verses have an impressionistic quality. They relate to each other as do the spots of color in a painting: if you stand close, you cannot tell why there is red next to blue, or green next to orange, but as soon as you take a few steps back, it all blends into a whole. The "whole" of the blues is the mood, the blues atmosphere. It creates its own continuity. Into the blues mood flows whatever comes up—events, memories, thoughts, fancies—and out comes, always, the blues.

Everything that exists in the world of the singer goes through the blues; all is contemporaneous. Nothing can be outside. Big Bill Broonzy, the singer, tells about how when he was a boy, he and his uncle caught a big turtle: ". . . We drug him home and my uncle told me to make him stick his neck out of his shell. I took a stick and put it in front of him. The turtle caught hold of the stick and wouldn't turn it loose. So my uncle said: 'Hold his head right there and I'll cut it off.' My uncle took the axe and cut the turtle's head off and we went in the house and stayed there a while. When we came back, no turtle. So we looked for him and the turtle was nearly back to the lake where we caught him. We picked him up, brought him back to the house and my uncle said: 'There's a turtle who is dead and don't know it.' And that's the way a lot of people is today: they got the blues and don't know it."

At the beginning of the blues stand the work songs and field hollers: the simple, archaic songs sung by the blacks at work in the fields or on the levees. They were sung because it was easier to work to the rhythms of a song than without it. The rhythm had an effect on the singers, and made even those perk up who otherwise would have worked sluggishly or not at all. "Lawd, cap'n, I's not a-singin' —I's just a hollerin' to help me with my work." That's why the white man wanted to see the Negro sing. "A singing Negro is a good Negro," says Francois Postif, describing the attitudes of a plantation owner or prison warden.

Folk song and folk ballad, frequently in the "white" sense, joined with work song and field holler. There were the old rounds with the regular, happy repetition of a refrain of a few lines, sung by the chorus of listeners.

Blind Lemon Jefferson, Big Bill Broonzy, Leadbelly, Robert Johnson, Elmore James, Blind Boy Fuller, Rev. Gary Davis, Bukka White,

Blind Willie McTell, Big Joe Williams, Sonny Terry, Brother John Sellers, John Lee Hooker, and Lightnin' Hopkins are famous representatives of blues folklore. Most accompanied themselves on guitar, and they often—as, for example, Muddy Waters and Lightnin' Hopkins—are wonderful guitarists. In the thirties some of them were ahead of their colleagues in the related field of jazz. Other blues singers—e.g. Sonny Terry and Little Walter—knew how to coax amazing sounds from a harmonica. Others record with well-known jazz musicians backing their folk-rooted blues vocals.

In most cases, the accompanying instrument meant more to the blues singer than mere background: It was a partner in conversation. It would inspire and excite; it could make comments in affirmation or protest, it anticipated or completed an idea.

Under no circumstances should the reader assume that we are speaking of things related to a distant past. Almost all well-known commentators on blues have consciously or unconsciously nurtured this feeling, as if they were the last of their profession with just time enough left to document a vanishing folklore art form. A feature of the white man's relationship to folklore of all kinds is that he links it to nostalgia, sentimentality, memories of the "good old days." As far as the blues is concerned, this response is wrong.

There are more blues movements and blues styles today than ever before, and they all live side by side. Not one of the old blues forms —folk blues, country blues, prison blues, archaic blues—has become extinct. In fact, new ones were added: city blues, urban blues, jazz blues, rhythm and blues, soul blues. . . . In addition there are different regional styles. The most easily recognizable are Mississippi blues (rough, archaic), Texas blues (mobile, flexible, jazz-related), and East Coast blues, from Florida or Tennessee, for example (often permeated with white country and hillbilly folklore). The folk blues of Texas and of the Midwest (the so-called "territories") shaped the California big city blues; the folk blues of Mississippi shaped the Chicago big city blues. But in this case too, the mixtures are no less interesting than the pure forms, which are illusory in the blues world, anyway—blues is by nature a mixture. The success of the Memphis blues since the sixties—of Otis Redding, to name one—lies precisely in its combination and urbanization of elements from Mississippi and Texas.

Almost all important blues singers are at home in several forms and styles—not only in the sense that they developed from one form to the other, as from country blues to city blues and on to urban blues (e.g. Muddy Waters, Howlin' Wolfe, B. B. King)—but also in the sense that they may practice several forms simultaneously (for instance, John Lee Hooker, who keeps switching between folk, country, and city blues; or Jimmy Witherspoon, T-Bone Walker, Ray Charles, who have all frequently played with jazz musicians).

Since the mid-fifties, the blues has penetrated popular music to a degree unimaginable up to then. First, black rhythm and blues—the rocking music of the black South and of the Northern ghettos—became rock 'n' roll. Bill Haley and Elvis Presley were the first white rock 'n' roll stars, but immediately following came black artists— Chuck Berry, Fats Domino, Little Richard—who enjoyed an immense success on the white "pop" scene that would have been considered impossible even shortly before. By 1963, the best of rhythm and blues had become so closely linked to the mainstream of American popular music that *Billboard* magazine temporarily suspended separate listings of "Rhythm and Blues" and "Pop." Separate listing was resumed later, but the magazine kept changing its policy—it had become uncertain, and still is. Outstanding black talent is also now part of the white scene. Younger readers will hardly be able to appreciate how unusual that once would have been. The term "rhythm and blues" was only introduced toward the late forties. Until then, that music had been called "race" music. This label makes it clear that for 50 years, black music had been played in a ghetto that was noticed by the white world only indirectly at best.

It was through musicians like Bill Haley, Elvis Presley, Chuck Berry, Fats Domino, Little Richard, and others, that the blues literally demolished the popular music of "Tin Pan Alley," and its babbling about schmaltzy, kitschy, dishonest feelings. If today's popular music is more realistic, clear, honest, and at the same time more poetic, musical, and emotionally richer than popular music before the mid-fifties, then this must be ascribed to the penetration of white popular music by the blues. Blues—and black music in general—has always *been* what white popular music only has recently become: realistic and full of social involvement, a commentary on the everyday life and problems of those who sang the blues.

What happened during the fifties was only the preparation for the "decade of rock," the term frequently applied to the sixties. For the U. S., it was Bob Dylan; then, initially in Great Britain and later simply for the whole world, it was the Beatles who created a new musical consciousness, so that artists who just shortly before had seemed to the personification of high musical standards—think of Frank Sinatra!—within a few years became "old fogeys" when confronted with this new consciousness. The musical standards of the world of popular music demolished in the process where the symbols of the moral, social, and political standards of the bourgeois world which had created the old pop music. These standards were the real target of the new movement.

Both Bob Dylan and the Beatles are unthinkable without the blues. The Beatles came from rhythm and blues, particularly Chuck Berry. Dylan comes from Woody Guthrie and the American folklore at whose center stands folk blues. It has been said that Dylan was "the first true poet of popular music." But in so saying, hundreds of black folk-blues singers, who since the turn of the century—and perhaps even earlier—have been the "true poets of popular music," are forgotten.

Both Dylan and the Beatles grew out of their respective bases of origin. When Dylan accompanied himself electronically for the first time (at the 1965 Newport Folk Festival) there was a storm of protest from his fans. But three years later, in 1968, he recorded his album "John Wesley Harding" with acoustic guitar and folk-blues harmonica; and, thus, he programmatically clarified for all his followers—and they did understand—how he viewed his musical and spiritual heritage.

There was a similar development with the Beatles. For years, they had continuously refined their rock 'n' roll heritage, sensitizing their music more and more, and had moved further and further away from the blues. In "Michelle," "In My Life," "Eleanor Rigby," and other songs, they had incorporated baroque elements; in "Yesterday" they had remembered the old Elizabethan English Madrigal culture; and, in George Harrison's songs, they had made reference to classical Indian music. "Sgt. Pepper's Lonely Hearts Club Band" was a rock symphony. But then, in 1968, their double album, "The Beatles," was released. And in this album—in reference to Chuck Berry, to early rock 'n' roll and rhythm and blues—they made it clear, as programmatically as Dylan in "John Wesley Harding," that they knew where they came from, and that they wanted their fans to know it too. For those who did not hear, John Lennon said it once more: "If there was another name for rock 'n' roll, it would be Chuck Berry."

It has been said that the Beatles and Bob Dylan changed the musical and social consciousness of a whole generation. In this context, it is important to realize that this change of consciousness is based on the blues and would have been impossible without it.

To be sure, from the standpoint of jazz and authentic blues, much of the blues derivations played in the rock era of the sixties and the rock 'n' roll of the fifties was inferior to the pure, uncommercialized product. But this holds true only for a minority of jazz and blues connoisseurs. For the majority, the reverse is valid: Through the blues, popular music of the fifties, and even more the sixties, gained a qualitative level previously unthinkable.

The fact that truly black feeling has entered the white world with the blues becomes apparent not only through the music, but also through the kind of dancing that goes with it.

In the world of blues—and in general in the black world, already in Africa—there has always been "open" and "individual" dancing. The actual partner of each individual dancer was and is the music; the dancer answers the music with his movements. In the white world, on the other hand, dancing had atrophied increasingly—as a pretext for social and physical contact for which the music merely furnished the barely noticed background. Dancing, like everything else in the rationalized white world, had to "serve a function"—as social contact and chance for physical contact. Dancing in the black world is done only for its own sake. The body becomes a musical instrument—as it has become also for the young white rock audience from the mid-fifties on.

Charles Keil (to whom I am indebted in this connection) assumes that, seeing today's young people dance in the U. S. or in Europe, ". . . a West African villager . . . would be delighted to see that Western men and women have at last cast aside the disgusting and lascivious practices of embracing, hugging, shuffling, and grappling in public and have adopted the vigorous, therapeutic pelvic exercise that has always been the pride and joy of his community."

At first, pure blues consciousness was stronger in Britain than in the U. S. Most of the successful British pop and rock musicians of the sixties for years had studied, imitated and copied black blues singers and blues instrumentalists; and on that basis found their own styles.

Since the late fifties, there had been a true "blues movement" in Great Britain—led by a guitarist and vocalist who was born in Vienna, educated in France, and settled in England, Alexis Korner, and later also by John Mayall. One could indulge in all kinds of speculation as to why this contemporary "blues consciousness" originated in Britain rather than the U. S., though the British Isles are much farther away from the creative blues centers of the American South or Chicago's South Side than are New York or Los Angeles. The question can be asked: Were there too many prejudices against black blues in the U. S., and did the American music world jump on the blues wagon only when it was realized how much money British groups like the Rolling Stones—or later Led Zeppelin or John Mayall—were making on the blues?

Another point cannot be made without bitterness: It is white musicians who are making fortunes in today's British and American scenes with black blues, while the black creators of this music—with a growing number of exceptions—are still the relatively obscure voices of a suffering proletariat.

At the beginning of this chapter, we quoted Leadbelly: "No white man ever had the blues." For decades, the blues were thought to be the "last retreat" of black music that no white man would ever be able to penetrate. In all areas of a music originally created by blacks, whites again and again had been more successful, had made more money than the black creators. Only in blues did the whites not succeed in producing really convincing sounds.

Since the sixties, parts of this "last bastion" have also been conquered. There are some white musicians who—at least as instrumentalists—can play authentic black blues. As we said, Britishers Alexis Korner and John Mayall paved the way for this, but both are still far away from the authenticity reached by the musicians following them: guitarists Eric Clapton or Rory Gallagher in Britain, and then also Americans—guitarist Mike Bloomfield and harmonica players Paul Butterfield and Paul Osher, all of whom learned in Chicago's black South Side (especially from Muddy Waters); the late guitarist Duane Allman; musicians of the blues-rock group Canned Heat; J. Geil; and others.

Still, there is a difference. White blues—especially where it is artistically serious—is more precious, more "accurate," cleaner, 'ess expressive, and also more vulgar, less subtle and less flexible than black blues.

Charles Keil tells of a survey about the nature of blues and soul made by a black Chicago radio station among its audience. In the answers, again and again the word "mellow" recurred. They're "mellow," the blues and soul. And "mellow" is exactly what white blues are not.

Above all, what we've said up to now refers to instrumental music. As soon as all these white musicians, "authentic" as they may sound as instrumentalists, open their mouths to sing, the illusion fades away. Even the layman can hear who is white and who is black, and there is no bridge over that gap. Not even Janis Joplin (the singer from Texas who died in 1970 and of all white singers came closest to the black sound) was able to to bridge that gap. That should be remembered later particularly when reading the chapters about the white male and female singers. Not without reason John Mayall, a man who should know and whom it concerns directly, has said: "When we talk about blues, we mean black blues. That's the real blues for us."

However, the sociological and social side of this matter should not be overlooked. The blues is black music, for one thing, because the living conditions of blacks in parts of the South and in the Northern ghettos are so different from those of whites, not only in degree, but in essence as well. American critic Ralph Gleason speculates that to the extent that this will change, white blues musicians will gain "equality" with black blues musicians.

Spiritual and Gospel Song

The singer who comes closest to Bessie Smith in vocal power and expressiveness is not a blues singer but a gospel singer: Mahalia Jackson, who died in 1972. The gospel song is the modern form of the spiritual, the religious song of the Negro—more vital, more swinging, more jazz-like than the old spiritual, which frequently shows a closeness to European church music, and above all a proximity to the white spirituals of the last century (which are often overlooked by the "race-romancers").

The blues is the secular form of spiritual and gospel song. Or the other way around: gospel song and spiritual are the religious forms of the blues. Thus it is not only in a relative, but in a literal sense that blues singer Alberta Hunter says: "To me, the blues are—well, almost religious. . . . The blues are like spirituals, almost sacred. When we sing the blues, we're singin' from our hearts, we're singin' out our feelings." And blues singer T-Bone Walker has said: "Of course, the blues comes a lot from the church, too. The first time I ever heard a boogie-woogie piano was the first time I went to church. That was the Holy Ghost Church in Dallas, Texas. That boogie-woogie was a kind of blues, I guess. Then the preacher used to preach in a bluesy tone sometimes. . . ."

The visitor to a church in Harlem or on Chicago's South Side will not find a great contrast to the ecstatic atmosphere that might be found at a jazz concert—say, by Lionel Hampton. He will find the identical rhythms, the same beat, and the same swing in the music. Frequently, he will find jazz-associated instruments—saxophones, trombones, drums; he will hear boogie-woogie bass lines and blues structures and see enraptured people beating time with their hands and feet and sometimes even dancing.

Winthrop Sargeant describes a church service in the South: "Minutes passed, long minutes of strange intensity. The mutterings, the ejaculations, grew louder, more dramatic, till suddenly I felt the creative thrill dart through the people like an electric vibration; that same half-audible hum arose—emotion was gathering atmospherically as clouds gather—and then, up from the depth of some 'sinner's' remorse and imploring came a pitiful little plea, a real Negro 'moan' sobbed in musical cadence. From somewhere in that bowed gathering another voice improvised a response; the plea sounded again, louder this time and more impassioned; then other voices joined in the answer, shaping it into a musical phrase; and so on, before our ears, as one might say, from this molten metal of music a new song was smithied out, composed then and there by no one in particular and by everyone in general."

Modern gospel songs are mostly composed pieces, marketed as sheet music. But these pieces are used freely in church services—certainly not quite as freely as jazz musicians treat a theme, but still as a basis for individual activity and interpretation. Leading black writers are sometimes authors of gospel lyrics. And the sheet music is often printed in larger editions than commercial tunes.

The most important gospel singer was—and will remain—Mahalia Jackson, born in New Orleans. In 1945, she became famous almost overnight with her recording of "Move On Up a Little Higher," a best seller in the category of the great hits: more than a million records sold!

Through Mahalia Jackson, the white world for the first time became familiar on a broader scale with the art of gospel singing. Prior to this, very few had any notion of what was happening each Sunday in the black churches.

Other important gospel groups, past and present, are St. Paul's Baptist Church Choir of Los Angeles, the Bells of Joy, the Gospel-aires, the Harmonising Four, the Dixie Humming Birds, the Original Five Blind Boys, the Stars of Hope, the Spirit of Memphis Quartet, the Christian Travelers, the Sensational Nightingales, the Staple Singers, the Golden Gate Jubilee Quartet, the Pilgrim Travelers, Dorothy Love Coates and her Original Gospel Harmonettes, R. H. Harris and the Christland Singers, the Stars of Faith, the Robert Patterson Singers, Brother Cleophus Robinson, and—above all—the late Bishop Kelsey and his congregation of Washington, D. C. On his records—such as "Little Boy"—one hears how in the course of his sermon, Rev. Kelsey gradually becomes the lead singer and how, suddenly and with gripping immediacy, the gospel singing of the entire congregation is "there."

Among the most likely candidates for Mahalia Jackson's vacated throne are Marion Williams and Bessie Griffin.

Many preachers and male gospel singers are masters of falsetto singing: a way of singing practiced in Africa for centuries as a sign of highly potent, bursting manhood. This manner of singing moved from spiritual and gospel song to the blues and, far beyond that, into modern jazz—as in Leon Thomas—or into contemporary rock and soul music—as in Percy Mayfield.

There are gospel songs with hillbilly and cowboy, mambo, waltz, and boogie-woogie rhythms. But most of all, gospel songs have a strong, full jazz beat. In gospel songs—as in blues—is everything that can be found in daily life: elections, skyscrapers, railroads, telephones. It may appear naïve to white people—with our characteristic notion of intellectual superiority—when someone expresses in song the wish to talk with the Lord on the telephone, or travel to heaven in a pullman car. Yet, in the great period of our own religious art, it was not different: the Flemish painters transferred the story of the crucifixion to the landscape of the Lowlands, and in the Christmas songs of Silesia, the people sing about the birth of Christ as if it had taken place in the ice and snow of their own mountains.

Spiritual and gospel songs are not, as is often thought, something belonging to history—something that existed at the beginning of jazz somewhere in the Southern countryside. Quite the opposite: in the course of jazz development, they have grown more effective, more dynamic and alive. From the fifties on, gospel and soul have broken into other areas of black music on a wide front; initially into jazz. Milt Jackson—the leading vibraharpist of modern jazz—once answered the question where his particular style and soulful playing came from: "What is soul in jazz? It's what comes from inside . . . in my case, I think it's what I heard and felt in the music of my church. That was the most important influence of my career. Everybody wants to know where I got my 'funky' style. Well, it came from the church."

In the liner notes to an early album by Ray Charles, Gary Kramer wrote: "The importance of the relationship between the religious music of the Negro and jazz is all too rarely emphasized. . . ."

Musicians such as Milt Jackson, Horace Silver and Charles generated a "soul wave" in the second half of the fifties that got its crucial impulse from gospel music and also broke into popular music during the sixties. Some of the most successful rock and soul singers of the sixties and seventies would be unthinkable without their gospel background: Otis Redding, James Brown, Aretha Franklin, Little Richard, Wilson Pickett, Isaac Hayes . . .

Soul is secularized gospel music. And the best soul singers, even at the high points of their careers, still love to sing in gospel churches for a black audience; Aretha Franklin, for instance.

Some jazz specialists claim that gospel music was more important in the development of the contemporary sounds of rock, pop, and jazz than was the blues. As Charles Keil points out, "there are still at least 40 store-front churches for every joint where blues or jazz is played in Chicago, the blues capital of the world."

Jazz and gospel singing are related in yet another respect: Many of the best female jazz singers got their start in church. Sarah Vaughan, for instance, who carried Charlie Parker's conception into jazz singing; or the late Dinah Washington, the successful "Queen" of rhythm and blues, who not only sang but also played piano in church; or Aretha Franklin, as we mentioned earlier.

In a reverse process, several great gospel singers also belonged to the jazz world: The late Sister Rosetta Tharpe sang in the thirties with the Swing bands of Cab Calloway and Lucky Millinder and had a successful night-club act; one of the best-known composers of gospel songs—Thomas A. Dorsey—got his start in Chicago in the twenties as a blues lyricist, singer and pianist.

Danny Barker, the guitarist, says about Bessie Smith: "If you had any church background, like people who came from the South as I did, you would recognize a similarity between what she was doing and what those preachers and evangelists from there did, and how they moved people. . . ."

In conclusion, we can go back to the very roots of jazz with guitarist Bud Scott: "Each Sunday Buddy Bolden went to church and that's where he got his idea of jazz music. They would keep perfect rhythm there by clapping their hands."

Harmony

In terms of harmony and melody, jazz does not offer much of a revolutionary nature, at least not until the beginning of free jazz in the sixties. Paradoxically, there is in this very fact a difference between jazz and concert music. In the realm of established musical culture, what is new and revolutionary is always so first and foremost in terms of melody and harmony. Jazz, on the other hand, though among the most revolutionary developments in the arts in our century, is relatively traditional in respect to harmony and melody. Its newness is based on rhythm and sound.

Almost the only novel and singular thing in jazz in the harmonic domain are the blue notes. Aside from these, the harmonic language of conventional jazz—that is, of the jazz prior to and apart from free playing—is identical with that of popular dance and entertainment music. The harmonies of ragtime, Dixieland, and New Orleans jazz are—beyond blue notes—identical with the harmonics of polkas, marches, and waltzes. They are based on the tonic and the dominant. Bix Beiderbecke brought certain Debussy-like chords and whole-tone effects into jazz. The great Swing musicians added the sixth to the major triad, and "enriched" sevenths with ninths—or even elevenths. Since bebop, passing chords are placed between the basic harmonies of a piece; or the basic harmonies are replaced by "alternations." Jazz musicians are—or at least were during the bebop and cool-jazz periods—proud of the developments in this realm of their music, and among them there was much talk of harmonic problems; but these problems—viewed from the position of European music—are more or less "old hat." Only very few chords with augmented or diminished fifths and ninths, characteristic mainly of modern jazz, do not exist in this form in conventional music, especially when such intervals occur in combinations. For example, harmonies occur that may have a flatted fifth in the bass and an augmented fifth in the treble, and above this one may occasionally find a diminished or augmented ninth. Example 4 shows two such chord combinations, with their respective resolutions.

Example 4

Example 5 shows the first four bars of the song "I Can't Give You Anything but Love," popular since the twenties. (A) indicates the simple, almost primitive harmonies on which the jazz improvisations of that day were based, while (B) shows how the harmonies were altered in later years—during the transition from Swing to bop. No doubt the simple harmonies of 5 (A) might just as well stem from a European folk dance. The more modern harmonies of 5 (B) could be employed equally well in modern popular music or in a commercial dance number.

Example 5

The developments of jazz harmonies from ragtime and New Orleans jazz to bebop and cool jazz are not peculiar to jazz. They run parallel to and are "synchronized" with harmonic developments in popular music from the polka to the slickly orchestrated sounds of Hollywood movie music. André Hodeir surmises that jazz was influenced by pop music in this respect—a thought which lies near to hand since jazz musicians, who listen open-mindedly to everything which appears to them valid or worthy of imitation in any kind of music, heard that here was something which could be learned and applied to what seemed to them unsatisfactory in their own music. The harmonic language of jazz, according to Hodeir, is "largely borrowed." *Because* this is so, it is quite in accord with the main line of jazz tradition. It is peculiar to the genesis of jazz that it united the best of two divergent musical cultures: European and African. The Negroes who sang the first shouts and work songs soon recognized that there was nothing in their own musical past which came even close to the ripe and rich harmonic expression in European music. On the other hand, there was nothing in European music that could come even close to the expressive power of "black" sonorities and to the vitality of Africa's rhythmic tradition. Thus both musical cultures contributed their "speciality".

In bebop and cool jazz, harmonies can be varied just as melodies were the basis for variations in traditional jazz. Thus Example 5 shows eight harmonies in the modern (B) version as compared to four in the old (A). The latter only has chords which are closely related to C-major. The modern version, however, creates a singable bass line which stands in contrapuntal relationship to the melodic line. The entire harmonic picture is loosened up and enriched. The chord sequence itself shows a steady succession of tension and relaxation—in terms of the tensions so important to jazz. Most of the added chords in the modern version 5 (B) are terminal chords, having a tendency to resolve in the subsequent chord. The older version 5 (A) shows only one resolution—in the fourth bar; the modern version shows three such processes. This, too, indicates how jazz history demonstrates an ever stronger and more intense concentration of jazzlike, tension-creating and tension-dissolving elements.

In the modern version a whole new chord structure comes into being. But this chord structure is not so new that it fails to indicate in each chord its relationship to the original harmonies. The new chords, so to speak, stand in place of the handed-down chords. The tonal relationship of the whole remains as ordered and neat as one could desire.

Many laymen, and friends of traditional jazz not conversant with the harmonic vocabulary of bop at first reacted to its sounds as "atonal." "Atonality," as the word itself makes clear, means that the music has no relationship to a tonal center and has no tonal center of gravity. But this is not the case in the prevalent forms of modern jazz. If many listeners could not hear the harmonic centers of gravity it was not because they are lacking, but because the listener's ear was unaccustomed to these harmonies. Indeed, harmony in music is a matter of custom. Any harmonic system, even in its most far-reaching variants, can be assimilated by the ear after a period of listening— even when the initial impression has been of absurdity.

Altogether, the development of harmony in jazz and modern concert music shows many parallels—with jazz tending to lag considerably behind. The flatted fifth—the bebopper's favorite interval in the forties—in many respects corresponds to the tritone, which plays an important role in modern concert music: in Hindemith, Bartók, Stravinsky, Honegger, Milhaud, etc. Hindemith devoted much space to the tritone in *The Craft of Musical Composition*—one of the main theoretical works on modern concert music. In this work he states: "With increases in distance the familial relationship is loosened until at the utmost note—the augmented fourth or the diminished fifth— the tritone, it barely remains noticeable." Elsewhere Hindemith says that the tritone is indifferent to the harmonic base. Thus Hindemith feels that the flatted fifth does not destroy tonality but stands in a neutral—"indifferent"—relationship to it. This is felt by jazz musicians as well. This "indifference" is the real reason for the popularity of the tritone in modern jazz. The tritone which, according to Hindemith, "neither belongs in the region of the harmonious, nor can be regarded as discordant," has renewed an old jazz tradition: the preference for the shimmering and the ambiguous, which can also be found in the blue notes of the blues. Not for nothing did the flatted fifth—as its novelty begins to fade—begin to take on the function of a blue note. Example 3 (in the chapter on the blues) shows the degree to which blue notes and flatted fifths have become equivalent.

The flatted fifths and blue notes of jazz and the tritone of modern symphonic music thus do not point toward a dissolution of tonality, but toward its loosening and broadening. The presence of the flatted fifth and blue notes in jazz can be explained from the same point of view from which Hindemith explains the tritone in the new symphonic music: "Harmonic and melodic power are arrayed in opposition." Where the harmonic power is weakest—in the flatted fifth—the melodic power is strongest. And power of melodic line is what counts.

The bop musicians—Charlie Parker, Dizzy Gillespie, Charlie

Christian, Thelonious Monk—who were the first to use flatted fifths certainly did not have the faintest notion of the tritone or of Hindemith's *Craft of Musical Composition*. In their own way they arrived at solutions which Hindemith (whose name here stands for an entire direction in modern concert music) had derived from European musical tradition.

The first few traces of atonality began to show a couple of years after the initial phase of bebop in some jazz forms of the fifties—as the work of Lennie Tristano, Charles Mingus, Teddy Charles, or George Russell. Russell, who wrote the famous "Cubana Be-Cubana Bop" for Dizzy Gillespie's big band in the late forties, created a system of tonality which he calls the "Lydian Concept of Tonal Organization." In many respects it resembles the scales of medieval church music. Lennie Tristano, with musicians of his school, created a freely improvised piece called "Intuition," in which Wolfgang Fortner—a well-known contemporary German symphonic composer—found tendencies toward the twelve-tone system.

Musicians like Tristano, Russell, Jimmy Giuffre, and Mingus paved the way for that sudden and explosive harmonic freedom which around the turn of the fifties made jazz come apart at the seams. Free jazz, whose first outstanding representatives were Cecil Taylor and Ornette Coleman, finally rejected the laws of conventional functional harmonics. Sounds and lines rub against each other wild and hard, lending an ecstatic character to the music—to a degree that goes far beyond what might have been felt as "ecstatic" in earlier jazz forms.

On the other hand, even in many of the freest jazz recordings, the music remains related to what musicians call "tonal centers". The word "tonal," however, is not used in the sense of functional harmonics, but is simply supposed to indicate certain crucial points—centers of gravity—from which the musicians take off, and to which they find their way back—or at least try—if they have not lost sight of each other in the collective heat of improvisation. (In this context, also see the chapter dealing with free jazz.)

In the chapters about Miles Davis and John Coltrane, we used the term "modal." In the manner of improvisation created by Davis and John Coltrane, the chords are no longer defined by the constantly changing harmonies of a harmonic structure; every chord that corresponds to the "mode," to the scale, is allowed. This is a way of playing that has been in existence for centuries in many of the great exotic musical cultures—for example, the Arab. On the one hand, it allows for harmonic freedom; on the other, it prevents caprice. Modal playing also means a further Africanization of the music; away from the dictatorship of European harmonies toward the free harmonization which exists in many African musical cultures (not only in the Arabianized and Moslemized ones). Modalisation thus creates a feeling of belonging in a dual sense: musically and racially—and in mood, too. That is the basis of its success.

In the meantime, the modal way of playing, improvising, and composing has come to shape almost all of jazz and rock music as well as a large segment of contemporary popular music. From Coltrane it moved to Jimi Hendrix and the psychedelic rock of the San Francisco groups, but also into modern soul music—singers like James Brown and Marvin Gaye. And above all, it is shaping jazz.

The jazz of the seventies combines the freedom of free jazz with the harmonic possibilities of previous jazz styles. The new aspects it seems to be achieving in terms of harmonies are rooted solely in the virtuousity and sovereignty with which harmonies from the most varied sources are dealt with. In Keith Jarrett's playing, for example— this pianist became known through his work with Charles Lloyd and Miles Davis and seems particularly representative of the harmonic possibilities of the seventies—one may find side by side, held together by modality, blues chords, Debussy-like whole-tone harmonies, traces of medieval ecclesiastical keys, romantic elements, exotic—for example Arab—elements; and in addition, the whole range of harmonic possibilities of conventional jazz. Often all these elements occur in such immediate transitions that even specialists no longer are able to localize the sources, but they appear in an order that seems necessary and logical, although no known system could explain the necessities and logic of such an order. That is exactly where freedom is founded: no longer on atonality, but rather in the mastery with which all the elements of tonality and atonality, European, exotic and jazz-like, classical and modern, are utilized. Thus, freedom also includes the freedom to be free—and the opposite: to forego being free, if that is what the musician wants.

This is also how the missionary and sectarian character of the freedom of the free jazz of the sixties is overcome—a conception of freedom which condemned all non-free playing as not only musically but also politically, socially, and morally regressive.

Melody

If one proceeds from the assumption made by modern musical theory that there is no basic difference between melody and harmony—melody is "horizontal harmony," harmony is "vertical melody"—almost everything that can be said about jazz melody has already been said in the preceding chapter. In the early forms of jazz there was hardly anything that could be called a "jazz" melody—with the exception of melodies containing blue notes. (Example 3 in the blues chapter.) The melodies were fundamentally similar to those of circus and march music, to the piano and drawing-room music of the late 19th century. To the degree in which jazz phrasing gained significance, melodies began to evolve in terms of this phrasing—with such far-reaching effect that this manner of phrasing finally changed and shaped the melodic flow itself, and something that might be called jazz melody came into being.

Jazz melody is primarily marked by its flowing character. Insofar as the melodic development is expressed in improvisation, there are no repeats, such as are often used structurally in European music. Repeats are excluded to begin with because the soloist mainly improvises from his subconscious, and thus is unable to repeat what he has just played without first having recourse to close study of a possible recording. Repeats are part of the relationship of music to time. When a melody is repeated, it is lifted out of the flow of time. It is as if one were to bring back a span of time which has already passed in order to re-live it once more. The absence of repetition in the flow of chorus improvisation makes it clear that jazz is more closely related to the realm in which music occurs—time—than is European music. The phenomenon of swing and other peculiarities of jazz also point to this. To give it exaggerated expression: if music—as almost all philosophies of music hold—is *the* art expressed in time, then jazz corresponds more fundamentally to the basic nature of the musical than European music.

Jazz derives one of its unique traits from the fact that it is instrumentally conceived. André Hodeir, who has expressed the most succinct ideas about the problems of melody and harmony in jazz yet published, said: "Composers in the European tradition conceive a phrase by itself and then make it fit the requirements of a given instrument. The jazz improviser creates only in terms of the instrument he plays. In extreme instances of assimilation, the instrument becomes in some way a part of him. . . ."

Since the instrument and, through it, the musician himself are "projected into" the melody, attack, vibrato, accentuation, rhythmic placement, etc., are so closely connected with a jazz melody that it may become meaningless without them. A European melody always exists "in the abstract" as well, but the jazz melody exists only in its concrete relationship to the instrument on which it is played and to the musician who plays it. It becomes nonsense (in the literal sense of the term) when it is removed from its creator. This is the reason why most attempts to notate jazz improvisations have remained unsatisfactory. The fine points of phrasing, attack, accentuation, expression, and conception cannot be expressed in notation, and since everything depends on these subtleties, notation becomes meaningless. When jazz melodies separated from these subtleties appear on note paper, they often seem primitive and banal.

In the course of jazz development, the improvisers have developed a facility for projecting subtleties into jazz which cannot be expressed in words. In order to accentuate the flowing character of jazz melody, the oppressively dotted quarter- and eights-notes so typical of the jazz of the twenties have been dispensed with. This kind of punctuation is now regarded as "corny"; it can still be found in popular music, especially when nostalgia for the "good old days" is in order (—but all of a sudden there were several free jazz musicians, most of all Albert Ayler, who had fun with such "old-fashioned" march, polka, and circus elements!). Miles Davis, Lee Konitz and Lennie Tristano have fashioned a manner of improvisation in which eighth-note stands next to eighth-note, almost without punctuation. Here are lines which look in transcription as "European" and "symphonic" as one could imagine. But when such lines are played by Davis or Konitz or almost any significant jazz musician today, they become the very essence of concentrated "jazzness." The jazz characteristic no longer lies in the crude, external punctuation and syncopation of notes —it lies in subtlety of conception. That is what jazz musicians mean when they say: "Jazz isn't *what* you do, it's *how* you do it."

Because all these refinements—almost ephemeral but extremely important differentiations in attack, phrasing, vibrato, accentuation, etc.—were further developed, it became increasingly possible to incorporate the beat, i.e., the rhythm section, into the melody line.

More and more one can hear unaccompanied jazz solos of just as much concentrated jazz essence as a solo improvisation with a rhythm section. We noted in the chapter about the jazz of the seventies that Coleman Hawkins was the first to record a whole piece without rhythm accompaniment: "Picasso," in 1947. This record was the actual forerunner of those freely swinging, long unaccompanied improvisations and cadenzas played by Sonny Rollins—or, for instance, in Germany by Albert Mangelsdorff—that became something of a trend during the seventies, filled with hidden romanticism.

One could say that from the mid-thirties on, it became the jazz improviser's prime concern to play long, fluid, flowing lines without crudely external jazz effects, and nonetheless convey real jazz intensity. This is also the source of the 'flowing,' 'pulsating' rhythmic conception developed by such musicians as drummer Elvin Jones in John Coltrane's group, or Tony Williams with Miles Davis.

It is only a step from here to the melodies of the free jazz musicians, who in the realm of melody more than anywhere else retained all elements of post-Lester Young and Charlie Parker jazz phrasing, in addition to the aspect of intensity expressed in an ecstatic manner. Free jazz melody is basically just a conventional jazz melody, over free harmonies, plus wild ecstasy, often with none of those hardly perceivable, subtle nuances that the cool-jazz people loved.

The ability to simply let certain notes "go by the board" becomes particularly important here. Anyone who has notated jazz improvisations knows of his phenomenon: The note is there, one hears it quite clearly, and it has to be included in the notation. But one does not hear it because it has been played, rather because it was *not* played: it was merely felt and hinted at. Faced with this, many a European musician capitulates. In the spring of 1958, Marshall Brown came to Europe to recruit a big band of leading European jazz musicians for the Newport Jazz Festival. He consistently admired their high musical standards, yet seldom was truly satisfied. "For example," he said, "it was difficult to find a musician who could throw away a note. Until we listened to these European musicians I had never realized that such subtleties are typical American."

The theme to be improvised on has become less and less important in the course of jazz development. The embellishment and ornamentation of the theme, so important to the old jazz, recedes further into the background. It still exists in the interpretation of "ballads"—slow pieces, mostly from the realm of popular music, with melodies or chord structures that appeal to jazzmen. Otherwise, improvisation is so free that the melody of a theme is hardly of significance. Often it cannot be recognized even at the start. Since the fifties, the jazz musician who plays fast pieces improvises not so much on a theme as on the harmonies of this theme. And thus—as Hodeir has said—the jazz variation is a "variation on no theme at all."

Example 6

Example 6 clarifies the process of untying the jazz improvisation from the theme. The example is transcribed from a record by the Max Roach Quintet, "Prince Albert." The actual theme is Jerome Kern's "All the Things You Are." The first bars of this melody are in row (a). Above the harmonies of this theme (b), trumpeter Kenny Dorham and tenor saxophonist James Moody have placed a riff figure (c)—a new theme closer to their jazz conception. This riff figure is introduced in unison by the two hornmen. Thus the original theme of "All the Things You Are" is never even heard on the record. The musicians improvise on the new theme which was gleaned from the harmonies (in jazz terminology, chord changes) of "All the Things You Are," and on which in turn alternated harmonies can be based. One of these improvisations and its related harmonies can be found in rows (d) and (e) (with a flatted fifth in the fourth bar).

Clearly, this chain can be extended. A new riff can be based on the (e) changes, and this riff can become the basis for a different improvisation which in turn possesses alternations. The relationship to

the theme is retained in all cases, and the jazz fan—if he is knowledgeable—at once feels that somewhere "All the Things You Are"
was the starting point.

This is radical usage of a tenet basic to all forms of music in which
improvisation is alive—such as baroque music—and in which the
melody is used as material. It is not a cause unto itself, as it is in
music of the romantic period. When the melody is a cause unto itself,
it becomes sacrosanct. Since our musical consciousness is romanti-
cized, we are accustomed to regarding melodies as sacrosanct, and
thus many people have no feeling for the "materiality" of melody.

Johann Sebastian Bach still had this feeling. It was not the melody
that played a role—as in romantic music—but what one made of it.
Executio took precedence over *Inventio*: execution came before invention, whereas the musical conception of romanticism created a
mystique of invention and placed it above all else. Because Bach regarded music as working material, he was able to take melodies
from other masters of his time—such as Vivaldi—and use them for
his own purposes without acknowledging his source. According to
contemporary conception this is musical theft. But to Bach it seemed
all right; and exactly in this sense it seems all right to jazz musicians.
Melody is the material, and so one can do with it as one wishes—
with the *proviso* that what is made of this material makes musical
sense.

The art of inventing new melodic lines from given harmonies has
become increasingly differentiated in the course of jazz development.
Often on older jazz recordings the improvisation actually only consists
of taking the harmonies apart: notes which in the basic chords were
superimposed on one another are strung out in the melodies. The
melodic movement has the flavor of cadenced triads and seventh-
chords. The melodies of modern jazz are more closely meshed. It no
longer depends on interpreting the chord, but on placing against it a
contrasting, independent melodic line. This creates tension between
the vertical and the horizontal—and the old jazz tendency to find
possibilities for tension is thus nourished.

The jazz melody—aside from free playing—obtains its structure
from the 12-bar form of the blues or the 32-bar AABA form of the
popular song—and in the newer stages of jazz, also from several irregular forms. There is a tendency among jazz musicians to cross
over formal sections. Here, too, as well, the indebtedness of music to
time becomes clear. This crossing over the formal sections would be

misread if one were to conclude that it results in a dissolution of form. The form—predetermined by the chord structure—remains perceivable, at least up to free jazz. Not following the formal bar structure is perceived as something special and out of the ordinary. One might almost say the formal structure is accentuated by the fact that it is not accentuated. Here, too, a new possibility for creating tension has been discovered: tension between the given, retained form and the free line that flows above it.

Related to the tendency to play across structural sections and displace them unexpectedly is the preference for long melodic lines in modern jazz—lines longer than in the older forms.

Kenny Clarke and Mary Lou Williams claim that the pioneers of bop consciously crossed bar lines so that musicians who were trying to "steal" their ideas would not be able to get themselves organized. Thelonious Monk said: "We're going to create something that they can't steal because they can't play it." Drummer Dave Tough told of the first time he walked into the place on 52nd Street where Dizzy Gillespie was playing: "As we walked in, these cats snatched up their horns and blew crazy stuff. One would stop all of a sudden and another would start for no reason at all. We never could tell when a solo was supposed to begin or end. Then they all quit at once and walked off the stand. It scared us." But—as Marshall Stearns points out—about a year later the selfsame Dave Tough was playing some of the things that had scared him with Woody Herman's band.

Independent of the structuring of 8-bar sections, blues choruses, or 32-bar song strophes is the natural structuring of tension and relaxation. The free jazz musicians went as far as to set this "natural form" in the place of predetermined structures. A collectively improvising free jazz group creates its own form by "breathing," by moments of orgiastic intensity followed by moments of quiet and relaxation, which in turn are built up into new "climaxes." This achievement of free jazz has also proven its lasting importance for the jazz of the seventies: Even the younger musicians who have returned to conventional, functional tonality love to create their own "breathed" forms independent of 12-bar, 16-bar, or 32-bar structures.

It is illuminating that the way for this was paved by the Kansas City jazz of the thirties, the so-called "riff style": The riff creates tension, and the subsequent improvised melodic line creates relaxation. The strong, rhythmic, heavily accentuated phrases called "riffs," often only two or four bars in length and capable of being repeated until the 32-bar song entity has been filled, are excellently suited to create tension.

Guitarist Charlie Christian—one of the musicians who played a part in the creation of modern jazz—built up his solos in such a way that new riff elements were constantly opposed to new melodic lines. His solos are sequences of riffs and free-swinging melodic lines; the riffs creating tension, the melodic lines relaxation. Charlie Christian's manner of improvising was adopted by many musicians and has had great influence—consciously and unconsciously.

This relaxation—the moment of relief—goes further and deeper than European music knows. Naturally, the moment of tension and relaxation belongs to every organic musical art. In jazz, however, it is projected into the old call-and-response principle of African music. In the improvisations of Charlie Christian, the riffs are the "calls," the subsequent free-swinging lines the "responses." In other words, the lead singer no longer holds a conversation with the answering chorus of listeners—as in African music or in the spiritual—but the improvising soloist holds a conversation with himself . . . and the loneliness of the creative jazz musician could never be made clearer than through this fact. Everything that goes into the give-and-take between call and response within the communion of a spiritual-singing congregation or a West African cult is now concentrated in the improvisation of a single soloist.

Of course this thought must not be pursued too far. The principle of call-and-response is not projected merely in the single individual. The "call" of the riff is frequently played by the other musicians during the improvisation—the "response"—of a soloist, and it is possible in this way to create an intensity that carries everything with it. This intensity is rooted in concentration. Call and response no longer follow each other, but are sounded simultaneously.

Rhythm, Swing

Every jazz ensemble—be it large or small—consists of a melody section and a rhythm section. To the former belong instruments such as trumpet, trombone, clarinet, and the members of the saxophone family; to the latter, drums, bass, guitar, and piano—of course only insofar as they do not step out in solo roles of their own.

There is tension between the melody and rhythm sections. On the other hand, the rhythm section carries the melodic group. It is like a riverbed in which the stream of the melodic lines flows. Tension exists not only between the two sections but within each group as well. Each line improvised by a horn has its own rhythm, and each member of the rhythm section plays various elements which in their entirety constitute the "fundamental rhythm" and often go beyond it.

Thus a many-layered rhythm is created which thoroughly corresponds to the many layers of melody found in, say, the music of Johann Sebastian Bach. To claim, as many people still do, that the rhythm of jazz is nothing but primitive pounding merely reveals that a person who holds such views is without feeling for the fact that rhythmic possibilities are as inexhaustible as melodic and harmonic ones. The lack of such feeling is of course in line with Western musical development. Hans H. Stuckenschmidt, one of Europe's leading music critics, and thus not a man of jazz but of concert music, once spoke of "the rhythmic atrophy in the musical arts of the white race." It is oddly ironic that the oft-heard complaint of primitiveness, directed against jazz and other similar phenomena, here turns back on the world whence it came: against our European-Western world in which there is this strange gap between admirable development of melodic, harmonic, and formal elements and—as Stuckenschmidt said—the atrophy of things rhythmic.

Not that there isn't any rhythm in European music. There are great rhythmic creations—for example in Mozart and Brahms, even more so in avant-garde concert music—but even these pale when compared to the grandiose rhythms of Indian or Balinese music, with traditions of rhythmic mastery as long and honorable as our music has in respect to form. One must not think only of jazz when it comes to recognizing the inferiority of rhythmic elements in European music.

It is simply an inferiority of rhythmic sense. What every street urchin in the Near East can do—beat out with arms and legs on boxes and pots rhythmic structures in which eight or nine different rhythms are complexly entwined—is within the European tradition not even possible for the percussionist of a symphony orchestra. In symphony orchestras, eight or nine different percussionists are frequently needed to achieve such complexity.

In jazz, the multiplicity of rhythms is anchored in the "beat": a regularly accented basic rhythm, the beating heart of jazz. As drummer Jo Jones has put it: "even breathing." This fundamental rhythm is the organizing principle. Through it, the musical happenings are ordered. It is maintained by the drummer, or in modern jazz often only by the steady 4/4 of the bassist. This regulatory function corresponds to a European need. Certainly swing is connected with the African feeling for rhythm. But in spite of this—as Marshall Stearns has pointed out—there is no swing in Africa. Swing arose when African rhythmic feeling was applied to the regular meter of European music—in a long and complex process of fusion.

In the styles of jazz can be found certain basic rhythms, represented in simplified fashion by Example 7. This example represents the drum parts: the notes in the lower row are played on the bass drum, those on the bottom on the snare drum, and the crossed notes on the cymbal. The carrier of the basic beat in New Orleans, Dixieland, and Swing style is the bass drum; in bebop and cool jazz it is the cymbal. The rhythmic accents are indicated by >.

In New Orleans style and ragtime (7a), the rhythmic emphasis is on the so-called "strong" beats: on 1 and 3, just as in march music. From here on in, jazz rises to an ever-increasing rhythmic complexity and intensity. Dixieland and Chicago style (7b), as well as New Orleans jazz as played in Chicago during the twenties, shifts the accents to 2 and 4, so that while 1 and 3 remain the "strong" beats, the accent now is on 2 and 4. Thus the peculiar "floating" rhythmic atmosphere from which swing takes its name was created for the first time.

Example 7

Both New Orleans and Dixieland rhythms are two-beat rhythms insofar as the bass drum, carrier of the basic beat, is assigned two beats per measure. Of course there were exceptions. Louis Armstrong—always the swing man!—requested drummer Baby Dodds to play an even four beats. Subsequently, Swing style was founded on four beats to the measure (7c), but tends to emphasize 2 and 4. Up to this point, jazz rhythm has a staccato beat—with its concomitant punctuation: the cymbal beat in the Swing example. Bebop brings a further concentration, replacing staccato with legato. The rhythm becomes—as French drummer Gerard Pochonet has said—a *"son continu,"* a continuous sound. The cymbal sounds steadily—thus the *"son continu."* On his other instruments—primarily on the bass drum —the drummer executes all kinds of rhythmic accents which serve to emphasize the basic rhythm: it is not so much "beat out" as it is "encircled." Compared to this bop rhythm, the rhythm of cool jazz seems like a throwback, combining rhythmic features of Swing and bop.

In free jazz, finally, the beat is replaced by what many free jazz musicians call "pulse": a pulsating, percussive activity so fast and nervous that single beats, standing by themselves, can no longer be isolated. The physiological shift of the beat from a correspondence to the heart beat to the faster, more nervous, jerky throbbing of the pulse has been repeatedly pointed to by musicians and listeners. Frequently, the melodic parts are played at quite moderate-medium tempo—to a basic beat which, though no longer marked by any one instrument, yet is clearly perceived as medium-fast—while the drummer contrasts to that a frenzied, multi-layered sounding of all his instruments. This certainly offers a new way of creating tension, and with stimulating results: several tempi—all different from each other —co-exist next to and on top of each other! There is no basic rhythmic formula that can be notated. On the contrary, the free jazz drummers use many rhythmic formulae that have been developed through jazz history, and also a host of new rhythms taken from African, Arabian, Indian, and other exotic musics—occasionally also from European concert music. Many musicians for whom the freedom of free jazz not only represents a liberation from conventional harmonies, but also has racial, social, and political implications, prefer the African elements—from pride in the traditions of their own race.

It is often proposed that within free jazz, swing—that basic constituent element without which jazz seems unthinkable—has ceased to exist. But what has ceased to exist is merely a certain metric symmetry. Our musical instincts perceived swing as rooted just in the friction between the symmetry of conventional, fundamental rhythm and the asymmetry of the various counter- and cross-rhythms that move above this fundamental rhythm and "contradict" it. Actually, what happened was that, in an even more concentrated and radical manner than when bebop rhythm was created, swing has been moved more "inward." Contemporary musicians have learned to produce swing through phrasing (and thus to include it in the flow of the melody line) to such an extent that they find the kind of swing that depends on the mere symmetry of a steady, basic beat—or on just a steady bass beat—much too obvious, and even "primitive" and outmoded.

At a time when the conventional way of swinging had been commercialized to an unprecedented degree, the free jazz musicians extended the tension between rhythm and melody to a point where it scarcely seemed to exist. One often has the impression that the drummer is playing something that has no relationship to the rest. But just how close, how absolutely precise this relationship really is, becomes clear the moment the drummer a group is used to is replaced by another. To the outsider, he may seem to produce exactly the same ecstatic, disjointed explosions as his predecessor, but the group is unable to really play with him. This fact was made particularly clear in 1966, when, just before the European tour of the Albert Ayler Quintet, Sunny Murray—one of the outstanding drummers of free jazz—was replaced by Beaver Harris: It was generally agreed that the group produced only a tensionless persiflage of its real music.

In the greatly expanded tension between melody and rhythm, the relationship between the two has become the more subtle and precise. The beat of the pulse—no matter how restlessly it may throb—reflects bodily activity less directly than the heart beat—but reflects it nevertheless.

When bebop came into being, the majority of critics and fans also responded: This music doesn't swing any more! But just a few years later, when they had grown accustomed to the new rhythms, these same critics and fans said: It swings more than ever. And even Dixieland bands used bebop drummers. It looks as if something similar—transposed, of course, to the jazz situation of the sixties and seventies—is taking place again.

Jazz of the seventies, in terms of rhythm, is in a similar position vis-a-vis the jazz of the sixties as, 20 years earlier, cool jazz was vis-a-vis bebop: The use of elements of earlier jazz forms is—in light of the newly gained freedom—once again held in high esteem. In addition, there are the rock elements, of which we spoke in the chapter about the seventies.

Of course, at the center of all jazz rhythms are still the rhythmical structures of bebop as they crystallized in the early years of modern jazz. These structures have gained such general acceptance that they are frequently used even by musicians who reject the modern jazz forms.

The rhythmic complexity of these structures is clarified by Miles Davis when he says: "Like, we'd be playing the blues, and Bird (Charlie Parker) would start on the 11th bar, and as the rhythm section stayed where they were and Bird played where he was, it sounded as if the rhythm section was on 1 and 3 instead of 2 and 4. Every time that would happen, Max (Roach, the drummer) used to scream at Duke (Jordan, the pianist) not to follow Bird but to stay where he was. Then, eventually, it came around as Bird had planned and we were together again." Davis called this—according to Marshall Stearns—"turning the rhythm section around," and adds that it so bewildered him at first that he "used to quit every night."

Stearns has shown, on the basis of African recordings, that no style of jazz before free jazz was rhythmically closer to Africa than bebop. In place of the simple, march-like meter of New Orleans music or the "reversed emphasis" of Dixieland (which is also march-like with the sole exception that the accents are placed not on the "strong" but on the "weak" beats) we now find rhythmic structures in which ancient African practices seem suddenly to have come to life again.

All this took place without any direct contact between the urbanized modern jazz musician and West African rhythms. It is as if the musicians had subconsciously undergone an evolution completed by their ancestors centuries ago. Or, to state it differently: as if they had gradually shaken off a burden which still weighted them down 30 years ago, and become increasingly 'free', rediscovering, consciously *and* unconsciously, their true rhythmic heritage. This is also supported by the fact that in free jazz—as with drummers Sunny Murray or Rashied Ali—there was a further "Africanization" of jazz rhythms.

As early as the fifties, Art Blakey travelled to West Africa to become acquainted with old African rhythms. Even earlier, in the late forties, Dizzy Gillespie had hired the conga drummer Chano Pozo, who was still a member of an African sect in his native Cuba. That bop musicians became so fascinated by Cuban rhythms can be explained by the fact that West African traditions remained alive in Cuba, to a much greater degree than in North America.

Meanwhile, what used to be the exception has almost become the rule on a host of newer jazz recordings: Frequently, percussionists who are exponents of Africanizing rhythms—Latin Americans, above all Cubans and Brazilians, and Africans—are included in the rhythm sections of jazz groups. No longer do we have to face a flaw that used to be so frequently prevalent in earlier combinations of jazz and African rhythms—a rhythmic gap. Miles Davis, for example, almost always included the Brazilian Airto Moreira in his recordings of the early seventies. A musician whose samba rhythms go back to the percussive tradition of the West African Yoruba tribes, Airto made the whole jazz world samba-conscious.

But all these remarks are insufficient. It may be possible to write down and notate the most complex rhythms by Max Roach or Art Blakey—or today, Tony Williams or Billy Cobham—only to discover that what has been written down and copied is merely a miserable skeleton of what the music really sounded like. You see, it swung— and swing cannot be notated. It cannot even be grasped in words. "It's a real simple thing," says Jo Jones, "but there are some things you can't describe, some things that never have been described. . . . The best way you can say what swinging is, is you either play with a feeling or you don't. It's just like the difference between receiving a genuine handshake or a fishy one."

Jo Jones thinks that the difference between jazz and European music lies in swing. In European music—"that approach to music is scientific"—the musician plays the notes that are placed before him. If one is sufficiently musical and has studied music, one can play the required parts. But in order to play jazz it is not sufficient to be musical and to have studied music long enough. Here lies the problem of all the jazz courses at conservatories and music schools, where jazz musicianship supposedly is taught. Surely much can be learned there. Almost all important representatives of modern jazz have studied music, and it is part and parcel of a good musician that he should know and understand his craft. But the decisive part cannot be taught: swing. One can hardly say what it is.

Thus the opinion gains ground that "symphonic jazz," if it is at all possible, will come from within jazz rather than from European music. It is only possible when the elements of both musical realms are joined together and preserved. But symphonic musicians who wish to write jazz have until now been unable to capture what jazz is —precisely because these things cannot be taught and because these musicians, coming not from jazz but from the European tradition, do not possess them. On the other hand, a jazz musician possesses these things—and he can study the European element.

But—back to swing. In the course of jazz development swing became ever more far-reaching and concentrated. "The phenomenon of swing," says André Hodeir, "should not be regarded as the immediate and inevitable result of a confrontation between the African rhythmic genius and the 2/2 beat. What we know about primitive jazz excludes the hypothesis that swing sprang into being like a spark at the collision of two stones. Pre-Armstrong recordings reveal, on the contrary, that swing was merely latent at first and took shape progressively over a long period. . . ."

The moment of tension and relaxation belongs to swing. Jo Jones says: "Another thing about rhythm is that when an artist is performing on his instrument he breathes in his normal fashion, and he has a listening audience that breathes along with him."

Steadiness of natural conditions of breathing create the uniqueness of swing. There are never two possibilities. "The only way I can describe swing," says ragtime pianist Wally Rose, "is it's the kind of rhythmic movement where you can place a note where and when it is due. The only thing that keeps you together is when the whole band meets on this beat, meets on the split second you all think the beat is due. The slightest deviation from that causes tension and frustration. . . ."

Swing gives jazz its peculiar form of precision, which cannot be compared with any kind of precision in European music. Conductors and composers of symphonic music have been among the first to admit this. The difference between the precision found in Count Basie's band and the precision of the best European orchestras—jazz as well as symphonic—is due to the fact that Basie's precision stems from swing, whereas the other kind of precision is the result of academic drill. Basie's musicians feel that the note is due, and since they all feel this at the identical moment, and from the basis of swing, everything is precise in a direct, unfettered way. The kind of precision gleaned from academic tradition, on the other hand, is neither direct nor unfettered.

To swing belong, furthermore, the multiple layers of rhythm and the tension between them—the displacements of rhythmic accents and all that we have said about them. This displacement is called "syncopation" in European music. But the use of this term in jazz reveals an essential misunderstanding of the nature of jazz. Syncopation can only arise when the syncopated displacement of a note is something irregular. In jazz it is something regular—and to such a degree that the absence of syncopations may have "syncopating" (if this word had any meaning in jazz) effects.

It must be clear by now: swing is not the task of a drummer who has to "swing" the soloists. A jazz musician who does not swing—all by himself and without any rhythm section—is no jazz musician. Thus, the considered opinion of many modern musicians that it is just as possible to swing without a drummer as with one. "The drive that creates the pulsation has to be within yourself. I don't understand why it should be necessary to have someone else drive you," says Jimmy Giuffre in the liner notes to an album in which he plays with a trio—clarinet or saxophone, trombone, and guitar—without any rhythm section and yet manages to swing considerably. Nat Hentoff states in this context: "The ability to swing must first be contained within each musician. If he is dependent on a rhythm section . . . he is in the position of the rejected suitor who can't understand that one must be capable of giving love if one wishes to receive it."

It becomes increasingly clear that such paraphrases, by the musicians themselves or by sympathetic critics, are more satisfactory elucidations of the phenomenon of swing than "exact" explanations made by musicologists who have no feeling for swing. It is particularly unedifying to see swing explained as off-beat accentuation, which is so often the case. Off-beat seems to take the place of swing. But the practice of playing off-beats—in other words, the accentuation away from the beat onto the "weak" beats commonly unaccentuated in European music—does not of necessity produce swing. Much of contemporary popular music—even when it does not swing —is full of off-beats.

Some of the most concise thoughts concerning swing have been expressed by the Swiss musicologist Jan Slawe. In his *Versuch einer Definition der Jazzmusik* he states: "The fundamental nature of swing is expressed in the rhythmic basis of the music as a whole . . . in particular, swing postulates a regularity of time in order to simultaneously be able to negate it.   The particular nature of swing is the creation of rhythmic conflicts between the fundamental rhythm and the rhythm of the melody; this is the musical-technical cornerstone of jazz."

But these definitions, too, remain unsatisfactory. Meanwhile, so much has been written about swing that one might tend to accept once and for all the dictum that swing cannot be verbally expressed. Maybe this is because swing involves a feeling for time for which there is no precedent in European music. Ethnology has shown us that the African's sense of time—and that of "primitive" peoples as a whole—is more unified and elemental than the differentiated time sense of Western man. Swing developed when the two concepts of time met. In all the polyrhythms of African music, often much more complex than those of jazz, there is still no swing—as is the case in European music. One might assume that its nature is rooted in the overlapping of two different conceptions of time.

Musicology knows well that music may occur in two different conceptions of time. Stravinsky calls these "pyschological" and "ontological" time. Rudolf Kassner speaks of "lived" and "measured" time. These two kinds of time cannot be equalized in those aspects of our being which count most—especially in art: one second of pain becomes an eternity, and one hour can be but a fleeting moment in a state of happiness. This is of significance to music. Music is art in time . . . as sculpture is art in space, and painting the art of the plane. But if music is art in time we may ask which time: psychological or ontological, relative or absolute, lived or measured.

This question can be answered only in respect to one particular musical style. It has been said that the relationship between lived and measured time is of considerable formative consequence to music. Thus romantic, and particularly late romantic, music is almost exclusively an art of lived, psychological time. Private and subjective experience of time is primary here. On the other hand, the music of a Bach is almost exclusively in measured, objective, ontological time, related in each note to the movement of the cosmos, to which it is of no concern whether a minute seems to us like an eternity, or eternity like a minute.

The question is: which is the time of swing? And here it becomes clear why Western man must "leap over the shadow of his time sense" if he wants to find out about swing. For there can be no doubt: swing is related to both levels of time at once—to measured, objective time through the basic, metrically undisrupted beat; to lived, psychological time through the individual, uncontrollable play of the melodic rhythms, which in turn negate, reconstruct, and negate again the basic beat. Swing is rooted in the awareness of a simultaneously desperate and joyous inability to find a common denominator for lived and measured time. More precisely: a common denominator for lived and measured time has been found, but the listener is aware of a duality—in other words, he is aware of swing.

A Definition of Jazz

The question, "What is jazz" calls for a dictionary and an encyclopedic answer. But a search through dictionaries and encyclopedias yields some odd examples. I was unable to find a single even halfway satisfying definition of jazz in the recognized, distinguished scientific encyclopedias. Webster's *New International Dictionary of the English Language* (1953 edition), for instance, has this to say: "An American style of music used particularly as accompaniment to dancing, evolved from ragtime through the addition of eccentric noises . . . hectic or subtly syncopated dance rhythms. . . ." In the face of that, one almost feels as if it were reason to rejoice that the *Grosse Brockhaus* (a respected German encyclopedia) already stated in 1931: "Jazz, a modern dance music and, developed from it, a style of music; it came into being among the Negroes of North America from English-Scots songs and operetta music and from the plantation songs and spirituals of the American Negroes and their native dances originating in Africa. . . . The essence of jazz is the driving rhythm, effective above all in syncopation; and in addition, the freely modifying embellishment of the melody lines, and a sound that is defined by drums, banjo, and horn instruments."

In a strangely paradoxical way, it becomes clear that the method often suggested to jazz critics as exemplary for arriving at an understanding of the phenomenon of jazz—the method of Western musicology with its impressive overtones of tradition—fails when it comes to jazz. Jazz can only be understood in terms of a genuine comprehension of its nature concerning which jazz musicians generally are better informed than the theoreticians. All attempts at a definition from other points of view—such as European music, or latterly, African music—remain unsatisfactory. That is why people involved with jazz at an early date took it upon themselves to find a useful definition of jazz. These attempts also have a history, and it is worth noting that each new attempt was based on all that preceded it. Important steps in this process were taken by Marshall Stearns and the California critic Woody Woodward. Bearing in mind their definitions, and the entire preceding body of work, I should like to suggest the following definition of jazz:

Jazz is a form of art music which originated in the United States through the confrontation of the Negro with European music. The instrumentation, melody, and harmony of jazz are in the main derived from Western musical tradition. Rhythm, phrasing and production of sound, and the elements of blues harmony are derived from African music and from the musical conception of the American Negro. Jazz differs from European music in three basic elements:

1. A special relationship to time, defined as "swing."

2. A spontaneity and vitality of musical production in which improvisation plays a role.

3. A sonority and manner of phrasing which mirror the individuality of the performing jazz musician.

These three basic characteristics create a novel climate of tension, in which the emphasis no longer is on great arcs of tension, as in European music, but on a wealth of tension-creating elements, which continuously rise and fall. The various styles and stages of development through which jazz has passed since its origin around the turn of the century are largely characterized by the fact that the three basic elements of jazz temporarily achieve varying degrees of importance, and that the relationship between them is constantly changing.

For one thing, this definition stresses the fact that jazz developed in the confrontation between "black" and "white," and thus is neither a completely European nor a completely African concern. In connection with this, the origin of the various musical categories—melody, harmony, rhythm, sound—in such differing musical cultures as the European and the African is indicated. Occasionally, since definitions demand brevity, it has been necessary to simplify. Thus, for instance, jazz instrumentation no doubt derives from Europe; but, among others, the banjo, which took the place of the guitar in early jazz, was an invention of the Negro. And the percussion apparatus developed by jazz in the course of its evolution differs significantly from that common to European music—then and now. From the opposite point of view, similar conclusions hold true for sonority. The jazz sound, as we have shown, is largely a black creation, but at the same time there are a multitude of vocal and instrumental sounds in jazz which are familiar to European music.

In all these points, we have related our findings to what has been stated in "The Elements of Jazz." Here the three significant characteristics—swing, improvisation, jazz sound/phrasing—were arrived at. The six points at the end of the chapter on improvisation may be taken as a further interpretation of Point 2 in the definition.

The final paragraph of our definition contains a thought not present in previous definitions of jazz. A history of jazz could certainly be written from the point of view of the three jazz characteristics of swing, improvisation, and sound/phrasing, and their relation to each other. All these characteristics are important, to be sure, but their relationships change, and these changing relationships are a part of jazz evolution.

That jazz sound and jazz phrasing stand in dialectic opposition has been pointed out already. In old New Orleans jazz, phrasing was largely dependent on European folk and light music. On the other hand, typical jazz sonority was particularly highly developed here. Later, this kind of sonority came to be regarded as exaggerated. No major musician in any phase of jazz has had a purely European sonority; nevertheless, jazz sonority and the sonorities of European music occasionally have come very close. On the other hand, jazz phrasing has become increasingly important. Thus jazz, since cool jazz, is as far removed from European music in terms of phrasing as old jazz was in terms of sonority.

In their extremes, jazz phrasing and jazz sonority seem mutually exclusive. Where jazz sonority is at its strongest—for example, in the "jungle" solos of Tricky Sam Nanton, Bubber Miley, or Cootie Williams with Duke Ellington's band—jazz phrasing stops. The "jungle" sound dictates the phrasing, and this sound exists for its own sake— beyond jazz phrasing. On the other hand, where jazz phrasing appears at its most highly cultivated stage—as in the tenor improvisations of Stan Getz, the flute solos of Hubert Laws, or the alto lines of the Lee Konitz of the fifties—jazz sonority seems largely suspended. The musical proceedings are so unilaterally dictated by the phrasing that it does not appear possible to produce sounds which have an expressive meaning outside the flow of the phrase.

Thus jazz sonority and jazz phrasing stand in a relationship of opposites.

A similar, if not quite as precise, relationship exists between swing and improvisation. Both are factors of spontaneity. Thus it may come about that when spontaniety is expressed in the extreme through the medium of swing, improvisation will recede. Even when a record by Count Basie's band does not contain a single improvised solo, no one questions its jazz character. On the other hand, when improvisation is given too free a rein, swing recedes, as in many unaccompanied horn solos or many free-jazz recordings of the sixties. This suppression of swing by freedom is illustrated by the very first totally free record in jazz history—Lennie Tristano's "Intuition."

Thus the relationships between the elements of jazz change constantly. In the thirties, when sonority in terms of New Orleans jazz had already receded and fluent phrasing in terms of modern jazz had not as yet been developed, swing celebrated such unquestioned victories that swing—the element—and Swing—the style—were not even differentiated in verbal terms. Always there are forms of jazz which seek to project the jazz essence into a single element of jazz. The ragtime pianists had swing, but neither improvisation nor jazz sonority. The New Orleans bands did have jazz sonority, but they had more march rhythm than swing, and a form of collective improvisation which sooner or later led to ever-repeated head arrangements. In the realm of Swing style there is a kind of big-band music in which improvisation, sonority, and—sometimes even—phrasing largely take a back seat—and yet it swings marvelously. During the fifties Jimmy Giuffre often projected the whole jazz essence into a single Lester Young-inspired phrase. On the other hand—as is made clear by just these "exceptional examples"—at the real peaks of jazz, all three jazz elements are present simultaneously, if in varying relationship to one another: from Louis Armstrong and Jimmy Harrison through Coleman Hawkins and Lester Young to Charlie Parker, Miles Davis, and Ornette Coleman.

It is important to note, too, that swing, improvisation, and sonority (or phrasing) are elemens of intensity. As much as they may differ from each other, just as much do they concur in creating intensity.

Swing creates intensity through friction and superimposition of the levels of time.

Improvisation creates intensity through the fact that the road from musician to sound is shorter and more direct than in any other type of musical production.

In sonority and phrasing, intensity is produced by the immediacy and directness with which a particular human personality is projected into sound.

It may thus be assumed that the main task and real meaning of the basic jazz elements rest in the creation of structured intensity. This meaning is also fulfilled by free jazz with its ecstatic glow, as idiosyncratic as the interpretation of the three basic elements in this music may often appear.

In all these differentiations the question of quality—stature—is decisive. One might almost be tempted to adopt it as a fourth "element of jazz" within our definition. If, for example, Dave Brubeck or Stan Kenton have found a place in jazz—a place that was perhaps disputed at some points of their development, but nevertheless basically is accepted—this is due to the quality and stature of their music, which are indisputable. Yet much might be said against these two musicians in terms of jazz essentials. But it is the same in other domains. Even if it were possible to give a precise definition of what "classical" music is, a music which contained all the elements of this definition yet lacked the stature of the great classical works would still not be "classical."

Quality and stature cannot be grasped through definitions. Hundreds of dance bands may improvise and phrase in jazz terms, and yet be counted as commercial groups, whereas for some jazz musicians a *single* element of jazz may suffice to insure their jazz character. Naturally, there is a difference between jazz and commercial music, but there is hardly a jazz element which cannot be applied within commercial music—if only as means to an effect. In hundreds of ordinary dance bands there may be one or two musicians who can improvise jazz-phrased solos. Yet the music of these bands remain commercial dance music and does not become jazz.

Not only are the basic elements of jazz to be found in commercial music: it may also acquire elements of jazz styles and elements of jazz playing. Dixieland counterpoint is a much-loved effect in commercial music, and boogie-woogie has almost entirely wandered off into this realm. Duke Ellington's "jungle" sound crops up as a movie-soundtrack cliché. Benny Goodman's combo music, once considered the epitome of Swing, is today suitable for any decent cocktail party. Big-band music *à la* Jimmie Lunceford or Goodman can be made today by any decent studio band and still, although the original is jazz, the copy is not.

Even Charlie Parker phrases have found their way into commercial music. And just the very greatest names in popular music would be inconceivable without personal, tangible jazz pasts: Sarah Vaughan, Billy Eckstine, Frank Sinatra, Nat "King" Cole, Glenn Miller, Ray Charles, Otis Redding, James Brown. . . .

The constant use of the elements, styles, musicianship, techniques, and ideas of jazz in commercial music forces the jazz musician to unceasing creation of something new. In this sense André Hodeir remarked that today's innovation is tomorrow's cliché.

The flair for the cliché is of course not only connected with the abuses of jazz in commercial music; it lies in the nature of jazz itself. Nowhere is this more obvious than in the blues. Almost every blues strophe can be turned into a cliché. All the famous blues lines exist as ever-recurring "entities": "I've been drinkin' muddy water, sleepin' in a hollow log . . . ," "My baby treats me like a low-down dog . . . ," "Broke and hungry, ragged and dirty too . . . ," " 'cause the world is all wrong . . . ," "But the meanest blues I ever had . . . ," "I'm just as lonely, lonely as a man can be . . . ," "Can't eat, can't sleep . . . ," "I wanna hold you, baby, hold you in my arms again . . . ," "I'm gonna buy myself a shotgun . . . ," "Take me back, baby . . . ," "I love you, baby, but you sure don't treat me right . . ."—and so forth. The great blues singers used them as they pleased, taking a line from here and another from there, sometimes stringing them together, and often not even that.

What holds true for the lyrics also applies to the music. When Jimmy Smith or Horace Silver record a blues, both the arrangement and the improvised solos are saturated with structural elements from half a century of blues history. Everything played by the modern bop musicians is saturated with elements from Charlie Parker records which, though not in themselves clichés, certainly lend themselves to cliché-making. Or, to reach back into jazz tradition: in every third or fourth blues by Bessie Smith one hears phrases, or even entire lines, which might just as well have been heard in other contexts from other blues singers. Every boogie consists of nothing but a constantly changing montage of "entities" made from ostinatos and indicated melodic phrases. Almost every improvised break on old records by the Hot Five or Hot Seven, by Johnny Dodds or King Oliver, by Jimmie Noone or Kid Ory, is mutually interchangeable. So are the breaks which set off the 4-bar blues phrases from each other—whether they be played by singers accompanying themselves on the guitar or by the most famous of jazz musicians. There are half a hundred—perhaps not even that many—"model breaks" from which all others are derived.

The further one goes back, the more apparent this model character becomes. What Marshall Stearns, Alan Lomax, and Alfons Dauer discovered of African elements in jazz consists almost without exception of such connective models and "entities"; they were not only taken over from African music as "entities" but often had this character within African music itself. Their model nature is so compact that they have survived through centuries almost without changing. Consider the tango: the rhythm was brought by the slaves from Africa, and today it exists in the jungles and in spirited South American folk dances, in modish bars and in boogie-woogie basses, and in hundreds of intermittent stages. Everywhere there is the identical ostinato figure—the model with its tendency toward the cliché.

All jazz consists of such "models." They are fragments—such as the downward-descending lines of old blues or modern "funk"—which have something of the aura of the words with which fairy tales begin: "Once upon a time. . . ." This, too, is a model element. And as it is in the fairy tales where elements-turned-symbols have penetrated into the content, so it is in jazz: the evil witch casts a spell on the noble prince, and the hard-hearted king turns soft when he catches sight of the lovely shepherdess, and at last prince and shepherdess find each other and the shepherdess turns out to be a bewitched princess—witch and prince, magic and hard-heartedness, King and shepherdess . . . all of these are elements of motif, which can be joined together in inexhaustible combinations.

While Western concert music in the process of its ever-increasing tendency toward abstraction has lost almost all the old models and entities; while there is hardly a structural element which has not been questioned—theme and variation, the sonata form, the triad—while we now long for the attainment of new and connective models and elements in our music, and can only attain them by taking up once again the old models and elements which in the meantime have become questionable; and while in doing this we are historicizing—meanwhile, all these things are present in jazz in the most natural, self-evident, and living way.

Model, element, entity, cliché may coincide—literally and note for note. But as model, as element, and as entity they have meaning; as cliché they are meaningless. But *since* they can coincide—literally and note for note—there is a constant tendency toward the cliché inherent in the models, elements, and entities. To a great extent, it is on the basis of this tendency that jazz constantly renews itself. The most fascinating thing about jazz is its aliveness. Jazz is counter to all academicism—that very academicism which has made the great European music the exclusive concern of the well-bred bourgeoisie.

The aliveness of jazz is such that standards are constantly overthrown—even where the old models and entities remain relevant. This complicates the position of jazz criticism. It has been reproached for being without standards.

Actually, it is remarkable that jazz criticism has so many standards. Often the evolution of jazz proceeds so rapidly that the kind of standards arrived at in European music—frequently formed one or two generations after the particular music has been alive—are meaningless. Jazz standards without flexibility tend to acquire violent and intolerant aspects.

We insist: It is not important to define standards and to test an art form against them; it is important to have the art and constantly reorient the standards in its image. Since this is inconvenient, one attempts to avoid it—within and outside of jazz. But it is above all jazz, as a music of revolt against all that is too convenient, which can demand of its listeners that they revise standards valid years ago and be prepared to discover new norms.

Seventy years after it began, jazz is still what it was then: a music of protest. It cries out against social and racial and spiritual discrimination, against the clichés of picayune bourgeois morality, against the functional organization of modern mass-society, against the depersonalization inherent in this society, and against that categorization of standards which leads to the automatic passing of judgments in areas where they do not apply.

Many American musicians, particularly blacks, understand protest as a matter of race. No doubt it is that. But their music would not have been understood all over the world, and it would not have received almost immediate acceptance by musicians of all races, colors, and political systems, if the racial aspect were the crucial factor. What *is* crucial is the protest against a social order perceived by thinking men all over the world, in every country and in every field —in short, by those who are shaping the judgment of our epoch by future generations—as a threat not only to themselves and their creative productivity but to essential human dignity and worth.

THE INSTRUMENTS OF JAZZ

The Instruments of Jazz

The Trumpet

The trumpet has been called "the royal instrument of jazz"—not only because of the abundance of brilliant trumpeters, but also because the lead in almost all ensemble passages in which a trumpet takes part almost automatically is assigned to it. This happens in the New Orleans collective as well as in the ensembles of the big bands, which are almost always dominated by the brilliance of the trumpet section.

With the trumpet belong, on the one hand—particularly in the older forms of jazz—the cornet, and, on the other—in the newer styles—the fluegelhorn. In the early days of jazz, "trumpet" almost always meant cornet. Later on, there were few cornetists—probably because the trumpet offers greater range and technical possibilities. Nevertheless, cornetist Rex Stewart ranks as one of the greatest technical virtuosos of the "trumpet" up to the beginnings of bop. Other technically able "trumpeters"—mainly in the realm of Dixieland—stayed with the cornet, among them Wild Bill Davison and Muggsy Spanier. In the more modern forms of jazz, however, the fluegelhorn became popular due to its round, flowing sound. There are fluegelhorn players in jazz who manage to lend their instrument a saxophone-like suppleness, and yet are able to preserve the brilliance of the brass sound. Among the best fluegelhorn players in modern jazz are Art Farmer, Thad Jones, and Clark Terry.

The first jazz musician to replace the cornet with the trumpet, at the beginning of the twenties, was Arthur Briggs, a musician in the

184 THE NEW JAZZ BOOK

New Orleans tradition who came to Europe early and became a resident of Paris. In the thirties, he was often on hand when the first representative jazz records were made in Europe.

The first generation of jazz cornetists is that of *Buddy Bolden* and his contemporaries, active around the turn of the century and immediately thereafter. They played jazz, or similar music—we might call it ragtime and march music with hot intonation. To this generation belong *Freddie Keppard, Emmanuel Perez, Bunk Johnson* (mentioned in our chapter on Bolden), *Papa Celestin, Natty Dominique,* and primarily *King Oliver*. His recordings provide rich material for study. They have that rough, earth-bound, hard sound, still lacking the triumphant tone which Louis Armstrong gave to the jazz trumpet.

Tommy Ladnier links this sound to a strong and expressive blues feeling, accentuated primarily in the lower registers of the instrument. Initially, Ladnier stems wholly from Oliver. In the twenties, he traveled as far as Moscow, billed as "Tommy, the talking cornet." Later he participated—with Mezz Mezzrow and Sidney Bechet—in the famous New Orleans recordings organized in 1938 in New York by the French jazz critic Hugues Panassié. His solo on one of these ("Really the Blues") enjoys great reputation among friends of traditional jazz. Ladnier—born in 1900—belongs to *Louis Armstrong's* generation, but one feels inclined to place him earlier in terms of musical conception. We have spoken of Armstrong in a special chapter: He did not switch from cornet to trumpet until 1928. Armstrong is the measure for all jazz trumpeting up to today.

Among the musicians who play most *à la* Armstrong are *Hot Lips Page,* Teddy Buckner, and Jonah Jones. Page, who died in 1954, was active in the Kansas City circle of musicians from the late twenties to the mid-thirties. An exceptional blues player, he sometimes played so much like Armstrong that he could be mistaken for him. As a singer, too, he was astonishingly close to Armstrong. *Jonah Jones,* who was among the most reliable big-band trumpeters of the Swing era—in Cab Calloway's band, for instance—made a comeback in the fifties. His playing, solid and full of humor, has won him a following among those who find modern trumpet too complicated and Dixieland trumpet too cliché-ridden.

To the first generation of white trumpeters belongs *Nick La Rocca,* founder of the Original Dixieland Jazz Band. His cornet retained the sound of the circus trumpeters of the time, in paradoxical contrast to his preposterous claims that he and his white orchestra had been the first jazz band.

In the realm of the old Dixieland, but considerably more musical and differentiated, was the trumpeting of *Sharkey Bonano*. He and Muggsy Spanier are among the white trumpeters who frequently are counted by traditional jazz fans among black New Orleans rather than white Dixieland. *Muggsy Spanier,* who died in 1967, made the first Chicago-style recordings in 1924 with his Bucktown Five. In 1939 he had a short-lived band—Muggsy Spanier's Ragtime Band—which made a deep and lasting impression with its musicianly and original Dixieland music. In 1940 he made records with Sidney Bechet—accompanied by guitar and bass only—which almost might be called a traditional premonition of one of the most successful cool-jazz combos, the Gerry Mulligan Quartet.

Along the line originating from La Rocca, but more polished and musical, are *Red Nichols* and *Phil Napoleon,* two musicians representative of "New York style." This term is common usage for the music of the white jazzmen in New York during the twenties, who did not have the privilege of steady, stimulating contact with the New Orleans greats, as did their colleagues in Chicago. On the other hand, they were often ahead of them in terms of academic training, technique, and craftsmanship. Comparison between Nichols and Bix Beiderbecke illuminates this point: Nichols' blowing was perhaps even more clean and flawless than Bix's, but he could not approach Bix where sensitivity and imagination were concerned. Both Napoleon's Original Memphis Five and Nichols' Five Pennies found great favor with their "purified" jazz, especially with commercial audiences.

Bix Beiderbecke brought elegance to the sound of the jazz trumpet. He had more followers than any other white trumpeter. *Bunny Berigan,* who died much too young, *Jimmy McPartland,* and *Bobby Hackett* are among these. The Bixian conception can be pursued well into cool jazz. Many solos by Miles Davis, and even more by Chet Baker, sound as if Beiderbecke's Chicago style had been "transformed" into modern jazz.

The most successful musician of the Beiderbecke succession was Bunny Berigan, who died in 1942. A pronounced big-band trumpeter, he worked with Benny Goodman and Tommy Dorsey in the mid-thirties and then formed his own band, with which he scored a hit that corresponds to Coleman Hawkins' "Body and Soul": "I Can't Get Started."

Stylistically, the most significant of Beiderbecke's followers is *Bobby Hackett*. His ballad interpretations are full of grace and genuine feeling. His music also enjoys great recognition among friends of modern jazz, since it draws on the harmonic and rhythmic experiences of the forties and fifties. It is a type of Dixieland jazz which is less dependent on stylistic purity than on polished, urbane musicality.

Indebted to Beiderbecke, but more closely related to Armstrong, are *Max Kaminsky* and Wild Bill Davison. Max emerged from the Chicago circle. *Wild Bill Davison* for years was the most exciting trumpeter of the Eddie Condon groups that became the focal point for traditional jazz in New York during the mid-forties and the fifties. Without his vitality and originality Condon's music might often not have been much more than "warmed-over" memories of old Chicago.

Beiderbecke had some influence on black musicians as well—for instance, on *Joe Smith,* a member of Fletcher Henderson's band. The contrast between the melancholy elegance of Smith's trumpet and the hard sounds of the Henderson band remains intriguing to this day. Henderson called Smith "the most soulful trumpet I ever had."

Rex Stewart copied some of Bix's solos during the years when Beiderbecke was the talk of all jazz musicians; mainly—with the Henderson band of 1931—Bix's celebrated "Singing the Blues," one of the most famous trumpet solos in jazz history.

With Stewart we arrive at a group of trumpeters who might be described as "Ellington trumpets." These are first and foremost the "jungle-style" trumpeters.

The first in this group was *Bubber Miley,* who gave the Ellington band of the twenties the characteristic coloration which until this day is associated with Ellingtonia. Bubber was first influenced by King Oliver: If one recalls Oliver's most famous solo—"Dippermouth Blues"—it illuminates how direct the link is to such things as Miley's famed solo on Ellington's first version of "Black and Tan Fantasy," which Bubber co-composed.

Ellington remained interested in the retention of the "Miley color." Stewart, *Cootie Williams, Ray Nance, Clark Terry,* and others had to see to this during various epochs in Ellington's career. Stewart, who died in 1967, has often been admired for the lightness and

assurance with which he could play at even the most rapid tempi—
and very expressively, at that. (He has a special position in German
jazz life. He was the first important jazz musician to visit the country
after World War II. The records that he made in July, 1948, in Berlin with a band of white German and black American musicians for an
East German record company [Amiga] are among the key documents of German jazz history.)

Cootie Williams plays growl trumpet with particular expressiveness. He is the soloist on one of Ellington's most significant recordings, "Concerto for Cootie" (1940).

An element of Stewart's style was the half-valve technique: the
valves of the trumpet are pressed down only halfway. Clark Terry
transplanted this style of playing into the world of modern jazz. He
has created a unique, completely personal style and is perhaps the only
modern trumpeter before free jazz who did not become enmeshed in
the back-and-forth between Dizzy Gillespie and Miles Davis.

Sidney De Paris was influenced by the growl style of the Ellington
trumpeters—and by King Oliver's sound. He belonged to a group of
Swing trumpeters who carried the New Orleans tradition into the fifties. In those years he worked with the *New* New Orleans Band of his
brother, trombonist Wilbur De Paris. This band disassociated itself
from the average output of the white New Orleans "revivalists." "To
us," Wilbur said, "that isn't jazz . . . just playing the old tunes doesn't
make jazz. . . . The best they can do is to play so it sounds as if *we*
were playing . . . these people only reproduce. But we play like the
old musicians would be playing if they were living today. . . . That's
the reason why I call my band 'Wilbur De Paris and his *New* New Orleans Jazz.' "

All trumpeters mentioned up to now actually belong to the immediate Armstrong school. In contrast to this school stands what might
be called—for simplification—the Gillespie school. It, too, is a product of what had come before. The Gillespie tradition actually begins
long before Dizzy, with *Henry "Red" Allen,* a musician who, if one
did not know what was to follow, would have to be counted among
the Armstrong trumpeters. Allen, who died in 1967, took King Oliver's place in the Oliver band when it was taken over by Luis Russell
in 1929. He played his most famous solos as a member of the 1933-
34 Fletcher Henderson band. The shift in emphasis from sonority to
phrasing is indicated for the first time in Allen's playing—if only in

spurts. Allen—at least when compared to his contemporaries—plays more legato than staccato, in a more flowing manner, connecting rather than separating his phrases.

The tendency toward this kind of playing becomes more marked with a group of trumpeters who came after Allen: *Roy Eldridge, Buck Clayton, Harry Edison* and *Charlie Shavers*. Eldridge became the most important exponent of his instrument between Armstrong and Gillespie. Fluidity now for the first time became an ideal for jazz trumpeters. The saxophone is the most "fluid" of jazz instruments, and here was revealed for the first time the impact of the saxophone on the sonority of modern jazz as a whole. Eldridge once said: "I play nice saxophone on the trumpet." Of course, he later abandoned this saxophone emphasis in his playing, but it remained an active influence.

Roy Eldridge excels in creative impulsiveness, *Charlie Shavers* in technical brilliance. Shavers, who died in 1971, was an all-round trumpeter to a degree matched perhaps only by Harry James. Yet he never went as far into commercial music as did James.

Buck Clayton and *Harry Edison,* finally, play the most gentle and tender trumpets of all the Swing musicians. Edison earned his nickname, "Sweets," from the supple tenderness of his playing. Harmonically speaking, he is the most modern trumpet before Gillespie, while Clayton tends more toward traditional harmonies. Both were among the star soloists of the classic Count Basie band of the late thirties. In the fifties, Edison became a busy Hollywood studio musician who participated in recording sessions with stars like Frank Sinatra. No other trumpeter so completely expresses the sensitivity of modern jazz in the idiom of Swing style, almost totally shunning the musical and stylistic means of modern jazz. Buck Clayton was the musical backbone of a series of jam-session recordings released by Columbia under his name: Swing-oriented, as vital as they were musical, and free from the exhibitionism of many more popular jam-session enterprises (for example, "Jazz at the Philharmonic"). Edison influenced a trumpeter who later played much the same role in the Basie band he himself had played from 1937 to 1950: *Joe Newman.* And Clayton is frequently mentioned when *Ruby Braff's* antecedents are under discussion. Braff is a unique stylistic phenomenon: a trumpeter of the jazz generation of the fifties who took his cues not from Dizzy or Miles, but from the trumpeters of the earlier jazz tradition—a perfectionist of the Swing trumpet, full of grace and charm in Swing and Dixieland.

Jazz trumpeters began early to make use of the stimulating effects of the highest registers of the instrument—playing far above conventional trumpet range. As with everything else in the history of the jazz trumpet, this too begins with Louis Armstrong. But Roy Eldridge was the musician who most influenced the high-note specialists: "Cat" Anderson and Al Kilian with Duke Ellington, and eventually *Maynard Ferguson,* who became known as a member of Stan Kenton's orchestra. Kenton scored with the record sales of Ferguson's skyscraper-climbing escapades, but the critics were almost unanimously antagonized by the tastelessness of this way of playing. Later, Ferguson showed that he is a musician with real jazz feeling and tremendous swing—mainly with his wildly swinging big bands, which he led in the late fifties in the U.S., later in Great Britain. From the point of technique and craftsmanship, Ferguson is the absolute peak among jazz trumpeters. With astonishing ease and assurance, he plays things other trumpeters would consider impossible. Most of all he does not just scream and screech when playing at skyscraper heights; even up there he hits each note accurately and phrases musically.

Dizzy Gillespie based his style of playing on the instrumental achievements of Eldridge and on the stylistic contributions of the other bop pioneers: antipodal to Armstrong and yet comparable to him in power and brilliance. Gillespie, too, has been discussed in a special chapter.

Just as all trumpeters of traditional jazz come from Armstrong, so do all modern trumpeters stem from Gillespie. The four most important in the forties were Howard McGhee, Fats Navarro, Kenny Dorham, and Miles Davis. The early death of *Fats Navarro* was as lamented by the musicians of his generation as Bunny Berigan and Bix Beiderbecke's passing had been mourned by the musicians of the Swing and Chicago periods. Fats' clear, assured playing was a forerunner of the style practiced by the generation of hard bop since the late sixties: the melodic arcs of Miles Davis with the fire of Dizzy Gillespie.

Miles Davis began as a Dizzy imitator, just as Dizzy had begun by imitating Eldridge. But he soon found his own, completely new style. Miles is the founder and chief representative of the second phase of modern jazz trumpeting: lyrical arcs of melody, in which the sophistication of simplicity is admirably cultivated, even less vibrato than Dizzy—and all this with a tone less glowing than melancholy, loaded with coolly smoldering protest. After Davis, the development of jazz trumpeting is contained in the interplay between Dizzy and Miles, frequently spiced with a shot of Fats Navarro. *Kenny Dorham* proved himself to be a musician in this mold who not by any means received the recognition due his talent. He died in 1972.

Chet Baker and Art Farmer started primarily under the Davis influence. Baker played his way to sensational success with his solo on "My Funny Valentine," recorded in 1952 with the Gerry Mulligan Quartet. For a short time he dominated all jazz polls. His phrasing is so supple that he occasionally was chided as "feminine." Starting in the early sixties, Baker developed into a trumpeter with a gripping attack, who impresses with the logic and form of his improvisations. On muted trumpet, *Art Farmer* combines liquid mobility with soulful expressiveness and strong jazz feeling. Art—and along with him *Johnny Coles*—are the only modern trumpeters who can equal the lyrical intensity of Davis without imitating Miles—in their own unmistakable ways. And it is indeed illuminating that just these two trumpeters, who are above any attempt at copying Miles, come closer to him in expressiveness than all the many musicians directly influenced by him. Art Farmer emerged in 1952 from the same Lionel Hampton band which also brought to light the most highly praised trumpeter after Miles Davis: *Clifford Brown,* who died in 1956 in a tragic automobile accident. "Brownie", as he was called, carried the Fats Navarro influence into the cool jazz era of the fifties, and was of great importance. The brilliance and wealth of ideas displayed in his solos are still lauded by all who played with him.

In many respects, Brown is something like the "father of hard bop." The black musicians, untouched by the wave of successful cool jazz, continued to play bop in the first half of the fifties. But "Brownie's" success was the beginning of the success of hard bop.

The musical experience of cool jazz in the first half of fifties and the vitality of the bop of the forties merged in hard bop. Donald Byrd, Thad Jones, Lee Morgan, Bill Hardman, Nat Adderley, Benny Bailey, Carmell Jones, Idrees Sulieman, Ted Curson, Woody Shaw, Blue Mitchell, Booker Little, and Freddie Hubbard are all trumpeters in this mold. They all are indebted to Clifford Brown—some leaning more toward Dizzy, others more toward Miles.

Donald Byrd combined ideas and inspiration with so much professional flexibility that he became one of the most frequently recorded trumpet players of hard bop. *Thad Jones,* an exceptional arranger, has been co-leader of the Thad Jones-Mel Lewis Big Band since the late sixties. He stems from the Basie Orchestra, and he blew some of his first notable solos in the at the time "experimental"-sounding Jazz Workshops of Charles Mingus. *Lee Morgan,* who died in 1972, and *Joe Gordon* worked with Dizzy Gillespie's big band in the mid-fifties. Morgan, who as an 18-year-old was featured extensively by Dizzy, became (as a member of Art Blakey's Jazz Messengers) a frequently recorded hard-bop musician of varying inspiration. *Carmell Jones,* who comes from Kansas City, plays tender, sensitive trumpet lines with a charm and amiability that scarcely any other trumpeter of this often so angry and protest-laden generation has matched. Carmell, who was first presented on the West Coast in 1960 in Gerald Wilson's big band, was in the Horace Silver Quintet for some time, but his conception did not blend very well with its funk and soul-oriented music. Since 1965, he has made his home in Berlin.

Among other creative jazz trumpeters living in Europe is *Benny Bailey,* who has won many friends with his great, full sound—a true trumpet stylist and, in addition, one of the best lead trumpeters one could wish for in a big band. If Bailey were living in New York, he would probably be as busy as Clark Terry, because his particular combination of inimitable improviser and perfect studio and section musician is very rare. *Idrees Sulieman* lives in Copenhagen. Stemming from bop, he has a good reputation as a big-band trumpeter of great dependability and precision. Jones, Bailey, and Sulieman are musicians of the type who can infuse jazz brilliance and jazz intensity into a trumpet section—or even a whole big band—consisting largely of non-jazz musicians.

The development of the trumpet, as far as it took place within 'tonal' jazz, brought little that was new until the mid-sixties—aside from a further, often astounding perfection of the fire of bop. After the much too early death of the very promising *Booker Little* (who had made some of his most beautiful recordings with Eric Dolphy), *Freddie Hubbard* became by far the most important representative of this way of playing. Hubbard is the most brilliant trumpeter of a generation of musicians who stand with one foot in 'tonal' jazz and with the other in the atonal camp. In this way, he reached equally high points in Max Roach's ensemble as (for example) in a studio band

Friedrich Gulda put together, as well as on numerous records under his own name which vividly reflect the development of jazz from hard bop through the period of free playing in the sixties to the electric sound of the seventies.

Hubbard himself influenced many musicians of his own generation and the one following, among them *Woody Shaw, Virgil Jones,* and, above all, the rapidly developing *Marvin Peterson,* one of the few musicians of the early seventies in whose playing there are indications of new trumpet possibilities.

Before we go further into the seventies, the most important trumpeter of actual "free jazz," *Don Cherry,* must be discussed. He blows a cornet-like "pocket trumpet"—more or less a child's trumpet. When he became known in the late fifties as a member of the Ornette Coleman Quartet, he seemed to most critics merely a good friend of Ornette who also happened to play the trumpet. Since then, he has become a 'poet of free jazz' of great, intimate, glowing expressiveness, commended even by so strict a critic as Miles Davis. Since the mid-sixties, Cherry has been living in Europe where he has made notable achievements—in a twofold sense. On the one hand—at the Baden-Baden Free Jazz Meetings, at the Berlin Jazz Days, and at the Donaueschingen Music Days—he created particularly unusual realizations of new big-band jazz that excel over all other attempts in this direction with their melodiousness and charm. On the other hand, he became an exponent of "jazz meets the world"—of the incorporation of elements of the great exotic musics into jazz. Cherry assimilates Balinese, Indian, Arabic and Chinese elements—often not only on his trumpet, but also on various flutes.

The immensity of Cherry's importance is illustrated by the fact that all other free-jazz trumpeters stand in his shadow—Lester Bowie, *Clifford Thornton* (who has made a name for himself on the valve trombone, too), *Dewey Johnson,* and Albert Ayler's brother *Don Ayler,* for instance, among the black musicians; and among the whites, *Don Ellis* and *Mike Mantler.*

Ellis, who became known in the late fifties as a member of George Russell's sextet, and after that lost himself in a somewhat uncreative period of "happenings" in jazz, scored a sensational success at the 1966 Monterey Festival, where he introduced his new big band. He plays a custom-made 'quarter-tone trumpet' which allows for the finest tonal nuances (before him, the Czech trumpeter Jaromir Hnilicka had already employed such an instrument, stimulated by the quarter-tone music of Czechoslovakian composer Alois Hába). Mantler, who hails from Vienna, made his name mainly as leader of the New York Jazz Composers Orchestra and as collaborator of composer (and pianist) Carla Bley. *Lester Bowie,* who grew out of the avant-garde circles in Chicago (the so-called AACM—Association for the Advancement of Creative Musicians) seems like a "Cootie Williams of the avant-garde" with his growl solos. Bowie, who lived in Paris for a while, has also shown interest in big-band realizations of the new jazz—above all in his "Gettin' to Know Ya' All" at the 1969 Baden-Baden Free Jazz Meeting and the 1970 Frankfurt Jazz Festival.

Among the trumpeters who have incorporated rock elements, *Randy Brecker, Bill Chase,* and *Lew Soloff* (of "Blood, Sweat & Tears") require special mention; but a musician like Freddie Hubbard has also shown his interest in rock elements in the early seventies with a new, "electricized" band. *Doc Severinsen,* known among the mass audience as a television personality, has tried on some of his big-band records to open the concept of the classic big jazz orchestra toward contemporary rock. Bill Chase, from Woody Herman's orchestra, combined the four-man trumpet section of big-band jazz with a rock rhythm section in his group "Chase," which we have mentioned. Randy Brecker—also an outstanding fluegelhorn player—made a name for himself through his work in Art Blakey's Jazz Messengers and in the Horace Silver Quintet. For several months (1967/68) he belonged to "Blood, Sweat & Tears;" he also gave trumpet brilliance to the group "Dreams." Probably more than other trumpeters, he is experienced in the realm of "jazz-rock": "Playing trumpet is often difficult in rock because you have to compete with all that electricity. . . . Certain elements of jazz have come to rock, but rock people still can't improvise on the level of a jazz artist. As a jazz musician, you feel like yourself. As a rock musician, you feel like a star."

The Trombone

The trombone began as a rhythm and harmony instrument. In the early jazz bands it was hardly more than a "blown bass." It supplied an additional harmonic background for the melody instruments— trumpet and clarinet—above which they could move, and it stressed the rhythmic accents. In big bands, the trumpets and trombones form the "brass section" which stands opposite the "reed section," the saxophone group.

In view of the substitute-bass role the trombone had to play in the marching bands of early New Orleans, it can be said that the style of the first jazz trombonist worth mentioning was already a sign of progress. This style is called "tailgate." The name stems from the fact that the trombonist took up more space on the "band wagons"—the carts on which the bands rode through the streets of New Orleans on festive occasions—and had to sit as far back as possible, on the tailgate. There he had room to work his slide. The tailgate position made possible effective, glissando-like fills placed between the melodic phrases of the other horns. *Kid Ory*, who died in 1973, was the most important representative of this style.

Honoré Dutrey, another New Orleans veteran, became famous in King Oliver's band. Dutrey was less concerned with tailgate effects than with the old harmonic and rhythmic functions of his instrument.

A trombonist of very personal conception within the New Orleans tradition is *Charlie Green*. Bessie Smith liked his accompaniments—as in "Empty Bed Blues"—which gives an indication of his style: blues trombone. He was a kind of Tommy Ladnier of his instrument.

George Brunies is an important early white trombonist. He was in the New Orleans Rhythm Kings, and his contribution can best be evaluated when one compares the trombone parts in the NORK recordings with those of the Original Dixieland Jazz Band. While the ODJB trombone functions almost exclusively as a bass, in the NORK it plays a subordinate but definitely important part in the Dixieland counterpoint ensemble.

Among trombonists in the New Orleans tradition still active in the sixties, *Jimmy Archey* is worth mentioning. He worked with King Oliver in the late twenties and stayed with the band when Luis Russell took it over. When Rudi Blesh organized his much-discussed broadcast and recording series in the late forties, "This Is Jazz," he was concerned with "reconstructing" the old New Orleans jazz as accurately as possible. He got hold of Archey.

The first jazz musician to play musically conceived, expressive, and melodically rich solos on the trombone was *Jimmy Harrison*. He has often been called the most important trombonist in jazz, and certainly is that in the realm of older jazz forms. He died in 1931 and was one of the leading soloists in Fletcher Henderson's band. He consistently extended the range of the trombone toward that of the trumpet.

Miff Mole is in many respects a white "counterpart" of Jimmy Harrison. Perhaps he lacked the former's mighty inspiration, but he was a flawless technician, and the white musicians of the day were made aware by his playing rather than Harrison's of the fact that the trombone had finally achieved "equal rights." Miff's trombone was an important voice in the Original Memphis Five led by Phil Napoleon, and along with the latter and Red Nichols made up the "triumvirate" of memorable New York-style brass musicians.

The Chicago-style trombonists were also influenced by Mole—for instance, *Tommy Dorsey* and Jack Teagarden. Dorsey evolved in the thirties into the "Sentimental Gentleman," leader of a successful big band and eventually hardly a jazz musician anymore. Yet he always remained a player of great technical ability and soulful feeling. *Jack Teagarden* came from a Texas family which gave three other talented musicians to jazz. He is among the traditional jazz musicians particularly recognized by modern jazzmen. Bill Russo—a former Stan Kenton arranger and an excellent trombonist—praised him as "a jazzman with the facility, range and flexibility of any trombonist of any idiom or any time; his influence was essentially responsible for a mature approach to trombone jazz." Teagarden—or Big "T," as he was called—was Louis Armstrong's favorite trombonist. Together, they played and sang on some of the most spirited and enjoyable duo-recordings in jazz. Both as singer and instrumentalist, Teagarden was a blues musician—with a very modern attitude toward the blues. He was perhaps the first to manifest the attitude toward the blues exemplified in the fifties in, say, the music of Jimmy Giuffre: indirect, reflective—yet genuine and from personal involvement.

There is a Duke Ellington group among the trombones as well, although they are not as closely related, stylistically, as the Ellington trumpets. These are *Joseph "Tricky Sam" Nanton,* Juan Tizol, and Lawrence Brown. "Tricky Sam" is *the* great man of growl trombone. *Juan Tizol* (with Ellington co-author of the famous "Caravan," the first Latin jazz tune) does not play the slide trombone—as most important jazz trombonists—but the valve trombone. He plays it softly and sweetly, and occasionally becomes a trifle saccharine. His sound has been compared to that of a cello. *Lawrence Brown,* stylishly melodic and often not very intense, is a musician of strong personal warmth with a preference for tuneful and sometimes faintly sentimental melodies.

Benny Morton, J. C. Higginbotham, Vic Dickenson, Dickie Wells, and Trummy Young are the great trombonists of Swing style. Their playing shares a vibrant vehemence. Morton, Wells, and Dickenson were all heard with Count Basie's band. Morton had previously worked with Fletcher Henderson; his playing has an intense, blues-like quality—something on the order of a Swing fusion of Jimmy Harrison and Charlie Green. *Dickie Wells* has been described as a musician of "romantic imagination" by André Hodeir. He is a romanticist not in the sense of overblown pathos but in terms of a forceful, imaginative sensitivity. Much of this romanticism is contained in the incomparable vibrato of his trombone sound.

J. C. Higginbotham is the most vehement, powerful trombone of the Swing period—his tone sometimes reminding of the earthy, tight sound known in the twenties as "gutbucket" trombone. Sometimes he plays with an abrupt explosiveness, as if the trombone had been struck rather than blown. *Vic Dickenson* has a lusty, pleasing sense of humor which sometimes seeps into even his slow solos. With his appealing and singable ideas, he is among those Swing musicians who —despite changing styles—continued to enjoy a remarkable recording career through the decades. He also frequently played in "Dixieland" groups.

Trummy Young is to the trombone what Roy Eldridge is to the trumpet. From 1937 to 1943 he was one of the principal soloists in the Jimmie Lunceford band. His "Margie" was a particular success from that period. Louis Armstrong brought in Trummy Young as the replacement for Jack Teagarden with his "All Stars" in 1952. With this group Trummy popularized—and sometimes banalized—his style.

Directly linked to Trummy Young—and in terms of tone related to the vehement verve of several Swing trombonists—is the trombonist who created modern trombone style and remains its personification: *J. J. Johnson.* Before discussing him, we must mention a white trombonist, *Bill Harris,* master of a brilliant virtuoso technique. Harris was a member of Woody Herman's band from 1944 to 1946, again from 1948 to 1950, and later played with Herman again from time to time. His solo on "Bijou," recorded with Herman in the mid-forties, was the most admired trombone solo of the time. His personality is marked by the contrast between the piercing, springy style of his fast work and the polished, studied vibrato of his slow solos. The contrast is so pronounced one might think two musicians were involved if one did not know that Harris, with his slightly professorial looks, was responsible for both. "Harris isn't playing, he's praying," is what Red Norvo said after Herman's 1946 Carnegie Hall Concert, where Harris scored with "Everywhere." Next to and along with J. J. Johnson, Harris for years was the strongest influence on trombonists. He died a forgotten man (at least in the U.S.A) in 1973.

J. J. Johnson became the Dizzy Gillespie of the trombone; what he plays is not just bop trombone but also "trumpet-trombone." He plays his instrument with that brilliant glow long associated with the trumpet; no other musician before him accomplished this feat on the trombone. Contrast to this the muted playing of J. J.: earthy, tight; reminiscent of Charlie Green's blues trombone but with all the mobility of modern jazz. Johnson went through the same development as Gillespie: from the nervousness of bop to great sobriety and quiet autonomy. J. J., also an outstanding arranger, went to Hollywood in the late sixites to start a new career as film and television composer and arranger. Since then, almost nothing has been heard from him on the trombone.

Kai Winding is the white counterpart of J. J. Johnson. Independent of J. J., he found a style often so reminiscent of J. J. that time and again they were mistaken for each other. It must be counted among the marvels of jazz that two musicians as different as Winding and Johnson should have arrived at similar styles. Kai, born in Denmark, was a member of Benny Goodman's band and later came to the fore through his playing with Stan Kenton; thus he was first and foremost a big-band musician. J. J. Johnson, from Indiana, black, combo-man of the bebop groups, came to the fore through his playing on 52nd Street.

In 1954-55 the two joined forces in the two-trombone combo, 'Jay and Kai,' which turned out to be pretty much the opposite of what had been expected, which was that a group in which the two only horns were the same—and additionally, played in similar style— would be colorless and monotonous. Actually, the charm of this two-trombone combo was specifically rooted in the many colors created by the two trombonists, with the aid of a whole arsenal of mutes employed in the most artful combinations.

Among the bop trombonists in the narrower sense of the term are *Benny Green* and *Earl Swope.* Green was already playing "bop" trombone before J. J. Johnson had become well-known, and still is somewhat closer to the Swing trombonists, particularly in terms of harmony. Swope had the tone and big-band experience of Kai Winding, coupled with a way of phrasing inspired by the early "nervous" Charlie Parker. He died young.

Ten years later—among the musicians of hard bop—*Curtis Fuller,* Jimmy Knepper, Julian Priester, and Slide Hampton (also notable as an arranger) are especially worthy of mention. Fuller is particularly typical of the Detroit generation of hard bop. *Jimmy Knepper,* discovered by Charles Mingus, blows a "piercing," vital trombone style in which Swing and bop elements are equally alive. Knepper is an all-round trombonist who masters everything from conventional big-band work to avant-garde experimentation. *Julian Priester* became known primarily through his work with the piano-less Max Roach Quintet. *Slide Hampton* emerged from Maynard Ferguson's band. His octet of 1959 linked up with the Miles Davis Capitol band of 1949, making it "contemporary," giving it a touch of soul. Meanwhile, Hampton moved to Europe. He has recorded with the most diverse European big bands—from Paris to Berlin to Finland—as arranger and band leader, as well as solo trombone.

J. J. Johnson and Bill Harris had an almost inestimable influence on all trombonists who came after. *Frank Rosolino* stems primarily from Johnson. His feeling for effects, his temperament, and his sense of humor often stood out in Stan Kenton's 1953-54 band. *Carl Fontana* plays without Frank's striving for effects, but with great flexibility and feeling for harmonic subtleties. He, too, is a big-band musician and emerged from the bands of Kenton and Woody Herman. Further trombonists of this line are *Frank Rehak* and *Eddie Bert*—the latter a particularly temperamental Bill Harris-influenced improviser. *Bob Enevoldsen* became one of the most frequently recorded trombonists of the fifties on the West Coast. He plays valve trombone, an instrument which permits a great, more saxophonelike mobility, though many musicians feel that it lacks the jazz intensity of the slide trombone. Trombone-like, too, is the sound of the bass trumpet solos recorded by *Cy Touff* with Woody Herman and with his own groups of the mid-fifties. The bass trumpet is an instrument which accommodates the trumpet tendencies of modern jazz trombone playing.

Rehak, Bert, Al Grey, Bill Watrous, and, most of all *Urbie Green* are flexible trombonists, able to cope with any style or demand—the "Vic Dickensons" of modern jazz. Urbie, who became known through his work in the Benny Goodman band of the fifties (during which stint he often "stood in" for Benny), has said: "My playing has been compared to almost every trombonist who ever lived. The reason probably is that I had to play in so many different styles—Dixieland, lead *à la* Tommy Dorsey, and later, modern jazz. . . ." To this flexibility, *Al Grey* adds the aspect of humor which has always had an especially live tradition among the trombonists—from "tailgate style" through Vic Dickenson and Trummy Young up to Albert Mangelsdorff, whom we will discuss later. Grey is a big-band veteran: from Benny Carter and Jimmie Lunceford to Lionel Hampton and Dizzy Gillespie up to Count Basie.

Particularly brilliant was *Willie Dennis,* who died in 1965. He emerged from the Tristano school and was the actual trombone exponent of the Tristano conception. Since he formed most of his notes with his lip, he did not have to move his slide very much, and in this way he achieved a fluidity on the slide trombone which few others have approximated even on the valve trombone. In addition, his tone gained much in singing grace.

The three most significant new trombonists of the late fifties/early sixties are probably *Jimmy Cleveland,* the above-mentioned Curtis Fuller, and Bob Brookmeyer. Cleveland is a "super J. J.," whose brilliant tromboning often seems almost explosive, especially since this explosiveness is combined with the fluency of a saxophone in the most natural way.

Valve trombonist *Bob Brookmeyer,* on the other hand, is a man of modern Lester Young-classicism, who "cooled off" the tradition of his home town, Kansas City, in quite a remarkable way. With Jimmy Giuffre, he recorded an album entitled "Traditionalism Revisited" which fully demonstrates the classicist position: the jazz tradition viewed from the standpoint of modern jazz. Here old famous jazz themes—such as Louis Armstrong's "Santa Claus Blues" and "Some Sweet Day," King Oliver's "Sweet Like This," Tommy Ladnier's "Jada," and Bix Beiderbecke's "Louisiana"—are transported into the world of modern jazz. In one of the pieces, Brookmeyer and Giuffre play the old solos of King Oliver and Dave Nelson note for note. These solos fit so well into the cool-jazz surroundings as to prove once again that it is mainly the arrangements and the external technical marks which change and may become dated in jazz: the improvisations remain valid.

In free jazz, Grachan Moncur III, Roswell Rudd, Buster Cooper, and Garnett Brown, among others, gained prominence—all musicians who widen and inflect the sound spectrum of their instrument, including noise elements in their music. *Roswell Rudd* deserves special attention in this field as he has a clearly recognizable Dixieland and blues approach to his tonally free excursions. Through the vocal qualities Rudd incorporates in his playing, he discovered the folk music of the world: "Suffice it to say that vocal techniques I had associated at one time only with the jazz singers of my own country were revealed to be common to the oldest known musical traditions the world over. What I had always considered the epitome of musical expression in America, the blues, could be felt everywhere in the so-called 'folk world.' " Roswell Rudd says this in a *down beat* article with the fitting title "The Universality of the Blues."

German trombonist *Albert Mangelsdoff*—like no other jazz player, even in America—has made lucid the logic of the development that leads from the Tristano school in the early fifties to free jazz in the sixties. He emancipated the long lines of alto player Lee Konitz—under whose influence he initially stood—in a gradual and seemingly necessary process, becoming ever freer harmonically, until they were —in the exact sense of the word—"freed." Since the beginning of the seventies, Mangelsdorff has been developing a technique which permits him—as far as I know, as the first trombonist in the world—to play "chords" on his instrument. By blowing one tone and simultaneously singing another, lower tone, Mangelsdorff gives the vocal tone the sound quality of the trombone. In addition to these two tones, Mangelsdorff creates—simultaneously!—three, four, and five-tone chords by playing with the over-tone scales generated through the friction between the blown and the sung tones. This conscious use of overtones is a specific discovery of the free jazz of the sixties—it occurred especially among the saxophonists, where overtones (as in tenorists Pharaoh Sanders, Dewey Redman, and Albert Ayler) frequently became more important than the *de facto* blown tones.

Among the trombonists of the seventies influenced by rock and soul, we shall name *James Pankow, Dick Halligan,* and *Dave Bargeron, Wayne Henderson* and *Glen Ferris.* James Pankow gave the "rock big band" "Chicago" its actual jazz quality. Halligan and Bargeron came to the fore with "Blood, Sweat & Tears;" Wayne Henderson with the soul jazz of the "Jazz Crusaders," a kind of California counterpart of Art Blakey's "Jazz Messengers." And Glen Ferris, who emerged from the Don Ellis Big Band, has a similar position among trombonists as Randy Brecker among trumpeters. These musicians are just beginning to explore the rock possibilities which the trombone has due to its combination of "sliding fluidity" and "brassy percussivity." The trombonist who might master all these possibilities some day—a kind of Kid Ory of rock with J. J. Johnson's technique —will have no reason to complain about lack of work.

The Clarinet

In all stages of jazz development, the clarinet has been a symbol of interrelation. The clarinet interlaced, and filled in between, trumpet and trombone in the old New Orleans counterpoint, entwining them like ivy. This has remained its position up to the present day, even in the few cases where it was used in the free jazz of the sixties. Not coincidentally did the clarinet have its greatest period during the Swing era, when jazz and popular music were largely identical.

Alphonse Picou is the first clarinetist from New Orleans whose style has become known. His famous chorus on "High Society" is one of the most copied solos in jazz history. Down to this day, almost every clarinetist who plays "High Society" is quoting Picou—just as every trombonist who plays "Tin Roof Blues" is quoting from George Brunis' solo with the New Orleans Rhythm Kings, or playing it entire.

The second important clarinetist from old New Orleans is *George Lewis*—though his influence was felt much later, in the New Orleans Revival of the forties and fifties. Born in 1900, he participated in New Orleans jazz life from the time he was 16. In the thirties, he worked on the docks until the New Orleans revival movement swept him along. In the music recorded by George Lewis and his bands of varying personnel during the forties and fifties one feels, more than anywhere else in modern recordings, something of the atmosphere of the archaic, ancient New Orleans jazz. All the joyousness is there—and the wrong notes.

It points up the multiple layers of jazz development that the great triumvirate of the jazz clarinet, *Johnny Dodds-Jimmie Noone-Sidney Bechet,* preceded Picou and Lewis in recording, while in a certain sense they built musically and stylistically on their way of playing. Picou—and, of course, Bechet, too—actually are merely the final and sole well-known representatives of a style cultivated in old New Orleans by many other Creole clarinetists. As late as 1964—on the island of Martinique, which is the center of the large Creole area that originally reached from Louisiana in the North to French-Guyana in the South—I heard an 80-year-old man who sounded virtually like Sidney Bechet play at a fair. He had never heard the name of that great clarinetist. On the other hand, Bechet, when he was introduced to music from Martinique, played many pieces of Martiniquan folk music as if they were—as they really actually are, in a way—old Creole dances from New Orleans.

But back to the 'triumvirate': Dodds-Noone-Bechet. Noone is best known for the gentleness and subtlety of his tone. Compared to him, the improvisations of Johnny Dodds seem almost wild and brutal. Dodds—a master of the lower register of his instrument—was Louis Armstrong's preferred clarinetist during the time of the Hot Five and Hot Seven recordings. Bechet, finally, of whom we shall speak again in the soprano chapter, is the embodiment of the jazz *espressivo*. The slow vibrato of his clarinet produced a sound recognizable even to the jazz layman. In France, where Bechet lived during his final years (he died in 1959), he was as popular as any *chanteur*. And even when much in his playing seemed to have become mannered, it was one of the especially moving human experiences in jazz to see this white-haired, dignified man from old New Orleans play amid the young Dixieland existentialists in Saint-Germain-des-Prés.

In Paris, too, *Albert Nicholas* made his home (he later moved to Switzerland, where he died in 1973)—playing in a clearly "clarinetistic," technically masterful style which in the fifties became somewhat Bechet-like, yet always retained that wealth of ideas and mobility which Bechet often seemed to have lost. Nicholas—also a Creole— emerged from the orchestras of King Oliver and Luis Russell, while the Bechet of the twenties is primarily represented by records made with the Clarence Williams Blue Five. In the thirties Bechet recorded with his own "New Orleans Feetwarmers." Among his most important clarinet recordings are those he made with pianist Art Hodes in the forties (on Blue Note).

Nicholas—along with Omer Simeon and Barney Bigard—belongs to what might be called the third generation of the jazz clarinet. *Omer Simeon* was Jelly Roll Morton's favorite clarinetist, while *Barney Bigard* became known mainly through the flowing, supple solos he recorded as a member of Duke Ellington's band from 1928 to 1942, and with Louis Armstrong's All Stars from 1946 to 1955, as one of the few jazz musicians who spent considerable time with both of these giants. Bigard is a sorcerer of melody—playing with strong feeling and with dynamics almost equal to those of Benny Goodman.

Bigard, though indebted to the New Orleans tradition, in his great period already belongs among the Swing clarinetists. Before going on to these, we must recapitulate the history of the white jazz clarinet. It begins with *Leon Rappolo* of the New Orleans Rhythm Kings, that famous white group of the early twenties. Rappolo is one of the Beiderbecke types so frequent in jazz who seem to burn themselves out in their music and their lives. Among his successors in the realm of Chicago style the most important are *Frank Teschemacher,* Jimmy Dorsey, and Pee Wee Russell. All three played with Bix Beiderbecke. Teschemacher, who died in 1932, loved to connect and smear his notes—perhaps subconsciously feeling that this would make him sound more like a black musician. He was a great influence on the young Benny Goodman. *Jimmy Dorsey* rose to fame with his big band, which he led from the thirties on, and through his collaborations with his trombonist brother Tommy, which were frequently interrupted by fights. Jimmy had a certain influence as a clarinetist, and perhaps ever more as an alto saxophonist, due to his technical assurance and craftsmanship. Charlie Parker, for example, always had praise for Jimmy Dorsey—with that touching tendency to overrate technical ability so frequent among musicians. *Pee Wee Russell* preferred the lower registers of the clarinet. He played with a vibrato and way of phrasing which puts him in a similar relationship to Lester Young and Jimmy Giuffre as Bix Beiderbecke seems to be in to Chet Baker. Willis Connover dubbed him "the poet of the clarinet." *Pete Fountain* has become one of the most successful Dixieland musicians of our time: a man who plays, with taste and instinct for success, a kind of tourist Dixieland for the sightseers on Bourbon Street, the main street of the French Quarter in New Orleans.

Finally, *Mezz Mezzrow,* a musician who reached renown through his friendship with the French jazz critic Hugues Panassié, must be mentioned among the Chicago clarinetists. From the standpoint of technique, he was mediocre, and as an improviser often had to limit himself to stringing triads together. Still, he played with a feeling for the blues surprising in a white musician of his generation.

"The race," Mezzrow wrote, "made me feel inferior, started me thinking that maybe I wasn't worth beans as a musician or any kind of artist, in spite of all my big ideas." Mezzrow's most important contribution is not so much his clarinet playing as his autobiography, *Really the Blues*, in which the flavor of Chicago in the twenties, and even more, of Harlem in the thirties and forties, has been so well captured that even Henry Miller expressed his enthusiasm. Though white, Mezzrow again and again described himself as a Negro, and on the several occasions when he was put in jail, he insisted on being placed in the black section. For a while he made his living selling marijuana in Harlem. The philosophy of his book is one of unbounded vitality: "That was what New Orleans was really saying—it was a celebration of life, of breathing, of muscle-flexing, of eye-blinking, of licking-the-chops, in spite of everything the world might do to you. It was a defiance of the undertaker. It was a refusal to go under, a stubborn hanging on, a shout of praise to the circulatory system, hosannas for the sweat-glands, hymns to the guts that ache when they are hollow. Glory be, brother! Hallelujah, the sun's shining!"

The clarinetist of whom the layman thinks first when jazz clarinet is mentioned is *Benny Goodman*. He, too, stems from the circle of Chicago style. He is the "King of Swing" of the thirties, whose scintillating and polished clarinet playing is the reason why the clarinet and the Swing era are largely synonymous. "B. G."—as he is known —is one of the great stylists of jazz, a musician of superlative charm, spirit, and gaiety. His clarinet playing is associated to equal degrees with his big-band recordings and those he made with various small combos: from the Benny Goodman Trio, with Teddy Wilson at the piano and Gene Krupa on drums, through the quartet in which Lionel Hampton first found public recognition, to the Benny Goodman Sextet in which guitarist Charlie Christian helped pave the way for modern jazz. In terms of expression, Goodman accomplished on the clarinet almost everything other instruments could not achieve until the advent of modern jazz. But he did this—and here is the heart of the matter—without the harmonic finesse and rhythmic complexity of modern jazz. This may be one reason for the disadvantageous position occupied by the clarinet in modern jazz. On the other hand, "B.G." is a master of subtleties. His dynamics range smoothly—as those of no other clarinetist—from softest pianissimo to jubilant fortissimo. Particularly astonishing is the skill with which Goodman manages to play even the softest notes and still—even when playing with a big band—capture the attention of the listeners in the very last row of a large concert hall.

Minor "Benny Goodmans" of a sort were Jimmy Dorsey, *Artie*

Shaw, and *Woody Herman,* all of whom had big bands to celebrate their clarinets in Goodmanesque fashion. *Jimmy Hamilton, Buster Bailey,* and, indirectly, Edmond Hall were also influenced by Goodman, as were all clarinetists who played alongside and after him —except Lester Young and the modern clarinetists who stem from him. Hamilton has played solos with Duke Ellington which are softer and more restrained than even Goodman. If the theories of the jazz-racists were correct, one would have to conclude—comparing Hamilton and Goodman on purely aural evidence—that the former was white and Goodman black, though the opposite is true. During the fifties, Hamilton evolved into an important clarinet voice in modern jazz, and it is regrettable that his name is so rarely mentioned in the same breath with Buddy DeFranco, Tony Scott, and Jimmy Giuffre. Perhaps this is because Hamilton, as a member of the Ellington band, was overshadowed by so many better known Ellington soloists: Harry Carney, Johnny Hodges, etc. Two other outstanding clarinetists of the Duke Ellington Orchestra are *Russell Procope* and *Harold Ashby,* whose main instruments, of course, are the alto and tenor saxophone, respectively.

Edmond Hall, who died in 1967, was the most important black Swing clarinetist and—alongside Benny Goodman—the towering Swing stylist on this instrument. He had a sharp, biting tone which often stands in contrast to Goodman's suppleness. During the forties and fifties, Hall played with Eddie Condon's New York Dixieland bunch. *Peanuts Hucko,* a clarinetist who plays "dixielandish Benny Goodman," also emerged from this group.

It is indicative of the organic rightness of jazz evolution that the approaches to the playing of different instruments have evolved on a parallel course. Nearly every instrument has its Roy Eldridge or Charlie Parker. The Eldridge of the clarinet is Edmond Hall; the Parker of this instrument became *Buddy DeFranco,* the only clarinetist who could outdistance Benny Goodman in terms of technique. He is an improviser of vital force—which led impressario Norman Granz to team him with Lionel Hampton and other great Swing musicians on numerous recordings. The brilliance of his playing is of such clarity it has sometimes been regarded as "cold." It is one of the paradoxes of jazz that the playing of so "hot" and basic an improviser as DeFranco should have impressed so many listeners as "cold." It symbolizes the difficult, almost hopeless situation of the clarinet in today's jazz that so brilliant a musician as DeFranco finally resigned himself to taking over the direction of the Glenn Miller Orchestra ". . . for reasons of economic survival . . . playing tiresome music and adding nothing to his own development," as Leonard Feather put it. In 1973, he left the band to try jazz once again.

It does not contradict Buddy DeFranco's position as the Charlie Parker of the clarinet to point out that a European musician should have been the first, strictly speaking, to play modern jazz on the clarinet. This was the Swede *Stan Hasselgard.* Benny Goodman made him a member of his sextet in the spring of 1948, the only clarinetist he ever tolerated alongside himself. A few months later—in November of the same year—Hasselgard was fatally injured in an automobile accident. Hasselgard was the second European jazz musician of stylistically creative consequence. The French gypsy guitarist Django Reinhardt, who had a considerable influence on almost all jazz guitarists between the late thirties and the late forties, was the first.

After DeFranco's "coldness," the "warmth" of *Jimmy Giuffre* seemed even stronger. Initially, Giuffre played almost exclusively in the low register of his instrument—the so-called Chalumeau register. He has on occasion pointed out that he did this because he was unable to do anything else. In fact, making the transition from low to high register fluently is the greatest problem involved in playing this instrument.

Giuffre's technical handicap became a stylistic identification. The dark warmth of his playing at last seemed to represent what had been missed for so long: a modern clarinet conception somehow corresponding to the "Four Brothers" sound of the tenor saxophonists. But Giuffre played his clarinet much like *Lester Young* had played his 20 years before—on the few recordings Pres had then made on this instrument: in 1938 with the Kansas City Six, and around the same time with Count Basie's band. Many experts do not doubt that Lester, had he played it more often, would have become as important on the clarinet as he was on the tenor. Lester himself said he played clarinet so rarely mainly because he could not find an instrument that suited him.

The paradox of the situation is that cool jazz actually has only two clarinetists whose playing corresponds to cool conception in its narrowest definition: Lester Young and Jimmy Giuffre; whereas among the tenor saxophonists the Lester Young-sound was multiplied to such a degree that Lester Young, the tenor man, seemed to be living in a world of mirrors. Indirectly, of course, a few tenormen have extended the cool Lester Young-conception when occasionally playing clarinet: *Zoot Sims, Buddy Collette,* and others. But this was usually perceived only as a surprising side effect, not as a genuine style—as, for example, Sims' way of playing tenor. Much later—in the early seventies—a musician who had come to attention through Miles Davis' "Bitches Brew," *Benny Maupin,* reminded us on clarinet and bass clarinet of the fact that the quiet balance of the Lester Young heritage can be particularly attractive even among the electronicized contemporary jazz sounds—especially when, as in Maupin, it is combined with free playing.

But back to Giuffre. During the second half of the fifties, he moved away from his preference for the low register of his instrument probably because the success of his dark-toned playing forced him to play clarinet so much that he overcame his technical handicap. By the sixties, finally, Giuffre stood out as a sensitive musician of a cool free jazz, with a restrained, chamber music-like conception.

A further level of abstraction of clarinet sound—almost bordering on a flute-like sound—was reached by *John La Porta* and *Sam Most.* Already in the fifties, both were considered "avant-garde," before the free jazz of the sixties had shown to what limits the "avant-garde" concept could go in jazz. La Porta, also an exceptional arranger, won high acclaim through his work in American jazz education.

Another important man who took up the struggle with the difficult position of the clarinet in modern jazz is *Tony Scott,* who is of Italian ancestry. He is a true "jam session" musician, one of the few still extant, with an immense drive to play—and, above all, with the "loudest sound of all clarinetists" (Perry Robinson)—a genuine clarinetist who feels the music through his horn, undisturbed by the unfavorable stylistic situation of the instrument. "I don't like funerals," said Scott when it seemed in the late fifties that the jazz clarinet was finally laid to rest. "That's why I went to Asia."

In Asia, Scott inspired and trained dozens of musicians. What all those 'Americans in Europe'—the American musicians who today live in every large and in many smaller towns of Europe—accomplished together, Scott achieved alone in the much more extended Asian territory. From Taiwan to Indonesia, from Okinawa to Thailand, he passed the message of genuine jazz on to a whole generation of young jazz musicians.

To be sure, the dilemma of the clarinet—that it simply didn't seem to fit into the 'saxophonized' sound of modern jazz—was not solved by Scott's flight to Asia. A solution was initiated by the great avant-gardist *Eric Dolphy,* who died in Berlin in 1964—however, not so much on clarinet as on bass clarinet.

Never before had the bass clarinet been a true jazz instrument. Dolphy turned it into one—with searing, wild emotional expression and also with a physically immense power that gave his listeners the feeling that he was not playing the traditional bass clarinet, which had always appeared somewhat old-fashioned, but rather a totally new instrument that had never been heard before. (Harry Carney, baritone saxophonist with Duke Ellington, and a few others had occasionally used the bass clarinet in more conventional contexts.)

Dolphy's way of playing bass clarinet quickly found followers, in Europe more than in the U. S. (it seems that Dolphy's influence in general is stronger outside the United States, in Europe and Japan). Dutchman *Willem Breuker,* Briton *John Surman,* German *Gunter Hampel,* and Luxembourger *Michel Pilz* have been playing bass clarinet with Dolphy's conception, yet—especially Breuker and Hampel —with their own clearly individual styles.

It was a European too, who first realized the possibilities Dolphy's clarinet style had opened up: German clarinetist *Rolf Kühn,* who lived in the U. S. from 1956 to 1959, and was designated "a new Benny Goodman" by John Hammond. In his "Encyclopedia of Jazz," Leonard Feather stated: "Kühn had the misfortune to enter the jazz scene at a time when his chosen instrument had suffered an apparently irreparable decline in popularity. Had it not been for these circumstances, he might well be a major name in jazz today."

Other clarinetists who have been appearing in the annual jazz polls of the late sixties and early seventies are *Bobby Jones, Roland Kirk, Eddie Daniels, Bob Wilber,* and *Paul Horn.* Jones, who came to the fore by playing tenor in the Charles Mingus Sextet, occasionally seems like an Edmond Hall of the seventies, with Hall's swinging expressiveness, but with greater, contemporary mobility. Kirk (about whom more in the tenor chapter) and Eddie Daniels tend toward a healthy, mainstream-oriented playing: the blind Roland Kirk with missionary black power, Daniels with a professionalism at home in all styles and ways of playing.

Bob Wilber further developed Benny Goodman's sophistication in an almost chamber music-like manner and carried it into our age, particularly through his clear, clever compositions and arrangements. On the West Coast, multi-instrumentalist Paul Horn (see also the flute chapter) became Eric Dolphy's successor in the Chico Hamilton Quintet when Dolphy went to New York in the late fifties to join Charles Mingus. Horn has an expressiveness that stands up in comparison with Dolphy, but his playing moves more along the lines of the versatile studio musician who has mastered all possibilities. Ian Underwood, known for his work in Frank Zappa's "Mothers of Invention," has carried some of the possibilities of contemporary clarinet playing into progressive rock.

The clarinetist who virtually personifies the state of the development at the beginning of the seventies is *Perry Robinson*. He has played with the Jazz Composers Orchestra; with Roswell Rudd, Charlie Haden, and Sunny Murray; with Gunter Hampel and the Darius Brubeck Group (a band led by one of Dave Brubeck's musical sons)—and all these names illustrate his universality. Universality is different from versatility. Unlike Paul Horn or Eddie Daniels, Robinson is not a well schooled, professional studio musician conversant with everything (which is not meant to be derogatory). He has—as John McLaughlin among guitarists—joined the different styles and playing techniques of free and cool jazz, bop, Swing, and rock into the new style that is the style of the seventies: "We want to be able to play any kind of music, yet we want to be ourselves. . . . The clarinet, it's incredible, because you have these different sounds. The only frustration thing about it that has to be overcome somehow is that it's too small; it won't carry the weight when you're trying to get through. That's why, when I went into the energy playing on clarinet, I made a study of it, and I learned a lot of things about sound, about overblowing. Like the need to express ourselves is sometimes such an urge, but there's other ways, the psychic ways, of breath control, thinking big, and thinking way out there." (Perry Robinson in an interview with Bob Palmer.)

The Saxophones

The ideal jazz instrument is an instrument that can be as expressive as the trumpet and as mobile as the clarinet. The saxophone is the only instrument to combine these two qualities, which are in extreme opposition where most other instruments are concerned. That is why it is important to jazz. But it became important only at the start of the thirties. One can hardly speak of a New Orleans saxophone tradition—at least not to the degree as with other instruments. The few saxophonists active in New Orleans were looked upon with the expressions reserved today for sousaphone or theremin players, regarded as odd characters rather than musicians. Generally, the saxophone belonged to sweet bands and popular dance music rather than jazz. During the days of Chicago style things changed. It is noteworthy that the New Orleans Rhythm Kings were without a saxophone when they came to Chicago from New Orleans in 1921; yet when they obtained the engagement at "Friar's Inn" that was their springboard to fame, they were forced to include a saxophone. The saxophonist stumbled and staggered about amid the collective ensemble of the NORK, and never really found his place—and as soon as the band quit the job at "Friar's Inn," he was let go.

Since no jazz tradition existed for the saxophone, the clarinet tradition had to do for jazz-minded saxophonists. The importance which saxophone—primarily the tenor—has achieved in modern jazz becomes clear with a single stroke when one realizes that at the outset of its jazz career, the saxophone was played more or less like a peculiar sort of clarinet, whereas in the fifties jazz clarinetists had a tenor-sax approach to their instrument.

The saxophones range downward from soprano through alto, tenor, and baritone to bass sax. The most important in jazz are the first four.

Adrian Rollini played Dixieland and Chicago-style music on the bass sax with its hollow, somewhat burping sound—with great agility and basically with the same intention that motivated Boyd Raeburn to use the instrument as the lowest voice in the sax section of his big band: to give depth and bottom to the sound spectrum. Joseph Jarman and Roscoe Mitchell use the bass sax in free jazz, creating similar "honking," exotic sounds as those produced in the beginning of the saxophone development in old New Orleans on the other saxophones. Thus, there still is hope for the bass saxophone.

The Soprano Saxophone

The soprano saxophone continues where the clarinet leaves off—because of its loudness, for one. It has the most disproportionate history of all instruments in jazz—even more disproportionate than the violin. In the beginning, there was only Sidney Bechet. Today, there are dozens of sopranoists. A tenor man is no longer acceptable in countless big bands and studio orchestras if he does not double on the soprano as an additional instrument.

For decades, we were told that soprano sax was used so rarely because of the difficulty in playing it "clean." Its overtone scales necessarily sound out of tune. Today, however, we know that this is the very advantage of the instrument: The "dirtiness" of sound, which has been of great importance in all phases of jazz history, is an integral part of the soprano. One could almost say that the soprano tends to flatten each note, to turn it into a "blue note," to turn the whole scale "blue." This is a tendency imminent from the start in folk blues and the archaic jazz forms. The three classical blue notes of jazz are compromises with the European harmonic system. Actually, the music of the African and the Afro-American tends toward slanting each individual tone, toward not accepting a note as it is, toward reinterpreting each note as a personal statement. The soprano does all this in an exemplary manner: It "Africanizes." The thesis that this is its actual strength can even be verified in a test: There are at least two sopranoists who have managed to produce "clean" sounds in spite of all the technical difficulties of the instrument—*Bob Wilber*, who plays soprano with the aesthetic clarity with which he plays clarinet; and *Lucky Thompson,* who transferred the perfect beauty of his tenor sound to the soprano. But both have remained relatively unsuccessful, in spite of the high degree of sophistication of their playing. Both are admired, but fail to truly excite and move.

Sidney Bechet is the Louis Armstrong of the soprano saxophone —he has Armstrong's majestic expressiveness. Bechet's personality alone makes it clear that the soprano is in succession to the clarinet. During the span of his rich life, which led from the New Orleans of pre-World War I days to the Paris of the fifties, he changed—gradually at first, but then more and more decidedly—from clarinet to soprano sax. It has been said he did so because with advancing age the soprano became more easy to play for him, since it requires less air for full-volume play. His main reason, however, was that the soprano makes possible a wider range of expression, and the maximum of *esspressivo* was Bechet's main goal. For good reason he has been called the forefather of the great ballad tradition of jazz. For the outsider, this tradition begins with Coleman Hawkins' "Body and Soul" in 1939. But actually, it began with Sidney Bechet—and, of course, with Louis Armstrong!

Bechet had only few soprano students: *Johnny Hodges, Don Redman, Charlie Barnet, Woody Herman,* Bob Wilber—and in a certain sense, even in the Coltrane era, *Budd Johnson* and *Jerome Richardson.* They all applied their Bechet experiences to the stylistic periods in which they belonged. Hodges, the most famous soloist of the Duke Ellington Orchestra, was devoted to expressiveness in a way similar to Bechet. But the soprano solos he played with Ellington in the twenties and thirties seem pale compared to the power of his alto sound. Hodges gave up the soprano altogether after 1940. Perhaps he also felt that playing the soprano would always keep him somewhat in the shadow of the great Bechet, to whom he was indebted in many other ways.

The close proximity between Hodges and Bechet in this aspect is made clear by Woody Herman: If he derives from Hodges as an alto player, he stems from Bechet as a soprano man.

We said that Bechet only had a few soprano students. But *John Coltrane,* too, is among Bechet's students on this instrument. With his solo on "My Favorite Things" in 1961, Coltrane created a sweeping breakthrough for the soprano sax. At that time, at the height of the success of "My Favorite Things," I visited the Guggenheim Museum of Art in New York with "Trane." As we looked at the modern paintings, Coltrane kept talking about Bechet and how he had studied Bechet's recordings. He asked me whether I could provide him with more Bechet records, especially those from Bechet's days in France. (I was happy to oblige.)

The development of the soprano saxophone again displays the continuity of growth so very characteristic of jazz: from New Orleans —from Sidney Bechet in this case—to the most modern and complex creations of Coltrane, and beyond that, to Wayne Shorter and his "students" and contemporaries.

Coltrane retained the expressiveness and "dirtiness" of Bechet. But he substituted for Bechet's majestic clarity, which is reminiscent of Louis Armstrong an Asiatic meditativeness. Coltrane's soprano sound calls to mind the shenai of northern India music, the nagaswaram of the music of Southern India, and the zoukra of Arabian music, His soprano sound virtually demands modality—and it becomes particularly clear at this point what modality actually is: the equivalent in jazz to the "modes" of Arabic music and the Indian ragas.

Without Coltrane's soprano work it is hard to conceive of the whole Asiatic movement in jazz—not only in the area of the soprano, but transcending to all other instruments. This is particularly true of those instruments which, since the sixties, have increasingly been incorporated into jazz or were imbued with a new approach: violin, flute, bagpipes, oboe, English horn, etc., etc. In fact, we must say that these instruments were incorporated into jazz or experienced changes in approach precisely because Coltrane's way of playing the soprano became the great example.

Still, Coltrane was not the first to play a modern type of jazz on the soprano sax. The first musician to do so was a European: the Danish sopranoist *Max Brüel,* a cool Norseman inspired by Lee Konitz. Unfortunately, he never found any attention outside Scandinavia.

The next sopranoist is an American, *Steve Lacy.* Steve has gone through an especially peculiar development: He moved from Dixieland directly to free jazz—bypassing the usual way-stations of bebop and cool jazz. Quite to the contrary, he did not discover bop until after he had been playing free jazz. In 1952, he played Dixieland with musicians like Max Kaminsky, Jimmy McPartland, and Rex Stewart; in 1956, he played with Cecil Taylor; and in 1960, with Thelonious Monk. He is one of the few horn players—and probably the only white among them—who fully understood and assimilated Monk.

The stations of Lacy's development—Kaminsky, Cecil Taylor, Monk—indicate his originality. He is the only well-known sopranoist in jazz who made the soprano his main instrument right from the start. Accordingly, he did not derive his way of playing from the clarinet, tenor, or alto sax. Lacy, who has been living in Europe since 1963, stands outside the three main currents in soprano playing— Sidney Bechet, John Coltrane, and Wayne Shorter. To the best of my knowledge, he was the first to produce sounds by blowing "in reverse": not by blowing into the instrument, but by sucking air "backwards" through the horn. Later, in free jazz, many others did this too.

Leonard Feather surmises that Coltrane first became interested in the soprano saxophone through Steve Lacy. This is suggested by the fact that before Lacy joined the Thelonious Monk Quartet, Coltrane had played with Monk. The club in which Monk then could be heard regularly was the "Five Spot" in New York, the meeting place of the in-group of jazz. It can be assumed with almost total certainty that Coltrane heard Lacy there.

"My Favorite Things," as we have said, became a hit. Soon, big bands and studio orchestras pounced on the soprano. The range of the saxophone section was extended. Some arrangers became specialists in incorporating soprano sound into this range: Oliver Nelson, Quincy Jones, Gil Evans, Gary McFarland, Thad Jones, others.

The soprano not only took up the legacy of the clarinet—in a certain sense it was also heir to the tenor saxophone. During the era of free jazz, many tenor men loved to "overblow" their instruments in a way reminiscent of the falsetto sound of blues and gospel vocalists—driving up into heights far beyond the normal range of the instrument. This tendency to play "high" has always been part of jazz. A hot way of playing is frequently achieved by playing "high"—in a way which prompted the German ethnomusicologist Alphons Dauer to suspect that the term "hot" actually was derived from the French *haut*—high. It is obvious that the overblown tenor saxophone is a very ecstatic, intensive instrumental sound on the one hand, but that it is musically rather limited on the other. The soprano offers the possibilities of the falsetto tenor in a simpler, and what is more, a musically correct manner. Thus, there is a group of soprano players who were initially specialists of falsetto tenor: *Pharaoh Sanders, Archie Shepp, Roscoe Mitchell, Joseph Jarman, Sam Rivers,* and Englishman *John Surman* (whose main instrument at first was the baritone, and who first used the soprano only as a "falsetto baritone"—until he made an increasingly decisive switch from baritone to soprano).

As a soprano player, Archie Shepp combines the old black saxophone tradition—of Coleman Hawkins, for one—with the Indian shenai sound in a particularly fascinating way. (Further discussion of the musicians whose main instruments are tenor, alto, or baritone, will be found in the chapters dealing with those instruments.)

Other important soprano saxophonists after Coltrane are *Oliver Nelson, Gary Bartz,* and *Cannonball Adderley* (all mainly alto men); *Dave Liebman, Steve Grossman, Roland Kirk* (who counts among his instruments the soprano-like manzello), *Jerome Richardson, Budd Johnson, Steve Marcus, Tom Scott, Captain Beefheart, Joe Farell, Sam Rivers,* the Englishman *Evan Parker*, and—most importantly—*Wayne Shorter.*

Steve Grossman and Dave Liebman played a "doubled Coltrane" in the Elvin Jones group of the early seventies, using the same style of playing in the same group. Tom Scott and Steve Marcus incorporate rock elements. Captain Beefheart, who will be discussed in the chapters on singers and rock combos, combines free jazz, rock, and folk blues in soprano eruptions which often seem amateurish but radiate a certain archetypical fascination, particularly because such sounds are scarce on the rock scene. Bartz and Rivers are influenced by Miles Davis. Richardson and Johnson (in whose playing the Sidney Bechet tradition can be felt) have become much in-demand soprano players in big bands and studio orchestras. Without compromise, Roscoe Mitchell, Joseph Jarman, and Anthony Braxton departed for the land of atonality—as did many European soprano players. Among these, Evan Parker deserves special mention because of his esoteric style. Jarman loves the typical dark "growl" which Sidney Bechet used in the low ranges to create "moody" blues and ballad improvisation.

Without Wayne Shorter, it would be difficult to talk about Grossman, Liebman, Marcus, Scott, Adderley, Bartz, and others.

At first, Shorter played tenor with Art Blakey, then he became the reed man for the Miles Davis of the sixties. "In a Silent Way" of 1969 was the first record on which he played soprano. Apparently, he and the producers thought this to be such a minor point that not even the personnel identifications on the record indicate his soprano contribution. But the jazz world immediately noticed and listened. "Bitches Brew," produced a year later, is unthinkable without Shorter's soprano sound. Shorter aestheticized Coltrane's legacy. Miles + Trane = Shorter, that is: Shorter combines Coltrane's meditativeness with Miles' lyricism. His soprano sound has, in a way, the expressiveness described in the beginning of the chapter on Miles Davis: loneliness, forlornness, "the sound floats like a cloud." As a soprano player—but not as a tenorist!—Shorter ranks among the truly great improvisers in jazz: The tone alone already implies the music and the complete musical personality of the improviser.

Shorter loves Brazilian music. One of his masterpieces is the transformation of "Dindi"—one of the earliest bossa compositions, dedicated by Antonio Carlos Jobim to the late Sylvia Telles, the first singer of bossa nova—into an exciting, hymnal free-jazz excursion, which yet retains in every note some of the Brazilian tenderness. Shorter's music is basically gentle, but at the same time gives the impression of immense intensity. Shorter says about his album "Odyssey of Iska": "I'm trying to get what you might call more of a sheer sound, instead of a hard and solid instrumentation."

The "sheer sound" in a gentle fashion: That is the source of the style and success of Wayne Shorter and of many other sopranoists influenced by him (who certainly will remain under his spell for a while).

The "sheer sound" seems to have been one of the reasons why Bechet found his way from the clarinet to the soprano saxophone.

The Alto Saxophone

The history of the alto saxophone differs from that of most other jazz instruments in that it only had its start in the Swing period. To the clarinet triumvirate "Jimmie Noone-Johnny Dodds-Sidney Bechet" of the twenties corresponds a trio of altos that set the pace for everything played on this instrument during the thirties: Johnny Hodges-Benny Carter-Willie Smith.

The Duke Ellington musician *Johnny Hodges,* who died in 1970, was a melodist of the rank of Armstrong or Hawkins. His warm, expressive vibrato and his way of melting notes in erotic glissandos made the Hodges sound one of the best-known instrumental signatures in jazz. Dark, tropical, and warm fulfillment seems to lie in this sound, which may occasionally approach sentimentality on slow pieces.

At faster tempi, Hodges remained the great, gripping improviser he had been since joining Duke Ellington's band in 1928. In 1951 he left the band; a few years later he returned. In the interval, and also during the sixties, he made a series of jump-oriented combo recordings.

Among the many Hodges disciples, *Woody Herman* is the most important. Even today Herman blows Hodges-inspired solos which stand in pronounced and sometimes amusing contrast to the more modern conceptions of the young musicians in his big band.

Benny Carter is Hodges' opposite. Where the latter loves melancholy and earthiness, Benny Carter has a buoyant clarity and airiness. During the forties Carter settled in Hollywood, where he composed and arranged for film and TV studios, becoming a kind of "Rock of Gibraltar" to the younger West Coast musicians. Carter is one of the most universal musicians in jazz, of equal importance as alto saxist, arranger, and orchestra leader, and also a notable trumpeter, trombonist, and clarinetist. We shall have more to say about Carter in the chapter on big bands.

Willie Smith, lastly, who died in 1967, was the Johnny Dodds of the altoists, his wild, unrestrained immediacy often breaking the limits of form and harmony in order to attain an expressive peak. Perhaps exposure to this peak is what caused the fire in Willie Smith to burn out rather quickly. In the thirties, Smith was a soloist in Jimmie Lunceford's band; his solo in Lunceford's "Blues in the Night" was highly acclaimed.

The maturity of the Hodges-Carter-Smith constellation seems all the more astonishing when one considers what preceded it. There was *Don Redman,* who as an arranger had a very powerful impact on the development of the big-band sound of the twenties and early thirties, and who played occasional alto solos with his bands; and then there was *Frankie Trumbauer* among the Chicago-style musicians, who recorded with Bix Beiderbecke. Trumbauer did not play the E-flat alto, but its relative, the C-melody saxophone.

After the Hodges-Carter-Smith constellation the whole development of the alto saxophone is concentrated in one towering personality: *Charlie Parker.* In the chapter dedicated to him and Dizzy Gillespie, we have attempted to clarify his singular position. Parker's importance was initially so great that there was hardly another bop altoist worth mentioning. The sole exception was *Sonny Stitt,* who vacillated between alto and tenor, and who—strangely enough—independently of Parker developed a Bird-like alto style of great clarity and expressiveness.

Only in the realm of Jump could be found a few altoists who more or less were free from the Parker influence. *Earl Bostic* and Pete Brown should be mentioned. Bostic, with his "Flamingo," "Temptation," and other recordings, scored big rock 'n' roll hits in the late forties and the early fifties. And *Pete Brown* found a way of playing in which the contrast between old-fashioned staccato and modern conception is unintentionally—and sometimes intentionally—humorous.

While all the other instruments during the great days of bop produced important musicians in addition to the leading representative on the respective horn, the alto saxophone had to wait for the start of the cool era for a considerable figure to emerge. This was *Lee Konitz.* Connected with the Lennie Tristano school, he is to this day its outstanding representative. The abstract, glittering alto lines played by Konitz around the turn of the forties on his own and Lennie Tristano's recordings later became more singable, calmer, and more con-

218   THE NEW JAZZ BOOK

crete. Of this change, Lee says that then "I played more than I could hear"; he feels better when "I really can hear what I'm playing." Since the late sixties, Konitz has occasionally electronicized his alto sound, thereby losing the immensely pure, personal sound that was his mark. Critic Larry Kart found that now his improvisations are often "more a meditation on the fact of improvisation than the thing itself," while Konitz—in contrast to the music that made him famous—sounds "deliberately anti-lyrical." The fact that Lee Konitz —uncompromising in his musical ideals as he may be—so rarely finds employment in American clubs seems incomprehensible to every European observer.

After Charlie Parker and Lee Konitz, the development of the alto saxophone takes place in the interplay between them. *Art Pepper* began more on the Konitz side. In the mid-fifties, after a prolonged period of silence, he found his way toward a mature, Parker-influenced style in which the blues had found a place. It is regrettable that this outstanding musician has so frequently been hindered in his career by personal problems connected with drugs.

Paul Desmond became the most successful figure of the Konitz line as altoist in the Dave Brubeck Quartet—and until the late sixties, when Gerry Mulligan joined Brubeck, surely the most significant jazz talent in this well-known group. Desmond's tone is a bit thin, but he has a bold, winning way of phrasing and a distinctive, imaginative, and lyrical cast of line.

The most significant altoists of West Coast jazz are Bud Shank, *Lennie Niehaus,* Herb Geller, and Paul Horn. Niehaus' racy, swingingly honed improvisations have the cold glitter of crystal. *Bud Shank* favored short, exciting phrases in which at that time one could discern a premonition of the coming tendency toward the dissolution of the phrase; *Herb Geller,* who moved to Germany, is a Benny Carter of modern jazz—or, if you will, a Carter who knows that Parker came between. *Charlie Mariano* played with Kenton and was affiliated with the Berklee Jazz School in Boston. He is a musician who during the sixties and seventies has combined Parker's message with the meditativeness and modality of the great Asian musical cultures.

The power of Parker's personality gains full clarity when it is realized that the 'Bird-influence'—after the ideas originating with Konitz had been digested—did not recede during the late fifties, but rather increased steadily: *Lou Donaldson* with his strong blues emotions;

Leo Wright, who used to play with the Dizzy Gillespie Quintet and now resides in Germany; *Cannonball Adderley,* who became highly successful with the soul and funk-inspired music of his quintet; *Jackie McLean,* who joins Parker's blues feeling with a 'freer,' less restrained expressiveness; *Gigi Gryce,* the arranger; *Sonny Criss,* who combines the archetypical world of the old blues tradition with that of Charlie Parker; *Charles McPherson,* who stems from the Detroit hard-bop circle; *Hank Crawford,* who emerged from the Ray Charles Orchestra, and who has a particularly strong ballad and blues expressivity; *Oliver Nelson,* who made his name especially as an arranger; and, finally, *Frank Strozier* and *James Spaulding,* who both mark the transition to free jazz—all of them have, in the final analysis, their roots in Charlie Parker. This is true about *Phil Woods* too: No other altoist transformed the Charlie Parker heritage so consistently into contemporary jazz. Swiss critic Peter Rüedi called him (in 1972) "the most complete alto player in today's jazz." It is significant to note that this completeness is shaped by the awareness of all the way stations Woods passed through in 25 years: Lennie Tristano's institution, Jimmy Raney's cool jazz, George Wallington's bop, Dizzy Gillespie's and Quincy Jones' big bands. . . .

While Bird's way of playing still dominated the scene, *Ornette Coleman* appeared at the Lenox Jazz School, which was under John Lewis' direction, in the summer of 1959. In the chapter devoted to him, the musical revolution this towering musician instigated is discussed in detail. The fact that he—as is true of all genuine innovators—did exactly what was 'in the air,' is significantly illustrated by the fact that other musicians were taking similar roads at about the same time, or just after him, without being directly influenced by him. Among the alto saxophonists in this group, we should particularly mention the immensely influential *Eric Dolphy.* Dolphy came out of Chico Hamilton's and Charles Mingus' groups and made recordings of lasting value with the late trumpeter Booker Little and with his own groups. With his emotionally charged intonation and the wild, free flight of his ideas, he created effects on a par with those of Ornette Coleman.

Beyond these musicians are the actual free-jazz altoists who seem to have left the realm of conventional music. Among them should be mentioned *Byron Allen; Marshall Allen; Giuseppe Logan* (who likes to play the Pakistani zoukra with its oboe-like sound); *Sonny Sim-*

mons; Marion Brown (who combines the virtuosity and clarity of a man like Benny Carter with the possibilities of free jazz); *John Handy,* who was first introduced by Charles Mingus (and who lives in San Francisco, where he occasionally played in marvelous empathy with the famous Indian sarod player Ali Ahkbar Kan, in probably the most beautiful combination of jazz and Indian music up to this point); *John Tchicai,* a black musician born in Denmark; as well as *Anthony Braxton, Roscoe Mitchell,* and *Joseph Jarman,* who are associated with the avant-garde circle of Chicago musicians. Some of them—especially the three first named—incorporate noise effects in their playing in such a radical manner that the alto sonority often is no longer recognizable. Anthony Braxton, also an outstanding soprano player, preserved Charlie Parker's—and Lee Konitz's—legacy in even his freest excursions, with a clear affinity and love for the contemporary European jazz scene.

In any event—and this state of affairs probably will not be overcome for a long time—even 30 years after he entered the scene and began to change jazz music, the alto sax cannot be played without a Charlie Parker consciousness. Indeed, there are only few exceptions to this rule: The more exact a musician's Parker-knowledge is, the better an altoist he is.

Among the alto players of the younger generation who have led the music back into more tonal realms—without forgetting the process of liberation of the sixties—and who join Parker, blues, and free jazz into the new jazz of the seventies, are: *Gary Bartz, Eric Kloss,* and John Handy, whom we mentioned above. British musician *Elton Dean* (who also plays the small "saxello," and is associated with the group Soft Machine), *Fred Lipsius* (who gained fame with Blood, Sweat & Tears), and *Ian Underwood* (who worked with Frank Zappa) incorporate rock elements, the latter two without actually being convincing soloists in the jazz sense. It can be said that, in general, the great stylistic synthesis of the seventies—as convincingly created by contemporary pianists, guitarists, drummers, and soprano and tenor saxophonists—has remained peculiarly pale among the altoists. There are two exceptions to that dictum—and they are not musicians of the younger generation, but quite to the contrary, "old beboppers," as they call themselves in amusing understatement—Phil Woods and Charlie Mariano.

The Tenor Saxophone

The evolution of the tenor saxophone is the reverse of that of the clarinet. While the latter begins with a wealth of brilliant names and then seems to ebb off into a decrescendo—albeit a wavy one—the history of the tenor sax is one imposing crescendo. At the beginning stands a single man. Today there are so many tenor saxists that it sometimes becomes difficult even for the expert to survey the subtleties which distinguish them. We have said before: from Lester Young to John Coltrane, the sound of modern jazz was "tenorized."

The single figure at the beginning is *Coleman Hawkins*. Until the end of the thirties, all jazz tenor playing took its cues from him: from his dramatic melodic structures, his voluminous sonority, and his rhapsodic improvisations. A Hawkins pupil then was quite simply anyone who played tenor. The most important are Chu Berry, Arnette Cobb, Hershel Evans, Ike Quebec, Ben Webster, Al Sears, Illinois Jaquet, Buddy Tate, Don Byas, Lucky Thompson, Frank Wess, Eddie "Lockjaw" Davis, Georgie Auld, Flip Phillips, Charlie Ventura, and Benny Golson. *Chu Berry* came closest to the master. During the second half of the thirties—while Hawkins was in Europe—he was a much-sought-after musician; the man who first came to mind when a tenor was needed. His solo on "Ghost of a Chance," recorded with Cab Calloway's band, became famous. *Arnette Cobb* was a member of the Lionel Hampton band in the early forties. His playing can best be characterized by the way he was advertised after quitting Hampton: "The Wildest Tenorman in the World." *Hershel Evans* was Lester Young's opposite in the Count Basie Band. Though Lester was the greater musician, Evans played the most renowned tenor solo in the old Basie band: "Blue and Sentimental."

"Why don't you play alto, man?" Evans used to tease Lester. "You got an alto sound." And Lester would tap his forehead: "There are things going on up there, man. Some of you guys are all belly." Basie found the contrast between the styles of Lester and Hershel so effective that he saw to a similar contrast in all his bands from then on. In his fifties band, for instance, these roles were taken by the "two Franks": *Frank Foster* representing the "modern" trend, *Frank Wess* the Hawkins school. Later, *Eddie "Lockjaw" Davis* took

Wess's place. Davis is a typical "Harlem" tenor, with hard, striking presence.

Before Hershel Evans, there was a tenor man in Count Basie's first Kansas City band whose place he took: *Buddy Tate*. When Evans died in 1939, Buddy returned to Basie. Later he dropped into comparative obscurity, until the Mainstream wave of the fifties and sixties brought him renewed attention. For many years, he led his own band in Harlem, enriching the style of the classic Harlem big bands (as played in the old Savoy Ballroom) with modern rhythm-and-blues tendencies.

Lucky Thompson is a master of sweeping, tuneful melodic lines. He often worked with Charlie Parker, Dizzy Gillespie, and other modern jazz musicians, and his improvisations unite, in a very personal fashion, the best of bop and Swing. *Don Byas*, who died in 1972, became known primarily for his "sensuous" vibrato and ballad interpretations. He played with Basie, was one of the first Swing musicians to work with the then young bebop people, and made his home in Holland from the late forties on. Whenever American musicians went to Europe and played with Byas, they found it deplorable that this musician, especially impressive for the richness of his sound, had lived on the other side of the Atlantic for so long that in his homeland only professional critics seemed to remember him.

Ben Webster—who died in Europe in 1973—was two things: a musician with a throaty, harsh vibrato on fast pieces, and a master of erotic, intensely felt slow ballads. Of all the musicians of the Hawkins school, his has been the strongest influence—on many musicians of modern jazz as well. In the early forties, Webster was a member of the Ellington orchestra, with which he recorded one of his most famous solos—"Cottontail." *Al Sears* took Webster's chair with Ellington in 1943. His stylistic bent is indicated by a rhythm-and-blues piece, "Castle Rock," he wrote for Johnny Hodges, which became a hit. Later *Paul Gonsalves* (who died in 1974) became Ellington's featured tenor in the Webster tradition. Gonsalves' marathon tenor displays very often stole the show at Ellington concerts: fast, torrid runs in flowing motion, almost free from repeated notes and honks, yet more exciting— and in addition musically more logical—than many solos played by tenor men whose honking ecstasy is outside the realm of music. Ellington took care to always have a musician who could take the spot of the great and, in the final analysis, unreachable

Ben Webster. In more recent times, *Harold Ashby* has been among these.

A stylistic phenomenon on the order of Ruby Braff—but without the latter's coolness toward modernism—is *Benny Golson:* a tenorist and arranger who emerged from the Dizzy Gillespie band of the mid-fifties and played with all the young modern musicians. Nonetheless, he is cast in the mold of the rich, mature ballad style of Thompson-Byas-Webster-Hawkins. "Out of the Past" is the title of one of Golson's most beautiful pieces—and out of the past, full of sadness and long-lost magic, are his tenor improvisations and otherwise highly modern arrangements.

Ike Quebec—to return to the great period of Hawkins' influence —first attracted attention with his playing in Cab Calloway's band, and was noted for intense solos played with a firm, strong Hawkins sound. *Illinois Jacquet,* finally, is perhaps the "hottest," most exciting musician of the Hawkins school. Long before the modern free-jazz tenorists, he was able to extend the range of his instrument into the extreme heights of steam whistle-like sounds. Jacquet came from Lionel Hampton's band, where he played his famous solo on "Flyin' Home." He is also renowned for his triumphs with the early tours of Norman Granz's "Jazz at the Philharmonic." Jacquet says: "Granz owes the world-wide success of JATP to me!"

Georgie Auld, Flip Phillips and Charlie Ventura are the leading white tenor men of the Hawkins school—the first two via Ben Webster. Auld, an experienced studio musician, came to the fore first with Bunny Berigan, then Benny Goodman, and later with his own groups. A substantial craftsman, he played more *à la* Pres with a medium-sized group at the height of the bop era; later, he made Jimmie Lunceford-inspired big-band recordings with more of a Hawkins orientation. For years, *Flip Phillips* was used as an effective crowd-pleaser with the "Jazz at the Philharmonic" troupe. But in Woody Herman's band in the mid-forties, and later also on records and in concerts, Phillips has played excellently structured ballads with a polished and "reduced" Hawkins sound. *Charlie Ventura,* lastly, became known with Gene Krupa and later through the medium-sized groups he led on and off from 1947 into the fifties. During the bop era he performed under the banner of "Bop for the People" and contributed much to the popularization of bop.

Bud Freeman, the tenor voice of Chicago style, who touched Les-

ter Young in his earliest period, preceded Coleman Hawkins in impact. Bud is still active today. He has become the most compelling
Dixieland tenor—a state of affairs which did not prevent him from
studying with Lennie Tristano in the fifties. *Gene Sedric* might be
called a black counterpart of Freeman, known from his playing on
many Fats Waller records of the thirties.

With these musicians we have for the present exhausted the Hawkins chapter of tenor history. *Lester Young* became the great man of
the tenor in the forties, and particularly in the fifties, but then, tension
between Hawk and Pres has remained alive—to the degree that a renewed predominance of the Hawkins tradition could be detected
among the tenorists of the Sonny Rollins school in the late fifties.

What fascinates tenor players about Hawkins is first of all the big
strong, voluminous tone. What fascinates them about Lester Young
are his lyrical, sweeping lines. Simplified, the tension that underlies
the history of the tenor sax is the tension between Hawkins' sonority
and Lester's linearity. This tension is already present in some of the
tenor players who have been mentioned as representatives of the
Hawkins line—Thompson, Byas, Gonsalves, Auld, Phillips, and
Ventura. To these must be added a group of tenor men who stylistically speaking are firmly in the Lester camp, but show a noticeable
tendency toward the Hawkins sonority. *Gene Ammons* is the most
important. The son of boogie-woogie pianist Albert Ammons, he was
in the Woody Herman band of the late forties and moved into the
limelight through the "battles" (those popular contests between two
practitioners of the same horn) he fought with Sonny Stitt. He has
the biggest, mightiest tone outside the Hawkins school: "Big as a
house, a 15-story apartment dwelling, and very vocal, too," says Ira
Gitler, who goes on to compare his playing with the blues singing of
Dinah Washington. Ammons died in 1974.

Otherwise, the tenorists of the Lester Young school may be
grouped—in much simplified terms—in two sections: the musicians
who have linked Lester's ideas to the ideas of bop, and the school of
modern Lester Young classicism, in which the bop influence receded
in proportion to the youth of the musicians. The most important tenorists of the "Lester Young plus bop" direction are Wardell Gray
James Moody, Budd Johnson, and *Frank Foster,* as well as the forerunners of Sonny Rollins we shall mention later.

Sonny Stitt, who will be discussed then, was an important influence
on Frank Foster, at that time Frank Wess's protagonist in Count Bas-

ie's band. *James Moody* was one of the more remarkable musical personalities of the bop era. Later, he seemed to have lost his stylistic identity in a shuttle between tenor and alto, and between different approaches to playing—until, in 1960, Dizzy Gillespie hired him for his quintet (to replace Leo Wright), in which Moody found new popularity and a new format. *Budd Johnson* emerged from the most influential big bands of the bop era: Earl Hines, Boyd Raeburn, Billy Eckstine, Woody Herman, Dizzy Gillespie; probably the only musician to play in all these great bands. Under this influence, he repeatedly reoriented his approach to playing to contemporary trends. Born in 1910, he belongs to the handfull of musicians of his generation to deal with the musical movements of the seventies.

Wardell Gray, who died in 1955 under mysterious circumstances (his body was found in the desert near Las Vegas), was a musician of supreme importance. He had Lester's linearity, the phrasing of bop, and his own distinctive hardness of attack and sparkling mobility, all joined in convincing stylistic unity. It is fitting that such genuine Swing musicians as Benny Goodman and Count Basie were attracted by Gray, but became aware of stylistic conflict when he began to play in their combos or bands. "The Chase," that characteristically titled tenor battle recorded in 1947 by Gray and Dexter Gordon (who is from a different branch), still ranks among the most exciting musical contests in the history of jazz.

Gray occupies a central position between the two tenor movements of the fiftes: the "Brothers," and the Charlie Parker school led by Sonny Rollins. In the former, Lester Young celebrated his real triumphs. The abundance of names belonging to this Lester Young classicism will be classified according to the manner in which the Basie-Young tendency has made itself increasingly felt: At the beginning of our list the bop influence is noticeable—Allen Eager, Stan Getz, Herbie Steward, Zoot Sims, Al Cohn, Bob Cooper, Buddy Collette, Dave Pell, Don Menza, Jack Montrose, Richie Kamuca, Jimmy Giuffre, and Bill Perkins. A remarkably large segment of these musicians either have worked with Woody Herman or are more or less connected with the California jazz scene. That is where the "Four Brothers sound" developed in 1947. "We had a band," *Stan Getz* tells, "in the Spanish section of Los Angeles. A trumpeter named Tony de Carlo was the leader, and we had just his trumpet, four tenors and rhythm. We had a few arrangements by Gene Roland and Jimmy Giuffre." Roland and Giuffre, in other words, created the "Four

Brothers sound." The four tenors in this band were Getz, Herbie Steward, Zoot Sims, and Jimmy Giuffre.

At the time, Woody Herman was about to form a new band. He happened to hear the four tenors and was so taken with the sound that he hired three of them: Sims, Steward, and Getz. In place of the fourth tenor he put Serge Chaloff's baritone, to add warmth to the tenor combination. The new sound was made famous by a piece written for Herman in 1947 by Jimmy Giuffre. It was called "Four Brothers"—whence the name of the sound. Along with the Miles Davis Capitol sound it became the most influential ensemble sound in modern jazz. Its warmth and suppleness symbolized the sound-ideal of cool jazz.

In the years to follow, a succession of tenorists passed through the Four Brothers sax sections of various Herman bands. The first was Al Cohn, who took Steward's place as early as 1948. Then came Gene Ammons, Giuffre, and many others, down to Bill Perkins and Richie Kamuca. Getz, who from the start counted as the *primus inter pares* among the "Brothers," made some combo recordings (for Prestige) in 1949 with Sims, Cohn, Allen Eager, and Brew Moore in which the Four Brothers sound was celebrated by five tenorists.

The following passage by Ira Gitler—a critic with particular affinity for the modern tenor scene—will give an impression of the fine distinctions among these tenor players: "An excellent example of inner differences in a similar area can be found in examining the work of Zoot Sims and Al Cohn and comparing it to the playing of Bill Perkins and Richie Kamuca. In the broad sense, all would be considered modernists in the Basie-Young tradition, but Sims and Cohn, who were originally inspired by Lester Young, grew up musically in the forties when Charlie Parker was at his peak and his influence at its most powerful. Although they do not play like Parker, they have been affected somewhat stylistically and very much harmonically.

"Kamuca and Perkins (active from the fifties) who for inspiration go back to the Pres of the Basie period and also to the Brothers (Sims, Cohn, Getz) are only touched by Bird through osmosis from the Brothers, and since it is twice removed, the traces are intangible."

The Parker traces are strongest in *Allen Eager* and—at least before his bossa nova period of the sixties—in Stan Getz. Eager was the first of the modern Lester Young perfectionists—in the splendid, stimulating solos he played with the Buddy Rich big band around 1945, such as "Daily Double" or "Nellie's Nightmare," on the long-defunct U. S. Army "V-Discs." Getz is the towering figure in this school, an improviser in the sense of truly great jazz improvising and altogether one of the outstanding white jazz musicians. He is a virtuoso who can play anything possible on the tenor sax. It is this technical element that distinguishes him from most of his Brothers-colleagues—primarily from the conscious simplicity of Al Cohn, Zoot Sims, Bill Perkins, Richie Kamuca, etc. Stan became known mainly through his ballad interpretations. Nonetheless, during the fifties, he had a Parker-inspired affinity for very fast tempos. Perhaps the best recordings of his career were made in 1953 at the Storyville Club in Boston with guitarist Jimmy Raney, and at a 1954 concert at the Shrine auditorium in Los Angeles with trombonist Bob Brookmeyer. It is characteristic of a musician like Getz that he seems to unfold more freely in contact with a night-club or concert audience than in the cold studio atmosphere.

After spending the late fifties with his Swedish wife in self-imposed exile in Denmark, depressed by various personal problems, he returned to New York in 1961—about the moment when bossa nova with its poetic, charming songs began to sweep the U. S. Getz was introduced to the bossa nova by guitarist Charlie Byrd, just returned from Brazil.

It has been said so many times that Getz was "inspired" by the bossa nova and that he "owes everything" to it, that it is necessary to point out that earlier there had been a reverse influence: from cool jazz (where Getz has his roots) to the Brazilian samba. Only from the interaction between cool jazz and samba did the bossa nova emerge. Thus, a circle was closed when Getz "borrowed back" (as he himself expressed it) Brazilian elements. This may be one of the main reasons for the fascination of his "Brazilianized," melodic cool-jazz transformations, although many creative Brazilian musicians called these recordings "falsifications" or "bastardizations." It is interesting to remember that the characteristic switch from the chorale-like *cantilena* to intensely rhythmic passages, so typical of Brazilian music, also existed in a different form in Getz's cool improvisations from the early fifties on—long before the emergence of bossa nova.

Since the mid-sixties, after the bossa nova wave died down, Getz has been combining his classicist Lester Young legacy with some harder, more expressive ingredients, originating mainly in Sonny Rollins. The expressive range of this great jazz musician has, in this way, become even more universal and towering.

Zoot Sims is considered "the most swinging of the Brothers." *Al Cohn* is the most expressive representative of this school. Sims is an untrammeled, vital improviser with a certain knack for emphasizing the upper ranges of his instrument, leading to his tenor an occasional alto sound; characteristically, he has experimented with the alto, too. Cohn mirrored the *conscious* turn toward Basie-Young classicism— not only in his playing but also as arranger and leader on countless recordings. One of his ensembles, modeled after Basie's Kansas City combos of the thirties, was called "The Natural Seven" because jazz in this format and instrumentation appears to Cohn the most natural and self-evident music imaginable. The little twists and turns he gives to his smooth Lester Young tone make his playing especially expressive: "Nobody can moan like Al Cohn," as someone once said. For several years Cohn and Sims co-led a two-tenor quintet which— within the confines of their similarity—gained attractiveness from their subtle dissimilarity.

Most of the remaining musicians on our list of Lester Young classicists are representives of West Coast jazz. *Bill Perkins* plays perfect, beautifully felt Lester phrases one is tempted to call "noble." *Jimmy Giuffre's* tenor playing has something of the quality of his clarinet—a great affinity for cool, "distilled" blue notes, transplanted into the jazz conception: a specifically "white" avant-gardism based on Young classicism, on modern "classic" concert music, and on a conscious preference for folk melodies. *Buddy Collette* is one of the few black musicians in the Hollywood studios. While the alto playing of this remarkable multi-instrumentalist veers toward Parker, his conception on other horns is more in line with the polished Young-Basie classicism of the West Coast. *Don Menza,* who for years lived in Germany, is among those who carried the "Four Brothers sound" into the vicinity of John Coltrane.

Eddie Harris illustrates how variedly fascinating the "Four Brothers" playing style is. In Chicago during the sixties—when the cool jazz era had long given way to a greater 'heat' in playing—he played the thin, cool, cultivated sound of the "Brothers." In the meantime, he electrified this sound and joined it with John Coltrane's phrasing—all in a very superficial manner oriented to the fashion of the day. But it has brought Harris great success.

Several musicians will not fit into either of the categories into which we have attempted to divide the Lester Young tenors. Among them are *Paul Quinichette,* Brew Moore, and Warne Marsh. Quinichette, who came out of Count Basie's band, was mentioned as a fascinating "mirror-image" of Pres in the chapter on Hawkins and Young. *Brew Moore,* too, belongs in Lester's immediate vicinity—without the detour via modern classicism. *Warne Marsh* is a product of the Tristano school, and plays "tenorized" Lee Konitz.

So far, it might seem as if the contest between the ideas of Hawkins and Young in the evolution of the tenor sax had ended with complete victory for Young. This picture became blurred in the course of *Sonny Rollins'* overwhelming influence during the second half of the fifties. The only significant innovations in the realm of improvisation during the year 1957, for example, were the records made by Sonny Rollins. Rollins the improviser became so important one tended to mention him right after Miles Davis. Nonetheless, neither Sonny himself nor his way of playing are "new" in the strictest meaning of the word. From 1946, he played with many important bop musicians: Art Blakey, Tadd Dameron, Bud Powell, Miles Davis, Fats Navarro, Thelonious Monk, and others. His style involves combining Charlie Parker lines with the voluminous sound of Coleman Hawkins—which Sonny developed into his very own, angular, edged, immensely individual sound—plus that slight Lester Young influence which no tenor player since Pres can completely escape.

This combination, which appeared so novel in the second half of the fifties, was *comme il faut* during the bop years. Not only Sonny Rollins played that way then. *Sonny Stitt,* and most of all *Dexter Gordon* are musicians of this lineage, related in many respects to the previously mentioned "Lester-plus-bop" line (James Moody, for instance). Gordon was *the* bop tenor man, with all the quicksilver nervousness belonging to bop, while Stitt primarily transferred the personal expressiveness of Charlie Parker to the tenor. In 1944, in a recording of Billy Eckstine's big band ("Blowing the Blues Away"), Gordon and Gene Ammons founded the musical practice of "battles" and "chases" of which we have spoken already in this chapter. In 1961, Dexter Gordon had a great comeback with his Blue Note record "Go." For some time now, he has been living in Denmark, and today plays with even greater maturity and mastery than in the early years of his career.

That Sonny Rollins nevertheless so suddenly achieved primary importance is due less to his innovations than to the temperament and vitality he brings to his improvisations—in short, to his stature. Thus, he can afford to treat the harmonic structures on which he improvises with an astonishing lack of constraint and great freedom, and indicate melody lines often only with widely spaced staccato notes, satirizing and ironicizing them in this manner. It is a freedom similar to that of Thelonious Monk's piano improvisations—and here again, it becomes clear that the innovations for which Monk laid the groundwork in the early forties were not really understood until the late fifties. Both Monk and Rollins are New Yorkers, and there's that typically quick and dry New York sense of humor in their music. "Sonny Rollins fears nothing," said the French tenorist *Barney Wilen* at a time when he was one of the many young musicians of the Rollins school. Others of this line are Hank Mobley, J. R. Monterose, Johnny Griffin, Yusef Lateef, Billy Mitchell, Charlie Rouse, Stanley Turrentine, Booker Ervin, Teddy Edwards, Roland Kirk, Clifford Jordan, Bobby Jones, et al. Even West Coast tenorist-arranger Jack Montrose—wholly a man of modern Young classicism during the fifties—leaned toward the Rollins school in the beginning of the sixties.

At the turn of the fifties, it became apparent that a sudden unrest was shaking the Young-inspired stasis in the tenor situation. Many tenor players seemed to be "overhauling" their styles, losing their identity in the process without immediately finding a new one.

Hank Mobley has a velvety tone which hangs like a veil over his long, seemingly self-perpetuating lines. *J. R. Monterose* has shown an interest in experimental jazz forms and consequently collaborated with Charlie Mingus and Teddy Charles. *Stanley Turrentine* applies a "modern" approach to the melodious lines of Ben Webster and Coleman Hawkins. The late *Booker Ervin*—who first became known through his association with Mingus—was one of the most solid improvisers of the early and mid-sixties with a marvelous wealth of blues-inspired ideas and vehement swing. In the liner notes to one of his records, *Johnny Griffin* is called a "symbol of the energy of jazz." With his melodic, humorous improvisations he has enthused many an audience.

Yusef Lateef stems from the Detroit circle of modern bop musicians. He has incorporated elements from the Arab and oriental musics into jazz—making inspiring, exciting recordings, on which he (aside from tenor) blows such instruments as diverse flutes of often exotic origin, and oboe and bassoon (used only rarely in jazz). *Harold Land*, who first became known through his work in the Max Roach-Clifford Brown Quintet that initiated (or, at least helped initiate) the transition from West Coast jazz to hard bop in California in the mid-fifties, still is one of the most dynamic and fresh improvisers of California jazz. *Pat LaBarbera* was for years—aside from the leader—the outstanding soloist of the Buddy Rich big band. He also has an intense interest in today's rock sounds. *Bobby Jones*, discovered by Charles Mingus in the late sixties, proves how inexhaustible the store of outstanding tenorists of this line still is. Most of these musicians have been active for a relatively long time span—from the early fifties until today—proving that they are playing a kind of music that is, in the best sense of the work, "timeless," independent of passing fashions.

And then, there is *Roland Kirk*: a blind musician who came to Chicago from Columbus, Ohio, in 1960, with three saxophones hanging around his neck, sometimes playing them all simultaneously—and, on top of that, a flute and about a dozen other instruments—blowing on a siren between choruses.

The question that was raised at the time—if Roland was just a circus musician or musical clown having fun with his pile of instruments—is no longer discussed. With his expressive energy and musicality, Kirk has blown away all doubts. He is one of the most vital, most communicative of today's jazz musicians; at the same time, he is like the folk musicians who packed up their bundle and wandered through the world. He is, therefore, a symbol for many things that have occurred in jazz during these years: sophistication rising from roots, naïveté from a genuine child-like attitude, sensitivity from vitality. Kirk says: "People talk about freedom, but the blues is still one of the freest things you can play."

Kirk plays out of the black tradition, and he has deliberately elevated this tradition into a program, not in the sense of historicizing backward looks, but quite to the contrary by incorporating it into the sounds of the seventies. Often, he has played with pop and rock groups: "I just want to play. I'd like to think I could work opposite Sinatra, B. B. King, the Beatles, or a polka band, and that people would dig it." Roland Kirk has referred to so many of the great black musicians—Duke Ellington, Charles Mingus, Sidney Bechet, Fats Waller, Don Byas, John Coltrane, Clifford Brown, Lester

Young, Bud Powell, Billie Holiday etc., etc.—that it may be said with special emphasis: Kirk plays "on" the black tradition as if it were an instrument. He says: "God loves black sound."

A distinction of many of these tenorists—certainly first and foremost of Sonny Rollins—is their relationship to rhythm. They play beyond the rhythm with the same free sweep that characterizes their approach to harmony; but since on the one hand they move far away from the basic beat while on the other never losing contact with it, they develop an intense, exciting rhythmic tension in which the real stimulation of their playing resides. In this respect, too, Rollins continues Charlie Parker's heritage. "Charlie Parker's Successors Play Tenor" said the headline in a French jazz magazine as the Rollins influence reached its peak in the late fifties.

At this peak the Rollins influence changed over into the perhaps even more engulfing *John Coltrane* influence. Coltrane, too (see the chapter devoted to him and Ornette Coleman), had originally begun under Rollins' sign. When he stepped into the limelight in the mid-fifties in the Miles Davis Quintet, some critics referred to him as a "student of Sonny Rollins." But soon, the student turned into the teacher and master of nearly all tenorists of the sixties and seventies.

These 'students' can be classified in three groups: those within the boundaries of tonality, those outside these limits (with all the different intermediate shades that must expressly be called to mind in such a generalizing classification), and those who have created the "great snythesis."

Part of the first group are *Joe Henderson, George Coleman, Sam Rivers, Joe Farrell, Billy Harper*—and for some years, *Charles Lloyd,* who in the meantime has become less significant. Coleman and Rivers became well known through "star-maker" Miles Davis—in the Miles Davis groups of the sixties. Rivers—who also likes to play completely "atonally"—was connected with Cecil Taylor, too. Farrell couples the power and vitality of a more conservative tenor style with contemporary sensitivity in a very personal way. It is characteristic of Farrell that so "romantic" a pianist as Chick Corea has repeatedly used him for recordings. Joe Henderson is a true outsider. He has led the great bop tradition—that of Wardell Gray and Dexter Gordon, for instance—into today's jazz.

Archie Shepp, Pharaoh Sanders, Albert Ayler, John Gilmore, and *Dewey Redman* stem from the camp of the initially wholly atonal New York avant-garde free jazz. Shepp, who also teaches college, plays his tenor lines, full of emotion and political engagement, from a masterful knowledge of the jazz and blues tradition, and with a sound reminiscent of Ben Webster. One of his pieces is devoted to the late blues-harmonica player Sonny Boy Williamson, another is entitled "Malcolm, Malcolm—Semper Malcolm." "I believe in his immortality," says Shepp about the great murdered black leader. And then: "My sax is a sex symbol." And here, too, Shepp is referring to black tradition. From the beginning, the tenor sax indeed had sexual implications in popular black music—not unlike the guitar in rock music. Of course, the wild, atonal exuberance of Shepp's beginning has subsided. His record "Attica Blues," released in 1972, proves that. It is timeless black music that reaches from folk blues through Charlie Parker to the freedom of the sixties, a "black classic."

Albert Ayler, who often appeared with his trumpet playing brother, Don Ayler, also showed an involvement beyond the realm of music (as almost all contemporary musicians have). Ayler's involvement was less political than religious, philosophical. "We play peace," was his motto. In the freedom of his tenor breaks, Ayler referred back to tradition in an especially peculiar, folk music-like manner: march and circus music of the turn of the century, folk dances, waltzes and polkas, or the 'dirges'—the music of the old New Orleans funeral processions. Ayler, who died in 1971 at the age of 34 (his body was found in New York's East River after he had been missing for 20 days), was "in many ways closer to [the old sound] of Bubber Miley and Tricky Sam Nanton than to Parker, Miles, or Rollins. He brought back to jazz the wild, primitive feeling which deserted it in the late thirties. . . . His technique knew no boundaries, his range from the lowest honks to the most shrill high harmonies being unparalleled." (Richard Williams)

Pharoah Sanders, finally, is the tenor man bursting with musicianly and physical power whom John Coltrane engaged in 1966 as the second horn player of his group, in order to grow through his challenge. As others among the newer tenorists, he extends the range of the tenor sax, by means of "overblowing," into the highest registers of the soprano. It is regretful that Sanders within a few years stereotyped and banalized a way of playing that had initially given rise to the highest hopes.

Around the turn of the decade from the sixties to the seventies, *Dewey Redman* finally became the congenial musical partner whom

Ornette Coleman had been seeking for so long. *Arthur Doyle* and *Frank Lowe* are among the young musicians who cultivate and develop the tradition. Lowe has played with Alice Coltrane; both have worked with drummer Milford Graves. Lowe: "What Milford is saying is that the saxophone is a drum itself, and that's why I'm affiliated with a lot of percussionists. . . ." Lowe began his career with Stax Records in Memphis, Tennessee, at a time when soul star Otis Redding had his biggest successes. But he also played in Sun Ra's "Solar Arkestra": That illuminates the extent of his musical range—and the range of many free-jazz musicians, who all (as before them Ornette Coleman and John Coltrane) got their start with rhythm and blues, and have preserved and are developing its power and expressiveness.

As with other instruments, the free way of playing struck especially fertile soil among Europe's tenorists, and has been developed along lines that will be made clearer in our final chapter. There is a host of European tenorists with a style totally their own, not comparable to any American musician. Dutchman *Willem Breuker* utilizes the European musical tradition—not coincidentally, also the tradition of Dutch and Low German folk music—in a way that corresponds to Roland Kirk's utilization of the black tradition. German tenorist *Peter Brötzmann,* who also plays other saxophones, has an unconditional drive for energy usually found only among black musicians. Brötzmann nevertheless realizes this drive in totally European—in fact, actually German—manner. British critic Richard Williams and other international observers felt Brötzmann's way of playing to be "teutonic." Clusters—"all notes at the same time"—are popular in the entire realm of free playing, but nobody plays clusters as radically as Brötzmann. Norwegian *Jan Gabarek* "spiritualizes" rock phrases in terms of free jazz, perceptibly stimulated by study of George Russell's Lydian system. Briton *Evan Parker,* mentioned in the soprano chapter, has abstracted the energy and freedom of this style in a way approaching modern concert music.

Among the tenorists who created "the great synthesis" of the seventies are *Wayne Shorter, Benny Maupin,* the Argentinian *Gato Barbieri, John Klemmer, Tom Scott,* and recently, also Archie Shepp. Shorter and Maupin were affiliated with Miles Davis. Also as a tenor man, Maupin fits into the picture we sketched of him as bass clarinetist. Shorter is a hymnic improviser of great melodic power and with great ability to give form to his music. Barbieri, who initially became known during the mid-sixties through his work with Don Cherry in Paris, calls his music "third-world jazz." However, it is less the whole third world than the Latin American world—and here, in turn, the Brazilian samba, the charming bossa nova of Rio, and the percussive sounds of Bahia—which he combines in a most impressive way with Coltrane's hymnic power *à la* "Love Supreme."

Almost all these tenor men are masters of long, raga-like modal improvisations, which require time to "get it together"—very much in the sense of Asian music—to reach their greatest intensity.

Aside from all these tendencies, there are many tenor players in popular black music who cultivate the great traditions of blues and Kansas City, Texas and Hawkins. The amazing thing is that these musicians, as "old" as their way of playing seems to be, find enthusiastic responses particularly among a young audience. This point is illustrated by the recognition *Trevor Lawrence* found so quickly. Singer Marvin Gaye loves to have Lawrence accompany him on the tenor in his self-assured songs about black dignity and the beauty obscured by the miseries of the ghetto.

Particularly secure in this tradition is *Grover Washington, Jr.*— realizing "black music today" as a tenor, alto and soprano player, not worrying about styles and schools. He does this not in terms of the contemporary utilization of a tradition, as Roland Kirk, but rather in the awareness that this tradition is anyhow so alive that it seems natural and doesn't need to be programmatically demanded (as with Archie Shepp).

It becomes ever more clear: this is the classical, and thus timeless, way to play the tenor. The best-known musician in this mold was *King Curtis,* who emerged from Lionel Hampton's band. King Curtis was murdered in New York in 1971. As leader of Aretha Franklin's back-up band, he had world-wide success. Coleman Hawkins, Buddy Tate, Illinois Jaquet, and mainly Gene Ammons (but also the great old folk-blues singers) figured in his music—a music that came from Texas, the state where Ornette Coleman was born. The fact that both Ornette's and King Curtis' music are typically "Texan" illuminates that tension between tradition and avant-garde—both of them rooted in old folklore—that we perceive as "contemporary."

The Baritone Saxophone

For decades, *Harry Carney* represented the baritone saxophone, more monopolistically than any other jazz musician represents any other instrument. In 1926 Duke Ellington received permission from the Carney family to keep 16-year-old Harry in the band, and since then Carney has been with Ellington. He is almost synonymous with the history and sound of the Ellington orchestra. He is a Coleman Hawkins of the baritone: of equal power and intensity of ideas. He plays his instrument with all the dark force and roughness it embodies. "No baritone player should be scared of the noise his horn can make. Carney isn't scared," says Pepper Adams, a baritonist of the generation which in the late fifties suddenly took up the Carney tradition again—as Sonny Rollins linked up with the Hawkins tradition among the tenors. Until the mid-forties, Carney ruled royally over the "baritone scene." Aside from him there was only *Ernie Caceres,* who managed to play Dixieland on the cumbersome horn, and *Jack Washington,* who provided a similar dark foundation for Basie's sax section as Carney gave his saxophone colleagues in the Ellington band—without, of course, Carney's soloistic brilliance.

Then came bop. And paradoxical as it might seem to play the nervous, mobile phrases of bop on the big baritone—suddenly there was a whole row of baritonists. *Serge Chaloff,* who came from a Russian Jewish family, was first. Critics have called him the Charlie Parker of the baritone, and, indeed, Chaloff applied all the new things played by Bird to the horn—as Buddy De Franco did on the clarinet and J. J. Johnson on the trombone. Chaloff is among the musicians who played big-band bop with Woody Herman's important 1947 band. Ten years later—when the original "Brothers" section was reconstructed for a record date—he had to be taken to the studio in a wheelchair. A few months later, he was dead of cancer.

The restless expressiveness of Charloff's baritone was smoothed out into cool sobriety by *Gerry Mulligan.* Mulligan began quite *à la* Chaloff in the combos of Kai Winding and Chubby Jackson toward the end of the forties. He worked in the big bands of Claude Thornhill and Elliot Lawrence, and was one of the important participants in the Miles Davis Capitol sessions—also as an arranger. From 1951 on, he became the increasingly influential baritone voice of Basie-Young classicism. Mulligan is of great importance as baritone saxophonist, arranger, band leader, but most of all as a catalytic personality. Few modern musicians are so firmly rooted in the "mainstream" of the Swing era. His "meetings" on record (Verve) with such Swing musicians as Harry Edison, Ben Webster, and Johnny Hodges are impressive proofs of this. The famous pianoless quartet which first made the name Mulligan popularly known in the early fifties, and will be discussed in our combo chapter, was organized on the West Coast. Though he himself never was a West Coast man, he had lasting influence there. Toward the end of the sixties, Mulligan took the place of altoist Paul Desmond in the Dave Bruebeck Quartet—at first only for a limited number of concert appearances. But then the Brubeck-Mulligan team effort proved so fruitful the two decided to stay together for a while. It is to Mulligan's credit to have blown a power and vitality into the Brubeck music which it rarely had displayed before.

The three baritonists of West Coast jazz are *Bob Gordon, Bud Shank,* and *Jimmy Giuffre.* For Giuffre and Shank, the baritone is a supplementary instrument. Shank reveals the altoist even when blowing the baritone. Giuffre, though he seldom takes up the big horn, recorded one of his most beautiful solos on the baritone: "I Only Have Eyes For You" (Capitol). At the height of the Mulligan influence, this was one of the few baritone solos not under its spell. If one wishes, one can detect traces of the clarinetist in Giuffre's baritone playing. Bob Gordon, fatally injured in an automobile accident in 1955, was an improviser of sweeping vitality—also a musician of Basie-Young classicism. The records he made with tenorist-arranger Jack Montrose are among the few truly fascinating combo recordings in West Coast jazz.

On the East Coast—and later in Copenhagen—*Sahib Shihab* developed into a baritonist who has received much too little recognition. Shihab had emerged from the bop circles of the forties. He plays his instrument with power and conviction, and often also with ironic humor, totally free of any mannerisms, and beyond the three modern 'baritone styles' signified by the names Chaloff, Mulligan, and Pepper Adams.

Since the bop days, the name of *Cecil Payne* has been mentioned frequently. And *Charlie Fowlkes* has earned himself a solid reputation as a "Jack Washington of the fifties and sixties" among the players with whom he made music in the Basie mold.

The man who got the whole new wave of interest in the baritone saxophone rolling is *Pepper Adams*. Before him, it seemed as if the possibilities of the baritone had been exhausted with Mulligan and the musicians of his direction, and that the only thing yet to come could be an increase in perfection. This opinion was blown down by Pepper Adams' "sawing" sound. Pepper emerged in 1957 from the Stan Kenton band. There he was nicknamed "The Knife." Drummer Mel Lewis says: "We called him 'The Knife' because when he'd get up to blow, his playing had almost a slashing effect on the rest of us. He'd slash, chop, and before he was through, cut everybody down to size." Adams is one of the musicians who ebulliently negate the belief that one can distinguish between "black" and "white" in jazz. Prior to the appearance of his first photographs in the jazz magazines, almost the entire European critical fraternity had thought him to be black. They were supported in this opinion by the fact that he comes from Detroit, the "Motor City," which in the fifties became a breeding ground for important black musicians. Adams matches the eruptive hardness of these Detroiters. Often one seems to feel in his improvisations traces of Sonny Rollins' ancestry. "Hawkins," says Pepper, "made a tremendous impression on me."

In the jazz of the seventies, the development of the baritone has remained—similar to that of the alto sax—peculiarly pale. As with the other instruments, we can differentiate between baritone players who lean toward free playing, who are rock-influenced, and who are classically inclined, playing along Mainstream lines. Of those in the first group, *Pat Patrick* deserves mention. He belongs to Sun Ra's "Solar Arkestra." Among the rock baritonists are *Ian Underwood, Trevor Koehler,* and *Euclid Sherwood.* Mainstream is represented by *Ronnie Cuber, Charles Davis,* and—most brilliantly in this group— *Nick Brignola.* A style of synthesis was created mainly by British musician *John Surman,* whom Japanese critics at the onset of the seventies called the most important baritonist of this time, "who has no competition to fear, even on the U. S. scene." Shortly thereafter, Surman left the music scene for a long stretch. When he began to play again, the soprano, which used to be his secondary instrument, had become his main horn, while the baritone had taken second place. Surman said in an interview at the time that the baritone by nature leans much more toward certain standard phrases and standard effects than the other saxophones, and that it tends toward cliché formation, even in totally free playing. Surman's remarks might also offer an explanation for the present lack of further development in baritone playing. . . . until some day, a convincing, great baritone player will come on the scene and blow away such speculations.

The Flute

Only a few years ago, the flute ranked among "Miscellaneous Instruments." But in proportion to the decline of the clarinet came the flute's conquest of the scene. At least since the late fifties, this instrument has taken the position of playful, airy, triumphant heights on jazz recordings which had been the domain of the clarinet during the Swing era . . . to which, since the mid-sixties, was added another "clarinet successor": the soprano sax under John Coltrane's influence.

By the end of the sixties, this development had gone so far that the young audience saw the flute as the contemporary wind instrument *par excellence*—at least more contemporary than trumpets, trombones, or saxophones. No other "horn" has seen such relatively frequent use in the more recent generation of rock recordings as the flute—probably most successfully in the group "Jethro Tull" led by flutist *Ian Anderson*. However, if one may assume that (as the polls suggest) Anderson is the "No. 1 flutist" of popular rock, then it is precisely that point—Anderson's weak intonation, his technical shortcomings, his tendency to always use the same effects—that illustrates how wide the quality gap is between jazz and popular rock. Not one flutist in rock has even approximated the technical, musical, and imaginative level of today's great jazz flutists—for instance, James Moody, Rahsaan Roland Kirk, Jeremy Steig, or Hubert Laws!

Still, the flute has only a relatively short tradition in jazz. The earliest flute solo I know of is on a 1933 recording by the Benny Carter band, "Devil's Holiday." The flutist *Wayman Carver* plays with a fluency that seems astonishingly modern. Chick Webb, too, occasionally used Carver's flute in his orchestra. But back then, the instrument still was a curiosity. Strange how suddenly this state of affairs changed when, in the early fifties, the appearance of a half-dozen jazz flutists—literally overnight—established the instrument in jazz.

The first musician to record modern flute solos—with a direct, vital bop feeling—was *Jerome Richardson*. Immediately after him,

Frank Wess and Bud Shank stepped into the limelight. We already mentioned Wess in the tenor saxophone chapter. He was in Count Basie's orchestra. And in this band, whose name stands for swing *par excellence,* he played the still alien flute with the same natural ease as a trumpet or saxophone.

Wess symbolizes the breakthrough that led to the acceptance of the flute. Of course, it could only become important in the post-Lester Young era of the fifties, after the priority of jazz phrasing over jazz sonority had reached the general consciousness. Lester Young is the "main culprit" in this shift of accent from sonority to phrasing, and thus, jazz flutists are initially shaped in his mold. Wess illustrates this point almost ironically: as a tenorist, he clearly is of the Hawkins tradition, while as flutist, he just as clearly is of the Young line. Wess recorded his most interesting solos on a date with Milt Jackson (vibraphone), Hank Jones (piano), Eddie Jones (bass), and Kenny Clarke (drums): "Opus de Jazz."

Bud Shank was the most important West Coast flutist. He emerged from Stan Kenton's band, where he already in 1950 had recorded an initially hardly noticed flute solo on "In Veradero." Later, his duets with Bob Cooper, into which Max Roach drummed swing, stirred much discussion. Cooper, too, played instruments on those records that were—and still are—unusual in jazz: oboe and English horn. *Yusef Lateef* is one of the few musicians to have played genuine jazz on the oboe—in a manner that shows his musical and religious orientation toward the Arab world of Islam. This Arab and oriental tendency is detectable in Lateef, the flutist, too. Aside from the usual concert flute, he has used a whole store of other, exotic flutes: Chinese bamboo flute, a flute of Slovak folk origin, cork flute, the Arab "nai" flute, Taiwan flute, and a "ma ma" flute he himself constructed.

Other good jazz flutists are *Sahib Shihab, James Moody, Leo Wright, Herbie Mann, Sam Most, Buddy Collette, Paul Horn,* the late *Eric Dolphy, Roland Kirk, Charles Lloyd, Joe Farrell, James Spaulding, Eric Dixon, Sam Rivers, Jeremy Steig,* and *Hubert Laws.* It should be noted here that many of these musicians first and foremost are saxophonists and play the flute as a second instrument. This is true, for instance, about tenor and alto player James Moody, whom we have mentioned in the tenor chapter, and who came out of the first bop circle of the forties. Although the flute is only one instrument among others for him, he has been considered one of the best jazz flutists for almost 20 years.

Probably the most successful jazz flutist is Herbie Mann; his records have become best-sellers. Mann incorporated many different exotic elements in his jazz recordings: Latin, Brazilian, African, Arabian, Jewish, Turkish—and in the seventies, of course, rock.

Herbie Mann won the Readers' Poll of *down beat* magazine—*the* authoritative popularity poll of the jazz world—from 1957 to 1970 —for 13 years! To everyone's surprise, Hubert Laws beat Mann by a narrow margin in 1971. Laws is a technically brilliant musician who has successfully attempted to create a number of jazz adaptations of classical music—compositions of Bach, Mozart, Debussy, Stravinsky, and others. He did this while frequently preserving the element usually lost in such adaptations: "jazzness."

Paul Horn, who became known in the second half of the fifties for his work with the Chico Hamilton Quintet, made a pilgrimage to the Ashram, the temple of his guru, the famous Maharishi Mahesh Yogi in India, in the early seventies. On this voyage, he made unaccompanied flute recordings in the Taj Mahal, on which the flute sounds echo back from the 100-foot dome of the marvelous edifice "like a choir of angels," multiplied a hundredfold, as in an acoustic hall of mirrors: meditational mantras transformed into flute music. The success of this Horn record, "Inside," was so great that it was soon followed by a second "Inside" disc, recorded in the U. S. and Canada: Paul Horn at the Pacific Coast of British Columbia in dialogue with a whale, in six or seven-track playback with Bach chorales and Palestrina masses.

New flutists keep coming. The reservoir seems inexhaustible. More and more saxophonists choose the flute as a supplementary horn— only to discover one day that it has become their main instrument— as it happened for a couple of years to James Moody or Frank Wess. One of the best new flutists was discovered in the late fifties by Duke Ellington: *Norris Turney,* who for several years unlocked the spectrum of the flute in the Ellington palette so richly and glitteringly one regrets that Duke did not start using flutes sooner. Perhaps Ellington should have given a "flute trio" a try: as a contemporary counterpart to the clarinet trios of the big bands in the twenties that were the germ cell for the development of the saxophone section. In the hands of a sound-magician like the Duke, a fascinating development might have started—in a sense that will be indicated at the end of the present chapter.

The European jazz flutists distinguish themselves through their solid classical training—musicians like the Bulgarian *Simeon Shterev,* Englishman *Bob Downes,* and Dutchman *Chris Hinze.* Downes, who has also stepped out as a composer of contemporary ballets, belongs to the realm of "classics" as much as to jazz. Hinze has a perceptible affinity for baroque music and contemporary jazz-rock. And Shterev is perhaps the technically best-trained flutist on today's scene, infusing the whole rich and solid musical tradition of his Balkan homeland into jazz.

Many of the flutists named above cultivate the "overblowing" technique, where, through simultaneous blowing and singing or humming, two voices become audible—and often, through overtones, even three or four voices—which create jazz intensity of an astonishing degree. Anybody who knows the flute from classical music—from baroque music, for instance—may not immediately think of the flute as an instrument that lends itself to jazz-like intensity in the same terms as, say, the tenor saxophone. Only by way of the technique of over-blowing has it gained this intensity, and only in that way could it have achieved its success on today's scene.

The first jazz musicians to over-blow the flute were *Sam Most* and *Sahib Shihab* in the mid-fifties. Today, this technique is applied by nearly all flutists, most intensely, most "hot" by Rahsaan Roland Kirk (whom we have already talked about). Occasionally Kirk's flute playing has the characteristic explosive power and heat of a highly pressurized musical steam engine just before departure.

A master of overblowing is *Jeremy Steig,* who occupies about the same position between jazz and rock "beyond all categories" among flutists that Gary Burton occupies among vibraphonists. Steig is the first flutist to structurally incorporate air and functional and finger noises in his music—while Kirk, for example, uses them only to increase ecstatic vitality.

Flutists in the actual rock-jazz field are, among others, *Jim Pepper, Chris Wood, Tom Scott,* and *Walter Parazaider* (of "Chicago"). It may be presumed that the flute horizon of jazz and jazz-rock will experience a further widening in the coming years.

"The" flute does not exist: no instrument is more universal. The history of the flute symbolically begins with Pan, the Greek god of the shepherds and of "the whole," the god who gives a soul to "everything." Every musical culture on earth has developed its own particular types of flutes. To the degree to which jazz musicians incorporate the musical cultures of the world do they discover flutes. Don Cherry is an example. To the recording sessions with his various "Eternal Rhythm Orchestras" in Europe—in Baden-Baden, Berlin, Donaueschingen—he brought 35 different flutes—among them a Chinese shuan flute made from ceramic, a Latin American Maya bird flute, a Bengali flute, a bamboo flute, a metal flute (in B-flat), a plastic flute in C, American Indian flutes, Japanese flutes, etc., etc. Some day in the future, flute orchestras will be formed—as string orchestras are now formed. The flute family is more varied and differentiated than the family of stringed instruments. The sounds of a flute orchestra might, thus, be more varied than those of a string orchestra—and more jazz-like as well!

The Vibraphone

"Percussion" instruments—i.e., instruments which are struck or hit—tend to be used primarily as rhythm instruments. If such instruments additionally offer all kinds of melodic possibilities, it can be assumed that they would make ideal jazz instruments. In this sense, the vibraphone is an ideal jazz instrument. The fact that so vitally rhythmic a musician as Lionel Hampton incorporated it in jazz—or at least helped to do so—points in this direction. If the vibraphone nevertheless has been slow to assert itself, it may be due to its inability to allow for the production of a horn-like jazz sound. The sound of the vibraphone can only be influenced indirectly, by way of its electrically adjustable vibrato—or by foregoing any electrical adjustment —or through the force with which it is struck.

Lionel Hampton and Milt Jackson are the outstanding vibraphonists—the former in the traditional realm, the latter in "modern jazz." Hampton is a volcano of energy. The tension between the sensitivity of some of his solo work and the fact that he seems to need a big band with trumpet, trombone, and sax sections behind him to feel happy constitutes the phenomenon of this musician. His big bands often pound away without consideration for intonation, blend, or precision, and these big Hampton aggregations seem to be the most "traditional" among the better-known modern big bands that have existed since Fletcher Henderson began to play big-band jazz in the twenties. Lionel Hampton, the vibraphonist, seems to derive so much inspiration for so many fine solos from the rhythmic riff orgies of his big bands that one would rather not do without them—questionable as they often seem to be.

Milt Jackson, ten years younger than Hampton, was born in 1923. In 1945 he was discovered by Dizzy Gillespie—as Hampton's vibraphone career had begun ten years before with Benny Goodman—and in subsequent years played with a variety of bop combos and in Dizzy's big band. From 1951 he has been a member of the Modern Jazz Quartet, which originated as the Milt Jackson Quartet and to begin with was hardly more than the combination of Milt Jackson's vibes and a rhythm section. The Milt Jackson Quartet became the Modern Jazz Quartet under the influence of John Lewis, and it has sometimes been said that the shape and form given by Lewis to this ensemble restricted Jackson's flow of ideas and improvisatory freedom. The fact is that Jackson has played the most beautiful solos of his career as a member of the Modern Jazz Quartet. In answer to the question whether playing in this group seemed to cramp his style, he said: "No, not at all. Maybe it sounds or looks like that, because everything is so well planned, but I can still play more or less what I want. I have complete freedom. When I first started with the MJQ, I felt that the planning of the music was a handicap, but now I look at it as an advantage . . . discipline can be a good thing. And discipline can be a help just when you want to feel most free."

Milt Jackson's improvisations deserve the adjective "flowing"—more than any other kind of jazz. They flow like a clear mountain stream. A provocative element of Jackson's playing is the seemingly unconscious way in which he makes the most complicated harmonies seem manifest.

Beside Lionel Hampton and Milt Jackson only a few vibraphonists initially seem significant. The history of the vibraphone began toward the end of the twenties with *Red Norvo,* who found his way to this instrument via the xylophone. Norvo developed in an intriguing way from Chicago style through Swing and bebop to cool jazz.

Among the vibraphonists of recent times are *Terry Gibbs,* Teddy Charles, Cal Tjader, Vic Feldman, Eddie Costa, Tommy Vig, Lem Winchester, and Mike Mainieri. Gibbs became known through his brilliant solo work with the Woody Herman band of the late forties. In 1960 he led a big band on the West Coast, which Leonard Feather designated as "the Lionel Hampton band of the young, more musical people." *Cal Tjader's* blend of jazz phrasing with mambo, conga, bolero, cha-cha-cha, and other Latin rhythms sometimes seemed a further development and sophistication of Cuban jazz, as initiated by Dizzy Gillespie, Chano Pozo, and Machito in the days of bop.

Lem Winchester, a policeman by profession, was a vibraphonist of great sensitivity. He was the first to display a feeling for the glittering, "oscillating" sound quality of his instrument. He died in 1961. The late *Eddie Costa,* British-born *Vic Feldman,* and Hungarian-born *Tommy Vig* (who, like the others, lives in California) are moving, stylistically convincing improvisers. The young *Mike Mainieri,* introduced by Buddy Rich, is a technical phenomenon of the first order, who meanwhile has also adopted the sounds of contemporary rock music. As early as the fifties—long before the era of free jazz—*Teddy Charles* came to the fore as an improviser in the mold of free playing with an extended tonality. Even back then, Charles expressed ideas about which young musicians are still concerned today. "That's what I really want to present: Jazz of today!" he said, "not jazz of ten or 15 years ago. And no futuristic, experimental contortions, but a representation of the ideas of some of my favorite musicians in terms of contemporary jazz and within a group which represents an organic connection of individual jazz talents. . . ."

"Jazz of today," as Teddy Charles meant it and Lem Winchester helped initiate it, is created by a generation of vibraphonists known since the first half of the sixties. Of this generation, we should mention, above all, *Bobby Hutcherson,* Walt Dickerson, Gary Burton, Dave Pike, Roy Ayers, Lynn Blessing, and the Germans Gunter Hampel and Karl Berger (who both alternately live in the U. S. and Europe). These are the musicians who after 15 years of unchallenged Milt Jackson reign have revolutionized the playing style of their instrument as dramatically as has happened only to the bass during this timespan. These musicians accomplished what Ornette Coleman had wanted to see replace the 'old rules of playing'—"a continuous exploring of all possibilities of the instrument." They found that the glittering, 'oscillating' quality of sound which we mentioned in connection with Lem Winchester fits their instrument better than simply "a continuation of standard bop by means of the vibraphone." It is self-evident that the simultaneously percussive and melodic possibilities of the vibraphone come into play in an especially vibraphone-like way. In this sense, Hutcherson has discovered surprisingly rich sounds that occasionally move into the vicinity of electronic music. *Walt Dickerson* seems to be strongly influenced by John Coltrane. *Dave Pike* and *Roy Ayers* have transferred some of the vitality—and showmanship—of Lionel Hampton into a more contemporary way of playing. *Gary Burton,* who initially came to the fore as a member of the Stan Getz Quartet of the sixties, plays with a fascinating combination of tender, floating lyricism and great virtuosity. He is the vibraphonist who has developed further than anyone else the ability to play with three or four mallets simultaneously, creating chordal effects similar to those of pianist Bill Evans, who influenced him. Another influence was the country and hillbilly music of his home state, Indiana. Burton joins all these elements into an independent, new whole so securely that he has been accepted equally by the jazz and the rock worlds. Burton is also among the musicians who initiated the contemporary tendency to play unaccompanied by any rhythm section, and brought this tendency to its most fulfilling heights.

The most radical among the newer vibraphonists, strangely enough —but, then again, also characteristically, because nowhere is there such a relatively wide basis for free jazz as in Germany—are two German musicians: *Gunter Hampel* and *Karl Berger.* Hampel (who has also distinguished himself as flutist, clarinetist, bass clarinetist, and pianist) is the more sensitive of the two, Berger the more dynamic. Both have a refined, developed instinct for the springy elasticity of their instrument, which they often strike so lightly that it seems as if the wind were playing it. It is precisely the "wafting," "windlike" sounds that Berger, Hampel, and a few other new vibraphonists elicit from their instrument which liberate the free tonality of the new jazz from any strained intentionality, and make it seem as "natural" as the "self-evident," tuneful melodies and phrases in "natural" functional harmonics.

Berger was in the Don Cherry Quintet in 1964/66 and came to New York with Don. He says: "Everybody talks about free playing, but I really became free inside through free jazz—all of us became free. You get ears as big as barn doors. You got to be able to listen. Listening: that's the most important thing."

The Piano

On the one hand: Since the history of jazz begins with ragtime, and ragtime was a pianistic music, jazz begins with the piano. On the other hand: The first bands on the streets of New Orleans had no pianos—perhaps because pianos could not be carried around, but perhaps also because the piano could not produce the jazz sound that seemed essential to the early hot players.

The history of jazz piano is acted out between these two poles. The piano offers more possibilities than most other instruments used in jazz. It is not limited to playing one note at a time, as are the horns. It can not only produce rhythm but can also harmonize this rhythm. It can not only state the harmonies, as can the bass, but also connect them with other musical possibilities. But a horn line is more intense than a piano line. In summary, we find:

On the one hand: The more the pianistic possibilities of the piano are exploited, the more the piano seems overshadowed by the horn-like, intense phrasing of jazz blowers.

On the other hand: The more the pianist adopts the phrasing of the horns, the more he relinquishes the true potential of his instrument—up to a point which can represent "pianistic suicide" for anyone familiar with pianistic virtuosity in European music.

Art Tatum and Bud Powell (who was too great to be capable of such "pianistic suicide," though it did exist within the piano school he represents) signify the extremes of this last dichotomy. These extremes have been sharpened since the eighties of the past century, when *Scott Joplin* began to play ragtime in the Midwest. Joplin was a "pianistic" pianist. He played his instrument well within the conventions of the romantic piano tradition.

Since New Orleans bands had no use for "pianistic" piano players, and since a horn-like piano style had not yet been "discovered," there was hardly one pianist in the jazz bands of old New Orleans. But there were pianists in the saloons and the bars, in the "houses" and cabarets—pianists in abundance. Every house had its "professor," and the professor was a pianist. He played ragtime piano. And even when he played blues and stomps and honky-tonk piano, ragtime was always in the background.

The great "professor" of New Orleans piano was *Jelly Roll Mor-*

ton. He can be distinguished from Scott Joplin by the following proposition: Jelly Roll Morton played ragtime piano with awareness of the marching bands on the New Orleans streets. Aware of his certainly considerable accomplishments, he became a victim of paranoid delusions: "I have been robbed of three million dollars all told. Everyone today [1939] is playing my stuff and I don't even get credit. Kansas City style, Chicago style, New Orleans style—hell, they're all Jelly Roll style. . . ."

The "professors," the "honky-tonk," and "barrel-house" pianists existed in New Orleans not only before actual New Orleans style, but also after—into our times. Only a few of them gained fame outside of the limits of the Delta City—as, for instance, *Champion Jack Dupree* and *Professor Longhair.* Fats Domino (mentioned in the blues chapter and later again in the singers chapter), who stands at the center of the rock 'n' roll movement of the fifties, emerged directly from this tradition. In the section dealing with jazz vocalists, we shall discuss the fact that New Orleans created styles twice in the history of black music—not only during the era of New Orleans jazz, but also 50 years later in rhythm and blues. The New Orleans piano "professor" bridges these two fields. Jelly Roll Morton made New Orleans jazz with his band; Fats Domino or Prof. Longhair "made" rhythm and blues and rock 'n' roll—although separated by half a century, all belong to the same "professor" and "honky-tonk" tradition.

Ragtime as played in the Midwest by Scott Joplin was clearly different from ragtime in New Orleans as played by Jelly Roll Morton —but both were music in which one could feel at least the elements of rag—the elements of "ragged time." Soon, there was ragtime in New York, and again it was different from the piano sounds in the Midwest and in New Orleans. From New York ragtime developed the great era of the Harlem jazz piano. But even if Scott Joplin did play in Sedalia, Missouri, since the 1890's, and Jelly Roll Morton names 1902 as the year he "invented" jazz, and the first ragtime pianists played in New York and Harlem around 1910, this still does not prove that the line of evolution led directly from Sedalia over New Orleans to Harlem. Styles—as we have mentioned—develop when the time is ripe, independently of causal schemes of evolution.

James P. Johnson is the first important Harlem pianist. He was a schooled musician; from the beginning there were many academically trained musicians among the pianists, in contradistinction to the players of other instruments. James P. Johnson had studied with a pupil of Rimsky-Korsakoff, and late in his career—during the thirties—he composed a series of symphonic and quasi-symphonic works.

With Johnson is revealed for the first time an aspect of jazz piano at least as important as all the brilliant solo achievements: the art of accompaniment . . . the art of adapting oneself to a soloist, to stimulating him and giving him a foundation on which to build. Johnson did this in unsurpassed fashion for Bessie Smith—on "Preachin' the Blues" or "Backwater Blues," for instance.

Harlem of the twenties was a breeding ground for jazz piano. *Duke Ellington* related: "Everybody was trying to sound like the 'Carolina Shout' Jimmy [James P. Johnson] had made on a piano roll. I got it down by slowing up the roll. . . . We went out every evening regardless of whether we had money or not. . . . I got a big thrill when I found *Willie 'The Lion' Smith* [one night]. . . . We made the rounds every night looking for the piano players. . . ."

Willie "The Lion" Smith is the second great Harlem pianist of the twenties—a master of charming melodies, which he set off with the mighty rhythm of his left hand.

The Harlem pianists—Johnson, Smith, Ellington, Luckey Roberts, and later, young Fats Waller—played for "rent parties" and in "cutting contests," all part of the whirling jazz life of Harlem. At the rent parties, jazz was a means of getting up the rent for one's apartment in a friendly atmosphere, and the cutting contests were play-offs among the leading pianists, ending only when one man had definitively "cut" all the others.

The most important pianist to come out of this Harlem tradition was *Fats Waller,* who died at 39 in 1943. Louis Armstrong said it: "Right now, every time someone mentions Fats Waller's name, why, you can see the grins on all the faces. . . ." Fats is two men: one of the greatest pianists in jazz history and one of the funniest and most entertaining comedians of popular music.

"Livin' the Life I Love" was the theme of his life and his music. He did not always bring it off—for all his comic sense, he still suffered when the public seemed to appreciate his showmanship more than his music. Gene Sedric, Fats' tenor man relates: "Fats was sometimes very unhappy about his music. You see, he was appreciated for his showmanship ability and for that amount of piano that he played on records, but very few of Waller's record fans knew how much more he could play than what he usually did on records. He didn't try to prove anything by his singing. It was a matter of fun with him. . . . Yet, he wanted to do great things on organ and piano—which he could do. . . ." Elsewhere, Sedric says: "As for the record sessions, it seems like they would always give him a whole lot of junk tunes to play because it seemed as if only he could get something out of them. . . ."

As composer, Waller wrote some of the most beautiful jazz themes, equally agreeable to all styles. "Honeysuckle Rose" and "Ain't Misbehavin' " are the most important. "Waller," says Coleman Hawkins, "could write tunes as fast as he could play the piano."

As a pianist, Fats had the strongest left hand in jazz history—a left hand which could replace not only a rhythm section but a whole band. He was altogether an "orchestral" pianist. His piano sounded like an orchestra. Quite relevantly, the most orchestral of all jazz pianists, Art Tatum, invoked Waller: "Fats, man—that's where I come from. . . . Quite a place to come from, too!"

The other great pianist to come from Fats Waller is *Count Basie*. Basie tells of his first meeting with Fats: ". . . I had dropped into the old Lincoln Theater in Harlem and heard a young fellow beating it out on the organ. From that time on, I was a daily customer, hanging on to his every note, sitting behind him all the time, fascinated by the ease with which his hands pounded the keys and his feet manipulated the pedals. . . . One day, he asked me whether I played the organ. 'No,' I said, 'but I'd give my right arm to learn.' The next day, he invited me to sit in the pit and start working the pedals. I sat on the floor, watching his feet, and using my hands to imitate them. Then I sat beside him and he taught me."

Today, one can sometimes still hear in the piano solos Basie plays with his band that he comes from Fats Waller. He plays a kind of "economized" Fats: an ingeniously abstracted structure of Waller music in which only the cornerstones remain—but they stand for everything else. Basie became one of the most economical pianists in jazz history, and the way he understands how to create tension between often widely spaced single notes is incomparable. Many pianists are influenced by this: *Johnny Guarnieri* in the Swing era, and during the fifties, *John Lewis,* the maestro of the Modern Jazz Quartet, in whom one senses behind Basie's unconscious economy of means a sage knowledge of all that economy and abstraction imply in music and art. And finally, it has been pointed out that Thelonious Monk is a late descendant of the stride piano school of Johnson and Waller. Along the line of James P.-Fats-Count-Monk, the economy becomes more stringent until the last retains only the skeletal structure of the absolutely necessary.

In the tributes to Basie of the fifties, West Coasters *Marty Paich* and *Pete Jolly* and Easterner *Nat Pierce* (with, among others, Woody Herman's big band) have played piano solos *à la* Basie. *Sir Charles Thompson*, too—the composer of "Robbin's Nest," a popular bop and Harlem-jump theme of the forties and fifties—shows a Basie influence.

However, another stream of jazz piano development flowed into Count Basie: the stream of great boogie-woogie pianists. Basie not only plays "economized" Fats Waller, but "economized" boogie as well.

In the early days, the ragtime and Harlem pianists always looked down a bit condescendingly on the "poor boogie-woogie piano-players." Chicago became the center of boogie-woogie—where Harlem rent parties and cutting contests jumped to the sound of stride piano, their counterparts on Chicago's South Side rocked to the beat of blues and boogie piano. Boogie-woogie, too, has its roots in the Midwest and Southwest, down to Texas. From Texas comes one of the few remarkable pianists who still, in the sixties, played genuine, uncommercialized boogie and blues piano: *Sam Price*. Memphis, St. Louis, and Kansas City were important boogie-woogie towns. *Memphis Slim*, who comes from Memphis, and now lives in Paris, is among the more recent masters of boogie. He made a name for himself primarily as a blues shouter, and there are many blues singers in the black sections of Northern and Southern cities who accompany themselves with convincing boogie-woogie piano, or even are outstanding boogie musicians—as, for example, Roosevelt Sykes, Little Brother Montgomery, and, above all, *Otis Spann* (who died in 1970).

The boogie-ostinato—the sharply accented, continuously repeated bass figures—may have developed in the South from the banjo or guitar figures with which the blues singers accompanied themselves. Anyhow, blues and boogie belong together since their origin. The first boogies were played as blues accompaniments, and to this day almost all boogies are in the 12-bar blues pattern. Often, the difference between blues and boogie is anything but distinct; and as might be pointed out here, the notion that all boogie-woogie is fast and bouncy is an erroneous generalization. It is just as false as the idea that all blues are slow.

If the search for the origins of boogie-woogie takes us beyond the early banjo and guitar blues accompaniments, we arrive at a time when the differentiation between Latin American (rumba, samba, tango, mambo, etc.) and North American (jazz-influenced) music was not yet so distinct. Thus it will be seen that the bass figures of boogie-woogie are nothing but condensed rumba or tango basses— actually, both rumba and tango basses and the boogie-woogie bass relate back to the same West African origins. *Jimmy Yancey*, the "father of boogie-woogie," and other boogie pianists have based some of their pieces on the bass figures of Latin American dances— from a partly conscious, partly unconscious feeling for their relatedness. (For example Yancey's "Lean Bacon Boogie," based on a tango figure.)

Yancey, Pinetop Smith, Cow-Cow Davenport, and Cripple Clarence Lofton are the first important boogie-woogie pianists. Yancey was originally a tap-dancer, which might have inspired his eight-to-the-bar playing. *Pinetop Smith's* "Pinetop's Boogie Woogie" gave the style its name.

Most brilliant of the boogie-woogie pianists is *Meade Lux Lewis,* who lost his life in an automobile accident in 1964. His "Honky Tonk Train Blues," first recorded in 1929, achieved legendary fame. In the mid-thirties, when the Negro audience for whom boogie-woogie had been played in the twenties on Chicago's South Side and elsewhere had long since gone beyond this style, the white world began to warm up to it. At that time, jazz critic John Hammond searched for Lewis and found him as a car-washer in a suburban Chicago garage. At New York's "Cafe Society" Hammond brought him together with two other pioneers of boogie-woogie piano: *Albert Ammons* and *Pete Johnson*. The records made by these three masters of boogie at three pianos are among the most exciting examples of boogie-woogie.

Yancey, too—though he was one of the most famous exponents of boogie-woogie in Chicago during the twenties—did not record until 1939, at the height of the boogie-woogie vogue. Not too much later, boogie-woogie rudiments were among the most welcome tricks of every cocktail-lounge pianist. Creative jazz musicians turned away from it. Dancing schools introduced courses in boogie-woogie, and the eight-to-the-bar became firmly established in commercial music. Fats Waller put it bluntly: "The fad of boogie-woogie piano playing is burning itself out. Why?   Because it's too monotonous—it all sounds the same."

As James P. Johnson and the other Harlem pianists belong to the ragtime branch, although they soon ceased to play the old, original rags and finally can only be designated as rag-influenced, so Chicago had pianists who clearly belong to the boogie-woogie branch and yet were only boogie-woogie influenced. The first of these is *Jimmy Blythe*—a sort of Hank Jones of blues and boogie, insofar as he was employed as frequently in the Chicago recording studios of the twenties as Hank Jones was in the New York studios in the fifties, when a tasteful, experienced, and versatile pianist of the "modern" piano school was wanted. Blythe was all of these in terms of blues, boogie, and stomps: tasteful, experienced, versatile—even though he may seem rough, monotonous, and untutored to listeners of today. In the meantime, our notions of what is tasteful, experienced, and versatile in jazz have simply become more demanding. Blythe, long before Basie, knew how to achieve boogie-effects without really playing boogie-woogie—as on his "Sunshine Special," where he "hides" the ostinato line, usually played by the bass, in the melody line.

As a stomp pianist, Blythe was not much different from the great Harlem pianists. The stomp is the connecting link between the boogie-woogie and the Harlem branch, and eventually also links up with the third line of pianistic development—horn-like playing. Before speaking of this, we must mention the white pianists of Chicago style and its wider radius. They more or less stand between the rag and boogie branches—*Joe Sullivan,* for instance, leaning more toward Waller, *Art Hodes* more toward the blues piano of the South Side pianists. The former has wonderful humor, the latter persuasive blues feeling.

The third branch of pianistic development—horn-like piano playing—was the latest to evolve: in the mid-twenties, during the great days of New Orleans music in Chicago. *Earl Hines* is the first musician of this direction. His playing has been called "trumpet style piano"—the mighty octave movements of his right hand sounded like a translation of Louis Armstrong's trumpet lines to the piano. Yet it is with Hines' as with most ways of playing in jazz: in the course of time they gain sharper contours. When Hines' way of playing the piano is heard with the horn-like phrases in mind that such pianists as Bud Powell played in the fifties, Earl's playing surely does not seem trumpet-like. But Earl Hines is the founder of the school which leads through Mary Lou Williams, Teddy Wilson, and Nat "King" Cole to Bud Powell and most pianists of the fifties and sixties.

This is particularly noticeable in *Mary Lou Williams,* since she lived through this entire school and developed parallel to it. Mary Lou is the only woman in instrumental jazz whose name can be mentioned in the same breath with those of the important males (though she has lately received competition in this area from Alice Coltrane; see the chapter on John Coltrane and Ornette Coleman). She began to play around 1930, in the blues and boogie-woogie style of the day. In Kansas City she became arranger and pianist for the Andy Kirk band. She has written some significant arrangements—as for Kirk, Benny Goodman ("Roll 'Em"), and Duke Ellington ("Trumpet No End")—which cannot be left out of any history of the arrangement in jazz. As a pianist she has evolved through Swing and bop into a mature representative of modern jazz piano—which has caused some to say that this "First Lady of Jazz" has no style of her own. She herself says with justified assurance: "I consider that a compliment, although I think that everyone with ears can identify me without any difficulty. But it's true that I'm always experimenting, always changing, always finding new things. Why, back in Kansas City I found chords they're just beginning to use now. What happens to so many good pianists is that they become so stylized that they can't break out of the prison of their styles and absorb ideas and new techniques. Some of them play the same things night after night—something I just couldn't do." At a time in which every talented young pianist gets his own record album, more attention should be paid to Mary Lou Williams. Her record album "Black Christ of the Andes"—with a choir, instrumental soloists, and herself as composer, arranger, and piano soloist—is the musical document of her conversion to Catholicism; and—aside from the gospel songs, of course, and from the religious concerts of Duke Ellington—it is one of the few successful examples of Christian religious jazz music in existence.

In the Swing style of the thirties the Earl Hines direction is embodied first of all in *Teddy Wilson.* He connects it with the format of the great black Swing horn players and with the elegance and affability which Benny Goodman brought to the jazz of that day. It is this connection which led to a point—25 years later—at which one seemed to be hearing Teddy Wilson in every other cocktail pianist. Wilson, as a member of the Goodman combos and as leader of his own ensembles, participated in some of the best and most representative combo recordings of the Swing era. During the thirties, he influenced almost every pianist—among others *Mel Powell, Billy Kyle, Jess Stacy,* and *Joe Bushkin.* Bushkin, of course, was also influenced by the "grand old man" of all jazz pianists: *Art Tatum. Marian Mc-Partland* has transferred the elegance of Wilson—with whom she also recorded a duo album—to the contemporary scene, incorporating many of the insights gained since then, particularly from cool jazz.

Everything created by the history of jazz piano up to the time of his renown—the mid-thirties—comes together in Art Tatum, with the addition of a pianistic virtuosity for which there is no point of comparison within jazz. Comparisons can only be drawn with Rachmaninoff, Rubinstein, Cherkassky, and the other great virtuosos of concert piano. The cadenzas and runs, the arpeggios and embellishments of the virtuoso piano music of the late nineteenth century are as alive in his playing as is a strong feeling for the blues—which he demonstrates in, say, his recordings with blues singer Joe Turner. Nurtured on the piano techniques of the nineteenth century, Tatum shows a certain preference for the salon pieces of that time—such as Dvořák's "Humoresque," Massenet's "Elégie," and others of this genre—a choice which is not wholly compatible with the ultimate in taste. But it is characteristic of the high esteem in which Tatum is held by almost all jazz musicians that a storm of protest arose when French jazz critic André Hodeir brought up this question of taste. Even musicians who otherwise could not be moved to write took pen in hand to send in glowing defenses of Tatum. When critic Leonard Feather polled 120 of the leading jazz musicians in 1956 concerning the most important representatives of the various instruments, 68 of them put the name of Tatum in the piano category. Next to Charlie Parker, who received 76 votes, this was the most overwhelming victory won by any musician in this poll.

Tatum, who died in 1957, was a soloist—period. Aside from a few combo recordings with all-star personnel, or the previously mentioned sessions with blues singer Joe Turner, he was accustomed to play solo or with his own trio.

After Tatum, the counterplay between the pianistic and the horn-like conceptions of jazz piano becomes particularly marked. *Bud Powell,* who died in 1966 under tragic circumstances, was the primary exponent of the horn-like approach and, in general, the most influential pianist of modern jazz. He is the Charlie Parker of jazz piano—and was similarly tormented and threatened as a human being. After his creative period—from the mid-forties to the early fifties—he spent more than half his time in asylums. At 18, he had already played with Charlie Christian and Charlie Parker at Minton's. At 19, he joined Cootie Williams' band. At 21, he suffered his first collapse.

The problem of Powell is an intensification of the problem of the jazz musician in general: the problem of the artist who is creative within a socially and racially discriminatory world. Moreover, it is a world in which many people only laugh when the word "creative" is mentioned.

Powell created those sharply etched lines which seem to stand free in space like glowing metal that has hardened. Yet Bud is also a romanticist, whose "Glass Enclosure" (an original composition) or whose ballad interpretations—for instance, "Polkadots and Moonbeams"—have the gentle charm of Robert Schumann's "Scenes from Childhood." This tension between the hardness of his horn-like lines and his romantic sensibility is always present, and perhaps it also was this tension between two ultimately incompatible extremes which contributed to the tragedy of this great musician.

From Tatum comes the technique, from Powell, the style. Tatum set a pianistic standard which seems unattainable. Bud Powell founded a school. Thus, there are more pianists in modern jazz who are "Powell students" than there are "Tatum students." Descended from Tatum are first of all *Billy Taylor, Hank Jones*, Phineas Newborn, and Oscar Peterson (who, of course, are also influenced to a certain degree by Bud Powell and other pianists). Taylor, as pianist and as observer of the jazz scene, has a wily and penetrating intelligence. Jones is a master of pianistic confections—mainly Tatum-inspired, but also with Teddy Wilson's affability and Count Basie's economy of means. *Clyde Hart,* the not very well-known pathbreaker of bop piano playing, was Tatum- and Wilson-influenced.

Phineas Newborn is technically astounding, and in 1956 he played his name into fame practically overnight with a plethora of pianistic filigree work. It took a few years until Newborn learned to differentiate between the important and the unimportant, and until he developed a truly strong jazz feeling beyond the filigree work.

Oscar Peterson—particularly in Europe, through his almost yearly concert tours—is one of the best-known jazz pianists alive. He is a swinging, moving improviser and has a strong personality, but after a while one can discover a certain trend toward the cliché behind the bravura and brilliance of his playing—overshadowed, however, by his exemplary musical vitality. Since the second half of the sixties, Peterson has increasingly taken to playing without accompaniment—that is, without rhythm section—until he finally dissolved his trio, which had ranked among the most successful small groups. Peterson's strong left hand, which became especially apparent in his unaccompanied playing, shows that his roots are not only in Tatum—to which he has referred again and again—but also in those musicians who themselves are Tatum's forefathers: Fats Waller and James P. Johnson, with their mighty bass lines.

From Bud Powell come Al Haig, George Wallington, Lou Levy, Lennie Tristano, Hampton Hawes, Pete Jolly, Claude Williamson, Dave McKenna, Japanese émigré Toskhiko Akioshi, Eddie Costa, Wynton Kelly, Russ Freeman, Ray Charles, Mose Allison, Red Garland, Horace Silver, Barry Harris, Duke Jordan, Kenny Drew, Walter Bishop, Elmo Hope, Tommy Flanagan, Bobby Timmons, Junior Mance, Ramsey Lewis, Ray Bryant, Horace Parlan, Roger Kellaway, Roland Hanna, Les McCann, and a legion of other modern pianists.

Al Haig and *George Wallington* played in modern jazz combos on 52nd Street during the formative years of bop. *Lennie Tristano* is the head of the previously mentioned Tristano school, which had such great importance at the time of the crystallization of cool jazz. He plays long, sweeping, sensitive melodic lines over complex harmonic structures. In the early fifties, there was a regular Tristano cult in certain circles of the jazz world. Tristano's influence reaches clear across all styles. Among those pianists who have paid allegiance to him are Dick Twardzik, Don Friedman, Clare Fischer, and above all Bill Evans; in the seventies, also a musician like Alan Broadbent. Tristano anticipated certain harmonic liberties of free jazz by as much as ten years.

Hampton Hawes, Pete Jolly, Claude Williamson, and *Russ Freeman* are among the pianists of West Coast jazz. Hawes has a strong blues and Charlie Parker feeling. Freeman, in many ways, is a "percussionist" on the piano in a Powell style. *Ray Charles* is the famous rhythm-and-blues singer, who in his lesser-known piano playing demonstrates persuasively that even the most modern piano styles are rooted in gospel and blues—creating that feeling of inner security of which we have spoken at the beginning of this book. In that context, we also mentioned *Mose Allison,* who represents an intriguingly direct connection between the old blues and folk songs and modern Bud Powell piano. *Red Garland* is a hard bop pianist who sparkles with ideas. He became known through his work with the Miles Davis Quintet in the mid-fifties. In his playing one often hears echoes of the yet to be discussed Erroll Garner. After Garland left Davis, his place was taken first by Bill Evans (of whom more later) and then *Wynton Kelly.* Kelly, and even more so *Junior Mance, Les McCann,* and *Bobby Timmons,* belong to the funk- and gospel-inspired young hard-bop pianists. Timmons' compositions "Moanin'," "This Here," and "Dat Dere," written in the late fifties when he was in Art Blakey's Messengers and Cannonball Adderley's quintet, became highly successful. In the early seventies, Les McCann combined his soul-piano conception, which he presented with great success in the fifties, with contemporary electric sounds. *Ray Bryant,* a master of sad, weighty blues improvisations, was involved with the Madison dance fad in Harlem around 1960 with pieces like "Little Susie," "Madison," and others. *Ramsey Lewis* leads a Chicago trio, which combines gospel and hard bop in a pleasant, often somewhat 'commercialized' manner. *Tommy Flanagan,* a musician of the Detroit hard-bop generation, has found a delicacy in the "hardness" of hard bop that nobody else has. *Barry Harris* has always been designated "genius" by the many musicians to come out of Detroit. He was the strongest and most individual personality behind the Detroit jazz scene. *Horace Silver* has extended the Powell heritage particularly convincingly—to a funk and soul-inspired playing style, coupled with a sober, audacious sense of form and affable vitality, which has become a (also commercial) success formula for himself and his quintet.

Thelonious Monk also belongs among the horn-like pianists. Chronologically, he comes before Powell, but his influence has been making itself more and more felt since the late fifties. Monk, a pioneer of modern jazz from Minton's, plays *"al fresco-*like," widely spaced, often only indicated lines. In terms of the dissolution of the phrase as a unit and harmony as a functional system, he went especially far before the emergence of free jazz. He has that harmonic freedom and proficiency which the self-conscious jazz experimenters have acquired intellectually and from modern European music. With Monk, these qualities stem from his strong, creative improvisatory talent. Much of what leads to Ornette Coleman, John Coltrane,

Eric Dolphy, and all the other avant-gardists of jazz is heard for the first time in his music—anchored in a strong blues feeling and saturated with a mocking, burlesquing sense of humor. Monk's own themes, with their rhythmic displacements and irregular structures, were the most original themes on the jazz scene of the fifties.

Randy Weston, Herbie Nichols, Mal Waldron, the late *Dick Twardzik* (and indirectly, Bill Evans) are pianists who seem to play along similar lines, whether consciously influenced by Monk or not. Weston, who, besides Monk, names Ellington as an influence, has been living in North Africa for years, where he has also worked with Arab music. Nichols played in Dixieland and blues bands before he had an opportunity to present his bizarre and novel compositions. Mal Waldron had great success in Japan around the turn from the sixties to the seventies, though he lives in Munich. His way of playing was initially referred to as "telegraph style:" his phrases sounded something like "long-long-short-long," like mysterious Morse code. Waldron was the last accompanist for the great Billie Holiday. He has developed an increasingly free style of playing, in which his awareness of the black racial and social situation in today's society plays an important role.

Of all these pianists, *Bill Evans* has received the greatest recognition. Evans is one of the few white musicians accepted within the narrower circles of hard bop—and yet his style is completely different from that of other hard-bop pianists: he was the first modal pianist. He might be designated a "Chopin of the modern jazz piano," with the eminent skill—without comparison in jazz—to make the piano "sound" in a way that places him (in terms of sound) in the vicinity of a pianist like Rubinstein. It is no wonder that such a unique and interesting combination of heterogeneous elements has been successful in commercial terms as well (the Bill Evans Trio).

It is also illuminating that Evans, 'tonal' as his music may be, has been a point of departure for a whole line of pianists who play harmonically freer. The most important among them are *Don Friedman* on the East Coast and *Clare Fischer* on the West, with their sensitive and clear piano improvisations.

Jaki Byard holds a special position. He emerged from the Mingus group and on the one hand plays very modern, nearly free improvisations with abrasive sounds; but on the other hand, he is rooted in the stride piano of the twenties. It is a happy mixture that has kept even Byard's most experimental excursions from having an experimental character. And it has made it possible for this musician with equal competence to play fascinating two-piano duets with Earl Hines and make music with—of course not totally uninhibited—avant-garde aggregations. Byard is a prime example of that group of musicians who master the art of innovation from a clear perspective on the old; Mingus, Roland Kirk, and Booker Ervin are others.

There are a few musicians who do not fit into the system we have tried to use in classifying the pianists. They should be discussed now, before going on. As a member of Lionel Hampton's band, *Milt Buckner* created a "locked hands style"—with intertwined, parallel octave movements—that has a strong, stimulating effect. Buckner manages to transfer whole big-band sections in all their brilliance to the piano. André Hodeir has called him one of the greatest stylists of jazz piano.

British-born *George Shearing* incorporated Buckner's style into the sound of his quintet. Combined with the bop lines of Bud Powell, he developed this style into a success formula. In the late forties, the name of Shearing was on every jazzman's lips, but though Shearing does not play very differently today, his playing—imbedded in the cliché-ridden sound of his group—no longer seems really exciting.

The pianists who are least definable in terms of schools are also equally successful: *Dave Brubeck* and Erroll Garner. Brubeck has incorporated a wealth of European musical elements, from Bach to Darius Milhaud (with whom he studied), in his playing. These elements all seem to be romantically obscured and strangely divested of their original meaning in his music. The question whether Brubeck "swings" has been debated for years. On the other hand, Brubeck is a marvelously imaginative and individual improviser. He and his alto saxophonist Paul Desmond (who was replaced by Gerry Mulligan in 1970) became mutually inspired during their collaborations—in the intuitive way of sleepwalkers. Brubeck often finds his way to great, moving climaxes. The way in which he builds to these climaxes over wide stretches and seemingly "shores up" to them is as admirable as the fluctuating exchange of ideas between him and Desmond (or Mulligan). When Leonard Feather initiated an inquiry as to who was the most overrated musician, Brubeck took the lead with ease. Thirty-seven percent of all those polled offered his name. Particularly in Brubeck's case, a behavior pattern among the "jazz fraternity" is evident, as can also be seen in other musicians of jazz history —even in Louis Armstrong's case: In the first half of the fifties, Brubeck was one of the most highly praised musicians on the jazz scene.

Again and again, he was chosen as best pianist and combo leader—
or, in more general terms, as "Musician of the Year." At that time, he
was considered *the* embodiment of avant-garde piano playing.
Then, he became successful—far beyond the limits of what can be
considered "normal" in jazz. And increasingly, the jazz fraternity began to move away from him—though he hardly plays any different
today from back then. On the contrary: his playing has become more
swinging, harder, more mature. Has the jazz world, one is forced to
ask, become so caught up in its clique-like self-isolation that it inter-
prets any success that goes beyond the usual limits as proof of trea-
son?

Less disputed than Brubeck is *Erroll Garner*. Since Fats Waller,
there has been no pianist whose name is so synonymous with a happy
feeling. Garner is also comparable to Fats—and to Tatum—in his orchestral approach to the piano. He sovereignly commands the entire
keyboard. "Concert by the Sea" is the title of one of his many successful records; and the title is appropriate not only because this concert was recorded on the Pacific Coast, but also because Garner's
piano cascades bring to mind the roar of the sea. Garner, who to this
day has not bothered to learn to read music, is the only pianist who
can play such cascades without creating the impression of a loss in
jazz feeling. This is primarily due to his incomparable sense of
rhythm, which is often reminiscent of the old two-beat feeling from
the early days of jazz, and is combined with a fascinating relaxation.
When Garner plays, the listener sometimes may feel that the beat has
been delayed too long, but when it comes, you know it fell just where
it belonged. Also masterful are Garner's introductions, which—often with cadenzas, often also with humorous intimations—seem to
delay the start of the theme and the beat further and further. Garner's world-wide audiences applaud enthusiastically when pianist and
audience finally arrive "back home" again, in the well-known melody
and the even better-known "Garner beat."

Garner has influenced many of the pianists previously mentioned,
especially in connection with Bud Powell. On the other hand, Garner
is so singular and original that only two pianists are really related to
him: *Ellis Larkins* and *Ahmad Jamal*. Larkins played some of the
most beautiful piano accompaniments in jazz history, on a record of
Ella Fitzgerald singing Gershwin. The younger Jamal occupies a curious position, evaluated in sharply contrasting fashion by musicians
and critics. While most of the latter hardly consider him more than a

gifted cocktail pianist, many musicians—primarily Miles Davis—
have called him a towering "genius." Jamal's timing and combination of embellishment and economy are masterly. Gunther Schuller
believes that Miles' high regard for Jamal is mainly due to the fact
that the Davis of the fifties adopted certain ways of embellishing and,
to a certain degree, his sophisticated simplicity from Jamal, and that
Miles' great success began with this adoption. At any rate, both Garner and Jamal occupy a position beyond the main schools of jazz
piano. And it is certain that, due particularly to Garner's stylistic independence, there is no other pianist who combines all the elements
and tendencies of jazz-piano history with such eminence and individuality—and as entertainingly—as Erroll Garner.

The next step in the development was taken by *Cecil Taylor,* in a
manner that had not been thought possible by even the most farsighted critics. In his 'clusters,' racing across the entire keyboard of
the piano, swings the world of Bartók's "Microcosm." Martin Williams claims that Taylor transforms modern concert music into the
idiom and technique of jazz as surely as Jelly Roll Morton transformed John Philip Sousa's marches.

There are musicians who have placed Taylor's influence above
that of Ornette Coleman—and in any case we must remember that
Taylor was already introduced at the 1957 Newport Festival, after he
had learned his trade in the groups of Swing musicians like Hot Lips
Page, Johnny Hodges, and Lawrence Brown, and thus chronologically stands before Coleman. The actual, overwhelming aspect of
Taylor's improvisations lies in the physical power with which he
plays. German pianist Alexander von Schlippenbach, strongly influenced by Taylor, has pointed out that any other pianist would be capable of generating such burning and bursting intensity for only a few
minutes, and that it is incredible that Taylor is able to keep up such
playing for an entire evening in long concerts or club appearances.

Stylistically between Taylor and the pianists mentioned before
him, but belonging to about the same era in time, are *Herbie Hancock,* Andrew Hill, Steve Kuhn, Denny Zeitlin, McCoy Tyner, Joe
Zawinul, Jan Hammer, and many more.

Among pianists, Hancock has about the same position as Freddie
Hubbard among the trumpeters: both have the same inspired sure-
ness and professionalism at both ends of tonality. With his Blue Note
records "Empyrean Isles" and "Maiden Voyage," Hancock has become a "jazz poet of the sea," who—without any of the effects of

program music, only by the means of jazz—captures the majestic rushing of the ocean as glitteringly and iridescently as Debussy did—though in a totally different musical world—in "La Mer." That, too, belongs to the possibilities of the new jazz—that it allows for such "tone poems" without extra-musical effects. Only ten years earlier, when Russ Freeman and Chet Baker wanted to evoke the sea on one of their recordings, they used sound tracks of rushing waves and chirping gulls. Since the beginning of the seventies, Hancock, who for a long time was the pianist in the Miles Davis Quintet, has been developing Miles' "electric jazz" into his own music, convincingly combing intensity and sensitivity.

Andrew Hill, from Haiti, grew up in Chicago, and has infused many African elements from his Caribbean homeland into modern piano compositions and improvisations. "Really listen to the avant-garde, and you can hear African rhythms. You hear the roots of jazz," he says. The fact that the African, Negroid, black nature of jazz is not only not being suppressed as the music's development continues, but on the contrary gains increasingly concentrated and valid prominence as the black music of America progressively throws off the shackles of European musical laws, becomes impressively clear with musicians like Hill (and a host of others). Old Afro-Creole voodoo magic is musically more alive in the elements Hill uses than in the music of a man like Jelly Roll Morton, who during the early days of jazz was so involved with voodoo.

Even more direct in his relationship to Africa is *Dollar Brand,* a musician who comes from Capetown, South Africa. Duke Ellington discovered him, and more recently he worked with Don Cherry. Dollar's father belonged to the Basuto tribe, his mother to the Bushman tribe. Brand fuses this heritage with an exact knowledge of Ellington and Monk, creating his own style, using also elements of baroque and romantic piano music.

San Franciscan *Denny Zeitlin,* a medical doctor and psychiatrist by profession, came to the fore in the mid-sixties with a modally conceived free jazz that was enthusiastically accepted, even by audiences who usually have an unappreciative attitude toward more recent developments in jazz. Though the proposition, "Zeitlin is a Dave Brubeck of free jazz," might be an oversimplification, it does hit the bull's eye in many respects.

McCoy Tyner is the most important 'modal' pianist. With his "floating chords," chosen in such a way that they establish a basis for almost any kind of melodic movement, he was one of the first to make conventional chord changes unnecessary. Small wonder, then, that for years he was John Coltrane's favorite pianist, until Coltrane's wife, *Alice,* took his place. In the early seventies, it seems that few pianists and groups have understood Coltrane's message in such a warm, loving manner as Tyner and his group.

Many of these pianists have been switching over to the electric piano since the end of the sixties—or play both acoustic and electric piano. The first impression was that in terms of expressivity the electric instrument was a step backward. A concert grand is a virtually perfect instrument with an unsurpassable wealth of technical and musical possibilities. Musicians like Erroll Garner, Teddy Wilson, Bud Powell, Art Tatum, Cecil Taylor, Keith Jarrett, and many others, have developed an unmistakable attack on the concert grand that makes them identifiable after only a few bars—like the great horn men of jazz. In the meantime, it has been proven that the best electric pianists of the seventies—through masterful control of the electronic possibilities—certainly were able to create the individuality of sound that is so important for jazz. It was also discovered that the electric piano sound is to the sound of the acoustic piano what the vibraphone is to the xylophone or marimba: clearer, more sparkling, more precise—and thus, in the final analysis, more percussive. And it is precisely this increase in percussiveness of sound that is so desirable in jazz.

In recent times, a generation of pianists has emerged who treat the electric piano not simply as an electrified conventional piano, but truly as a new instrument with its own laws. Among them are Herbie Hancock, the Austrian *Joe Zawinul,* the Czech *Jan Hammer,* and *George Duke.* Some have added to the electric piano a wide range of electronic accessories and other electronic keyboard instruments. We shall discuss this whole field of keyboards (together with the organ) in a special chapter.

Zawinul initially was a blues and soul-oriented pianist, who accompanied singer Dinah Washington, and for years had had one great success after another—also as composer—in the Cannonball Adderley Quintet. In the late sixties he collaborated with Miles Davis, and it is possible that he was not only influenced by Davis' modal conception but also himself played a crucial role in Miles' transition to "electric jazz."

Hammer was the pianist in John McLaughlin's first Mahavishnu

Orchestra, particularly brilliant in developing his own, individual electric piano sound.

Some of the above-mentioned musicians already lead us to the next group of pianists—that kind of transition is always in flux. They are the pianistic representatives of free jazz, who either play totally free, or are oriented to so-called "tonal centers" (in the sense of a "rudimentary tonality"). Included in this group are such diverse players as Paul Bley, Carla Bley, Burton Greene, Don Pullen, John Hicks, Chick Corea, Keith Jarrett, Richard Abrams, Alice Coltrane, Dave Burrell, Sun Ra, Lonnie Liston Smith, Bayete, and many more.

In ironic simplification, we might designate *Paul Bley* as a "James P. Johnson of free playing." *Carla Bley* gained fame mainly as a player of her own tender, delicate compositions, perhaps the most original jazz compositions this side of Thelonious Monk. Carla's "chronotransduction," which she created with writer Paul Haines, "Escalator over the Hill," is a kind of jazz opera: With its six record sides, the largest complete work that has so far emerged from jazz— by far transcending the limits of jazz, to be sure, in the direction of a "total music" incorporating elements of rock, Indian music, European music, etc. The language creation "chronotransduction" illuminates what the point is here: Time and Space are being transcended in a musical and poetic sense, the terms "musical" and "poetic" implying "the Cosmos."

Chick Corea and *Keith Jarrett* have both been members of the Miles Davis groups. Jarrett (whom we already talked about at the end of the chapter on harmony) is an especially versatile, particularly eclectic musician, typical of the jazz of the seventies, a master of "spiritualization" and sublimation of rock phrases. And Corea is a romanticist of the contemporary jazz piano, not only as a pianist, but also as a composer. Critics have compared his affable piano pieces with the nineteenth-century piano music of Schumann, Mendelssohn, Schubert, or Rubinstein—but failed to notice the imminent, highly sensitized, often barely perceptible jazz tension with which Corea "fills" his romanticism. This "filling" of romanticism with modern tension is, in many ways, a real challenge to the music in the seventies. It can also be found in a similar way in the playing of Jarrett, Gary Burton, John McLaughlin (when he plays without accompaniment and amplification) and also in many other artistic phenomena of our time, far beyond the limits of jazz.

Finally, let us turn to the rock-influenced pianists—and here again, we are only listing those who seem interesting from the jazz point of view: *George Duke* (who became known through his work with Frank Zappa and Cannonball Adderley), and *Nicky Hopkins, Don Preston, Keith Emerson,* and *Leon Russell* (who are rock stars of the biggest order). Particularly in the realm of this music, the musicians —unhampered by stylistic doubts—again and again refer back to elements of tradition: Emerson (who will be discussed in the keyboard chapter) refers mainly to the music of the nineteenth century, in a manner largely devoid of meaning—understood only in technical terms (and thus, misunderstood). Russell, on the other hand, (and others) refers back to where jazz piano began: to ragtime around the turn of the century, with good-humored borrowings that have an attractive double-entendre effect: direct and ironically aloof. All of a sudden, there is a real ragtime movement—in jazz as well as in rock. In jazz, it is surfacing in the renewed popularity of old, almost forgotten rag pianists and rag records. In rock, it shows itself in recordings such as "Fixin' to Die Rag" by Country Joe & the Fish, or "Rag Mama Rag" by The Band.

Thus, the circle of this chapter closes. And it is fitting that in 1971 the last great authentic ragtime pianist, *Eubie Blake,* enjoyed an astounding comeback at age 88. "I composed this piece in 1899," is how Eubie usually introduces his performances. Louis Armstrong was born a year later.

The Guitar

For the modern jazz musician, the history of the jazz guitar begins with Charlie Christian, who joined Benny Goodman in 1939, and began to play in the Minton circles shortly thereafter. He died in 1942. During his two years on the main jazz scene, he revolutionized guitar playing. To be sure, there were guitarists before him; along with the banjo, the guitar has a longer history than any other jazz instrument. But it almost seems as if there are two different guitars: as played before Charlie Christian, and as played after.

Before Christian, the guitar was essentially an instrument of rhythm and harmonic accompaniment. The singers of folk blues, work songs, and blues ballads accompanied themselves on guitar or banjo. In the whole field of jazz prehistory—the field of the archaic, West African-influenced folk music of the Southern slaves, the guitar (or banjo) was the most important and sometimes sole instrument. This was the beginning of the tradition which singers like *Leadbelly* and *Big Bill Broonzy* carried into our time, playing melodic lines which jazz guitarists per se discovered considerably later. Another outstanding example of this folk tradition is Atlanta-born *Blind Willie McTell.* On his 12-string guitar, he hinted at possibilities —albeit in an archaic, rustic manner—that John McLaughlin is now realizing within the electric jazz of the seventies.

The surveyable history of the jazz guitar begins with *Johnny St. Cyr* and *Lonnie Johnson.* Both are from New Orleans. St. Cyr was an ensemble player—with the bands of King Oliver, Louis Armstrong, and Jelly Roll Morton in the twenties—while Johnson, almost from the start, concentrated on solo work. The contrast between the rhythmic chord style and the soloistic single-note style which dominates the evolution of the guitar, is emphasized from the very beginning in St. Cyr and Johnson. Bud Scott, *Danny Barker,* and later, in the Swing era, Everett Barksdale descended straight from St. Cyr. Barker recorded with Charlie Parker, and the collaboration between the New Orleans guitarist and the great bop musician was not at all as paradoxical as one might assume. *Everett Barksdale* is known primarily for his work with the Art Tatum Trio.

The supreme representative of the rhythmic chord style of playing is *Freddie Green,* most faithful of all Count Basie band members: from 1937 to the present. Indeed, what is meant by the concept "Basic" is in no small degree to Freddie Green's credit: the tremendous unity of the Basie rhythm sections. Nowhere else in jazz did rhythm become "sound" to the degree it did with Basie, and this sound, basically, is the sound of Freddie Green's guitar. He hardly ever plays solos or is featured, yet he is one of the most sought-after guitarists in jazz history. Green is the only guitarist who surmounted the breach created by Charlie Christian as if there had been no breach at all.

An intermediate position is occupied by *Elmer Snowden,* who in 1923 formed the "Washingtonians," who later developed into the Duke Ellington band—at first, not Duke was slated to play the piano, but Fats Waller. Snowden, once a player of background music for silent movies, is a master of so-called "Harlem banjo," which has its roots not so much in the New Orleans tradition as in Midwestern ragtime.

The guitarists of the New Orleans tradition who combined the chord style of St. Cyr and the single-string style initiated by Lonnie Johnson in the most personal way are *Teddy Bunn* and Al Casey. Bunn made some of his most beautiful recordings with Tommy Ladnier in 1938—among them "If You See Me Comin'," on which he also proved himself an expressive vocalist. *Al Casey* is more in the Swing tradition. He became known through his many recordings with Fats Waller and played the—in his time—most inventive single-note solos outside the Charlie Christian realm.

Lonnie Johnson was the main influence on *Eddie Lang,* the most important Chicago-style guitarist, and also made duet recordings with him. Lang came from an Italian background, and reflects the tendency toward the *cantilena* and the *melos* of the Italian musical tradition noticeable in so many jazz musicians of Italian origin. The other important Chicago-style guitarist is *Eddie Condon* (who died in 1973), more influenced by St. Cyr, purely a rhythm player and for decades the tireless guiding spirit of the New York Chicago-style scene.

If one had heard everything played by these guitarists well into the second half of the thirties, and then had gone to Europe to hear *Django Reinhardt,* he would have understood the appeal of Django to all American musicians who encountered him in Europe. Django came from a gypsy family which had trekked through half of Europe. He was born in Belgium, but the Reinhardt's, as the name implies, are a large German gypsy family, and even today there are Reinhardt gypsy groups in Germany playing à la Django. Django's playing vibrates with the strong-feeling of his people—whether they play violin, as the Hungarian gypsies, or flamenco guitar, as the Spanish gypsies of Monte Sacre. All of this—combined with his great respect for Eddie Lang—came alive in Django Reinhardt's famed Quintet du Hot Club de France, consisting solely of stringed instruments: three guitars, violin, and bass. The melancholy strain of the ancient gypsy tradition lent a magic to Reinhardt's music; down through his last years (he died in 1953), he found his greatness in slow pieces. Often the very titles of his compositions capture the enchanted amosphere of Django's music: "Douce Ambiance." "Mélodie au crépuscule," "Nuages," "Songs d'automne," "Daphne," "Féerie," "Parfum," "Finesse". . . . In 1946, none other than Duke Ellington took Django Reinhardt on an American tour.

Reinhardt is one of the few Europeans mentioned when the formative musicians of jazz are asked about their models or influences. As late as in the fifties, John Lewis named Django as a man who had influenced him through the climate of his music: Lewis named "Django," one of the Modern Jazz Quartet's most successful pieces, in memory of Reinhardt. The phenomenon of Django has often been cause for amazement. How was it possible for such a musician to emerge from the European world? In all probability, the only possible explanation—if one is not satisfied with the statement that Django simply was there—is sociological: European gypsies were in a social situation comparable to American blacks. Again and again, ethnic minority groups have been the sources of great jazz musicians —in the U. S. (besides the blacks) Jews and Italians; and in the Europe of the thirties and forties, particularly Jews.

This sociological interpretation has frequently been offered, particularly by contemporary black spokesmen in the U. S. Thus Dizzy Gillespie answered the question: "Is there a difference between black and white musicians?" with the assertion that the difference is not based in skin color but in environment. In the case of Django, this seems the only possible answer.

Django's position as an outsider is somewhat related to that of *Laurindo Almeida,* a Brazilian musician of the rank of the great concert guitarists, such as Segovia or Gomez. Almeida employed the Spanish guitar tradition within jazz—or rather, he carried on this tradition. But since he did so as a member of Stan Kenton's band in the late forties, it acquired jazz traits—less through his playing itself than by way of its "environment." The solos he recorded with Kenton give off more warmth than almost anything else recorded by this orchestra.

Ten years later, in 1957, *Bill Harris* (not to be confused with the trombonist of the same name) attempted to play modern jazz on unamplified guitar, and actually seemed to have succeeded in combining the Spanish guitar tradition with the modern jazz idiom and a strong blues feeling, although within the technically narrow confines of his abilities. Such confines do not exist for *Charlie Byrd.* For years, he presided over the most disciplined and attentive audiences in any U. S. jazz club: at the Showboat in Washington, D. C. Nobody dared say a word when Byrd played one of his famous selections from the great literature for the Spanish guitar, which he mastered in a manner reminiscent of Segovia. For his next piece, Byrd would switch to a swinging, modern jazz improvisation—in command of everything that can be expressed on the guitar, from Bach to folk music and from Spain to jazz.

The connection of the Iberian baroque guitar tradition with the modern age and a West African rhythmic feeling was made even more convincingly by the great guitarists of Brazil. Although their place is outside of jazz, they have fascinated many jazz musicians. The most important is *Baden Powell.*

But back to Django Reinhardt (who also featured, in a totally different cultural environment, but in a similar process of acculturation, many Ibero-Spanish elements). The melodic lines he initially played on unamplified guitar seemed almost to cry out for the technical and expressive possibilities of the electrically amplified guitar. *Charlie Christian* gave the electric guitar such renown that almost all guitarists switched from acoustic to amplified instruments at the turn of the thirties. Yet Christian was not the first to play amplified jazz guitar. First came *Eddie Durham,* sometime arranger, trombonist, and guitarist in the bands of Bennie Moten, Jimmie Lunceford and Count Basie. In Basie's 1937 recording of "Time Out," the contrast between Freddie Greene's rhythm guitar and Durham's solo guitar is charming. More recent guitarists as well—for example, Tal Farlow in the fifties or John McLaughlin in the seventies—have frequently made use of the possibilities for contrast between electric and acoustic guitar. As far as Durham is concerned, however, he did not yet know how to exploit fully the potential of the electric guitar. He continued to play it as if it were the old acoustic instrument, only electrically amplified—as in the late sixties many pianists initially approached the electric piano as if it were a grand with an electric sound. An outstanding musician with especially keen foresight was needed to recognize the new possibilities of the electric guitar. Charlie Christian was that man.

Christian is comparable to both Lester Young and Charlie Parker. Like Young, he belongs to the Swing era and to the pathbreakers; like Parker, he belongs to the creators of modern jazz.

Christian is the outstanding soloist on some recordings made privately at Minton's around 1941: "Charlie's Choice" and "Stomping at the Savoy." These records were later issued publicly and must be regarded as the first of all bebop records.

Christian charted new territory in terms of technique, harmony, and melody. Technically, he played his instrument with a virtuosity that seemed incredible to his contemporaries. The electric guitar in his hands became a "horn" comparable to the tenor sax of Lester

Young. His playing has been described as "reed style"—he played like a saxophone.

Harmonically, Christian was the first to base his improvisations not on the harmonies of the theme, but on the passing chords which he placed between the basic harmonies.

Melodically, Christian replaced the tinny staccato which almost all guitarists prior to him had employed with a legato sound. He played interconnected lines which radiated some of the atmosphere of Lester Young's phrases. Not in vain had Christian played tenor sax before becoming a guitarist.

Whoever comes after Charlie Christian has his roots in him. To begin with, there is the first generation of "post-Christian" guitarists: Tiny Grimes, Oscar Moore, Irving Ashby, Les Paul, Bill de Arrango, Barney Kessel, and Chuck Wayne. The most important is *Barney Kessel,* who—as a member of the Oscar Peterson Trio and with his own groups—made many Swing-oriented recordings in the U. S. and in Europe. Strange how that which had seemed revolutionary in Christian appeared in Kessel, already at the end of the fifties, as solidly grounded in the jazz tradition. Of all successful modern guitarists, Kessel is the most "traditional."

If Kessel could be designated the most rhythmically vital guitarist of the jazz of the fifties, Jimmy Raney is the harmonically most interesting and Johnny Smith the one with the most subtle sound. But before Raney and Smith comes *Billy Bauer.* He emerged from the Lennie Tristano school, and in the early fifties played the same abstract, long lines on the guitar that Warne Marsh played on tenor or Lee Konitz on alto. With Konitz, Bauer made some of the most beautiful duet recordings in jazz—just guitar and alto sax—among them, the slow, deeply felt "Rebecca." *Jimmy Raney* is also indebted to the Tristano school, but his melodies are more concrete and singable. Where Bauer played "dissonant" chords and pointed leaps in which the thresholds are barely exploited, Raney featured richly nuanced harmonies, whose interrelatedness seems rounded, logical, often almost inevitable. *Johnny Smith* unfolded these harmonies to the last note: he strummed chords on his strings as if Art Tatum were strumming on the strings of the piano. A whole universe of satiated, late-romantic sounds evolved—the world of *L'Après-midi d'un faune* brought into jazz; a fatigued, decadent faun who relaxes in the warm sun of late summer . . . or in "Moonlight in Vermont." The mood of this ballad has never been more subtly captured than by Johnny Smith—and, of course, Stan Getz!

All this comes together in *Tal Farlow*. Farlow initially stems from Raney, but with his big hands he had quite different possibilities. After Tristano, and before Sonny Rollins, hardly any jazz musician swung such long, ceaseless, seemingly self-renewing lines above the bar lines of choruses, sequences and bridges as Farlow. But these are not the abstract lines of Tristano; they are the concrete lines of modern classicism.

Beyond the constellation Bauer-Raney-Farlow, yet inspired by it, stand the other guitarists of modern jazz: Jim Hall, Herb Ellis, Les Spann, Gabor Szabo, Grant Green, George Benson, Larry Coryell, and finally the most significant: Wes Montgomery. *Jim Hall*—with his beautifully melodious, tuneful improvisations—gained renown, initially, through his work in Jimmy Giuffre's trio; *Herb Ellis* through his long cooperation with Oscar Peterson. Ellis often has the fire and stylistic elements of Christian, plus a shot of country music (in which he has roots). And Jim Hall, when less and less was heard from the other great cool jazz guitarists (Farlow, Raney, and Bauer), became a master of delicate, sensitive guitar improvisations that have proven themselves truly ageless, as indebted to cool jazz as they may be.

Detroit-born *Kenny Burrell* could initially be designated *the* outstanding hard-bop guitarist, but in the meantime—on electric as well as Spanish guitar—has grown in the most diverse directions. He has played with Dizzy Gillespie, Benny Goodman, Gil Evans, Astrud Gilberto, Stan Getz, and Jimmy Smith—which proves his versatility and openness.

Ralph Gleason, the San Francisco critic, said that *Wes Montgomery,* who died in 1968, was "the best thing to happen to the guitar since Charlie Christian." Wes was one of three musical Montgomery Brothers from Indianapolis (the others are pianist-vibraphonist Buddy and bassist Monk), who first became known in San Francisco. He combined a fascinating, at the time almost inconceivable octave technique with hard and clear self-restraint, in statements in which the blues figured prominently. Even when he moved into pop-jazz as he did frequently during the last years of his life. In this realm as well, his guitar—recorded with a big-band background—remained an unmistakable voice.

After Montgomery's death, it first seemed that *George Benson* would be built up as the new, successful guitar star—but Benson, imaginatively as he improvises, lacks Montgomery's technical virtuosity. *Grant Green's* playing is fascinating, intensified in contrasting inter-action with a "cooking" organist as he combines the tradition of rhythm and blues with hard bop.

Around the turn from the sixties to the seventies, four basic lines of contemporary guitar playing crystallized, each equally alive and relevant: jazz guitarists cultivating the cool-jazz heritage, jazz-rock guitarists, blues guitarists, and pure rock guitarists.

In the first group, of which the most brilliant member is Jim Hall, are *Joe Pass, Howard Roberts, Pat Martino, Dennis Budimir*, and *Attila Zoller.* The connecting element between these musicians is a highly developed sensitivity. Martino has also shown interest in Arabic music. In Budimir, one finds the special brand of relaxation associated by those knowledgeable about the older jazz forms with Lester Young. Zoller, who emigrated from Hungary, Austria, and Germany to the U. S., in 1959, was initially indebted to the Tristano school and Tal Farlow. First among guitarists, he transferred the long, charming, singable melodic lines he had learned back then into the freer realm of the new jazz—working with, a.o., pianist Don Friedman. And even though he has taken, occassionally, to using the rock-associated wah-wah pedal—as have many other jazz guitarists —his music always retains an air of noble restraint. It is hard to understand why a man of such talent is still only known by the insiders on the American jazz scene!

The free-jazz guitarist par excellence is *Sonny Sharrock,* who initially came to prominence through his work with Pharaoh Sanders, but has also frequently been featured in the groups of Herbie Mann. Sharrock plays "clusters" on his guitar, sounding all the notes imaginable simultaneously (as do modern concert pianists), with the ecstatic vitality of harmonically unchained free jazz.

Such "clusters" are popular among jazz-rock guitarists, too—such as *Larry Coryell, Jerry Hahn, Gabor Szabo,* and *Joe Beck.* The first two became known through their work in the Gary Burton Quartet, and (like Burton) stand beyond the categories "jazz" and "rock." In cooperation with the great Spanish flamenco guitarist Sabicas, Beck created one of the most beautiful encounters of jazz and rock with a foreign musical culture: a mature and sensitive "Jazz-Rock Meets Flamenco" record, which regrettably has remained relatively unknown. The opposite can be said about another guitarist (also an immigrant from Hungary), Gabor Szabo. On his "Jazz-Raga" album, he recorded a totally fashion-oriented, superficial, and tasteless "combination" of jazz and Indian sounds.

Between this group of players and the one to follow stands *Cornell Dupree*. Since the end of the sixties, he has become a kind of "Freddie Green of rock and black soul music"—a musician who plays what has long been considered *passé* for other guitarists, proving that (if done his way) one can still create contemporary sounds in this field. He plays rhythm guitar (though he occasionally, of course, plays solo excursions). He fills in the "rhythm sound" of modern rhythm-and-blues records in as unmistakable a manner as Freddie Green has been doing with Count Basie for more than 30 years.

In the group of blues guitarists, clearly the blues tradition is as alive and creative as ever—along with all that goes with it: black folklore, gospel music, and spirituals. A center of this tradition, as mentioned in the blues chapter, is Chicago's South Side—with musicians like *Muddy Waters, Jimmie "Fast Fingers" Dawkins, Buddy Guy,* and many others. From this school emerged a white guitarist who stands authentically in the black tradition: *Mike Bloomfield.* Other outstanding blues guitarists are *T-Bone Walker, Albert King, Shuggie Otis* (who became known at 13), and—most important of all—*B. B. King.*

B. B. King is the father of all guitar playing in rock and popular music of the sixties and seventies. He "rides" on the guitar sound: He lets it approach, jumps in the saddle and bears down on it, spurs it on and gives it free rein, bridles it again, dismounts—and jumps on the next horse: the next sound. It was King who fully realized the development that began with Charlie Christian: the guitar sound grew increasingly longer, was further and further abstracted from the instrument. Of course, this development in actuality began before Christian; at the moment when first the banjo, then the guitar were used in Afro-American music. A development leads straight from the metallic chirpings of the banjo in archaic jazz (so brief in duration one often could barely hear them), through Eddie Lang and Lonnie Johnson, who (still without electric potential) waged a constant battle against the brevity of their sounds, and via the saxophone style of Charlie Christian and the great cool guitarists of the fifties, to B. B. King—and from him, as we shall see, on to Jimi Hendrix. This development has a single goal: the continuous, determined elongation (and the related individualization and malleability) of the sound. The aim of this development—the fact that one can do almost whatever one wants with the sound of the guitar, more so than with any other instrument—is the reason for the immense progress and popularity of guitar playing in rock and pop music of the sixties and seventies. This popularity is without precedent in the history of music. However, the disproportion between quantity (tens of thousands of young guitarists throughout the world) and quality (much fewer qualified musicians than in the narrower field of jazz) cannot be overlooked. Many rock guitarists electronically alienate the sound of their instrument to such a degree that it is often barely recognizable as coming from a guitar. The best of them, however, are unthinkable without the blues—for instance, the Briton *Eric Clapton* (see the chapters on blues and jazz combos) or *Duane Allman,* who accompanied Aretha Franklin, Wilson Pickett and King Curtis prior to forming the Allman Brothers Band (he died in 1971).

Other notable guitarists in this field are *Steve Katz* (of Blues Project and Blood, Sweat & Tears), *Carlos Santana* (with a wonderful feeling for the integration of percussive sound, and of particular charm and elegance), as well as *Jerry Garcia, Jorma Kaukonen, Frank Zappa,* and the towering Jimi Hendrix. Frank Zappa is so significant as composer, band leader and in general, stimulating personality (see the section on big bands) that one tends to overlook how excellent his guitar playing is. Its racing phrases conceal the biting cynicism so prevalent in Zappa's compositions.

Jimi Hendrix was a magician of multi-faceted and iridescent ideas, a man whose playing radiated with vision and whose wealth of ideas expanded not merely the musical scene, but also the consciousness of his listeners. Among instrumentalists, he probably was the real genius of the rock era of the sixties. Hendrix played "on" electronics and not as if he were playing an instrument. For him, electronics was a new idea, something spiritual that radiated not only over his guitar, but over all instruments—in fact, over sound *per se.* The new, electrifying aggressiveness of sound (also to be found in as meditative a man as John McLaughlin, for instance) stems from Hendrix and concerns not only all guitarists who follow him. It also concerns, for example, the best electric pianists in contemporary jazz (Herbie Hancock, George Duke, Jan Hammer); it even concerns the horn men who use electronics—insofar as they use them more imaginatively than merely for "effects" and "gags."

Jimi was black, and he admired the black blues artists—above all, Elmore James, B. B. King, and Muddy Waters. But he only admired them and learned from them; he did not soak up their tradition as had the black guitarists of the South or Chicago's Southside. He admired them—as he also admired Bob Dylan, and later Eric Clapton. Linda Keith, Keith Richard's girl friend, who brought Hendrix to England, says he kept asking her: "If you take me to England, will you take me to meet Eric?"

Perhaps Jimi Hendrix was the sole outstanding black musician of those years who was actually not conscious of the color of his skin. His mother was of Indian descent, his step-mother Japanese, his grandmother (who raised him) was a full-blooded Cherokee. Gerry Stickells, his road manager, says: "He didn't think like a colored guy, and he certainly didn't appeal to a colored audience at all. He wasn't playing colored music." Here lies the riddle of Jimi Hendrix, the black who had become so alienated from his heritage that he himself and his friends ceased to see him as black—and who nevertheless of course remained black. His iridescent, glittering, mystical uncategorizable ambiance was part of his success—and part of the aura of mystery surrounding him that the press exploited—up to the largely invented stories about his death. Hendrix did not die of an overdose of narcotics. He never was a junkie; he only occasionally smoked some hashish or marijuana—as did all the others. He had swallowed too many sleeping pills, but that wasn't the cause of his death either. It was his own vomit that made him suffocate.

John McLaughlin unites the four guitar groups—and everything that came before. The wealth of McLaughlin's music is based not so much in innovation as in his sovereign command of what already exists. McLaughlin plays "double-barreled" with the fret board of the conventional guitar plus that of the 12-string instrument of the folk-blues singer. One is almost tempted to say that he plays all guitars simultaneously. His range extends from folk blues through the great guitarists of the fifties—in particular Tal Farlow—to the Indian sitar. (See also the chapters on jazz of the seventies and combos.)

McLaughlin, first introduced to U. S. audiences by Miles Davis and his drummer, Tony Williams, is British. Even after his years of success in America, the knowledgeable listener still can hear in his playing that he emerged from the British—and in general, the European—scene. The eclecticism of his playing is typically European—as the most eclectic group of the rock scene, the Beatles, was so typically European (if in a totally different context). As far as guitar is concerned, McLaughlin certainly is *the* towering figure of this development; but particularly in Europe, there is a surprisingly large number of guitarists who indicate a similar direction: the Belgian Philip Cathérine, the Germans Toto Blanke and Volker Kriegel. . . .

For reasons of space, we must confine ourselves to the American scene, and thus mention only non-American musicians of stylistic significance. Among the guitarists in particular, there are two Europeans, still almost completely unknown in the U. S., who nevertheless have broadened the possibilities of their instrument as have no American guitarists: the British *Derek Bailey* and Norwegian *Terje Rypdal*. Both have created sounds in free playing that no longer have anything to do with the traditional guitar conventions. Both are realizing the abundant sound potentials of larger groups on their instrument. For this reason, Bailey prefers to appear as solo performer. And Rypdal, who studied George Russell's "Lydian Chromatic Concept of Tonal Organization" with Russell himself, and also was introduced by Russell, generates "flowing sounds" that also incorporate the experiences of modern concert music—of Ligeti, for example. "He bows on his instrument with a violin bow, coaxing from it clusters reminiscent of splintering glass. . . . He is a painter in sounds and time. . . . Rypdal often works with rock elements, with rhythmic patterns and riffs, but does not—as customary in rock—use them as filler material, but on the contrary eliminates the superfluous . . . and creates structures by placing all these elements in completely new relationships." (Achim Hebgen) We quote this passage because it is not only characteristic of Rypdal, but of jazz of the seventies in general.

However tight today's guitar scene may be, new approaches to playing always force their way in. In the early seventies, *Ralph Towner* proved, to the surprise of the scene, that (even in our electronic era) new ways of playing can still be created without the use of electronics—new ways not traditional, but on the contrary, progressive in nature.

The guitar has come a long way—from the African banjo to the instrument of John McLaughlin and Terje Rypdal, from folk blues to the "electronicon" of rock. Like the flute, the guitar is an archetypical instrument. Gods have blown on flutes, angels have played guitars. Psychologists have pointed to the phallic image of the flute and the similarity of the guitar to the female body. Like a lover, the guitarist must woo the body of his mistress, stroke and caress it, so that she not merely receives love, but also returns it. And while the singer sings and his instrument, the guitar, answers, lovers speak to each other—love becomes an audible happening. The singer and his guitar symbolize the couple *per se,* symbolize love.

However, when certain rock stars shatter, burn, or stomp on their guitar at the conclusion of their performances, eroticism is reduced to sex. It becomes depleted: climax has been reached, the body has done its job, it is no longer needed. "It's a Man's World." However, what is destroyed here is not the archetypical guitar. It is what is left of that archetype—its electronic remains, which actually imply completely different instruments—instruments of the future, electronic and nothing else, which also relinquish the pretext of the guitar, its remains.

The Bass

In 1911, Bill Johnson organized the Original Creole Jazz Band, the first real jazz band to go on tour from New Orleans. He played bowed bass. In the course of a job in Shreveport, Louisiana, he broke his bow. For half the night, he had to pluck the strings of his bass. Ostensibly, the effect was so novel and interesting that the bass has been played pizzicato ever since.

This tale, told by jazz veterans from New Orleans, is probably an invention, but has the advantage of reflecting much of the spirit of those years. Thus, it is "true" on a higher level. On the everyday level, it is true that the string bass had much competition from the tuba in old New Orleans. The tuba tradition was so strong that many of the great jazz bassists—such as John Kirby or Red Callender— still could play tuba well into the thirties.

The bass provides the harmonic foundation for the jazz ensemble. Since this foundation is indispensable, the bass is of the greatest importance—though it may not seem so to the layman, since its sound is not very loud. It is the backbone of a jazz ensemble. At the same time, the bass has a rhythmic task. Since bop, the four even beats to the measure played by the bass are often the only factor keeping the basic rhythm firm. Since the plucked string bass can fulfill this rhythmic function with more precision than the blown tuba, bass replaced the tuba at an early date. Thirty-five years later, the electric bass is in the process of replacing the contrabass. The evolution thus moves from tuba via stand-up bass to electric bass guitar: In the course of this evolution, the rhythmic impulse has become more precise, shorter, sharper. In the course of the same development, on the other hand, the sound has become less personal and direct. Many of the great bassists have pointed out that the acoustic bass is such a sensitive, highly developed instrument that it will probably never be completely replaced by modern electronics. It might well be that the stand-up bass has an ideal median position between the two extremes of the tuba on the one hand and the electric bass on the other, because it fulfills the needs of sound and rhythm optimally. Yet, in many groups in the early seventies, the trend is toward electric bass, probably mainly because it is better suited to the other electric instruments in today's bands.

The history of the bass can be approached from the same point of view as that of the guitar. As modern guitar history begins with Charlie Christian, so the story of modern bass starts with *Jimmy Blanton*. Both Christian and Blanton stepped onto the main jazz stage in 1939. Both died of lung disease in 1942. In two short years, both revolutionized the playing of their respective instruments, made "horns" of them. This function is established as clearly in the duo recordings made by Blanton in 1939-40 with Duke Ellington at the piano as it was by Charlie Christian with Benny Goodman during the same period. The Ellington band of the early forties is considered the best band of Ellington's career primarily because Jimmy Blanton was on bass. He gave the Ellington band a rhythmic-harmonic compactness that often has been missing—despite the brilliance of the horns and the rich colors of the sound. Blanton was 23 when he died. He made of the bass a solo instrument of such importance that leading modern jazz arrangers have dedicated miniature "concerti" to it.

From Blanton stretches the impressive line of modern jazz bassists: *Oscar Pettiford* is the second. Soon after the death of Blanton he became Ellington's bassist. And as Duke had recorded duets with Blanton's bass, he now made quartet recordings with Pettiford on cello. Harry Babasin was the first jazz cellist, but Pettiford was the man who gave the cello its place in jazz. The road from the deeper sounds of the bass to the higher range of the cello seemed a natural consequence of the evolution of the bass from harmonic to melodic instrument. Since then, there have often been bassists who choose the cello as secondary instrument, and often even seem to favor it, as did Ron Carter and Peter Warren for a while during the sixties and seventies.

Pettiford, Ray Brown, and Charles Mingus are the great post-Blanton bassists. Pettiford, who died in Copenhagen in 1960, played on 52nd Street in the mid-forties with Dizzy Gillespie, and at that time really disseminated the new "Blanton message." Several times during his career Pettiford organized big bands for recording purposes. His mobility on the bass was consistently amazing. He knew how to create tones on the bass that sounded as if he were "talking" on a horn. There may be more perfect bassists, but nobody could "tell a story" as O. P. could. In the two years before his death when he lived in Europe—first in Baden-Baden, then in Copenhagen—he had a strong and lasting influence on many European musicians. (And if the author is permitted a personal word of gratitude here, I should like to say that I have not learned more from any great jazzman than from those night-long talks and record-listening sessions with O. P., who always considered it a special challenge to spread the "message"—as he called it—of jazz.)

Ray Brown is the rhythmically most dependable and firmest of modern bassists. He was featured in a bass concerto, "One Bass Hit," recorded by Dizzy Gillespie and his big band in the late forties. Later, he recorded an album with a big band led by arranger-pianist Marty Paich, which seems a complete, grandiose "concerto" for bass and big band. This record also contains a solo for bass alone: it has the aura of "Picasso," Coleman Hawkins' equally unaccompanied tenor-sax solo. For years, Brown was Norman Granz's preferred bassist for the "Jazz at the Philharmonic" tours. For a long time, he was also a member of the Oscar Peterson Trio, and many connoisseurs found his playing in this group more notable and influential than Peterson's own. He settled in Hollywood in 1966.

Charles Mingus, finally, played traditional jazz with Louis Armstrong and Kid Ory in the early forties, then joined Lionel Hampton. Hampton's best band—that of 1947—gained much from Mingus' arrangements and personality. Through his work with the Red Norvo Trio in 1950/51, he gained renown as a soloist. Subsequently, he increasingly turned his attention to breaking new paths for jazz, never fearing powerful and exciting harmonic clashes. There was probably more collective improvisation in the Mingus groups of the fifties and early sixties than in any other significant jazz combo of that time. It has been said his were modern collective improvisations in the spirit of old New Orleans (where collective improvisation was also of great importance). As a bassist, Mingus led and held together the many different lines and tendencies that were taking shape within his group with the certitude of a sleepwalker. More than any other musician, he paved the way for the free, collective improvisations of the new jazz. In spite of his uncompromising conception—and a complex psychological tension which makes dealing with him rather difficult and repeatedly has had disastrous effects on his concert tours—he also had many great commercial successes.

During the mid-sixties, Mingus lived in comparative seclusion. But since 1970, he has enjoyed a world-wide comeback. It did not start in the U. S., but on a great European tour, prompted by years of repeated invitations to appear at the Berlin Jazz Days. The new Mingus of the seventies looks back on the whole history of jazz. One of his pieces from 1970, for example, is based on "Tin Roof Blues," made famous by the New Orleans Rhythm Kings in the early twenties.

We have presented the triumvirate Pettiford-Brown-Mingus. This constellation seems even more brilliant when seen in the light of a host of other outstanding jazz bassists, among them Chubby Jackson, Eddie Safranski, Milt Hinton, George Duvivier, Percy Heath, Curtis Counce, Leroy Vinnegar, Red Mitchell. . . .

Safranski and *Chubby Jackson* (who plays a specially built five-string bass) became known primarily through their work in the bands of Stan Kenton and Woody Herman. *Duvivier* and *Hinton* are "musicians' musicians", not so well-known among the fans, but highly regarded by musicians for their assurance and dependability. *Percy Heath* has become a much-admired musician through his superior, firm playing in the Modern Jazz Quartet. *Leroy Vinnegar* turned the California-based rhythm sections built around Shelly Manne upside down, insofar as Shelly found many melodic potentials in the drums, while Leroy's bass delivered the rhythmic foundation that made the swing felt. He, and before him *Curtis Counce* were the most frequently recorded bassists during the period of West Coast jazz. *Red Mitchell* is a wonderful soloist who phrases with saxophone-like intensity and mobility. The late *Paul Chambers* had the same characteristics, and in addition the expressiveness and vitality of the young Detroit generation. He was also a master of bowed bass, and plays *arco* with intonation and phrasing reminiscent of Sonny Rollins' tenor sax.

With Chambers, we have arrived within the circle of hard-bop bassists: *Jimmy Woode* (who emerged from the Duke Ellington band, and since has become one of the most indispensable "Americans in Europe"), *Wilbur Little, Jymie Merritt, Sam Jones,* the late *Doug Watkins, Reginald Workman,* and others belong to this group. Some of them have been pathbreakers for the development that was carried out by *Charlie Haden* and *Scott LaFaro:* the second "emancipation" of the bass—after Jimmy Blanton.

Since the turn from the fifties to the sixties, Haden has frequently worked with Ornette Coleman, and he was—in the beginning perhaps even more so than Don Cherry—an essential partner of Coleman. His "Liberation Music Orchestra," for which Carla Bley wrote arrangements, expands not only musical but also political consciousness: music conceived as the guiding torch of freedom—using themes and recordings from East Germany, Cuba, and the Spanish Civil War. Scott LaFaro, tragically killed in a 1961 auto crash at 25, was a musician on the order of Eric Dolphy, creating new possibilities not from disdain for the harmonic tradition, but from superior mastery of it. Hearing LaFaro improvise with the Bill Evans Trio makes clear what the bass has become through its second emancipation: a kind of super-dimensional, low-register "flamenco guitar," whose sound has so many diverse possibilities as would have been thought impossible for the bass only a short time before, but which still (when there is demand for it) fulfills the traditional functions of the bass. An especially convincing example of these "flamenco-bass" effects was created by *Jimmy Garrison,* John Coltrane's bassist, in the long solo which he plays at the begininng of the 1966 recording of Trane's hit, "My Favorite Things." Technically perhaps even more amazing is the bass work of *David Izenzon,* who was in the Ornette Coleman Trio during the mid-sixties, and presents his "guitar-like" bass sounds with the drive of a percussionist.

From this juncture grew the bassists of the younger generation who have come to attention during the late sixties and early seventies: *Art Davis, Wilbur Ware, Ron Carter, Richard Davis, Chuck Israels, Gary Peacock, Steve Swallow, Barre Philips, Eddie Gomez, Cecil McBee, Buster Williams, Malachi Favors, Alan Silva, Henry Grimes,* and *Stanley Clarke;* as well as a number of European musicians, of whom only those who have gained recognition on the American scene are mentioned here: The Dane *Niels Henning Örsted-Pedersen,* Britisher *Dave Holland,* and Czechs *Miroslav Vitous* and *Jiri (George) Mraz.*

For years, Richard Davis and Ron Carter have been the most frequently heard New York bassists. Davis is one of those universal musicians who has mastered everything from symphonic music through all styles of conventional jazz to free playing. Carter and Dave Holland became known through their work in various Miles Davis groups. Carter also has a special affinity for Brazilian music, as, for example, in recordings with Chick Corea and Airto Moreira. Holland is particularly mobile and expressive in free playing. Vitous plays with a flowing ease that defies the imagination. One of his "special sounds" is the bowed bass played through a wah-wah pedal. Stanley Clarke combines Vitous' fluidity with Oscar Pettiford's "soul." Gary Peacock, who lived in Japan for a long time, seems like a younger Scott LaFaro. Steve Swallow is the favorite bassist—and also one of the favorite composers—of vibraphonist Gary Burton. He, and also Chuck Israels, Peacock, and Barre Philips distinguish themselves through particular sensitivity. Eddie Gomez gained fame through his bravura playing with pianist Bill Evans. Cecil McBee made a name for himself particularly in the realm of Pharaoh Sanders' and Alice Coltrane's ecstatic free playing. Other largely "free" bassists are Malachi Favors (from the Chicago AACM avant-garde group), Henry Grimes, and Alan Silva, who is also an excellent viola player. Orsted-Pedersen, on the other hand, almost appears to be a "traditionalist" in this list of avant-gardists. He became known in the U. S. mainly through his work in the Oscar Peterson Trio—an association that also characterizes his way of playing in stylistic terms.

Some of the above-mentioned musicians have also been using electric bass in recent years, but their main instrument has remained the conventional acoustic bass. The electric bass is virtually the exclusive instrument for thousands of rock bassists all over the world, among whom, in this context, we mention only those also notable by the solo standards of jazz: The Englishman *Jack Bruce,* who became a "super-star" of rock in the group "Cream" in the second half of the sixties; *Jim Fielder* of "Blood, Sweat & Tears;" *Jack Casady* of "Jefferson Airplane;" and *Chuck Rainey,* who with guitarist Cornell Dupree and drummer Bernard Purdie formed a key rhythm section in the field of soul music of the seventies, which in tightness and dependability forms a contemporary counterpart to Count Basie's old Swing rhythm section with Basie (piano), Freddie Green (guitar), Jo Jones (drums), and Walter Page (bass).

If this wealth of names—and we have by no means mentioned all —is compared with what existed in the era of the "unemancipated" bass before Jimmy Blanton, a recapitulation need not be lengthy. *John Kirby* and *Walter Page* are the most important names of the elder bass generation. Kirby, who emerged from the Fletcher Henderson band in the early thirties, was in the late thirties leader of a small group which cannot be omitted from the history of the jazz combo. Walter Page (who died in 1957) was a member of the classic Basie rhythm section. Jo Jones says it was Page who really taught him to play in Kansas City: "An even 4/4."

Further Swing-era bassists who should be mentioned are *Slam Stewart* and *Bob Haggart*. Haggart was the backbone of the Swing-attuned Dixieland—or the Dixieland-attuned Swing—of the Bob Crosby band, and has continued this tradition in the sixties and seventies as co-leader of the "World's Greatest Jazz Band." Stewart is best known for the way he sings in unison with his *arco* playing: the humming effect of a bee, which can be very amusing if not heard too often. (A contemporary successor to his style in the sixties is *Major Holley*.)

All these bassists relate back to *Pops Foster,* a musician who oddly rounds out the history of the bass: back home in New Orleans, he started out on the instrument on which Oscar Pettiford reached a peak in the years of modern jazz—the cello. Foster worked with Freddie Keppard, King Oliver, Kid Ory, Louis Armstrong, Sidney Bechet, and all the other New Orleans greats, and easily can be identified by his "slapping" technique. This way of letting the strings snap back against the wood of the bass—rejected by the bassists of the fifties as a sign of extreme technical inability, but used again by the free-jazz bassists to increase sound and intensity gave Foster's playing much of its rhythmic impact. During the thirties, Foster was chosen several times as the all-time bassist of jazz. In 1942—the year when Jimmy Blanton died and the Blanton influence became noticeable among bassists—he went to work for the New York Subway system, but could still frequently be heard on New Orleans-style recordings. He died in 1969.

The Drums

To the person raised in the tradition of European concert music, jazz drums initially appeared to be noise-making devices. But—paradoxical as it may seem—this was because the drums serve this very purpose in European music. The tympani parts in Tchaikovsky or Richard Strauss, in Beethoven or Wagner, are "noisemakers" insofar as they create additional *fortissimo* effects. The music "happens" independently of them; the musical continuity would not break down if they were left out. But the beat of the jazz drum is no mere effect. It creates the space within which the music "happens": the musical continuity would become disrupted if it could not be constantly "measured" against the beat of a swinging drummer. Rhythm, as we have already shown, is the ordering principle.

It was no accident that there were no drum solos in the early forms of jazz—indeed, there were no drummers then with developed individuality. Concerning early jazz history, we know of Buddy Bolden and Freddie Keppard and the Tio family, we know of trumpeters, trombonists, even violonists—but we hardly know anything of drummers. Since the beat was the ordering principle—and only that! —the drummer had no task but to mark the beats as steadily as possible, a task which was performed the worse the less neutrally (i.e., the more individually) he drummed. Only later was it discovered that jazz could add to the tension so important to it through the individuality of a drummer—without loss to the ordering function. Quite the contrary: unvaried, metronomic regulation developed into organically nuanced artistic order.

At the beginning stand *Baby Dodds* and *Zutty Singleton,* the great drummers of New Orleans. Zutty was the softer, Baby the harder. Zutty created an almost supple rhythm; Baby was vehement and natural—at least in the terms of that day. Dodds was the drummer in King Oliver's Creole Jazz Band, later with Louis Armstrong's Hot Seven. He can be heard on many records with his brother, clarinetist Johnny Dodds. Baby was the first to play breaks: brief drum eruptions, which often fill in the gaps between the conclusion of a phrase and the end of a formal unit, or set off solos from each other. The break is the egg from which drummers—primarily Gene Krupa— hatched the drum solo.

Oddly enough, white drummers initially expressed more strongly the tendency toward accentuating the weak beats (2 and 4) so characteristic of jazz. The first two are the drummers of the two famous early white bands: *Tony Spargo* (Sbarbaro) of the Original Dixieland Band and *Ben Pollack* of the New Orleans Rhythm Kings. Pollack later founded a larger band in California (1925) in which many Chicago-style musicians—among them Benny Goodman, Jack

Teagarden, and Glenn Miller—became known. In the late twenties, *Ray Bauduc* held down the drum chair in the Pollack band. Ray is one of the best white drummers in the New Orleans-Dixieland tradition.

Within the Chicago style circle "white" drumming developed in a different direction: toward virtuoso play with rhythm, in which the play occasionally became more important than the rhythm. The three most important Chicago drummers were Gene Krupa, George Wettling, and Dave Tough. *George Wettling* was the only one who remained true to the musical tradition of Chicago style until the end of his life—he died in 1968. Wettling was also a gifted abstract painter. He remarkéd that jazz drumming and abstract painting seemed different to him only from the point of view of craftsmanship: in both fields, he felt rhythm to be decisive. To someone who expressed amazement that Wettling should be both abstract painter and jazz drummer, he conveyed his own surprise that he should be the only one active in both spheres, since in his opinion they belonged together. George Wettling was one of those fascinating personalities who demonstrate the unity of modern art simply through their work, without much speculation about it.

Gene Krupa, who died in 1973, became the star drum virtuoso of the Swing era. "Sing Sing Sing," his feature with the Benny Goodman band, in which he played a long solo (in part with Benny's high-register clarinet soaring above him), drove the Swing fans to frenzy. Technically, Krupa was topped only by the drummers of modern jazz. He was the first who dared to use the bass drum on recordings in the twenties. It had been the practice to dispense with this part of the drummer's equipment, due to the danger that its reverberations would cause the cutting-needle to jump on the still rather primitive recording equipment.

The most important of the drummers of the Chicago circle is *Dave Tough,* who died in 1948. He, too, was a man who knew something about the unity of modern art—if not as a painter, then as a would-be writer. Throughout his life, he flirted with contemporary literature as Bix Beiderbecke had flirted with symphonic music. Tough is one of the most subtle and inspired of drummers. To him, the drums were a rhythmic palette on which he held in readiness the right color for each soloist. He found his greatest fame around 1944 as the drummer in Woody Herman's "First Herd." He helped pave the way for modern jazz drumming, as did *Jo Jones* with Count Basie's band and it is interesting to note how a white and a black drummer here arrived at more or less the same results.

More about Jo Jones later, but let us point out that here is a fact vividly illuminating the element of inevitability in jazz evolution. Aside from Baby Dodds, the white Chicago drummers hardly drew much from other black drummers. Even though there were constant relations with black musicians, one could say that for 20 years "white" and "black" drumming in the main developed independently of each other. Nevertheless, the two evolutionary branches arrived at similar ends. Dave Tough prepared the way for the new style in Tommy Dorsey's band, which he joined in 1936. At this time, Jo Jones was doing basically the same thing with Count Basie. (See Chart II.)

Jo Jones developed under the influence of the great black New Orleans and Swing drummers. Along the line which leads from Baby Dodds to Jo Jones, there are four important drummers. The most important is *Chick Webb,* whose elemental power conjures up a giant rather than the crippled, dwarfish man he actually was. The term "elemental power" must not be misunderstood. It is not the sort of power that reveals itself in violent thumping that ruptures the drumhead. There are recordings by Chick Webb's band in which his drums are barely audible, and yet each note conveys the excitement which emanated from this tiny man.

Big Sid Catlett, Cozy Cole, and *Lionel Hampton* follow Webb. Big Sid and Cozy are Swing drummers par excellence. Cozy made his first recordings in 1930 with Jelly Roll Morton. In 1939 he became the drummer with Cab Calloway's band, in which he was frequently featured in solos. In the late forties, he was the drummer in Louis Armstrong's best All-Star group, and in 1954 he founded a drum school with Gene Krupa in New York.

Cole and Catlett were for a long time considered the most versatile drummers in jazz history, equally in demand for combo or big-band work, for New Orleans, Dixieland, and Swing recordings (and both even in a few records important in the history of bop)—in other words, in all the different fields in which other drummers were forced to specialize. Catlett, who died in 1951, was with Benny Carter and McKinney's Cotton Pickers in the early thirties, then worked with Fletcher Henderson. At the turn of the thirties, he was Louis Armstrong's preferred drummer. "Swing is my idea of how a melody should go," he said—not a scientific definition, but a statement which the musicians of the time, and jazz fans of all times, have understood better than all the fancy theories.

The difference between traditional and modern drumming becomes clear when one compares Cozy Cole and *Jo Jones*. Both are great musicians, but Cole is completely absorbed in the beat, staccato-fashion, and relatively unconcerned with musical shading of what the horns are playing. Jones also creates an imperturbable, driving beat, but legato fashion, carrying and serving the musical happenings. The Count Basie rhythm section in its classic period (with Jones' drums, Freddie Green's guitar, Walter Page's bass, and Basie's piano) was known as the "All American Rhythm Section," and surely still deserves this title.

Jo Jones is the first firmly committed representative of the even four-bar unit. He says: "The easiest way you can recognize whether a man is swinging or not is when the man gives his every note its full beat. Like a full note four beats, and a half note two beats, and a quarter note one beat. And there are four beats to a measure that really are as even as our breathing. A man doesn't swing when there's anticipation." *Kenny Clarke* followed this dictum through: The even four beats became the *son continu*—the ceaseless sounding of the rhythm. The basic beat was displaced from the heavy, pounding bass drum to the steadily resounding ride cymbal.

Clarke, the drummer of the Minton circle which included Charlie Christian, Thelonious Monk, Charlie Parker and Dizzy Gillespie, is the creator of modern drum technique. It seems to me that he is often overlooked in this capacity by jazz friends in the United States, perhaps because he has been living in Paris since 1956 and has become the respected father figure of all the many "Americans in Europe." Clarke's playing is still much admired: in the Clarke-Boland Big Band, formed by American and European musicians in Germany, in which a second drummer—Englishman Kenny Clare—provides additional metric consistency. *Max Roach,* of course, has developed this manner of playing to its most complete maturity. He is the prototype of the modern percussionist: no longer the more or less subordinate "drummer" who must beat out his 4/4, but a complete musician who has studied, generally is able to play an additional instrument, and often knows how to arrange. It is almost the opposite of what used to be: once, drummers almost always were the least schooled musicians in the band; today they are often the most intelligent, as interesting in personality and education as in their playing. Roach once said: "To do with rhythm what Bach did with melody." This was not just meant as an impressive slogan; jazz rhythm has literally achieved the multilinear complexity of baroque play with melodic lines.

Roach was the first to drum complete melodic lines. There are private recordings, made at the historic bop sessions at the old Royal Roost in New York in the late forties, on which Roach, in dialogue with Lee Konitz, consistently completes phrases Konitz has started. You can sing along with Roach's drumming just as well as with Konitz's alto playing. And vice versa: What Lee plays on alto is rhythmically as complex as what Max plays on the drums. The drums are no longer exclusively a rhythm instrument, and the alto sax no longer just a melody instrument. Both have enlarged their range in a complex joining of what earlier could more readily be distinguished as "melody," "harmony," and "rhythm" than today. Thus, Roach could manage without a piano in his quintet of the late fifties. His sidemen said: "He does the piano player's comping on the drums."

Roach has effectively destroyed the belief that jazz can swing only in 4/4 time. He plays entire drum solos in thorough, accurately accented waltz rhythm and swings more than many a musician who limits himself to 4/4. And he superimposes rhythms tightly and structurally—almost as in a fugue—such as 5/4 over 3/4. Roach does all this with a lucidity and restraint which gives meaning to his expression: "I look for lyricism." No one has proved more clearly then Roach that lyricism—poetic lyricism—can be conveyed through a drum solo. His "Freedom Now Suite" is the most important jazz work so far dedicated to the black liberation struggle in America.

And so the drums became a melody instrument . . . or more precisely, became a melody instrument as well. Certainly the drums did not suddenly give up their rhythmic function. Through the increasingly complex and musical conception of rhythmic function, the melodic function arose almost by itself. Logically and inevitably the drums went the way of all the instruments in and around the rhythm section. First came the trombone, which had only furnished the harmonic background in New Orleans; Kid Ory, with his tailgate effects, began and Jimmy Harrison, with his solo work with Fletcher Henderson, completed, the emancipation of the trombone. Then came the piano, which insofar as it was used at all in New Orleans bands, was purely a rhythm-and-harmony instrument. Earl Hines emancipated it: not relinquishing the rhythmic-harmonic function, but gaining a melodic one. Guitar and bass went the same way. The evolution of the guitar from Eddie Lang to Charlie Christian is one of increasing emancipation. On the bass, Jimmy Blanton brought about this emancipation with one stroke. And finally, Kenny Clarke and Max Roach made the drums an "emancipated instrument."

The interest expressed by Roach and the bop musicians in the West African ways of Cuban rhythms thus appears logical. Jazz percussionists and Cuban drummers now combined the arsenal of the jazz drummer with the arsenal of all the Latin American rhythms—claves, chocallo, guiro, cabaza, maracas, quijada, cencerro, bongos, conga drums, timbales, pandeira . . . .

Art Blakey incorporated many Afro-Cuban rhythmic figures in his playing. He has made duet recordings with the Cuban bongo drummer Sabu, which are on the order of constant interplay between jazz and West African rhythms. In the late fifties, Blakey finally put together whole percussion orchestras: four jazz drummers—Jo Jones among them—and five Latin drummers, using all kinds of rhythm instruments and playing together under the slogan "Orgy in Rhythm." And of course: Once the drums are emancipated—i.e., once they have acquired melodic possibilities from the complexity of the rhythms—orchestras of percussionists had to become possible, just as there are orchestras made up of brass players or saxophonists.

In the sixties, other jazz drummers—among them Max Roach—also formed percussion orchestras, using not only African percussive elements, but also elements from European contemporary concert music. Still, the African influence has continually gained in importance for the jazz drummers from the late fifties on. Many theoreticians and ethnomusicologists believe that the African heritage was strongest in the original jazz forms and has been lessened ever since. But that is true, at best, for certain forms of folk music. Beyond that, jazz instrumentalists—and mainly drummers (parallel with their growing political and sociological awareness and identification) have infused more African elements into jazz since the days of hard bop —even more so in free jazz—than the instrumental, urban jazz music from New Orleans via Chicago to Harlem ever had to show.

Blakey is the wildest and most vital of all the jazz drummers to emerge from bop. His rolls and explosions are famous. Compared to this, Max Roach seems more subdued and musical. Philadelphia-born *"Philly" Joe Jones* attempted to merge the two approaches. He plays with the explosive vehemence of Blakey, but without the latter's almost hostile tension toward the horns—rather with some of the musical cosmopolitanism of Max Roach. Even more "musical" —in the refined sense this word has acquired in the terminology of jazz musicians—is the playing of *Joe Morello,* a musician who is something of a phenomenon. From the start, he had the maturity, if not the vitality, of Max Roach. He continued from there with a nearly somnabulistic feeling for the improvisations of his colleagues. Morello joined the Dave Brubeck Quartet in 1957. Through him, Brubeck gained a rhythmical awareness which he had lacked before. Ten years later, *Alan Dawson* replaced Morello. Dawson also teaches percussion at Berklee College in Boston, the most famous of all jazz schools. He combines intellect and spirit with a swing and drive that seem to harken back to Chick Webb and Baby Dodds.

Particularly integrated into melodic play is the percussion work of *Connie Kay* with the Modern Jazz Quartet. Kay, who first became known as Lester Young's drummer, has undergone an impressive development. Since his playing is so intimately connected with the ensemble to which he belongs, we will have more to say about him in the combo chapter.

The drummers of hard bop—Art Taylor, Louis Hayes, Dannie Richmond, Pete LaRocca, Roy Haynes, Albert Heath, and (although he has gone far beyond hard bop) Elvin Jones, to mention only the most important—link up to Blakey and Roach. *Dannie Richmond* is the only musician to remain affiliated with Charles Mingus for a considerable time. The suppleness and precision with which he was able to follow the constant tempo changes of Mingus' music have frequently caused admiration. *Roy Haynes* gave the successful, bossanova influenced Stan Getz Quartet of the sixties a kind of jazz feeling that it probably would not have had without him. Like Roach, he is a master of well-structured drum solos, and he has never stopped developing within his art. *Elvin*—the third member of the *Jones* family from Detroit, which gave us two other remarkable talents in pianist Hank and trumpeter-composer Thad—plays a kind of "super-bop" which musicians feel to be a new way of "turning the rhythm around"—after all that has already been done in this area by Charlie Parker and Kenny Clarke. At a period when one could hardly imagine that further concentration and compression of the rhythmic happenings in jazz was possible, Elvin Jones and his cohorts proved that the evolution continues.

Before we can attempt to show where this development might

lead, we must refer back to a number of drummers who stand outside the realm of these tendencies, and represent a basically timeless modern Swing approach, in which new developments are hardly of a stylistic nature, but tend mainly toward even greater professionalism and perfection. *The* main representative of these drummers is *Buddy Rich,* a *ne plus ultra* of virtuoso technique. His astonishing drum solos and no less astonishing personality were highlights of the big bands of Artie Shaw, Tommy Dorsey, and Harry James, as well as of his own brilliant big bands. At a drum workshop at the 1965 Newport Festival, he "stole the show" from all the other drummers— and among them were Art Blakey, Jo Jones, Elvin Jones, Roy Haynes and Louis Bellson. However, Rich often gives one the impression that he is almost more a great vaudeville artist—a circus artist who performs the most breathtaking *salti mortali* without a net— than a genuine jazz musician in the sense of Roach, Blakey, or Elvin Jones. It certainly is psychologically illuminating that Buddy Rich was born into a family of vaudevillians.

Louis Bellson, also an excellent arranger, put *two* bass drums in the place of one, and played them with an agility comparable to the footwork of an organist. During his years with Duke Ellington— 1951 to 1953—the band gained a new, typical "Bellson" sound. Ellington's *Sam Woodyard* retained the two bass drum setup, and 15 years later double bass drums became standard equipment for many rock drummers.

The name *Denzil Best* stands for a way of playing known as "fill-out" technique. Kenny Clarke, Max Roach, and Art Blakey "fill in" the musical proceedings, placing their accents wherever they deem appropriate. This is the "fill-in" technique. But Best "fills out" the musical space evenly, placing no (or hardly any) accents, but stirring his brushes continuously on the snare drum, and thus creating his own special *son continu* swing. This, too, is an end result of the legato evolution initiated by Jo Jones and Dave Tough. After the great success of the George Shearing Quintet around 1950, when Best was a member, his way of drumming has been copied in hundreds of modern cocktail-lounge groups.

From Dave Tough descend a number of excellent big-band percussionists, such as *Don Lamond,* Dave's successor with Woody Herman, or *Tiny Kahn,* who died much too young and also was a gifted arranger whose themes are still being played. Other drummers of this lineage are *Gus Johnson, J. C. Heard,* the late *Osie Johnson* and

Shadow Wilson, Oliver Jackson, Grady Tate; and the outstanding big-band drummers *Mel Lewis, Sonny Payne, Sam Woodyard, John Von Ohlen,* and *Rufus Jones.*

Wilson, Gus Johnson, and Payne were Jo Jones' successors in the Basie band. Heard participated in many "Jazz at the Philharmonic" tours and is in some respects a "modernized" Cozy Cole or Sid Catlett. Grady Tate is much in demand for modern Swing and pop-jazz recordings. Mel Lewis is perhaps the only drummer who is keeping alive today the great big-band drum tradition of men like Chick Webb, Dave Tough, or Don Lamond—although younger musicians are of the opinion that Rufus Jones (who has drummed with Ellington, Maynard Ferguson, Count Basie, and Woody Herman) is also in the process of becoming a worthy successor to this tradition.

On the West Coast, there were two kinds of development, and much interaction between the two, during the fifties. *Shelly Manne* took a step which was as logical as Art Blakey's, though it led in the opposite direction. Manne is an absolute melodist among jazz percussionists. His way of playing is spare and subtle, spirited and animated, but frequently quite removed from what swing means in terms of the line leading from Webb to Blakey. He became well known as the percussion star of Stan Kenton's band in the late forties and through hundreds of records which made the term "West Coast jazz" a trademark of success in the mid-fifties.

Manne appears most in character on a duet recording with pianist Russ Freeman (Contemporary). In the liner notes to this album, a good many things about the rhythmic and musical conception of Manne and of modern jazz as a whole are clarified. The notes were assembled from a taped conversation between Manne and Freeman. Russ says: "I think playing without a bass gives me a lot more freedom with my left hand." Shelly: "This way we can be a little more flexible with the time . . . we do play four beats to the bar but we might take one phrase a bit shorter or longer, yet maintain the time . . . ." Russ continues in this vein: "It doesn't have that metronomic feeling." Shelly: "Russ has a way of inverting time, and it stimulates me. . . . When I'm playing, I think along melodic lines . . . drums are a very sympathetic instrument and I can sometimes sound like I'm playing the melody without being right in tune. Naturally, I don't have the whole keyboard at my fingertips. I've only four drums to work with, so I do the best I can with them to point out the melodic line." About the playing of a theme by Charlie Parker, Russ says: "Neither of us played a set 4/4 pattern; we each had complete freedom. We do these free things within the set structure of the 12-bar blues." And finally Shelly: "Instead of separate drum or piano solos, we play at the same time, trying to interweave. . . . In the drum intro, I tried to play along the lines of the melody which was coming."

Ever since rock became important to jazz—and jazz became relevant for rock—Manne has been leading a number of "rejuvenated" groups in which he assembles musicians of the free-jazz and post-free-jazz generation—occasionally also using rock elements and electronic instruments—around his drums, which he still plays masterfully.

The other way of drumming worked out on the West Coast is connected with the name *Chico Hamilton*. With his quintet, Chico recorded two drum solos in the mid-fifties, "Drums West" and "Mister Jo Jones" (Pacific Jazz). His ideas really become clear when one merges these titles. Chico plays a "West Coast Jo Jones." In 1953, he was a founding member of the Gerry Mulligan Quartet, and he represents the strongly "cooled" drumming style of modern Basie-Young classicism—often, however, doing somewhat self-consciously what comes naturally to the others. From the beginning of the sixties, Hamilton has moved his quintet into the realm of a moderate avant-gardism.

One of the symptomatic works that makes the whole history of jazz percussion from Baby Dodds to Shelly Manne and Art Blakey more clear than many words is "Drum Suite," written by Manny Albam and Ernie Wilkins, two of the leading arrangers of modern jazz, for big band and four percussionists (RCA Victor). The four drummers are Osie Johnson, Gus Johnson, Teddy Sommers, and Don Lamond. Gus generally lays down the fundamental beat. The others play around him. No drum solo is more than eight bars in length. Each beat is integrated into the musical proceedings. In one of the six movements of the suite the four drummers play in *concertante* with four horns—Joe Newman (trumpet), Hal McKusick (alto), Al Cohn (tenor), and Jimmy Cleveland (trombone). In another, the cymbals are used coloristically with unusual instrumental combinations of oboe, French horn, and woodwinds. Throughout, there are spirited exchanges among the four drummers, or among individual drummers and single horns, often in "fours" (four-bar exchanges). Nowhere are the drums used differently from any of the horns.

The "in group" of New York jazz—that small elite from whence almost everything important in jazz originates—has long passed this point. Its development leads from *Elvin Jones*—here we tie up with the paragraph in this chapter where we first mentioned this outstanding drummer—via Tony Williams to Sunny Murray, and from there to Billy Cobham and beyond.

Elvin took the *son continu* that began with Kenny Clarke to the extreme limits of perceivable, symmetrical meter—in fact, in some recordings of the Coltrane group of the mid-sixties (as in Trane's "Nature Boy," recorded in 1965 at the Village Gate), he already went beyond those limits: the meter ceased to exist. However, when Coltrane wanted Jones to carry on this development even further, Elvin resigned from the Coltrane group. He was replaced by *Rashied Ali,* in whose playing meter has been almost totally dissolved.

Meanwhile, in 1963, Miles Davis had hired *Tony Williams* (only 17 at the time) for his quintet. Williams arrived—from a different point of origin—at a most extreme reduction of the jazz beat to a nerve-like vibration and swing. In the chapter about jazz rhythm, we spoke of the fact that there is a clear physiological parallel to this reduction: from heartbeat to "pulse." Thus, a new physiological level, heretofore virtually blocked to any musical and artistic approaches, was made accessible to the musical experience. The physiological level of great classical music was breathing, that of previous jazz forms the heartbeat, that of the new jazz the pulse.

A number of drummers have also undergone this development, if less creatively than Williams. Among them are *Joe Chambers* and *Andrew Cyrille.*

Before all this, however, three drummers who had worked with Ornette Coleman since 1959 had already shown that the liberation from the meter does not mean a liberation from the function of accompaniment. These three were *Billy Higgins, Ed Blackwell,* and *Charles Moffett*—the latter the most "traditional". (There have been attempts to describe Moffett as a "Sid Catlett of the free jazz.") Blackwell is from New Orleans, and has said that he sees no contradiction between what the drummers of his home town have always been doing and his own conception. (We have pointed to Coleman's own relationship to the archaic folk blues of his home state, Texas.)

The most extreme representative of the new possibilities of free-jazz rhythm is *Sunny Murray*. In a radical fashion, the marking of the meter is here replaced by the creation of tension over long passages. When Murray was with Albert Ayler in the mid-sixties, especially when Ayler was playing folk-music themes, there were clearly per-ceptible metric pulses in the horn melodies. Murray played above them, with slight, often barely audible, pulsating beats that seemed to be collecting energy, and suddenly broke out into wild rolls utilizing the entire spectrum of his instrument. "Murray," wrote Valerie Wil-mer, "seems obsessed with the idea of strength and intensity in music."

There can be no doubt that Murray's music swings with an im-mense density and power. It swings without beat and measure, meter and symmetry—all that which only recently was thought indispensa-ble to swinging—simply by virtue of the power and flexibility of its tension-arcs. One is tempted to wonder whether this fact might not call for revision of all previous swing theories. No doubt, this way of playing creates tension, too; in fact, it increases tension, in an ecstatic sense, far beyond anything previously known. And swing in earlier jazz can be subsumed under this, too: swing as an element of ten-sion-building.

There is a whole group of other free-jazz drummers of comparable style surrounding Murray—though none of them has achieved the dy-namic effects of Murray. Among them are the "cooler" *Milford Graves, Idris Muhammed* (who also has a strong interest in African rhythms), *Beaver Harris, Bob Altschul,* and the afore-mentioned Charles Moffett and Rashied Ali.

Murray says: "I work for natural sounds rather than trying to sound like drums. Sometimes I try to sound like car motors or the continuous cracking of glass . . . I have such a magnitude of strength about myself that I often destroy something that has set upon its own basis to be very way out and creative. . . ."

When the seventies began, the great synthesis took shape—more perhaps among drummers (and guitarists) than among any other in-strumentalists: the freedom of free jazz was preserved, but it was rec-ognized that freedom can turn into chaos if one does nothing but rely on freedom and insist on it. On the contrary, one is genuinely free if one is able—if he so desires—to play not only free, but also bop, cool, hard bop, Swing, and even Dixieland: in other words, what had been considered *taboo* among a certain group of musicians as "square" and "un-hip." Added to that was the emotionalism, the communicative power of rock.

Rock rhythm is not very flexible. In some respects, it returned to Cozy Cole and Sid Catlett of the thirties: it reverted the accent away from the cymbals and back to where it had been—to the bass drum. Thus, it cannot react as easily and effortlessly to the soloists' playing as a rhythm "played on top." But it is direct and clear. One can tell where the beat "one" is—which occasionally was no longer possible in the playing of jazz drummers in the sixties.

The task of the new type of drummer to gain significance since the beginning of the seventies has been, in other words, to merge the emotionalism and communicative power of rock with the flexibility and complexity of jazz. The two drummers accomplishing this most perfectly are *Billy Cobham* and Tony Williams.

We have already mentioned Williams. Since he left Miles Davis, he has been leading his own "Lifetime" groups, but never quite succeeded in balancing and integrating these groups—the crucial problem seems to be his "ego," and it perhaps implies a positive process of psychological awareness that Tony called one of his albums of 1971 "Ego."

During the late sixties, Williams' "Lifetime" became the U. S. launching pad for British guitarist John McLaughlin, founder of the Mahavishnu Orchestra. The first drummer of that aggregation was Billy Cobham. He reaches the optimum combination of rocking expressivity with the "many-voiced" rhythmic complexity of jazz, and it seems he does this by incorporating elements from the basic "two-beat-tendency" of Latin rhythms—as opposed to the "four-beat-tendency" of jazz. It is certainly not coincidental that Cobham comes from Panama. Dutch drummer Pierre Courbois went so far as to say that sensitive rock drumming in the style of Cobham is just another way of Latin drumming—without, of course, the Latin character of the melody. After Cobham became leader of his own group—electric, of course—his influence became even greater. Among the dozens of young drummers under his spell is his successor in the new Mahavishnu Orchestra, *Michael Walden,* who plays in a simplified Cobham style.

Aside from Cobham and Williams, a number of drummers are headed in a similar direction: *Eric Gravatt* (who was with Weather Report); *Billy Hart* (who played in Herbie Hancock's Mwandishi group); *Jack De Johnette* (who emerged from the Miles Davis

Quintet of the late sixties, and in his group "Compost," has modernized the boogaloo rhythms of the black tradition, and occasionally also incorporates elements of West-Indian steel band and calypso music); and (characteristically) several British drummers connected with groups such as Soft Machine and Nucleus, and with British pianist Keith Tippett: *John Hiseman, Robert Wyatt, John Marshall, Brian Spring.* . . .

The two most important drummers in this field—next to Cobham, of course—may be *Paul Motian* and *Al Mouzon.* Motian was for many years a perfect and sensitive accompanist for Bill Evans, but suddenly, in the early seventies, seemed to have sovereignly mastered the rhythmic and percussionistic possibilities of the whole world— from flamenco to Vietnam, from China to the American Indians. And Mouzon, in groups like those led by McCoy Tyner and Larry Coryell, has gained a stature which prompted some critics to call him "the next step after Cobham."

Bernard Purdie extracts his communicative power not so much from rock as from Soul and the real black music, gospel and blues. His position among drummers is somewhat like that of Chuck Rainey among bassists or Cornell Dupree among guitarists: a modern Cozy Cole who has become an outstanding accompanist for a singer like Aretha Franklin. Musicians of his kind are the ones who assure the true continuity of the black tradition: their playing is as contemporary as it is timeless.

Among rock drummers in the narrower sense (Billy Cobham, Tony Williams, etc. are jazz-rock drummers) some merit attention from the jazz standpoint: *Buddy Miles* (who made some of his most representative records with John McLaughlin and Carlos Santana), *Bobby Colomby* (of Blood, Sweat & Tears), Englishman *Aynsley Dunbar* (who has mastered admirably the many complicated rhythm changes of Frank Zappa), and also *Ginger Baker,* another Englishman, who after emerging from the British jazz scene at the turn of the fifties became world famous in the blues-rock group "Cream," and has frequently visited Africa, mainly Nigeria, since the early seventies.

Ginger Baker did with rock rhythms what Art Blakey did with bop rhythms in his "Orgies in Rhythm": he "Africanizes" them. Especially from this point of view, it was interesting to witness a drum "battle" between Blakey and Baker at the jazz festival in conjunction with the 1972 Olympics in Munich. Although most of the youthful audience had been lured by Baker's name, the "battle" was decided in Blakey's favor according to majority opinion. The musicians and most of the critics present agreed and it was proven at this very juncture that jazz rhythms are still more complex, rich, and many-faceted than rock rhythms—even when they are in the hands of so excellent a drummer as Baker.

The Violin

What had happened to the flute during the fifties came true for the violin during the second half of the sixties: All of a sudden, it was at the center of attention—there was talk of a "violin wave." This seems particularly paradoxical in view of the inferior role the violin had previously played in the history of jazz. Though the violin is by no means new to jazz—it is as old as the cornets of New Orleans—its softness of sound long kept it from playing an equal role in the swinging consortium of trombones, trumpets, and saxophones.

Early New Orleans bands frequently included a violinist, but only because it was a 19th Century custom to have a violin in that sort of a band. The violinist in the old New Orleans orchestras was the counterpart of the "stand-up fiddler" of Viennese *Kaffeehaus* music. As late as the fifties, this *Kaffeehaus* tradition still cast its shadow over the jazz violinists. As soon as they were no longer "modern," they wound up where their instrument—as far as jazz was concerned— came from: in commercial music. This was the fate, temporarily, of among others, *Joe Venuti* and *Eddie South,* the first two important jazz violinists.

Venuti was associated with the Chicago-style circle and became famous for his duets with guitarist Eddie Lang. Even in the seventies, the "old man" generated an amazing vitality, outplaying many of the younger violinists. Eddie South lived in Paris during the late thirties, and played there with Django Reinhardt and Europe's most important jazz violinist, *Stephane Grappelly.* An amazing recording made by these three is the "Interprétation swing et improvisation swing sur le premier mouvement du concerto en ré mineur pour deux violons par Jean Sebastian Bach." Here, South and Grappelly play the main segment of the first movement of the Bach D-minor concerto for two violins, with Reinhardt taking the orchestra part on guitar. This re-

300   THE NEW JAZZ BOOK

cording is one of the earliest, and perhaps the most moving, testimonies to the admiration so many jazz musicians have for Bach's work. During World War II, the German occupation authorities in Paris melted down the entire pressing of this record as a particularly monstrous example of "degenerate art" (*Entartete Kunst*). Fortunately, a number of copies in private hands survived, and the recording was later reissued.

Stephane Grappelly is the "grandseigneur" of the jazz violin with a very French sort of amiability and charm. From 1934 on, he was, with Django Reinhardt, the key member of the famous "Quintet du Hot Club de France," the first important combo in European jazz. During the German occupation, he lived in England. Since the late forties, he has played with many well-known European and American musicians in Paris. When the "violin wave" started, he made a true come-back. One of his most beautiful new recordings was made with one of the great American musicians of the young generation, vibraphonist Gary Burton. There is often a wonderfully tender melancholia in Grappelly's improvisations. In 1973, he made a remarkable album with the classical violinist Yehudi Menuhin.

In the meantime, in the U. S.—beginning with his 1936 record of "I'se a Muggin' "—*Stuff Smith* had become the great jazz violinist. He was the first to use electronic amplification. With the sovereignty of a master, he ignored all the rules of the conservatory. A well-bred concert violinist might cringe at Stuff's violent treatment of his instrument, but he achieved more jazz-like, horn-like effects than any other violinist prior to today's "violin wave."

Smith, who died in Munich in 1967, was a humorist of the calibre of Fats Waller. During the second half of the thirties, he led a sextet on 52nd Street in New York with trumpeter Jonah Jones which combined jazz and humor in a wonderful way. In the fifties, Norman Granz teamed Smith's violin with the trumpet of Dizzy Gillespie, and the resulting Verve album is almost symbolic of the violin's position in jazz: No matter how brilliantly this most "horn-like" violinist in jazz history bows away, he does not achieve a fraction of the effect —to say nothing of the intensity—that Gillespie reaches with almost playful ease on the trumpet. *Ray Nance* has united this *ad absurdum* in his person. For years, Nance was a trumpeter in Duke Ellington's orchestra and also played occasional violin solos. But on violin he played mostly moody, sentimental melodies, while his trumpet solos belong with the great examples of the genre in jazz. On the other hand; it is an illustration of the growing importance of the jazz violin that the instrument became increasingly essential to Nance in the course of the sixties. Now, in smaller groups, he played happy, swinging violin solos that showed his roots in terms of style and phrasing to be where he originated as a trumpeter as well: in Louis Armstrong.

It was primarily a European who initiated the great success of the violin in the new jazz: *Jean-Luc Ponty,* born in 1942, the son of a violin professor. To be sure, an American, *Dick Wetmore,* had played violin in contemporary jazz style earlier. But Wetmore failed to attract attention even among connoisseurs, to say nothing of the general public. It was left to Ponty to change the position of the violin—with a style of phrasing that corresponds to early and middle John Coltrane and with a brilliance and fire that seems even more noteworthy in a European musician.

Ponty electrified the violin. Since Ponty, the jazz violin has been a different instrument. His position is thus the same as Charlie Christian's among guitarists or Jimmy Smith's among organists. This cannot be sufficiently emphasized: The electric violin has as little in common with the jazz violin before Ponty as the electric guitar of Charlie Christian had with the guitar of Eddie Lang. Ponty, who studied classical violin (he was a first-prize winner at the Conservatoire Nationale Supérieur de Paris), has made recordings in a wide field of contemporary jazz, jazz-rock and free jazz: in a violin quartet with Stuff Smith, Stephane Grappelly, and the Dane Svend Asmussen ("Violin Summit"), accompanied by pianists like Kenny Drew, George Duke, Wolfgang Dauner, and Joachim Kühn; and with rock star Frank Zappa.

Next to (and with) Ponty, *Don "Sugar Cane" Harris* is the dominant violinist of the contemporary jazz world. As Ponty stems from the violin concerto—to put it in a simplified way—Harris comes from the blues. For years, he toured around the U. S. with Johnny Otis' Blues Show. Ponty is as French as Harris is black. The position Coltrane occupies in Ponty's work is taken in Harris' music by the great black blues singers.

But the list of extraordinary contemporary violinists only begins with Ponty and Harris. There are also such players as *Mike White, Jerry Goodman, Richard Green, Papa John Creach,* the Pole *Michal Urbaniak,* and many, many more. White, from San Francisco, who early in his career—and occasionally even today—had problems with sound and intonation, became well known through his work with the John Handy Quintet and the important if much too little noticed jazz-rock group "Fourth Way." Since then he has recorded with Pharaoh Sanders and under his own name, always shaped by the spirit of John Coltrane.

Richard Green comes from the "Blues Project," from which—through Al Kooper and Steve Katz—grew Blood, Sweat & Tears on the one hand, and—through Green himself—"Seatrain," on the other. Green, who has also played with Gary Burton, merges folk, rock, and jazz. Jerry Goodman, former leader of the rock big band, "The Flock," is the real eclectic among the violinists, uniting rock, country, hillbilly, the Nashville sound, Mingus, gypsy music, jazz, and classical music. Papa John Creach is a musician of the older generation, of classic blues. Toward the end of the sixties, in his work with the Jefferson Airplane he found a degree of recognition on the California blues-rock scene which—had his instrument not been so unpopular during those years—he would have had 20 years ago. Michal Urbaniak from Poland combines the intelligence of Ponty with a special flair for electronics.

The dominating and far too little-noted violin voice of free jazz—in the narrower sense—belongs to *Leroy Jenkins.* His wide-ranging, cluster-like violin sounds have a kind of manic drive. In his hands, the violin is used as a percussion instrument, horn, keyboard, or simply a noise; aside from being masterfully employed on its own terms —as a violin.

Alan Silva plays "free" on his viola. And *Ornette Coleman,* whose violin playing was mentioned in the chapter about him, should again be mentioned here, as a violinist whose playing is totally without technical perfection but generates the sounds he wants and needs. It was Ornette, too, who collaborated in creating a four-part violin-ensemble sound for Alice Coltrane characterized by particular expressivity and mobility: at last, there was an authentically jazz-like violin-quartet sound, free from the classical ideal which up to that point had haunted all jazz experiments with violin quartets.

At any rate, it is evident that in no other instrument used in jazz is the European heritage as strong as in the violin. Among the violinists discussed in this chapter, five are Europeans, and Americans Eddie South, Stuff Smith, and Alan Silva all have lived in Europe for long periods. Sugar Cane Harris was first introduced in a manner befitting his position by a European record company with which he remained connected for years. In this context the fact that the very first jazz violinist to become well known—Joe Venuti—was born in Europe, puts an ironic dot on the "i". During the twenties, Venuti used to say he had been born on the Atlantic Ocean, in transit to the U. S., possibly because it was then not very promising for a jazz musician to have been born in Europe. But when Joe was 70, he could afford to tell the truth. He was born in Northern Italy, near Lago di Como.

Organ, Keyboards, Synthesizer

The organ: Originally, it was the dream of exalted church music, resounding in hallowed cathedrals, the "royal instrument" of the European tradition.

The realization of a dream was the starting point of the organ in jazz. It began with *Fats Waller*.

John S. Wilson wrote: "Like the inevitable clown who wants to play Hamlet [Fats] had a consuming desire to bring to the public his love of classical music and of the organ . . . ." And Waller himself, in reference to a Chicago music critic, who had written that "the organ is the favorite instrument of Fats' heart, and the piano only of his stomach," said: "Well, I really love the organ . . . I have one at home and a great many of my compositions originated there . . . ."

To be sure, the organ was also the instrument of escape for Fats Waller: It symbolized a world—a distant, unreachable world—in which the artist is accepted solely on the basis of his musical abilities, without racial or social prejudice, and also without regard for his talents as showman and entertainer. If one hears the organ records made by Fats Waller—such as his famous version of the spiritual, "Sometimes I Feel Like a Motherless Child"— today, one encounters an element of sentimentality that makes clear that Waller had only a fuzzy notion of the world into which he wanted to escape.

Waller passed his love of the organ on to his most important pupil, *Count Basie*. And from Basie come several musicians who use the organ in a rhythm-and-blues manner: *"Wild Bill" Davis, Milt Buckner,* and others.

This rhythm-and-blues organ tradition has remained alive until today; in fact, the organ, with the guitar, is the most important instrument of the non-vocal music of America's black ghettos. Particularly popular are the combinations organ-guitar, or organ-tenor sax.

Among the organists who, in this sense, play their instrument in a rhythm-and-blues way, 20 years after Wild Bill Davis and Milt Buckner, and also have assimilated all the musical and stylistic innovations made during that period, are *Jack McDuff, Johnny Hammond, Don Patterson, Lou Bennett, Richard "Groove" Holmes, Lonnie Smith, Jimmy McGriff, Charles Earland,* and many others. *Shirley Scott* has brought some of the relaxation and amiability of Erroll Garner to this way of playing. Since *Ray Charles* (who also plays organ) became successful, the soul and gospel element of the black churches has become the more significant, the younger the organists. At the risk of over-simplification, it can be said that in the beginning, blues was dominant; then blues and gospel music converged, the gospel element gradually growing stronger while the blues element became correspondingly weaker—until today there are organists in popular music who play unadulteratedly in the style of the gospel churches.

A host of rock organists have taken over the traditions of rhythm and blues and of gospel music; among others, *Stevie Winwood, Al Kooper,* and the black, particularly soul-oriented musicians *Billy Preston* and *Booker T. Jones.* Dick Halligan—who mainly played trombone with Blood, Sweat & Tears—made promises on that group's second album in his interesting intro to "Blues Part II" which he regretably has not fulfilled. In his group "Booker T. and the M. G.'s," Booker T. Jones—utilizing gospel, soul, and blues influences —helped create the so-called "Memphis sound" that has become a world-wide success in popular music.

Musicians like Richard "Groove" Holmes, Jimmy McGriff, Charles Earland, Booker T., Billy Preston, and many others, bring to mind that the technique of playing the Hammond organ was already quite developed in the gospel churches when it was only in its infancy in jazz. It is, generally speaking, significant to note that for both black and white audiences, the organ has—superficially—a similar tradition; but that this tradition implies a totally different musical background for each. For both, the organ comes from church. But "church" for black listeners is associated with the cooking sounds of the gospel churches; for white listeners, with Bach and such . . . .

We have gone far ahead in time to clarify the position of the blues and soul tradition in jazz organ playing. Before the road was free to travel for all the organists coming after Wild Bill Davis and Milt Buckner, *Jimmy Smith* had first to appear on the scene. Smith did for the organ what Charlie Christian had achieved for the guitar: he emancipated it. Only through him did the organ gain equal footing to the other instruments in jazz. Probably his most important record, made in 1956, is an improvisation on Dizzy Gillespie's "The Champ" (Blue Note). Nobody had accomplished this before: achieving effects on the organ reminiscent of a big band—in this case of the most exciting Dizzy Gillespie Big Band of the late forties—by employing a huge, overpowering dynamic range built on wide, steadily rising arcs of sound.

Smith can also be compared to Christian because he was the first to consciously play the organ like an electronic instrument—similar to Christian's transition from acoustic to electric guitar. Certainly, Wild Bill Davis, Milt Buckner, and others played Hammond organ before Jimmy Smith. But they played it more like a piano with an electric organ sound. It was left to Smith to realize that the electric organ is an independent, new instrument that only has the keyboard in common with the piano or the conventional organ. Indeed, the realization that electronics do not simply electronicize and amplify an instrument, but rather make of it something new, has penetrated the consciousness of only a few progressive musicians—and certainly not yet the public at large. Electronics—I emphasize again—means a revolution—for organs, guitars, violins, bass and other instruments.

Later, during the sixties, Smith made many commercial pop-jazz recordings of doubtful value. But that does not cast doubt on his historic achievement: He made the organ a vehicle for jazz improvisations of the highest artistic quality.

Jimmy Smith came on the scene in 1956. Nine years later came the next step in the development of the organ: through *Khalid Yasin* (at that time still known as *Larry Young*). Yasin plays the organ in the spirit of John Coltrane. It is illuminating that he became well-known at the moment when Jimmy Smith, through continuous repetition of blues and soul clichés, more and more seemed to have become a roaring Frankenstein of Hammond Castle. Understandably, organists and audiences initially became enraptured with the instrument's immense range of dynamics, its fortissimo possibilities. Yasin discovered the potential of the organ played pianissimo.

Yasin belongs to the generation of musicians that carried the Coltrane legacy into advanced rock. He was the organist in Tony Williams' Lifetime groups. It is regretable that he has not yet enjoyed a truly great commercial success. But his influence is omnipresent in the organists of modern jazz and rock.

It is especially notable in *Brian Auger* and *Mike Ratledge*. The latter gives the British group Soft Machine its "intellectual" image. He was trained by an organist at Canterbury Cathedral. "Ratledge's relationship to rock is indirect, similar to that of Frank Zappa . . . In terms of sound and style, his playing seems to be free of influences of the organ tradition . . . One of the main reasons why his organ playing sounds so 'different' is his use of an unusual organ model—a 'Lowrey,' whose sound range deviates from the usual models (Hammond, Farfisa, etc.)." (Achim Hebgen)

Alice Coltrane developed Yasin's way of playing toward the free modality John Coltrane cultivated during the last years of his life. There are also echoes of Pharaoh Sanders in her organ playing, but above all one can tell by her organ cascades that her favorite instrument is the harp!

In Europe, Frenchman *Eddie Louiss* (whose family comes from Martinque) has developed the Coltrane influence into an individual, hymnal, singing, triumphant style. A man as critical as Stan Getz has stated that Louiss is one of the most original organists on today's scene. Too bad that, due to various personal problems, he has not had the recognition he deserves. Louiss is also a brilliant composer, and extremely original in this area, too. He carries the melodiousness and singability of the tunes of his Caribbean home into the modal climate of John Coltrane.

Those who love system-building can view the development of the organ as follows: First, blues and gospel are applied to the organ (this application remains and is continuously intensified); then, this blues and gospel approach is applied to rock; simultaneously, Charlie Parker is applied, then Coltrane, and finally, the "Coltranized" organ playing is applied to rock.

Since the turn of the sixties, a new group of musicians has developed who play the organ, but whom I hesitate to call organists in the sense of the term as used so far in this chapter. For them, the organ is an instrument among several others: acoustic and electric piano, synthesizer, and such accessories as wah-wah pedal, fuzz, vibrator, Echoplex and Echolette, phase shifter, ring modulator, etc. These musicians are referred to as "keyboard artists." Among them are some musicians already discussed in the piano chapter: *Jan Hammer, Joe Zawinul, Herbie Hancock, George Duke* . . . ; musicians mostly from the circle of Miles Davis' "electric jazz." These musicians have masterful command of the various keyboards which offer them the differentiation possibilities of an entire orchestra.

The synthesizer, developed by R. A. Moog in the late fifties, gained sudden popularity in 1968 through the world-wide success of Walter Carlos' record "Switched-on Bach," which presented electronic versions of some of Johann Sebastian Bach's compositions. Here, the electronics "simulate" the original instrumental voices—there are hardly any signs yet of a truly autonomous use of the new sounds and new instrumental possibilities. In his next work, however —the soundtrack to Stanley Kubrick's "Clockwork Orange"—Carlos took a crucial step forward that attracted wide attention in the jazz and rock worlds.

The musicians of the concert realm, besides Carlos, were first to experiment with the synthesizer—for example, John Cage and Terry Riley (about whom more later).

Then jazz musicians like Paul Bley and Sun Ra began to experiment with the synthesizer. Herbie Hancock made particular strides, truly using electronics as a new means of expression subject to its own laws. Others—for instance, Jan Hammer—at first limited themselves to playing the synthesizer like some sort of piano. George Duke—or the Europeans *Jasper van t'Hof* and *Dave McRae*—are not using the synthesizer at the time of this writing, but are achieving synthesizer-like effects through ingenious use of organs and electric pianos—with the added advantage of not sounding as synthetic as the sound effects of the synthesizer.

Using electronics, Hancock and van t'Hof were the first in jazz music to create that kind of *"Klangfarbenmelodie"* established in modern concert music by Arnold Schönberg—first in 1909, in the third of his Five Orchestral Pieces, opus 16 (the famous "Colors"); and theoretically, in his theory of harmony in 1911. Of course, there were no electronics then, but many of Schönberg's and Webern's discoveries did in fact anticipate and demand the use of electronics. The consequence is rooted not only in Schönberg's ideas, but in the electronic medium itself. I know it to be true in van t'Hof's case (and would suspect it in the case of Hancock) that without conscious knowledge of Schönberg's theories he reached a kind of "Klangfarbenmelodie" simply through his own understanding—truly having felt his way into the laws of electronics. It may, however, be presupposed that Hancock and other contemporary keyboard players listened to Jimi Hendrix: Here begins a real musical playing "on" electronics—Hendrix was the first to aim for what is being continued today on keyboards and synthesizers. (See the chapter on guitar—and also what is said about the synthesizer in the chapter "1970.")

Today, synthesizers are made not only by R. A. Moog, but by many manufacturers. The synthesizer realizes "sounds *per se*," abstract and not bound by particular mechanical vibration generators; i.e., the synthesizer is the master of "all" sounds. The mathematically calculable possibilities reach into the millions, and billions.

The sheer endless range of possibilities makes it difficult to work practically with the synthesizer. All synthesizer-players complain that they discovered a sound some time ago—yesterday or maybe last week—which they, now that they need it, can't find again. Some synthesizer players—such as Keith Emerson—have begun to record the various sound possibilities in card catalogues. Another difficulty in the use of the synthesizer is the fact that it has to be programmed through the use of patch cables. This takes time and impedes spontaneity. For that reason, several companies have constructed smaller model, the "Mini Moog," f.ex., which handle much more simply.

The synthesizer is only the beginning of a development the extent of which is almost impossible to foresee. Nearly everything played on synthesizers today is more or less in the experimental stage. For this reason, most musicians use it only in addition to their other keyboard instruments. When Paul Bley, mentioned in the piano chapter, plays the synthesizer, one can appreciate the degree of calculated, unsatisfying, conscious effort still necessary when experimenting with this instrument.

In rock, *Don Preston* has made interesting synthesizer sounds on Frank Zappa's records. Most of the synthesizer players in rock use the instrument superficially, unmusically, aiming only at exterior effects. The general public would probably name Keith Emerson the "best" rock synthesizer player—and keyboard player in general—because he is backed by the full advertising power of the record media. Emerson is one of those outwardly perfect musicians who mistake expansiveness for expressiveness. Frequently, he creates fantastic sounds never before achieved by any musician, but much too seldom are these sounds organically integrated into the musical context—they remain effects only.

Emerson plays his diverse instruments—organ, piano, synthesizer, other keyboards, accessories—in a "Wagnerian," bombastic sense, literally subjugating the audience to displays oriented only toward commercial success.

So far, I know of only one musician whose synthesizer playing really possesses the power, greatness, and expressivity of spontaneous jazz improvisations—in the sense, for example, of a tenor sax with immensely enlarged possibilities. This is band leader *Sun Ra,* of whom we'll have more to say in the big-band chapter. Sun Ra says he plays "music of the cosmos," of "new galaxies," and his synthesizer improvisations—played mostly on the Mini Moog—give the impression of some of the power and scope of the experiences future astronauts may have on entering new dimensions of time and space.

At performances by the "Sun Ra Arkestra," the musicians may often be seen sauntering, promenading, dancing, playing among the audience. Sun Ra remains on stage alone, surrounded by six or seven keyboard instruments—organ, Mini Moog, piano, clavinet, rocksicord, electra piano, spacemaster—sitting in the center of all this electronic equipment that it takes a whole day to set up—like an astronaut in the cockpit of his space ship. And while his musicians are somewhere "out in space," he takes off for someplace with "colored noise," with streaming synthesizer sounds, with "shot" sounds, hammering out clusters, drumming forth organ power—one hand on the synthesizer, the other on one of his other keyboards, masterfully dominating the instruments, changing, switching and recombining them.

And then there is *Terry Riley.* Riley not only plays organ, but also soprano sax and diverse other instruments—and he plays them not so much as main instruments, but rather as means to an end in which their instrumental character disappears. The impulses Riley exudes do not lend themselves to categorization—even less than most of the other tendencies of the contemporary scene. This musician does not belong anywhere—neither to jazz nor to rock nor to avant-garde concert music—but he has influenced musicians in all these areas. Many of them—for example, Don Cherry, the Soft Machine, or Steve Reich (to name three names from the three different areas)—speak of him with highest admiration, through Riley is far from being an organist with the kind of technical mastery taken for granted among contemporary players. He plays at low volume, carefully, modestly, as a sort of aid to meditation. His music is supposed to be felt rather than heard. It is music for a person's aura rather than for his ears. Riley's music might be called "minimal music," since it hardly seems to change. The listener has the impression that the same tonal movements are constantly being repeated, but in the course of these repetitions, imperceptible changes take place, so that at the end of a Riley piece something new, something different is reached, while the listener is still under the impression of hearing the same tonal movements, phrases, and sounds with which the piece began a long time ago. Riley's phrases are "mantras" that develop and grow in meditation—hardly noticed by the meditating subject— and begin to be effective in a spiritual world, according to their own laws. Riley has dematerialized the organ—certainly a significant accomplishment with an instrument that just a short while before (as with Jimmy Smith, Jack McDuff, or Keith Emerson) had seemed to be one of the most material, robust, and solid of all instruments. But he also brought the organ back to where it had been before it became electronic: to the spiritual realm—not, however, to a regressive spirituality, but rather to one that progresses into new spaces.

Miscellaneous Instruments

For 50 years—until about 1950—only a relatively small "family" of instruments was used in playing jazz. They were basically the same instruments that had been employed in early New Orleans jazz: two instruments from the brass group (trumpet and trombone), saxophone and clarinet from the reed group, and, of course, the rhythm-section instruments—drums, bass, guitar, and piano.

Nevertheless, there have been shifts in emphasis within jazz instrumentation—to such a degree that the entire history of jazz can be viewed in terms of individual instruments. In this scheme, the piano would stand at the beginning; it ruled the ragtime period. Then the trumpet blew its way to the forefront: first in New Orleans, where the "Kings of Jazz" always were trumpeters (or cornetists), then in the great Chicago period, when trumpeters like King Oliver, Louis Armstrong, and Bix Beiderbecke came to the fore. The Swing era was the time of the clarinet. And with the appearance of Lester Young and Charlie Parker, the saxophone became the main instrument—initially tenor, then for a while alto, and after that again tenor. Since the second half of the sixties, finally, electronics have become the determining sound factor—to such a degree that the electronic sound is frequently more important than the original sound of the instruments electronically amplified or manipulated. Electronics similarize the sound of instruments. This is true even for instruments as diverse as organ and guitar. There are rock groups which have disbanded because the musicians thought that the electric organ and electric guitar sounded so much "alike" they felt they could do without one of them. Differentiation within similarity, on the other hand, is one of the most attractive chapters in the annals of jazz. It was a fascinating challenge to differentiate between the various instruments of the saxophone family or between the Four Brothers saxophonists of the fifties. Today, it is just as fascinating to differentiate between the various electronic sounds of the seventies.

But we have made a leap in this discussion. Twice there were changes in jazz instrumentation—first, through the Lester Young-initiated switch of jazz-consciousness from sonority to phrasing, then through electronics.

After Lester Young had cleared the path for the recognition that the jazz essence was no longer tied, for better or worse, to jazz sonority, jazz could be played on practically any instrument offering possibilities for sufficiently flexible, clear jazz phrasing. Thus, instruments were "discovered" for jazz which previously had hardly ever (or never) been in jazz use. The flute, the French horn, and the violin are examples for this phenomenon. While some of these instruments could be summarily discussed under the heading "Other Instruments" in prior editions of this book, they now require chapters of their own: flute, violin, organ.

The "Miscellaneous Instruments" chapter had become too large. We had to cut it down in order to avoid its breaking apart at the seams a second time. After all, Philadelphia-born saxophonist *Rufus Harley* has proven that convincing jazz solos can be played even on the bagpipes.

Most of the "miscellaneous instruments" are used as secondary instruments, and we have mentioned them where a certain musician's primary instrument was discussed: The cello in connection with bassist *Oscar Pettiford;* the bass clarinet that was introduced by *Eric Dolphy* in the clarinet chapter; oboe and bassoon in connection with *Yusef Lateef* in the tenor and flute chapters. *Roland Kirk* was also presented there. In addition to all his other instruments, he also plays two archaic instruments from the saxophone family: the stritch and the manzello.

How the limits of jazz instrumentation have expanded in the meantime becomes clear when one hears the harp improvisations of *Alice Coltrane*. In the fifties, *Corky Hale* from the West Coast and *Dorothy Ashby* from New York had already attempted to play in a jazz vein on this instrument; *Johnny Teupen* did something similar in Germany. (Curiosity: the first traceable jazz harp was played by Adele Girard in 1938, on recordings with her husband Joe Marsala and His Chicagoans, on pieces like "Jazz Me Blues"!) But only the modality of the new jazz seems to have cleared the way for this difficult instrument, which has to be constantly retuned. Alice Coltrane was the first to develop a jazz-harp sound into something more than just a curiosity.

Two instruments have come full circle: harmonica and tuba. In the early days of jazz, the tuba—as we've mentioned—was used as a string bass substitute. Today, musicians like *Howard Johnson, Don Butterfield,* and *Dave Bargeron* (of Blood, Sweat & Tears) are playing tuba solos of almost trumpet-like agility. And Johnson, behind blues singer Taj Mahal, used an entire tuba section as accompaniment on a record aimed at the young rock audience. Since one tends to forget the man who initiated this whole development, it should be pointed out at this juncture that as early as the fifties, in Los Angeles, bassist *Red Callender* tried to incorporate the tuba into the then dominant West-Coast sounds.

The harmonica is the "harp" of the folk-blues singer. The two *Sonny Boy Williamsons, Sonny Terry, Junior Wells, Shakey Jake, Little Walter, Big Walter Horton, James Cotton, Whispering Smith,* and many others have played marvelously expressive, "talking" harmonica solos—usually in the simple blues groups that existed (and continue to exist) in the South or on Chicago's South Side. Nevertheless, this instrument has always been afflicted with the stigma of a certain folklore-like primitiveness. Since the emergence of electronic amplification, it has been given equal rights in the family of jazz instruments. The harmonica has also made inroads in contemporary blues-rock music where it is played by white musicians like *Paul Butterfield* or *John Mayall* in the style of the great black "harp" men. Outside the narrower blues confines, Belgian *Toots Thielemans* has developed a mobility and wealth of ideas on the harmonica that brings to mind the great saxophonists of the cool-jazz era.

The horizon of instruments grows even larger when it is extended to the exotic instruments that became available in the course of the opening of jazz to the great musical cultures of the world. *Don Cherry,* for example, has used Balinese gongs (gender and saron), *Charlie Mariano, Clifford Thornton,* and others have played the Indian shenai; *Han Bennink* and other percussionists have used the tabla; *Bill Plummer* the sitar, Bennink, the dhung (a gigantic Tibetan alphorn). And *Airto Moreira* has made today's musicians aware of the wide range of Brazilian percussion instruments: cuica, agogo, caxixi, berimbau, reco-reco, afuche, ganza, chocalhos, surdo, pandeiro, zabumba, atabaque, and many others, including those he has "invented".

There is virtually no instrument left in the world on which somebody has not played jazz at one time or another. The chapter on "Miscellaneous Instruments" can only be a suggestion if it is not to become endless.

THE VOCALISTS OF JAZZ

The Vocalists of Jazz

The Male Singers

BEFORE JAZZ, there were blues and shouts, work songs and spirituals —the whole treasury of vocal folk music sung by both black and white in the South. There was what Marshall Stearns has called "archaic jazz." From this music jazz developed. In other words, jazz developed from vocal sources. Much about the sounds peculiar to jazz can be explained by the fact that horn-blowers imitated the sounds of the human voice on their instruments. This is revealed with particular clarity in the growling sounds of trumpets and trombones in the orchestra of Duke Ellington.

On the other hand, jazz is today so exclusively an instrumental music that its standards and criteria derive from the realm of the instrumental, even the standards of jazz singing. The jazz vocalist handles his voice "like an instrument"—like a trumpet or trombone or —today especially—a saxophone. Thus the criteria important to European vocal music, such as purity or range of voice, are inapplicable to jazz. Some of the most important jazz singers have voices which —according to "classical" criteria—are almost ugly. Many have a vocal range so limited that it would hardly encompass a Schubert song.

The dilemma of jazz singing can be expressed as a paradox: all jazz derives from vocal music, but all jazz singing is derived from instrumental music. Significantly, some of the best jazz singers are also players—above all, Louis Armstrong.

In the literature of jazz, critics of the most diverse persuasions

317

mean to be laudatory when they say of an instrumentalist—such as alto saxophonist Johnny Hodges—that his sound "resembles that of the human voice." On the other hand, nothing more flattering can be said of a singer than that he or she knows how to "treat the voice as an instrument."

The symbol of the jazz-vocal dilemma is that almost all the jazz polls in the fifties gave first place to a man who is not a jazz singer— *Frank Sinatra*. The reason for this was not the oft-claimed intrusion of commercial values on the jazz field. Many uncompromising jazz instrumentalists voted for Sinatra. And undoubtedly, no "modern" singer *within* jazz at that time sang with the sensitivity and musicality of Sinatra. In the field of commercial music, Sinatra set the standards for almost all who came after him. Thus, "Frankie's" place in the jazz polls is not based on erroneous judgments, but is a direct result of the jazz-vocal dilemma.

Only two domains are beyond this dilemma: blues and gospel. But it is precisely this that makes clear the vicious circle in which jazz singing moves. For decades, almost all jazz singers who found favor with the general public were outside the stream of real blues, whereas the first-rate singers of authentic blues and gospel—at least until the big success of blues in commercial music from the sixties on —were hardly known. This breakthrough began—as early as the late fifties—with *Ray Charles*. A real blues singer from the tradition of folk blues and gospel was accepted by the whole world of modern jazz, and found a wide audience beyond both blues and jazz. It has been rightly said that no one did more to assure the return of the blues to the common consciousness of America than Ray Charles in the fifties. But Charles was only the final link—for the time being!— in an unending chain of blues singers whose earliest representatives disappear somewhere in the darkness of the South of the past century. And simultaneously, he was the first link in the still growing chain of black singers who sing authentic blues, yet have great success even with white audiences.

The first well known representatives of this blues folklore are probably *Blind Lemon Jefferson*, a blind street musician from Texas, and *Huddie Leadbetter*—called *Leadbelly*—who served time in Angola State Penitentiary in Louisiana, first for murder and a few years later for attempted killing. From them, the line runs via *Robert Johnson*, who came from Mississippi and was poisoned in Texas, to *Big Bill Broonzy* and *Son House* and the many blues singers who made

Chicago the blues capital of the U. S. A. (though all are natives of the South): *Muddy Waters, Little Brother Montgomery, St. Louis Jimmy, Sunnyland Slim, Little Walter, Memphis Slim, Howlin' Wolf* . . . many others. *John Lee Hooker,* who lives in Detroit, also belongs here. Almost all the blues singers are also excellent guitarists. And when they play piano, they accompany themselves with exciting boogie-woogie bass lines. (Other great folk-blues singers are mentioned in the blues chapter.)

In an unending stream, over the decades more and more new blues singers became known as they migrated from the South to the cities of the North and West. There are two main streams in this great blues migration, and two main states: Mississippi and Texas. Mississippi-born blues people generally migrate to Chicago, those from Texas go to California. The two streams differ musically, too: The Mississippi stream is rougher, "dirtier;" the Texas stream softer, more flexible and supple. It was the Texas stream that merged with the Midwestern big bands during the Swing era, leading to Swing blues and jazz blues. But, here, too, there are of course all imaginable kinds of crossings and mixtures.

The blue stream from Mississippi and Texas (and all the other Southern states) has been flowing uninterruptedly for more than 50 years. But the South remains full of great blues talent. Many blues people resist all the temptations of North and West—such as the wonderful *"Lightnin' " Hopkins* from Texas. To this day, he sings his songs in the bars and hangouts of Houston, his lyrics mirroring the life of his city.

The blues is as alive in the seventies as it was during the twenties and thirties. Since the sixties, a new generation of blues singers has appeared filled with the consciousness of race and social protest that can be found in many contemporary jazz musicians as well. Members of this new blues generation include singer/harmonica player *Junior Wells,* or singer-guitarist *Buddy Guy* and *Albert King,* or *Taj Mahal,* who has found success with contemporary rock audiences. They no longer hope—as did Trixie Smith and many other 1920's blues vocalists, filled with the despair and irony which co-exist in the blues, that some day "the sun will shine in their back door". (The irony is in the conscious avoidance of the front door!) Rather, filled with sense of self they demand—like singer-pianist *Otis Spann*—"I Want a Brand-New House."

When I visited Angola State Penitentiary in the summer of 1960, I heard several young blues singers every bit as good as the well-known Chicago names. The day before my visit, there had been a thunderstorm. One of the prisoners told us he had nearly been struck by lightning. He was still under the spell of the fear which had possessed him. I suggested that he would someday write a blues about his experience—and right away, he strummed a few chords on his guitar and improvised his "Lightning Blues." The surprise was the lyrics, which reflected his experience with intensely realistic expression. These blues lyrics are the real "jazz and poetry." Here the difference between "jazz" and "poetry" is one of terminology, not substance.

The realm of folk blues, difficult to survey in its entirety, has been divided into "country" and "city" blues, but this division is often merely theoretical. Even the singers who never left the South, where they still sing so-called country blues, live in large cities: Lightnin' Hopkins in Houston, or *Brother Percy Randolph*, who pushed his rag cart through the French Quarter in New Orleans. Even Leadbelly, often cited as a prime example of country blues, sang city blues as well.

The most successful singer-guitarist of authentic big-city blues today is Mississippi-born *B. B. King,* a cousin of Bukka White, the great old folk-blues man. In the 1966 edition of Leonard Feather's "Encyclopedia of Jazz," it is stated that King "would like to see Negroes become unashamed of blues, their music." Indeed, King himself has been an essential mover toward the fulfillment of this wish, though (especially in the middle class) there still are many blacks who look down on blues as rustic, primitive, and archaic, and want to dissociate themselves from it. The black American will have found the road to the freeing of his own inner self—and thus to true equality—only when he takes as much pride in the blues as a German can take in Beethoven or an Italian in Verdi. . . .

From the start, the borderline between folk blues as a realm distinct from jazz and the domain of jazz itself has been fluid. A number of singers who are authentic blues singers have been counted as belonging to the jazz world at least as much as to the world of blues. The first of these—and founder of the vocal swing tradition—was *Jimmy Rushing,* who died in 1972. Rushing, from Oklahoma—a state that always was within the sphere of Texas blues influence—became the blues singer of Swing style par excellence. He was the first not to sing "on the beat"—as the folk-blues people did—but in front

or behind the beat, to "sing around" the rhythmic centers and counter them with his own accents, thus creating greater tension. During
the thirties and forties, Rushing was Count Basie's singer, and his
singing was the exact counterpart of Basie's instrumental theme of
those years: "Swingin' the Blues." Other singers of this brand are
Jimmy Witherspoon, who today lives in California, and *Big Miller*
from Kansas City. In the Basie band of the fifties, *Joe Williams* took
the role of Rushing. He is a fine musician, who on the one hand en-
dows his ballads with a blues-like intensity and on the other sings the
blues with the sophistication of a modern jazzman.

Joe Turner, who now lives in New Orleans, is the blues shouter of
boogie-woogie. In the thirties he worked with the great boogie pianists; a generation later, he had a second round of success—as did
many other bluesmen—with the emergence of rock 'n' roll. *"Champion" Jack Dupree* from New Orleans ("Champion" because he
started as a boxer), *Memphis Slim,* resident of Chicago and later of
Paris, *Roosevelt Sykes* from Louisiana, and the late Otis Spann are
also among the blues and boogie musician-singers.

Leon Thomas combines the blues tradition with the music of the
post-Coltrane era in free, cascading falsetto improvisations, for which
he also found inspiration in exotic folklore—such as the music of
Central African pygmy tribes.

The line that leads from Blind Lemon Jefferson through the South
Side of Chicago to the modern blues of Ray Charles and B. B. King
is the backbone of all jazz singing. This line could be designated the
"blues line" of jazz singing to differentiate it from the "song line".
But it is important to see the continuous, intensive interrelationship
between these two. This is illustrated by the first and most significant
singer of the "song line," *Louis Armstrong*. Armstrong's music remains related to the blues even when it is not blues—and in the or-
thodox sense of the word, it rarely is. Armstrong's singing is exemplary of the instrumental conception basic to all jazz singing, a conception revealed particularly clearly by vocalists who are also instrumentalists: from the old blues singers, who usually also played the
guitar, via trombonist Jack Teagarden, to today's singer-instrumen-
talists.

Some years ago, on the occasion of an Armstrong visit, the *London Times* noted: "Of course, this voice is ugly when measured
against what Europe calls beautiful singing. But the expression which
Armstrong puts into this voice, all the soul, heart, and depth which

swings along in every sound, makes it more beautiful than most of the technically perfect and pure, but cold and soulless singing in the white world of today."

The late *Hot Lips Page*—at times almost an Armstrong double—came close to Satchmo not only as trumpeter, but also as singer. Trombonist *Jack Teagarden* made some of the most humorous and spirited vocal duets in jazz with Armstrong. Teagarden is a master of "sophisticated" blues singing, and was that as early as in the thirties, long before the ironic sophistication of the blues became "modern" in the late fifties. Later, in a more modern field, one finds in *Woody Herman* a similar sophistication, tasteful and musicianly, but not as expressive as Teagarden or the great black vocalists.

The male singers who have maintained a position in the realm of jazz *per se* have almost without exception been instrumentalists. Most others who began somewhere within jazz or close to it have gone over to commercial music: *Bing Crosby, Frankie Laine,* and the musically outstanding *Mel Tormé,* who—wavering between jazz and commercial music—tries to combine both. Appropriately, *Nat "King" Cole* was a first-rate jazz vocalist as long as he was mainly a pianist. Later, as he became a successful singer in the commercial field, his piano playing was pushed further and further back. Nevertheless, a jazz past remained clearly noticeable in his singing to the end. This is one reason why American commercial music is the world's best: so many of the popular stars have a jazz background and "paid dues" in jazz before attaining commercial success. (Outside of the vocal realm, Glenn Miller, Harry James, and Tommy and Jimmy Dorsey are examples of this fact.)

The jazz instrumentalist, as we said, is especially qualified also to be a good jazz singer. Examples of this can be cited not only from the times of Hot Lips Page and Jack Teagarden, but also in the sixties and seventies: drummer *Grady Tate*, trombonist *Richard Boone,* organist *Jimmy Smith*, and trumpeter *Clark Terry* are notable singers in their stylistic area—Terry with lots of joy and humor, Boone with a combination of traditional blues and contemporary satire, Smith with lyrics full of racial and political consciousness . . . .

In the forties *Billy Eckstine* was to male singers what Sarah Vaughan was to the females. Eckstine had the greatest vocal gift since Louis Armstrong and Jimmy Rushing. He belonged to the bop circle around Gillespie and Parker, and was so full of enthusiasm for the music that he took up an instrument—the valve trombone. Today, of course, Eckstine has left jazz entirely, and it is difficult to recall, listening to a sentimental recording by "Mr. B.," the assurance with which he drew from the blues tradition within the modern jazz of the forties in "Jelly, Jelly" and other hits.

In the more narrow realm of bop itself, male singers worth mentioning are *Earl Coleman*, whose sonorous baritone was once accompanied by Charlie Parker; and *Kenneth "Pancho" Hagood* and *Joe Carroll,* who both worked with Dizzy Gillespie. Carroll reminds of Dizzy in mobility of voice and sense of humor. Of course, one must not forget *Dizzy Gillespie* himself when speaking of bop vocalists. Dizzy's high-pitched, slightly Oriental-sounding voice corresponds as closely to Dizzy the trumpeter as Satchmo's voice related to *his* trumpet. *Jackie Paris* carried the bop vocal conception into cool jazz. *Mose Allison* translates the black and white blues and folk songs of his home state, Mississippi, into the modern jazz idiom. *Oscar Brown, Jr.,* a personality of great radiance, is a singer, nightclub artist, and lyricist. *Johnny Hartman* is a "musicians' singer," whose supple, flowing phrasing—as in his ballad recordings with John Coltrane—has been much admired by connoisseurs. *Bill Henderson* and *Mark Murphy* sing with a healthy, Basie-inspired Mainstream conception.

No doubt the yield of great male jazz singers—aside from the great blues singers and Louis Armstrong—is slight. This fits our conception of the jazz vocal dilemma. Jazz singing, beyond blues, is the more effective the closer it approximates instrumental use of the voice. The female voice has the greater potential in this respect.

From the realm of bop stems a development which led to the most successful vocal group in modern jazz. From the early fifties on, *Annie Ross* (born in England and raised in California) and vocalists *King Pleasure* and *Eddie Jefferson*—the latter mainly as a member of James Moody's combo—had equipped famous recorded solo improvisations (by Wardell Gray, Moody, Lester Young, Lars Gullin—all saxophonists!) with lyrics, and sung them note for note. They were mostly happy, amusing lyrics with the climate of jazz—and of the "hipsterism" of that time—exuding from each note. *Dave Lambert* (who died in 1966), had been singing bop prior to this. His 1945 recording of "What's This?" with Gene Krupa's big band must count as the first bop vocal. Later, Lambert directed vocal ensembles and choral groups, using musical materials from modern jazz. *Jon Hendricks,* finally, was not only a bebop singer but also a bebop lyricist. He made possible for the first time outside the blues, a "jazz of words." Thus, Dave Lambert, Annie Ross, and Jon Hendricks belonged together musically prior to forming the *Lambert-Hendricks-Ross* Ensemble in 1958. The group began with vocalizations of Count Basie pieces, and went on from there to discover an entertaining, pleasurable style of their own. When Annie Ross returned to England in 1962, Ceylon-born *Yolande Bavan* took her place, until the trio finally broke up in 1964 . . . .

We have talked about the "blues line" and the "song line" of male jazz singing. Both lines merge in rock singing. The key figure in opening up this realm was Ray Charles. He was the first to introduce the traditions of the folk, classical, and big-city blues to a large, modern audience. It was also Charles who established the concept of "soul," which transformed black religious music into contemporary pop music (also see chapter on spirituals and gospels, and what was said in the section "1950—Cool, Hard Bop").

From Charles, first of all, come all the great black soul singers— each even more successful than the last—whose central personality remains *Otis Redding.* Redding founded the success of Stax-Volt records in Memphis, who produce soul records the way Ford and G. M. make cars. The private airplane, which has become the symbol of success for so many black artists in a white world became Otis' doom. In December 1967, he was killed in a crash.

Other soul singers of Redding's circle are *Joe Tex* (who for a while engaged on a career in gospel singing), the duo *Sam & Dave, Wilson Pickett,* and also *James Brown.* These singers infuse their songs and vocal technique with not only the gospel tradition, but also the heritage of rhythm and blues—the popular music of the black ghettos from which the white rock of the fifties grew. In rhythm and blues, there were *Little Richard, Sam Cooke, Big Joe Turner, Fats Domino,* and others whose influence can hardly be overestimated here. (A phenomenon like Elvis Presley is unthinkable without black rhythm and blues—and white hillbilly music!)

Domino and other singers in this style stem from New Orleans. It should be recognized that this city was the point of origin of style-setting impulses in music at least twice: not only around the turn of the century with New Orleans jazz, but also in the fifties during the great period of rhythm and blues. In fact, one feels that for the third time, New Orleans is shaping a musical style: During the seventies, in a combination of rhythm and blues, soul, and the rhythms resonating from the Caribbean, particularly Jamaica and Trinidad, to the U. S. This connection between New Orleans and the Caribbean is certainly nothing new. It already existed around the turn of the century, and dates back even further, to an era when the French *La Nouvelle Orléans* was oriented not toward the north, the United States, but on the contrary toward the south, as the northernmost point of that French-Creole area of which only Martinique and a few other islands and language enclaves remain today—as Trinidad and St. Lucia, as well as French Guayana on the South American continent. New Orleans is situated—not only musically, but also geographically—at the borderline between the Creole area on the one hand, and the black music area that begins directly to the north of it on the other.

Mick Jagger of the Rolling Stones has become *the* embodiment of masculine-agressive sexuality for show in the white world of pop music. But Jagger told in an interview with the magazine *Rolling Stone* where he took his cues from: *James Brown*. "Sex Machine" Brown projects aggressive sexuality onto a black consciousness; one stands for the other, sexuality for self-assurance, and vice versa. This projection mechanism, which can be found in many black artists, has resulted in Brown becoming—not only in the U. S. and Europe, but also in West Africa—a black *hero*. "James Brown is the secret—and actually no longer so secret—King of Africa," a reporter wrote in the early seventies. In the double talk of black ghetto jargon, he is called "Super Bad Brown"—"bad" has been turned into "good."

No speech by Eldridge Cleaver, Rap Brown, Stokeley Carmichael —or by Martin Luther King or Malcolm X—has done so much for the growing self-awareness of the black masses all over the world as Brown's cry: "Say it loud: I'm black and I'm proud!"

Brown and the other black soul and blues singers cued a generation of successful white rock singers: *Joe Cocker, David Clayton-Thomas, Wayne Cochran, Rod Stewart,* and many, many more. In the final analysis, all white rock singing is unthinkable without black rhythm and blues and soul.

The wealth of expressive possibilities begun by the black blues and soul tradition appears inexhaustible; for the time being, at least, no end seems in sight. If one considers that the simple 12-bar blues form and the equally simple call-and-response structure of the gospel song have unceasingly generated new styles, fashions, trends—and, yes, gimmicks too—in popular music for the last 60 or 70 years, one may fathom the depth of creativity and vitality hidden beneath these only seemingly "simple" structures.

Tim Buckley and *Captain Beefheart* are examples of the fact that this tradition can still produce individual, notable, personal styles clearly outside of dominant fashion. The former "sophisticates" the rhythm-and-blues tradition; the latter ironicizes it—his wanton, cynical sarcasm is just another form of the uncompromisingly sincere search for understanding of self for which the black tradition is apparently a more honest starting point than the white. Beefheart, with his "drunkard's" voice, liberates the country tradition of the Mississippi delta—of Robert Johnson, for instance—into "free rock," as Ornette Coleman liberated black Texas folklore into free jazz. But in this process of liberation, the country blues remain Beefheart's source of power. His more recent recordings give reason to warn him not to move too far away from this power source.

Many white singers have escaped into the world of the seemingly "beautiful"—into a world which, at least from the perspective of black music, often appears like an imaginary wonderland. Above all, this is true about such contemporary singer-songwriters as *James Taylor, Neil Young,* Irishman *Van Morrison, Leon Russell,* etc. Morrison displays much of the jazz heritage, Russell the gospel and ragtime traditions.

For the modern "singer-songwriter," the "song line" of jazz singing is as important as the "blues line" has been for the others. And yet a third element becomes perceivable here: the element of American folklore that is not only black but also white. This was made clear to the general public during the early sixties by *Bob Dylan,* but Dylan was only the final link in a chain that leads back through *Woody Guthrie, Pete Seeger,* etc., to *Leadbelly* and the other early blues-folk singers. For the great expansion of consciousness of the sixties, Dylan was as essential in the U. S. as the Beatles were in the whole world (also see discussion of Dylan and the Beatles in the blues chapter). In this jazz book, we can only marginally note these pheonomena and their interpreters; they require a book of their own.

The Female Singers

In the history of female jazz singers, there is also a "blues line" and a "song line." However, while these two lines run parallel in equal strength among male singers, the blues is clearly predominant among the females, in the beginning and again today. Between these periods, the "song line" was relatively dominant (although, of course, there was blues sung by women during this time, too).

The history of female blues singing starts later than male blues singing. No female singers from "archaic" times are known to us. Folk-blues singers like Blind Lemon Jefferson or Leadbelly did not have female counterparts, as even their contemporary successors don't. The simple, rural world of folk blues is dominated by the man —the woman is an object.

This changed as soon as the blues moved into the big cities of the North. At that time—in the early twenties—the great era of classic blues, whose "mother" was Ma Rainey and whose "empress" was Bessie Smith, began. In the chapter on Bessie, we discussed the classic blues period in detail. Singers like Bertha "Chippie" Hill, Victoria Spivey, and Sippie Wallace carried a faint glow of this era into the fifties and even sixties, but as early as the late twenties the musical and social climate changed so radically in the wake of the great depression that public attention shifted from the "blues line" to the "song line."

The first girl singers important in this field (who are worth listening to even today) are *Ethel Waters, Ivie Anderson,* and *Mildred Bailey.* Ethel Waters was the first to demonstrate—as early as the twenties—the many possibilities for jazz singing in commercial tunes, especially good ones. Ivie Anderson became Duke Ellington's vocalist in 1932 and remained for almost 12 years; Duke called her the best singer he ever had. Mildred Bailey—of part Indian origin—was a successful singer of the Swing era with great sensitivity and mastery of phrasing. She was married to Red Norvo; and with him, Teddy Wilson, and Mary Lou Williams she made her finest recordings. Her "Rockin' Chair" became a hit of considerable proportions; it was a blues, but an "alienated," ironic blues. That was the dominant attitude toward the blues during the Swing era, overcome by only a few truly great black musicians—above all Billie Holiday.

The songs of the female singers in this "song line" were—and are —the ballads and pop tunes of commercial music, the melodies of the great American popular composers—Cole Porter, Jerome Kern, Irving Berlin, Geroge Gershwin—and sometimes even tunes from the "hit parade," all sung with the inflection and phrasing typical of jazz.

In this area, improvisation has retreated to a final, irreducible position. The songs must remain recognizable, and of course the singers are dependent upon the lyrics. But in a very special sense there can be improvisation here, too. It lies in the art of paraphrasing, juxtaposing, transposing—in the alteration of harmonies, and in a certain way of phrasing. There is a whole arsenal of possibilities, of which *Billie Holiday*, the most important figure in this branch, had supreme command. Billie was the embodiment of a truth first expressed—I believe —by Fats Waller (and after him by so many others): in jazz it does not matter what you do, but *how* you do it. To pick one example among many: In 1935, Billie Holiday recorded (with Teddy Wilson) a banal little song, "What a Little Moonlight Can Do"—and what resulted was a completely valid work of art.

Billie Holiday sang blues only incidentally. But through her phrasing and conception, much that she sang seemed to become blues.

Billie Holiday made more than 350 records—among them about 70 with Teddy Wilson. She made her most beautiful recordings in the thirties with Wilson and Lester Young. And in the intertwining of the lines sung by Billie Holiday and the lines played by Lester Young, the question which is lead and which is accompaniment—which line is vocal and which instrumental—here becomes secondary.

Billie Holiday is the great songstress of understatement. Her voice has none of the volume and majesty of Bessie Smith. It is a small, supple, sensitive voice—yet Billie sang a song which, more than anything sung by Bessie Smith and the other female blues singers, became a musical protest against racial discrimination. This song was "Strange Fruit" (1939). The "strange fruit" hanging from the tree was the body of a lynched Negro. It was the most emphatic, passionate musical testimony against racism before Abbey Lincoln's interpretation of Max Roach's "Freedom Now Suite" of 1960.

Billie Holiday's way of understatement is more effective than the grandest gesture and the most passionate, unrestrained expression. The restraint and caution of understatement are more powerful. Listening to Billie Holiday, one felt that everything really was much more weighty than she stated it, and so each listener was forced to supply from within what he required for a full emotional measure. Thus the avalanche of internal activity one always heard about when Billie Holiday appeared was set into motion.

Yet there is also pathos in Billie Holiday's singing. Listen to "Tell Me More," recorded in June, 1940 with Roy Eldridge and Teddy Wilson. But charm and urbane elegance, suppleness and sophistication are the chief elements in the understatement of Billie Holiday, These elements can be found everywhere—for example, in "Mandy Is Two" (1942), the song about little Mandy, who is only two years old but already a big girl. And this is expressed so straightforwardly and warmly! How simple and unpretentious it is! Nothing rings false, as is the rule with commercial ditties attempting childlike naïveté. It is almost inconceivable that something seemingly destined by every known law to become *kitsch* could be transformed into art.

A cool tenor saxophone was almost always the yardstick for comparisons with good modern ballad singing until the late fifties, and this, too, may be traced back to Billie Holiday. Billie's singing has the elasticity of Lester Young's tenor playing—and she had this elasticity prior to her first encounter with Lester. Billie was the first artist in all of jazz—not just the first woman or the first jazz singer—in whose music the influence of the saxophone as the style and sound-setting instrument becomes clear. And this took place, only seemingly in paradoxical fashion, before the beginning of the saxophone era, which actually only began with the success of Lester Young in the early forties. This is apparent already in Billie Holiday's first recording—"Your Mother's Son-in-law," made in 1933 with Benny Goodman. Modern jazz really began in the realm of song, with Billie Holiday.

The life story of Billie Holiday has been told often, and even more often has been effectively falsified: from servant girl in Baltimore through rape and prostitution to successful song star—and through narcotics all the way downhill again. In 1938 she worked with Artie Shaw's band, a white group. For months she had to use service entrances, while her white colleagues went in through the front. She had to stay in dingy hotels, and sometimes couldn't even share meals with her associates. And she had to suffer all this not only as a black, but also as the sole woman in the band. Billie felt she had to go through all this to set an example. If it could work for *one* black artist, others could make it too. She took it . . . until she collapsed.

Before that, she had appeared with another great band, that of

Count Basie—and had suffered the reverse kind of humiliation, possibly even more stinging than what she had to endure in Shaw's band: though Billie was as much a Negro as any of Basie's musicians, her skin color might have seemed too light to some customers and it was unthinkable at that time to present a white girl singer with a black band. At a theater appearance in Detroit, Billie had to put on dark make-up.

In the last years of her life, Billie Holiday's voice was often a mere shadow of her great days. She sang without the suppleness and glow of the earlier recordings; her voice sounded worn, rough, and old. Still, her singing had magnetic powers. It is extraordinary to discover just how much a great artist has left when voice and technique and flexibility have failed and nothing remains except the spiritual power of creativity and expresssion.

Billie Holiday stands at the center of great jazz singing. Her important recordings with Teddy Wilson, Lester Young, and other greats of the Swing era are convincing testimony to the fact that the dilemma of jazz singing affects only lesser practitioners. Indeed, it is from the almost paradoxical overcoming of this dilemma that great art can be wrought. That is why we have concerned ourselves with Billie Holiday at such length.

After Holiday came a wealth of female singers who applied Billie's discoveries to their respective stylistic surroundings. So many were the members of the "song line" that it is impossible to list them all. Many are so well-known beyond jazz that they scarcely require introduction.

First come the female singers connected with the three centers of instrumental jazz in the forties: the circle surrounding Dizzy Gillespie and Charlie Parker, the one around Woody Herman, and the one around Stan Kenton.

Sarah Vaughan came from the Parker-Gillespie circle and became particularly successful—beyond jazz as well. She is generally regarded as the most important female jazz singer next to Ella Fitzgerald. Her vocal range is equal to an opera singer's.

Mary Ann McCall was the vocalist of Woody Herman's Herd of the late forties. She had a musicianly conception which corresponds to that of Woody's soloists at the time, for instance Serge Chaloff or Bill Harris.

June Christy was the voice of Stan Kenton's band, and the warmly human climate of her singing won her many friends time and again, even when one could not go along with her all the way as far as intonation is concerned. June Christy replaced *Anita O'Day* with Kenton, and Anita is still probably the most expressive of white female singers—with a musical assurance of virtuoso caliber and great improvisational capacity.

In the fifties almost all female singers in the "song" field were more or less strongly influenced by the three aforementioned instrumental circles . . . and by Billie Holiday. *Chris Connor,* for instance, belongs to the line which leads from Mildred Bailey and Holiday through Anita O'Day to June Christy. *Carmen McRae, Dakota Staton, Ernestine Anderson, Lorez Alexandria,* and *Abbey Lincoln* are all remarkable singers in the field of modern jazz. McRae, who was once married to Kenny Clarke, is the most important. She has the sober musicianship, stylistic assurance and taste of Sarah Vaughan and Ella Fitzgerald, but unfortunately not their popularity charisma. Dakota Staton is handicapped by certain mannerisms and the artificiality characteristic of stereotyped blues clichés. Ernestine Anderson had to find success in Sweden before being discovered as "one of the freshest new voices in jazz of the fifties" (Ralph Gleason) in the United States. Her comment, "If I had my way, I'd sing true like Ella and breathe like Sarah Vaughan," describes the musical ideals of many modern female singers.

Jackie Cain became known in the ensemble of Charlie Ventura in the early fifties. She is equally outstanding as a scat singer, in swinging tempos, or in slow ballads; always with a little bit of cheerful irony in the voice. Roy Kral was the pianist and fellow vocalist in the Ventura group and Jackie and Roy have been together ever since. Their spirited, pleasant, sensitive, often humorous music make them the most perfect vocal team in jazz history.

Helen Merrill, who found a wide audience in Japan, is a ballad singer of special sensitivity and sophistication. *Nina Simone,* full of black pride and self-assurance, transforms elements of the black tradition into modern song, infusing her material with a social protest message. *Abbey Lincoln* distinguished herself above all in the songs —frequently of angry content—by her ex-husband, Max Roach for which she often supplied lyrics. The strong, sincere expressiveness of her voice, each syllable clearly understandable, has made her the best interpreter of Roach's outstanding "Freedom Now Suite." *Nancy Wilson* has long been—and still is—one of the most successful black nightclub acts, with more or less strong jazz undertones and much radiance. Two singers continuing the classic line into the seventies are *Maxine Weldon* and *Dee Dee Bridgewater.* The former impresses in recordings made with Ernie Wilkins as a young, contemporary Sarah Vaughan. The latter has appeared mainly with the Thad Jones-Mel Lewis Big Band, and fills the high musical demands of this band with the special "hipness" of the seventies.

Sheila Jordan, Jeanne Lee, and—in Europe—the Norwegian *Karin Krog* and British *Norma Winstone* are among the few girl singers to carry their art into free jazz. Sheila became known especially for her work with George Russell—as in the grandiose-satirical "You Are My Sunshine." In recordings made in Europe and the U. S. with German multi-instrumentalist Gunter Hampel, Jeanne has created gentle, multi-layered textures of vocal and instrumental lines and sound: "natural sounds," the songs of birds and mountain streams that have become contemporary free music. Karin Krog is the "intellectual" among these singers, also incorporating into her vocal excursions elements of avant-garde concert music, say, of Ligeti. Norma Winstone has made excellent recordings with the cream of British jazz musicians (John Surman, John Taylor, Alan Skidmore, etc.), combining the discoveries of free jazz with the characteristics of the great ballad.

In the early seventies, a fifth voice was added to this quartet: Indian singer *Asha Puthli,* whose fame had been spreading for years from Bombay to the Western jazz world, and who found initial support in New York from John Hammond and Ornette Coleman. Asha accomplishes something that has been in the air since John Coltrane: she vocalizes contemporary jazz by way of the feeling of her own Indian tradition.

In his uncompromising endeavors to use the human voice as instrumentally as possible, Duke Ellington first employed *Adelaide Hall,* then *Kay Davis,* the former in the twenteis, the latter in the forties. Kay Davis' voice was used as a kind of coloratura above the orchestra, often scored in parallels with clarinet, creating a strange meshing of sounds. Kay Davis is probably the only jazz singer who has the vocal equipment of a genuine operatic coloratura and also possesses jazz feeling. Since the mid-sixties, this combination of a jazz voice with the sound of an ensemble or full band has become commonplace, and few remember that this, too, began with Duke.

Some of the aforementioned singers have taken cues from the instrumental conception of jazz singing and have done scat vocals, stringing together "nonsense" syllables with complete absence of lyrics. *Louis Armstrong* "invented" scat singing way back in the twenties; the story goes that he came upon it when he forgot the lyrics while recording. Scat singing is probably the most intense form of jazz singing, outside of the blues.

Anita O'Day, June Christy, Sarah Vaughan, Carmen McRae, Dakota Staton, Jackie Cain, Annie Ross, Betty Roché, and others have created excellent scat vocals, but the mistress of this domain—and of jazz singing as a whole since Billie Holiday—is *Ella Fitzgerald*. In the thirties, her big hit "A Tisket, a Tasket"—done with the Chick Webb band—was a naively playful song dressed up in Swing style. In the forties, she fashioned scat vocals on such themes as "How High the Moon" or "Lady Be Good" with so pronounced a bebop conception that there was talk of "bop vocals," as if this were something new. Later Ella developed a mature ballad conception. Her interpretation of the "songbooks" of the great American songwriters—Gershwin, Kern, Porter, Berlin—belongs among the great documents of American music. Hardly another jazz singer can hold thousands spellbound in a great hall for several hours, as Ella Fitzgerald can.

Even today, no matter how much she may have changed during all these years, Ella still has some of the simplicity and straightforwardness of the teenage girl who was discovered in January, 1934, in an amateur contest at Harlem's Apollo Theatre—as were so many other great jazz talents (for example her greatest competitor, Sarah Vaughan). The "prize" Ella won back then was a "short" engagement with Chick Webb's band—but the engagement did not even end with Chick's death five years later. In 1939, Ella took over nominal leadership of the Webb band.

This is the key to the phenomenon of Ella Fitzgerald: unharmed by passing fashions and trends, she has retained her rank and superiority from the thirties on up to this day, longer than any other singer in jazz history.

Fitzgerald has remained the great diva of jazz singing, but meanwhile, the "blues line" of jazz singing (which Ella, of course, also masters with fitting virtuosity) has increasingly moved into the foreground. Let us for the moment backtrack a little. Since the fifties, the concept "modern blues" had become more firmly established, represented among the male singers with particular excellence and wide influence by Ray Charles. Among the female singers in this field are *Helen Humes* (who paved the way for it as early as the thirties),

Ruth Brown, LaVern Baker, Betty Carter, Etta Jones, Dinah Washington (who died in 1963), and *Esther Philips*. Dinah Washington, who appeared with Lionel Hampton and his orchestra early in her career, was the most successful of them all—the "Queen of the Blues," full of biting, cynical humor. In the early seventies, Esther Philips was in the process of becoming Dinah's successor. In 1949, at 13, she already was a rhythm and blues star as "Little Esther," and with her "Double Crossing Blues" had a million-seller hit. Twenty years later, after difficult drug experiences, she has become a mature blues artist, full of disillusioned sarcasm. "Home Is Where the Hatred Is" is the title of one of her best songs.

Meanwhile, at the 1967 Monterey Pop Festival, a San Francisco rock group called Big Brother and the Holding Company had made a notable appearance. The group itself was of no particular importance, but its girl singer was to make headlines until her death three years later: *Janis Joplin*. To jazz listeners, it seemed as if the voice of Bessie Smith had returned to the scene in a barely credible, eerily distorted manner (and the voice of another more recent black blues singer, Big Mama Thornton, as well). The difference was only that Janis Joplin was white, a young, whisky-drinking Texas girl, driven by a fierce will to live and to love. Her singing was always a little harder, cruder, louder, more aggressive than Bessie Smith's and Big Mama's art. "I'd rather not sing than sing quiet," she supposedly said once.

At this point, it again becomes clear to what extent many white musicians—especially those who seem "authentic" in their relationship to the blues—have vulgarized and coarsened the message of their black models. Speaking of Bill Haley's relationship to the great black rhythm-and-blues artists—for example, Joe Turner—in 1954, at the beginning of the rock 'n' roll era, Carl Betz says in his *Story of Rock*: "Haley tended to shout his lyrics rather than clearly 'vocalizing' them." This holds true for dozens of other white singers and instrumentalists who derive from black blues.

Janis Joplin did to the male rock audience what Mick Jagger or James Brown did to the female fans: She was a sex idol. Every note she sang, every syllable she spoke, every move she made was full of aggressive, gripping, demanding sexuality.

As a human being, she was driven; a woman who seemed to live in a continuous state of explosion. Even when she sings—in an unaccompanied solo—about wanting a Mercedes-Benz because all her friends have Porsches, or a color TV to be delivered before three, this humorous request sounds like a mystic incantation, a desperate prayer.

There are echoes of Joplin in countless other girl singers on the contemporary rock scene—for example, in *Maggie Bell,* who comes from a Glasgow slum, or in Czech-born *Genya Ravan,* now living in the U. S. But one thing is certain: no singer, in the foreseeable future, will equal Janis Joplin—her hectic pace, her drivenness, her explosiveness.

In the course of the sixties, the heritage of the black spiritual and gospel tradition even more strongly entered into the mainstream of female singing. The white world had become conscious of this heritage through the recordings of *Mahalia Jackson,* who died in 1972 —but Mahalia was only one of the many wonderful singers of black religious music. Others are *Dorothy Love Coates, Marion Williams,* the late *Clara Ward, Bessie Griffin.*

The combination of this gospel tradition (discussed in an earlier chapter) with the blues and jazz heritage gave rise to a unique artist corresponding to Ray Charles in importance:*Aretha Franklin,* who meanwhile has surpassed even Charles' success. Aretha is the daughter of Rev. C. L. Franklin, the preacher of New Bethel Baptist Church in Detroit. From childhood on, she heard the rousing gospel songs in her father's church. When she was able to carry a tune, she joined the church choir; and at 12 or 13, she became a soloist. As her first important influence she named Mahalia Jackson; later, she pointed in particular to the significance of jazz musicians in her musical development: Oscar Peterson, Erroll Garner, and Art Tatum. Aretha herself is also a good, soul-inspired pianist.

Aretha Franklin, as a critic once put it, sings "with the sweetness of black women," with those floating nasal sounds one feels rather than hears.

One can appreciate how great an experience it must have been for her to record her 1972 gospel album, "Amazing Grace," at the New Temple Missionary Baptist Church in Los Angeles, in front of and with the congregation. This was not only a homecoming to the musical world from which she originates—that alone would have meant much—but a conscious, jubilant rediscovery of her own roots.

Aretha Franklin's career illustrates that even—perhaps especially! —so outstanding a singer depends on the conception of her record producers. Her first start, at Columbia-CBS Records, was a flop, although Aretha was handled by experienced A & R men—among them John Hammond. Only after she joined the Atlantic label did she gain world-wide popularity within a few years. Here, Aretha was guided by the two most successful producers of black music, Jerry Wexler and Ahmet Ertegun—two men who are veritable geniuses in feeling out who their artists are and what their potential is, and who •have been as important to the history of rhythm and blues since the fifties as its most famous artists.

Among the female singers, too, there is a grouping that corresponds to the soul specialists clustered around Otis Redding, Wilson Pickett, etc. In this group, above all, are *Tina Turner* and *Diana Ross*. With her volatile temperament, Tina became the female sex symbol of soul music. Diana Ross, who emerged from the vocal girl trio "The Supremes," has become more than just a soul specialist. As early as 1969, Lennie Tristano said: "I think Diana Ross is the greatest jazz singer since Billie Holiday"—a statement that was then greeted with incredulity in the jazz world. However, opinions have changed since Diana Ross' excellent acting and singing in the role of Billie Holiday in the film "Lady Sings the Blues." Regrettably, her part in this movie is its sole redeeming feature; otherwise, it is a cheap, sentimental cliché drama *à la* Hollywood and has next to nothing in common with the true story of Billie Holiday.

In rock, only a few white female singers can be mentioned here— for instance, *Grace Slick* and British singer *Julie Driscoll*. Neither simply imitates soul or rhythm and blues, but both have found their own styles. Grace Slick was a member of the Jefferson Airplane, the group that more than any other made the "San Francisco sound" world-famous in the later sixties. Grace put into song Timothy Leary's message, the message of the drug revolution, rocking word yarns of flowers and incense and love-ins, of trips and cosmic discoveries and three-way sex. Julie Driscoll, married to British jazz pianist-arranger Keith Tippett, could be one of the greatest female vocalists of today's scene if psychological problems had not so often interrupted her career. "Jools," who became known in 1968 through her recordings with organist Brian Auger's "Trinity," fell victim to her métier. The multi-faceted extreme sensitivity that makes her singing such a ripe and unsettling experience became a handicap when she had to deal with managers and agents, publicity hacks, journalists and the whole machinery of the music business.

She only had one real hit: "This Wheel's on Fire." But even that was just a hit of small proportions, a promise—as was her success in the polls. To one critic, she seemed to be a "mystique," and that probably hits the spot.

Among the girl singers as well there is a group of singers-songwriters. Most notable in this field are *Carole King* and *Laura Nyro*. Neither is a great singer in terms of voice and technique, but each is a congenial interpreter of her own compositions, which often sound as simple and light as modern folklore, but in reality are highly developed and sophisticated "art songs" in this realm. Laura Nyro is urbane, "New Yorkish;" Carole King is more rustic.

The wave of male folk singers, of which we spoke in the preceding chapter, of course has its counterpart among the ladies. The most important girl singer in this field is probably *Judy Collins*. In her song "Farewell to Tarwathie," she incorporated the yearning songs and signals of the whales in a wonderful way; and in her recording of "Amazing Grace," in an unaccompanied vocal chorus, she intellectualizes and "cools down" the gospel tradition in the manner of contemporary folklore.

Let us finally mention the probably most successful female singer on today's scene: *Roberta Flack*. She breaks through categories: Friends of jazz, rock, and pop all regard her as one of their own. Dan Morgenstern has pointed out that Roberta Flack "is very probably the most accomplished musician among today's pop artists." Which means that she knows the professional tools of her trade better than anyone else. She herself says that she longs to direct a symphony orchestra. At 16, she was already Musical Assistant to the President of Howard University in Washington, D. C.; at 19, she directed a university production of Verdi's "Aida." Among those who have influenced her, she names not only the great singers, male and female, of the black tradition, but also folklore singers like Odetta, Judy Collins, Joan Baez, and Bob Dylan.

Above all, however the burden of melancholy and the tragic intensity of Billie Holiday have been recreated for the seventies in Roberta Flack. For the time being, she represents a respectable final link in that great chain of black women singers signified by the names Bessie Smith, Billie Holiday, Mahalia Jackson, Sarah Vaughan, Ella Fitzgerald, Aretha Franklin and . . . Roberta Flack.

THE BIG BANDS OF JAZZ

The Big Bands of Jazz

IT IS DIFFICULT to determine where big bands begin. What a moment ago was New Orleans music in the next moment has become big-band jazz, and we stand at the doorstep of the Swing era. In "The Chant" by Jelly Roll Morton's Red Hot Peppers (recorded in 1926), there are traces of big-band sounds, though the idiom is purest New Orleans jazz. And when King Oliver yielded his band to Luis Russell in 1929, the orchestra, though it scarcely had changed, turned from a New Orleans group into a big band. How fluid these transitions were can be clearly seen in the case of *Fletcher Henderson*. The real big-band history of jazz begins with him. From the early twenties through 1938, he led large orchestras and exerted an influence comparable only to Duke Ellington. (We are omitting Ellington from this chapter because his music and his spirit run through nearly all stages of big-band jazz; an entire chapter about Duke may be found in the first part of the book.)

At the outset, Fletcher Henderson played a kind of music which differed little from the New Orleans music of the time. Between 1925 and 1928, he fittingly made records under the name of "The Dixie Stompers." Slowly and almost imperceptibly, sections were formed, joining related instruments in groupings. For the next 40 years, the sections were to be the characteristic of big bands. Among the first "sections" were the clarinet trios. They can be found in Henderson, and in Jelly Roll Morton as well. The development from the nine or ten men Henderson had at the start—a personnel which today would be called a combo, but then was the ultimate in "bigness"—to the typical ensemble work of the compact trumpet, trombone, and saxo-

341

phone sections of the height of his career, is smooth and barely perceptible.

Fletcher Henderson and the Beginning

Fletcher Henderson had a real instinct for trends. He was not a man like Ellington, who spearheaded evolution. He followed—but not without first giving format and content to what the trend happened to be. It is fitting that he did not retain his musicians for long periods of time, as Ellington did, but changed personnel frequently.

In Henderson's various big bands the musicians found a freedom which seems contrary to the general opinion of big-band work. This freedom extended to external matters: In 1932, John Hammond supervised a recording session with the Henderson band. It was called for 10 a.m. By 11:30, five men had arrived. At 12:40, the last man showed up: John Kirby with his bass. The freshness and spontaneity of Henderson's music is the sunny side of such goings on which, however, are not unfamiliar in jazz recording work up to today.

Henderson, who died in 1952, was a great arranger; there are experts who rate him as the most important man in this field, next to Duke Ellington. At any rate, he and Duke were the first who knew how to write for big bands with a sure feeling for improvisation.

The versatility of the Henderson band was great. Around 1930, a program might consist of Jelly Roll Morton's old "King Porter Stomp," "Singin' the Blues," with Rex Stewart soloing à la Beiderbecke; a number featuring the big sound of Coleman Hawkins' tenor sax or the fluent trombone of Jimmy Harrison; then perhaps a showpiece from the repertoire of the old Original Dixieland Jazz Band such as "Clarinet Marmalade;" and finally "Sugar Foot Stomp," patterned on King Oliver's famous "Dippermouth Blues," with Stewart playing Oliver's original trumpet solo. And in between, some real stomp numbers tailored to the taste of the Harlem audience (a taste which since then has changed, if at all, only in terms of an even stronger beat and—related to this—a simplification of the traditional blues elements), pieces like "Variety Stomp," or "St. Louis Shuffle" —and now and then also one of the commercial tunes of the day, such as "My Sweet Tooth Says 'I Wanna' But My Wisdom Tooth Says 'No.' "

Henderson always had an amazing knack for using the right soloists. Musicians who played in his band have been mentioned in almost every chapter on instruments in this book. Among the most important are alto saxophonists Don Redman and Benny Carter; tenorists Coleman Hawkins, Ben Webster, and Chu Berry; clarinetist Buster Bailey; trumpeters Tommy Ladnier—with the blues sound; Rex Stewart, Red Allen, Roy Eldridge, and Joe Smith; trombonists Jimmy Harrison, Charlie Green, Benny Morton, Claude Jones, and Dickie Wells; drummers Kaiser Marshall and Sid Catlett; and Fletcher's brother Horace Henderson, who played piano (as did Fletcher) and often lent his name to the band. Many of these musicians later became band leaders, primarily Redman and Carter.

Don Redman is one of the names that might well be offered in answer to the oft-asked question about the most underrated musician in jazz history. "I changed my way of arranging after hearing Armstrong," he has said. From 1928 on he made recordings with McKinney's Cotton Pickers; from 1931 to 1940 (and intermittently after that until his death in 1964) he led his own band. Many of the musicians who played with Henderson have also been with Redman's bands. Redman refined the music of Henderson. But then, this is a common denominator for the whole evolution of orchestral jazz: a steady, uninterrupted refinement of the ideas of Fletcher Henderson.

In 1931, Redman put together the first big-band line-up in a modern sense. It consisted of three trumpets, three trombones, a four-piece saxophone section and a rhythm section of piano, guitar, bass, and drums. In 1933, the four saxophones grew to five—for the first time in Benny Carter's band. This constitutes the standard big-band instrumentation—with the qualification that the brass section, occasionally in the late thirties and generally from the forties on, might consist of four or even five trumpets and four trombones. That would add up to a total of 17 or 18 musicians, and it is characteristic of the nature of jazz that such an instrumentation is conceived of as a "big" band. From the standpoint of European music, this is still a chamber ensemble. "Big" would mean the 100-man apparatus of the symphony orchestra. Thus the reproach of overdone trappings certainly does not fit jazz. The impressive multiplication of the same voices, employed in the great symphonic forms—a multiplication often purely for the sake of volume or effect—is contrary to the nature of jazz. Jazz tends toward linear instrumentation of each voice: each instrument has a distinctive, perceivable musical purpose, it is used as a "voice".

Benny Carter briefly led McKinney's Cotton Pickers—the manager was named McKinney—after Redman had left. Carter became the prototype of the band leader as he would appear with increasing frequency from then on: leaders who were first and foremost arrangers, and led bands only because they wanted to hear their ideas translated into the kind of sounds they had in mind. Carter's career as a band leader, accordingly, was unhappy and full of interruptions, and yet he became the true specialist of the saxophone section—and a master of melodic delineation. No one knows how to make a saxophone section "sing" like Carter . . . like a multivoiced "saxophone-organ." The saxophone sounds discovered by Carter in 1933—on such recordings as "Symphony in Riffs" or "Lonesome Nights"—signified an entirely new tone color, which was to gain ever-increasing importance in jazz. It is in no small measure due to the wealth of possibilities discovered by Carter in the five-piece saxophone section that some modern band leaders would rather make do with a trombone or trumpet less than without one of their saxophonists.

The Goodman Era

From Fletcher Henderson came first of all the most successful big-band man of the thirties—*Benny Goodman,* "the King of Swing." Then came all the Henderson- and Goodman-influenced big white orchestras of those years, such as the bands of *Tommy* and *Jimmy Dorsey,* and the Artie Shaw band mentioned below. They combined the Henderson influence with that of white bands of the twenties more or less close to Chicago style: Ben Pollack, The Wolverines, Jean Goldkette.

The Goodman band played a polished Henderson music, cleansed of "impurities" of intonation and precision. It became the symbol of the Swing era. The crest of the B. G. wave (which began in California in 1935 when Goodman and his musicians had almost given up hope of ever breaking through) was the famous 1938 Carnegie Hall concert—the decisive entrance of jazz into the hallowed halls of "serious" music. Goodman (and jazz enthusiast John Hammond) had hired members of the Duke Ellington and Count Basie bands for this concert. They performed alongside the well-known soloists of the big Goodman band: trumpeters Harry James and Ziggy Elman, drummer Gene Krupa, pianist Jess Stacy—and the soloists of the

Goodman small groups: pianist Teddy Wilson and vibraphonist Lionel Hampton. In point of fact, Goodman—and later Artie Shaw—was the first who dared to feature black musicians in white bands; if at first only in the "diplomatic" form of added solo attractions, so that racists would not have to face the fact that white and black musicians were sitting side by side in the same band.

The Goodman band retained its Henderson stamp well into the forties. Actually, it still bears that stamp today, no matter how many other arrangers Goodman has employed. Only Eddie Sauter gave the Goodman band of the early forties a "new sound"—in such pieces as "Superman," with Cootie Williams as trumpet soloist, "Clarinet à la King," a showcase for Benny's clarinet, and "Moonlight on the Ganges." Sauter no longer used the sections in contrasting opposition throughout, as had Henderson, but sometimes merged them and sometimes created new "sections" by combining instruments from different sections only to dissolve them again—all according to the flow of the music. Here Sauter began what he would carry to a point of perfection—in collaboration with arranger Bill Finegan—in the *Sauter-Finegan Band* of the fifties. In this band, much of the artistry of concert music—not least the frequent use of percussion instruments beyond the jazz beat—was combined with a thoroughly Americanized, jazz-minded sense of humor.

Clarinetist *Artie Shaw*—after a not very successful 1936 attempt to use a string quartet within a big band—played the most refined and subtle big-band jazz of the late thirties and forties—with the exception of Duke Ellington, of course. There often was an impressionistic, Debussy-like sensitivity in Shaw's music—and yet he retained the powerhouse vigor of the great Swing big bands. Again and again, he used black musicians in his band: Billie Holiday, and trumpeters Hot Lips Page and Roy Eldridge. The indignities these musicians had to suffer during the successful tours of the Shaw band—when hotels refused to admit them, restaurants where the others ate refused to serve them, and the establishments where the band was performing would let them in only through the back entrance—have been touched on before, when speaking of Billie Holiday.

Three white Swing bands are outside the Henderson-Goodman circle in certain respects: the *Casa Loma Band,* and the orchestras of Bob Crosby and Charlie Barnet. Glen Gray's Casa Loma Band was a hit with the college crowd even before Benny Goodman. In the stiffness of its arrangements and its mechanical ensemble playing it was a forerunner of the Stan Kenton band of the late forties—the band for which Pete Rugolo was the arranger and which was connected with the "progressive jazz" slogan. Gene Gifford was the "Rugolo" of the Casa Loma Band. He wrote pieces which then seemed as imposing and compact as did the Kenton "Artistry" recordings 15 years later —"White Jazz," "Black Jazz," "Casa Loma Stomp."

Bob Crosby played Dixieland-influenced Swing, pointing back to the Ben Pollack band (which he took over in 1935) and the New Orleans Rhythm Kings, and ahead to the modern brand of commercialized Dixieland music. He had an ideal Dixieland rhythm section consisting of Nappy Lamare (guitar), Bob Haggart (bass), and Ray Bauduc (drums). Since the late sixties, *The World's Greatest Jazz Band* has been bringing the old Bob Crosby tradition back to life.

Charlie Barnet founded his first big band in 1932, and led bands almost continuously until the fifties—bands which were all shaped by Barnet's strong feeling for the music of Duke Ellington. Perhaps it is fair to say that Barnet's relationship to Ellington corresponds to that of Goodman to Henderson.

The Black Kings of Swing

Fletcher Henderson not only influenced most of the successful white bands of the thirties, but himself led the first successful Harlem band. This concept, the "Harlem" band, became a stamp of quality for jazz bands, just as the word "New Orleans" is the stamp of quality for traditional jazz. Even Benny Goodman had the desire to play for the big-band audience of Harlem, which had made the Savoy Ballroom into a famous center for music and dance in the Swing era. In 1937, he played a musical battle with the then most popular band in Harlem, that of Chick Webb—and lost! Four thousand people jammed the Savoy Ballroom, and five thousand more stood outside on Lenox Avenue to witness this friendly battle.

From Henderson the "Harlem" line leads straight through Cab Calloway, Chick Webb, and Jimmie Lunceford to Count Basie and the various Lionel Hampton bands; and beyond these to the bebop big bands of Harlem in the forties and finally to the jump bands of the fifties *à la* Buddy Johnson; or to the back-up band for *Ray Charles'* appearances.

Cab Calloway, the comedian of scat singing, took over a band in

1929 which had come to New York from the Midwest: The Missourians. From then on through the late forties he led a variety of bands of which the later are important primarily for the musicians who played in them: Ben Webster, Chu Berry, Jonah Jones, Dizzy Gillespie, Hilton Jefferson, Milt Hinton, Cozy Cole.

Tiny, hunchbacked *Chick Webb* presided over Harlem's Savoy Ballroom. Duke Ellington says: "Webb was always battle-mad, and those guys used to take on every band that came up to play there. And most times they did the cutting, regardless of the fact that half the time the other bands were twice the size. But the unforgettable and lovable Chick ate up any kind of fight, and everybody in the band played like mad at all times." Gene Krupa, who was "drummed out" by Webb while with Benny Goodman, said: "I was never cut by a better man." And pianist-arranger Mary Lou Williams remembers: "One night, scuffling around Harlem, I fell in the Savoy. After dancing a couple of rounds, I heard a voice that sent chills up my spine. . . . I almost ran to the stand to find out who belonged to the voice, and saw a pleasant-looking, brown-skinned girl standing modestly and singing the greatest. I was told her name was Ella Fitzgerald and that Chick Webb had unearthed her from one of the Apollo's amateur hours."

Even more important is *Jimmie Lunceford*, orchestra leader par excellence. Through him the concept of "precision" gained real importance in the playing of large jazz bands. From the late twenties until his death in 1947, he led a band whose style was mainly developed by arranger Sy Oliver, who also played trumpet in the band. This style is marked by a two-beat "disguised" behind the 4/4 Swing meter, and by the effective unison work of the saxophone section, with its tendencies toward glissandi. Both the Lunceford rhythm and the Lunceford sax sound were widely copied by commercial dance bands in the fifties, most of all by Billy May. The Lunceford beat was so potent in its effect that the general designation of "swing" did not seem to suffice. The Lunceford beat became "bounce." Lunceford's music "bounced" from beat to beat in a way that emphasized the moment of "lassitude," as Erroll Garner does in his piano playing. Oliver's section writing was the first really new treatment of the sax section since the work of Redman and Carter. From this developed the first typical orchestra sound—aside from Ellington's growl sounds and the clarinet trios of Fletcher Henderson's and Ellington's bands. Such sounds and tricks of instrumentation, which stuck to a band like a trademark and made it identifiable after just a few bars, now became increasingly popular.

With *Count Basie,* the stream of Kansas City bands merges with that of the successful Harlem bands. To Kansas City belong the *Benny Moten* band (which Basie himself took over in 1935); the bands of *Jay McShann* and *Harlan Leonard,* in both of which Charlie Parker played; and, prior to these, primarily *Andy Kirk and his Twelve Clouds of Joy.* All were blues- and boogie-oriented, with a well-developed riff technique, using short, reiterated blues phrases as themes or to heighten tension, or employing such riff phrases as contrasting elements. Andy Kirk's pianist and arranger was Mary Lou Williams, and it was mainly due to her influence that the Kirk band developed beyond the simple blues-riff formula of the other Kansas City bands.

At first (and in some of his recordings until today), Basie retained the Kansas City blues-riff formula, but he made much more than a formula of it. In it, he found the substance which gives his music its power. Later, almost everything brought forth by the evolution of big-band jazz came together in Basie's music. Basie has led big bands since 1935, with but a single interruption. In the Basie band of the thirties and forties the emphasis is on a string of brilliant soloists: Lester Young and Hershel Evans (tenors); Harry Edison and Buck Clayton (trumpets); Benny Morton, Dickie Wells, and Vic Dickenson (trombones); and the previously mentioned "All American Rhythm Section." In the modern Basie band, the emphasis is on precision, but of a sort which develops in the most natural way from an almost somnambulistic swing. It has been said that Basie is "orchestrated swing." The Basie band of the fifties also had good soloists: trumpeters Joe Newman and Thad Jones; saxophonists Frank Foster, Frank Wess, and Eddie "Lockjaw" Davis; trombonists Henry Coker, Bennie Powell, and Quentin Jackson; and, last but not least, Basie himself, whose sparing piano now as before swings a band as no other pianist can. In the old Basie band, Jimmy Rushing took care of the blues, not only as musical material, but also as vocal and verbal message. Joe Williams did the same for the Basie band of the fifties.

Around 1967, Basie's still indestructible "Swing machine" consisted of baritonist Charlie Fowlkes, tenorists Eric Dixon and Billy Mitchell, trumpeters Al Aarons and the still masterful Harry Edison (who had temporarily returned to Basie from Hollywood), bassist Norman Keenan, drummer Eddie Shaughnessy, and alto man Marshall Royal (who masterfully led the Basie sax section for some 20 years). Basie has become an institution: something no one else but Duke Ellington has accomplished.

Woody and Stan

In 1936 *Woody Herman* became front man for a collective of musicians from the disbanded Isham Jones orchestra. Swing *à la* Benny Goodman was the last word then. Nevertheless, Herman did not play Swing but blues. He called his band *"The Band That Plays The Blues."* "The Woodchopper's Ball" was the band's most successful record. When the war broke out, the band that played the blues began to dissolve, but soon thereafter the brilliant line of "Herman Herds" began. The *"First Herd"* was perhaps the most vital white jazz band ever. "Caldonia" was its biggest hit. When Igor Stravinsky heard this piece on the radio in 1945, he asked Herman if he could write a composition for his band. Thus the "Ebony Concerto" came into being; a piece in three movements in which Stravinsky combines his classicist ideas with the language of jazz.

Bassist Chubby Jackson was the backbone of the First Herd. The drummers were first Dave Tough, then Don Lamond. Flip Phillips was on tenor; Bill Harris established himself with one stroke as a significant new trombone voice with his solo on "Bijou"; John La Porta played alto; Billy Bauer, guitar; Red Norvo, vibraphone; and Pete Candoli, Sonny Berman, and Shorty Rogers were among the trumpets—in short, a star line-up which no other white band of the time could match.

Indicative of the spirit of this band is Jackson's recollection that the musicians frequently would congratulate each other on their solos after a night's work.

In 1947 came the Second Herd. This grew into the *Four Brothers Band,* mentioned in the tenor saxophone section. This, too, was a bebop band—with Shorty Rogers and Ernie Royal (trumpets); Earl Swope (trombone); Lou Levy (piano); Terry Gibbs (vibraphone); the previously mentioned tenor men, and singer Mary Ann McCall. "Early Autumn" written by Ralph Burns, was the big hit of the Four Brothers band. George Wallington's "Lemon Drop" was characteristic of the Second Herd's bop music.

In the fifties came the *Third and Fourth Herman Herds*—and so on; the transitions are blurred. Herman himself once said: "My three Herds? I feel as if there'd been 80." Ralph Burns wrote a "book" (i.e., library of arrangements) for the Third Herd in which the Four Brothers sound became the trademark of the band. (This had not been the case in the actual Four Brothers band, where the typical Brothers section of three tenors and one baritone was used alongside the traditional five-voiced sax section with the alto as lead.)

In spite of all the talk about the end of the big bands, Woody Herman has swung so successfully through the sixties and well into the seventies that even his closest followers have stopped counting Herds. Herman adapts the more musical rock themes to his big-band conception—pieces, say, by the "Doors" ("Light My Fire"), Burt Bacharach or Jim Webb. And he discovered a fascinating new arranger: New Zealand-born *Alan Broadbent*, a musician who studied at the Berklee School in Boston and with Lennie Tristano, and proves that even today new, exciting sounds can be generated from the tried and true big-band instrumentation. Broadbent also wrote some pieces and a concerto that the Herman Herd performed with the Dallas Symphony Orchestra.

"The Band That Plays The Blues" was Woody Herman's start in 1936. Thirty-five years later, in 1971, he teamed his band with one of the best-known young white blues musicians, guitarist Mike Bloomfield.

Stan Kenton has also led various bands of differing styles, and so more space must be devoted to him than to any single bands. Perhaps the most typical Kenton piece is "Concerto To End All Concertos"—typical in title as well. It opens with poorly copied Rachmanioff-like bass figures by pianist Kenton. The whole late-romantic musical climate lurks behind these figures, along with the notion that sheer size and volume equal expressive power—this seemed to be the peculiar Kentonian world of ideas. From this climate sprang Kenton's first well-known piece, "Artistry in Rhythm," in 1942. It was followed in subseqent years by a series of other "Artistries": in Percussion, in Tango, in Harlem Swing, in Bass, in Boogie. Arranger Pete Rugolo is often linked with this effect-filled and elaborate style, but Kenton himself clearly had already established the "Artistry" style when Rugolo, then still in the army, first offered him an arrangement in 1944. Rugolo, who studied with Darius Milhaud, the important modern French composer, is primarily responsible for the second phase of Kenton's music, "Progressive Jazz" in the narrower sense, even more powerful and elaborate, laden with massive chords and multi-layered clusters of sound. During the late forties—the main period of Rugolo's influence—Kenton was enormously successful. His soloists led in the jazz polls: drummer Shelly Manne; bassist Eddie Safranski; tenorman Vido Musso; trombonist Kai Winding—and most of all, singer June Christy. Hers was the most engaging voice in the band.

Encouraged by success Kenton built himself a large concert orchestra in 1949, reinforcing his jazz line-up with a string section and extra woodwinds. For this project, Kenton again found a pretentious title: "Innovations in Modern Music." But these were "innovations" which Hindemith, Bartók, Stravinsky, and the other great modern composers had introduced 20 or 30 years earlier. Typical was Pete Rugolo's "Conflict," with June Christy's voice used as an instrument and stark contrasts between etherealized string sounds and roaring brasses—or, from the second series of "Innovations," the late Bob Graettinger's "House of Strings," with sounds reminiscent of Bartók's "Music for Strings." Graettinger's big suite, "City of Glass," conjured up the images of the title with coldly abstract, shimmering, ghostly sounds.

Then in 1952-53 came the most significant Kenton band from a jazz standpoint. Kenton seemed to have forgotten his past and decided to make a swinging music, perhaps not directly influenced by Count Basie, but nevertheless extremely well suited to a time in which the Basie spirit had come to life to the degree that hardly anyone in jazz could escape it. Kenton had many gifted soloists in this band, and the emphasis was on solo work as never before in Kenton's career. Zoot Sims and Richie Kamuca played tenors; Lee Konitz was on alto; Conte Candoli on trumpet; Frank Rosolino on trombone. Gerry Mulligan wrote such arrangements as "Swinghouse" and "Young Blood," and Bill Holman—obviously inspired by Mulligan—furnished artfully simple examples of sections employed in contrapuntal ensemble play.

In the following years, Kenton involved himself more and more deeply in work at American colleges and universities. He established "Kenton Clinics," in which he and his musicians acquainted thousands of young students with the problems of contemporary jazz, particularly of big-band music. In the process, Kenton did not shrink from personal sacrifices, often furnishing arrangements and musicians free of charge or below usual rates. "Stan is the driving force in jazz education in America," says Dr. Herb Patnoe of De Anza College in California.

From the end of the sixties on, Kenton has been experiencing a comeback hardly anyone had expected. He has surrounded himself with young, contemporary musicians with whom he plays more directly, simply, and straightforwardly than in his "Progressive" and "Artistry" periods, if still with the Kentonian power and his own incomparable pathos. He has recorded some of his best work at concerts held at universities, such as Redlands and Brigham Young.

Kenton severed relations with Capitol Records, the label with which he had been affiliated since the start of his career, and markets his records by mail order on his own "Creative World of Stan Kenton" label. This has prompted an entire wave of independent record companies distributing their records in the same way. Experience has shown that mail-order firms often can reach their customers faster, simpler, and more effectively than labels employing conventional marketing methods. The latter are often handicapped by ignorance of jazz needs on the retail level.

The Bop Big Bands

In the meantime, bebop had arrived, and there were various attempts at big-band bebop, for the first time in the *Earl Hines* band. The great pianist, identified with the trumpet style of piano in Louis Armstrong's second Hot Five, led big bands almost uninterruptedly from 1928 to 1948—along lines in which Harlem Jump and bop could merge smoothly. *Billy Eckstine,* a Hines alumnus, made the first deliberate attempt to play big-band bop when he formed a band in 1944. He himself and Sarah Vaughan were the vocalists. Dizzy Gillespie, Fats Navarro, and Miles Davis successively played in the band—the three most important modern trumpet voices; Art Blakey was on drums; and the saxophones included Charlie Parker, Wardell Gray, Dexter Gordon, and Leo Parker.

The aforementioned "Jelly, Jelly" was a great hit for Eckstine and his band—a piece that still lives, as the thunderous applause after just a few bars proved when Mr. B. sang it at the great "Newport in New York 1972" festival. In 1947, the orchestra had to disband, but by then *Dizzy Gillespie*—who for a time had been musical director of the Eckstine band—had brought about the final transformation of bop into big-band jazz. Gillespie, Tadd Dameron, John Lewis, and Gil Fuller furnished the arrangements. Lewis was at the piano, Kenny Clarke on drums, Milt Jackson on vibraphone, Al McKibbon (later Percy Heath) on bass, James Moody and Cecil Payne among the saxes; and Chano Pozo added the Cuban rhythms so characteristic of this band—rhythms that remind one of the *Machito* band—not a real jazz band, yet one that must be cited among the important big bands of the time. The Machito band was the witches' cauldron in which the mixture of Cuban rhythms and jazz phrases was most thoroughly brewed. At times, the horns would consist of North American musicians and the rhythm section of Cubans. Dizzy Gillespie—as a matter of fact, Stan Kenton too—was fascinated by this music. One of Dizzy's reasons for hiring Chano Pozo was that he wanted to capture the Machito atmosphere.

Gillespie was in the process of forming his big band when President Truman warned the Japanese in the summer of 1945 that they must surrender or experience "ultimate destruction." When the first atomic bomb was dropped, the Gillespie band had just become ready to play. This fact takes on almost ghostly symbolism when listening to a piece like "Things To Come." This is the Gil Fuller "Apocalypse in Jazz" mentioned in our Parker-Gillespie montage, with its jabbing, hectic, decaying phrases.

It is illuminating that the visions of a world blown to pieces created by "Things To Come" arose again as much as 20 years later —in the big-band attempts of free jazz. . . .

In the realm between Kenton and Herman a string of bands worth mentioning existed. *Les Brown* provided dance music, but it was so sophisticated and musical that jazz fans, especially jazz musicians, often responded to it. *Claude Thornhill* played his calm, atmospheric piano solos amid a big-band sound that inspired the conception of the Miles Davis Capitol Orchestra in the late forties. *Elliot Lawrence* played swinging arrangements by Gerry Mulligan, Tiny Kahn, and Johnny Mandel—both simple and musically interesting.

Boyd Raeburn led a band in the mid-forties that in many respects paralleled Kenton's. "Boyd Meets Stravinsky" was a representative title. Soloists such as pianist Dodo Marmaroso, bassist Oscar Pettiford, and drummer Shelly Manne (on one occasion even Dizzy Gillespie), brought much jazz feeling to the complex arrangements by, among others, George Handy and *Johnny Richards*. The latter wrote the arrangements for Dizzy Gillespie's 1950 recordings with strings —the most jazz-oriented string arrangements created up to that time —and in the mid-fifties he put together a band that attempted to extend the ideas of Progressive Jazz. The Richards band featured huge, piled-up blocks of sound and focused on irregular meters. Interest in 3/4 time has increased steadily among jazz musicians since Thelonious Monk recorded his "Carolina Moon" and Sonny Rollins proved that you can improvise over 3/4 and swing as readily as over 4/4.

Basie as Basis

In the mid-fifties, the conviction that there is a contradiction between swing and elaborate production effects which cannot be bridged beyond a certain point seemed to gain ground everywhere. This conviction is quite in line with Basie classicism. Big bands of this persuasion make music beyond experimentation. *Maynard Ferguson,* who emerged in 1950-53 from the Kenton band, organized his "Dream Band" in the mid-fifties for an engagement at Birdland in New York. It really was a dream band. Every musician in it was a famous exponent of his instrument, and all these musicians had the same musical ideal: to play swinging, blues-based jazz—vital and musically interesting in equal measure. Jimmy Giuffre, Johnny Mandel, Bill Holman, Ernie Wilkins, Manny Albam, Marty Paich, and others furnished the arrangements. Eventually, Maynard decided to form a permanent band instead of an orchestra whose members were unable or unwilling to leave New York. He found a bunch of excellent young musicians who made a brand of big-band jazz as fiery and wild as Woody Herman's First Herd, yet more clearly rooted in the language of modern Basie-Young classicism. "Fugue," written by trombonist-arranger Slide Hampton for Ferguson is perhaps the most swinging fugue to have yet emerged from jazz.

Since 1967, Canadian Ferguson has been living in Great Britain, where he formed a band that in drive and fire need not fear comparison with his earlier American aggregations. Ferguson says: "I'm not interested in nostalgia. You have to move along with the times . . . you just have to take and use the current rhythms. In the so-called golden era of the big bands, the great bandleaders of the day all played the better tunes of the day—so why not now?" And so, Ferguson's British band plays Isaac Hayes' "Shaft," David Clayton-Thomas' "Spinning Wheel," and John Lennon's "Hey Jude."

But back to the fifties, when Basic's influence was stronger than Ellington's. *Shorty Rogers* made a kind of Basie jazz with a West Coast conception, full of original, spirited inventiveness. Arranger Quincy Jones, bassist Oscar Pettiford, trombonist Urbie Green, Boston trumpeter Herb Pomeroy, and others made big-band recordings in which the Basie influence is strongly apparent.

Quincy Jones called his first album (with such marvelous soloists as Art Farmer (muted trumpet), Lucky Thompson and Zoot Sims (tenors), Phil Woods (alto), Herbie Mann and Jerome Richardson (flutes), Jimmy Cleveland (trombone), Milt Jackson (vibraphone), Hank Jones and Billy Taylor (pianos), and Charles Mingus and Paul Chambers (bass)): "This Is How I Feel About Jazz." He wrote in the liner notes that the music reflected his feelings about "the less cerebral and more vital or basic elements contained in jazz." He continued: "I would prefer not to have this music categorized at all, for it is probably influenced by every original voice in and outside of jazz, maybe anyone from blues singer Ray Charles to Ravel. . . . We aren't trying to prove anything except maybe that 'the truth doesn't always hurt.' . . . Our prime objectives in this album were soul, groove and honesty. . . ."

Jones always had a great liking for Europe. In 1959 he brought to the Old World the first American big band to be permanently based in Europe. The band was to supply the music for the show *Free and Easy*. The musicians were extremely well integrated into the show, not just as musicians, but also as actors; but other things about the show were weak and the tour collapsed. With great difficulty Quincy managed to keep the band together for a time—with work in Paris, Sweden, Belgium, and Germany. Among the members were Phil Woods, Sahib Shihab, Budd Johnson, and Jerome Richardson in the sax section; Quentin Jackson, Melba Liston, Jimmy Cleveland, and Sweden's Ake Persson in the trombone section. The music was moving and healthy, simple and honest; in many ways the most enjoyable big-band jazz of the turn of the fifties besides Ellington and Basie. To be sure, Quincy offered nothing very new. But he perfected the old, and made it shine as hardly anyone managed to do. Too bad that

Jones—after his band returned from Europe and continued to work together for several months in the U. S.—gave up fighting for its survival in the face of lack of commercial possibilities.

Meanwhile, Jones has become one of Hollywood's most successful film and TV arrangers and composers. One can feel the jazz tradition in everything he writes, and occasionally a big-band record by Quincy is released, joining commercialism and jazz quality with a cleverness totally Quincy's own.

Of similar interest in this context are the big-band recordings of *Gerry Mulligan*—almost like a "sophistication" of Basie. And *Bill Holman* was the first to achieve something on the order of a big-band realization of hard bop—with intense and concentrated arrangements of such bop themes as Sonny Rollins' "Airegin." A little later (in 1960), there was a big band of "funk" and soul and gospel jazz, if only for recording purposes: tenor man *Johnny Griffin's* "Big Soul Band" with arrangements by Norman Simmons.

On the West Coast during the sixties, *Gerald Wilson* came to the fore with a big band that found great admiration in the jazz world. Wilson, who wrote arrangements for Lunceford, Basie, Gillespie, and other important orchestras also does not want to "prove anything new," but rather sums up with power and brilliance the "mainstream" of the development of orchestral jazz so far.

Gil Evans and George Russell

The one man whose big-band jazz really seemed "new" in this period was *Gil Evans*. Gil, who emerged from the Claude Thornhill band, wrote for the Miles Davis Capitol Band, and once again teamed up with Davis in 1957—to produce those warmly glowing, impressionist orchestral sounds discussed in the Miles Davis chapter. The Evans band became the big-band realization of Miles Davis' trumpet sound. Occasionally—regrettably much too seldom—Evans also created similar sounds for other soloists—as trumpeter Johnny Coles and guitarist Kenny Burrell.

Evans—though he has been a gray-haired veteran for some time —also opened himself to the free music of the sixties. His "most modern" album up to this writing is not his U.S.-made "Svengali," but was recorded in Japan in 1972 with the Masabumi Kikuchi Big Band and two American soloists—trumpeter Marvin Peterson and saxophonist Billy Harper. Gil Evans is not a "diligent" arranger—as, say, Quincy Jones. He lets his music ripen within himself, and seldom writes anything finished and final. Even during recording sessions, he often whittles away at changes and reconstructs entire compositions and arrangements. That is why they are—regrettably—much too few records by this immensely personal and incomparable musician.

The other great loner among arrangers is *George Russell,* already mentioned several times. He also emerged from the jazz revolution of the forties. During the fifties, Russell created his "Lydian Chromatic Concept of Tonal Organization," the first work deriving a theory of jazz harmony from the immanent laws of jazz, not from the laws of European music. Russell's concept of improvisation, "Lydian" in terms of medieval church scales, yet chromatic in the modern sense, was the great pathbreaker for Miles Davis' and John Coltrane's "modality." Russell came to Europe for the first Berlin Jazz Days in 1964, and since then has been living alternately in Scandinavia and Boston. With European as well as American musicians, he has created numerous works which are as individual, as different from the mainstream of what most of jazz arrangers write, as only the works of Gil Evans.

The possibilities for orchestral jazz within the limits of conventional big-band instrumentation are rather narrow. If one considers what a wealth of sounds and ideas has unfolded within solo jazz on the road from Louis Armstrong via Charlie Parker to Ornette Coleman, one is forced to admit that the developments within big-band jazz have remained much narrower once Fletcher Henderson, Don Redman, Duke Ellington, and Benny Carter had created the basic instrumentation. Principally, the developments have consisted only of further perfection and refinement. To be sure, this tendency toward ever greater perfection also exists in solo jazz, but what interests us in that area is mainly stylistic development. That is where the emphasis lies. Of course, this stylistic development in solo jazz is also mirrored by the big bands, but here the emphasis is less on style—and thus on spiritual and artistic content—than on ever greater perfection —i.e., on skill and technique. That is why the interest of the public in big-band jazz has steadily declined since the triumphs of Stan Kenton and Woody Herman in the forties; and this point also gives rise to the hopeful question that has been asked over and over again: "Are big bands coming back?"

Free Big Bands

Meanwhile, free jazz entered the scene, and the question must be asked pointedly: What does the new, free jazz sound like when played by big bands?

The musician who stands out most clearly in the transition from tonal to atonal orchestral jazz is bassist *Charles Mingus* with his big-band concerts at New York's Town Hall and the 1964 Monterey Jazz Festival. While the Town Hall concert failed because of Mingus' personal and psychological difficulties, he accomplished an impressive and astonishing realization of his sounds and ideas (also known from his combo recordings) in Monterey.

A little later, composer (and pianist) Carla Bley and trumpeter (and arranger) Mike Mantler presented their *Jazz Composers Workshop* first in New York and then at the 1965 Newport Festival.

From this, the *Jazz Composers Orchestra* evolved with soloists such as Don Cherry, Roswell Rudd, Pharaoh Sanders, Larry Coryell, Charlie Haden, Gato Barbieri—in general, the top of the New York avant-garde—under *Michael Mantler's* direction. If one realizes how difficult it is to find an audience for such avant-garde productions in the U. S.—definitely much more difficult than in Europe—he can speak of Michael Mantler's personal contribution with only the greatest respect.

There is also a "political" program for the Jazz Composers Orchestra, in which Mantler refers to Samuel Beckett: "If it will kindly be considered that while it is in our interest as tormentors to remain where we are, as victims our urge is to move on and that, of these two aspirations warring in each heart, it would be normal for the latter to triumph, if only narrowly. . . ."

The Jazz Composers Orchestra was also involved in the Jazz Opera, "Escalator Over The Hill," by Carla Bley and Paul Haines, which was mentioned in the chapter on pianists.

The other, even more important name in free big-band jazz is *Sun Ra.* As early as the mid-fifties, Sun Ra, who had learned his trade thoroughly as pianist with the Fletcher Henderson band of the late forties, had formed a big band in Chicago, incorporating percussive and other sounds totally new for the time—sounds which their composer and creator perceives as "cosmic sounds," as "music of the outer galaxies" and of the "Heliocentric Worlds." On one of his album covers, Sun Ra had himself depicted with Pythagoras, Tycho Brahe, and Galileo.

Sun Ra's music is more than just avant-garde, free big-band jazz. It certainly is that, but behind it stands the whole black tradition: Count Basie's Swing riffs and Duke Ellington's saxophone sounds; Fletcher Henderson's "voicings;" old blues and black songs; African highlife dances and Egyptian marches; black percussion music from South, Central, and North America, and from Africa; Negro show and voodoo ritual; trance and black liturgy—celebrated by a band leader who strikes one as an African medicine-man skyrocketed into the space era.

Sun Ra's music is free from the sections common to conventional big bands—even more than in the Jazz Composers Orchestra. The instruments play together in ever changing combinations. Especially notable are the saxophone players of the Sun Ra "Cosmic Arkestra," among them John Gilmore, Marshall Allen, Pat Patrick, and Danny Davis. Their saxophone and woodwind sounds are as new and revolutionary today as Benny Carter's saxophone sections were in the early thirties. The "Arkestra" includes, among other rarely used instruments—original constructions by band members, such as the "Sun Horn,"—as well as oboe, bassoon, bass clarinet, English horn, violin, viola, cello, and a group of dancers, occasionally even a fire-eater.

Sun Ra's compositions have titles like "Next Stop Mars," "Outer Spaceways Incorporated," "Saturn," "It's After the End of the World," "Out in Space," etc. Many uninitiated listeners have smirked at such titles and at the show Sun Ra puts on as naïve. They joke about the dancers and acrobats Sun Ra makes jump all over the stage; or about a film which he has shown with his music: Sun Ra as a Christ figure, a dozen times in 20 minutes. They mock the glittering "Saturn gowns," "galaxy caps," and "cosmic rosaries," which the Sun Ra musicians and dancers wear. Occasionally, the culmination of a Sun Ra show involves a telescope which the master sets up next to his organ, and through which he searches for his "home planet Saturn" during special "cosmic climaxes."

But naïveté does not exist where black art is concerned. It did not exist when the chorus girls of the Cotton Club in Harlem during the twenties took on the hullaballoo of white Broadway musicals, accompanied by Duke Ellington's jungle sounds; it does not exist when the preacher of a black Revival church expresses his hope that his parishioners may "go to Heaven tonight! right now! by subway;" it did not exist when Louis Armstrong sang "I Hope Gabriel Likes my Music." It existed only in the heads of white critics; and while they diagnose him as a naif or even a charlatan, they say nothing about Sun Ra's music—and definitely nothing about the man Sun Ra—but a lot about themselves. Sun Ra's music—to LeRoi Jones—is the most exact expression of ancient black existence today. And Sun Ra says himself: "I paint pictures of infinity with my music, and that's why a lot of people can't understand it . . . . Intergalactic music concerns the music of the galaxies. It concerns intergalactic thought and intergalactic travel, so it is really outside the realms of the future on the turning points of the impossible. But it is still existent, as astronomy testifies."

Unlike the U. S., Europe offers a mass of free big-band jazz: by *Alexander von Schlippenbach,* one of the first; his "Globe Unity" is mentioned in the last chapter ("European Jazz Today"); by *John Tchicai,* who recorded his "Aphrodisiaca" in Copenhagen; by *Lester Bowie,* who produced "Gittin' To Know Y'All" at the Baden-Baden Free Jazz Meeting with the Chicago Art Ensemble and some European musicians; or by the *London Jazz Composers Orchestra,* which plays compositions by Barry Guy, Paul Rutherford, Kenny Wheeler, and others. And *Don Cherry,* the former partner of Ornette Coleman, has developed into a master of free orchestral sounds in Europe (mentioned in the trumpet chapter), while in the U. S. he is known almost exclusively for his recordings with small groups. Don Cherry's big-band music has a poetic contemplativeness which has nothing to do with the hectic eccentricity of most free jazz.

John Coltrane's pathbreaking "Ascension" and the preceding double-quartet record "Free Jazz" by Ornette Coleman (both cited in the chapter on Coleman and Coltrane) have been key experiences for almost all free big bands. Here the form was created: exciting, hectic collective improvisations, from which emerges a solo which—in turn—intensifies to the point that the next collective improvisation (which, again, will "give birth" to a new solo) becomes inevitable. This form has been further developed by others—differentiated, sublimated, and structured.

Rock Big Bands

There are three main currents in the big-band jazz of the early seventies:

1. Continued development of free big-band jazz.
2. Continued development of conventional big bands, utilizing contemporary themes and tendencies.
3. So-called "rock big bands."

And of course there are widely varying combinations of these three.

Let us first discuss rock big bands. The word "big" should actually have been put in quotation marks because we are here dealing mostly with groups of seven to 11 members—in other words, relatively small according to the conventions of big-band jazz. Still, it is customary to call them "big bands," because they really are, compared to the usual four to five-member rock group, and because—with help of electronics—they show tendencies to play in "sections." Keep in mind, too, that the big jazz band, in its early stages, also consisted of no more than eight to 11 musicians. It may well be that a development has come full circle here, or perhaps the rock big band stands at the beginning of an evolution similar to that of the jazz big band in the twenties. However, there is no evidence for this, with the exception of Frank Zappa. More likely, the rock big bands will disappear as quickly as they emerged.

There is no—or hardly any—development among the rock big bands. Frequently they strike the listener with a strange stiffness and immobility, reminiscent in many respects of Stan Kenton during the forties. Since so many young big-band rock musicians have emerged from the university and college bands shaped by Kenton and his clinics, one might perhaps find a connection here.

The rock big band that has shown more growth than any other is *Blood, Sweat & Tears,* which—for a while—became more and more flexible and jazz-like from one record to the next, from one line-up to the other. *"Chicago"* sounded promising at first, but has bogged down in stereotyped repetition of what already was on the first record. (It is interesting to note that many rock big bands existed only for very short time spans—among them *"Dreams"* with trumpeter Randy Brecker and drummer Billy Cobham (who later joined John McLaughlin's Mahavishnu Orchestra), and *The Flock*, which prac-

ticed collective improvisation in such a refreshing manner—reminiscent of free jazz (and of Mingus!)—and lost its most important musician (violinist Jerry Goodman), also to the Mahavishnu Orchestra.)
Particularly massive, commercially successful effects are produced by
the *"C. C. Riders"* (who back up singer Wayne Cochran), the rock
big band first assembled by blues-rock singer *Edgar Winter* and then
by *Jerry La Croix;* and *Chase,* whose leader and several members
were killed in a 1974 plane crash. All attempted to solve the problem—and that is the main goal, in the final analysis—of combining
jazz horns and a rock rhythm section.

The initial problem for all these groups is technical: the balance
between acoustic horns and the basic electronic instrumentation of
the rock groups. Even with electronic amplification and manipulation
of the horns, this problem, in most cases, could only be unsatisfacto-
rily solved. The degree of sensitivity on the part of the members of
such groups must, therefore, be particularly high.

While conventionally staffed big bands can often record a whole
LP in two to three sessions, rock big bands require weeks—often
months—to obtain suitable results. Thus the high degree of human
fatigue and exhaustion among the members of these groups. Blood,
Sweat & Tears changed its personnel three times in a few years, until
in 1974 only one of the original musicians were left.

The musical results often are in grotesque contrast to the effort involved. Unlike most other forms of rock, its big bands have failed to
utilize and sophisticate tradition, particularly the jazz tradition. On
the whole, horn parts are hardly more than orchestrated guitar riffs.
The use of horns is often so primitive that the impression is that be-
ginners who do not have the slightest idea of the mysteries of orchestral arrangement—neither in jazz nor concert music—are at work
here.

In a way, *Santana* belongs to the rock big bands. The group added
to the usual rock instrumentation Latin percussion instruments and
occasional horns, and thus created a true pandemonium of exciting rhythms. Especially impressive is Santana's album "Caravanserai," a musical allegory caravan moving in future dimensions of
space and time—the caravan of the human self on its eternal voyage
from reincarnation to reincarnation. John Coltrane's meditativeness
and Gil Evans' many dimensions have here been artfully contrasted
in the percussiveness of Santana's music.

Still, up to now only *Frank Zappa* has found in rock—if one can still call it rock—musical avenues which reach the level and complexity of the great masters of big-band jazz. Significantly Zappa did not start with jazz or blues or rock, as did all the others. In interviews he has repeatedly said he was prompted to become a musician by the works of Edgar Varese, the great modern composer who as early as in the twenties treated and solved many problems relevant for today's music scene: problems of noise integration, electronics, percussion, collage techniques, musical density, etc. In the early fifties, Zappa, then unknown and unnoticed, attended the *"Kurse für Zeitgenössische Musik"* (Courses in Contemporary Music) in Darmstadt, Germany, where almost all the composers who have so radically changed the contemporary avant-garde music scene lectured or studied: Boulez, Stockhausen, Nono, Zimmermann, Ligeti, Henze, Kagel, Berio. . . . That is the world that shaped Zappa—and which he longs for even today—only one is not supposed to notice: thus his eccentricity, his bizarre humor, his pose—at once ironic and sincere—as a fighter for sexual freedom. In this day and age, doesn't he seem like a Don Quixote struggling against windmills? And doesn't he love to appear this way?

Since Zappa's film "Two Hundred Motels" (an especially revealing example of dressing up a highly developed intellectuality in the style of a bizarre, contemporary Don Quixote), and since "Chunga's Revenge" and "Waka Jawaka," Zappa's actual roots have become clearer. In "Waka Jawaka," he produces big-band effects through intensive use of multi-track playback techniques. It has become apparent that Zappa's many records with small groups were only anticipations of his big-band productions of the early seventies. That is why we are discussing Zappa in this chapter, not in the following.

Most critics feel that with the album "The Grand Wazoo," released in 1972, Zappa's music reached its culmination point so far. The production is said to show influences by—I will simply list the names—Miles Davis, John McLaughlin, Manitas de Plata, Gil Evans, Kodaly, Prokofieff, Stravinsky, Kurt Weill, etc. Harvey Siders calls one of the pieces from "The Grand Wazoo" one of the "most successful weddings of jazz and rock in the book."

The album's personnel, which varies from track to track, consists of six saxophones and woodwinds, five brass horns, two percussionists, George Duke on keyboards and Don Preston on Mini Moog, two guitars (one of them Zappa's), bass, and drums (Aynsley Dunbar). A contrabass sarrusophone also belongs in the band: "Sounds like an elephant playing soprano sax," says one of the members.

"The Grand Wazoo" is a megaphone through which Cletus, the "Funky Emperor," calls into battle an army, which Zappa in passing reveals as actually being a big band. Before the battle, Cletus regretfully disposes of "the ones who refuse to alter their unmusical ways. . . . It bubbles and fumes for a few moments, finally gulping them all down."

Cletus' army consists of "5000 brass players (assorted) which is The Air Force, 5000 drummers (assorted) which is The Artillery, 5000 players of electronic instruments (assorted) which is The Chemical/Biological/Psychological Warfare Section . . . ," etc.

This army fights against the "Mediocrates of Pedestrium," which also includes a "string section—alternately, The Sweetener. . . . The main difference between the two armies, however, is The M. O. P. is heavy on vocals. . . . The M. O. P. has 5000 dynamic male vocalists in tuxedoes . . . 5000 more dynamic performers of indeterminate sex who can't sing at all, but dance good and do hot moves with the mike wire . . . 100,000 girl back-up singers (assorted). . . . As if that weren't enough, there's another 5000 girl lead singers, many of which are so sensitive they're invisible. . . ."

We quote at length because this "battle" between the armies of the "Funky Emperor" and the "Mediocracy of the Pedestrians" with its singers and its "Sweetener" has been fought in Zappa's soul as long as Zappa the artist has existed. For the first time, Zappa has succeeded in also expressing instrumentally that which he has been ridiculing in vocals, comedy routines, and clowning. He has now mastered, instrumentally, his love for the bizarre and obscene and black humor.

I quote Zappa also because in writing a book such as this, one learns often enough how futile it is to describe music with words. Only a few thousand words apply to music, but there are millions of musical possibilities. That is why a musician's thoughts are often more able to express what is behind the music than an outsider's technical analysis.

Zappa has two record labels: "Bizarre" and "Straight." Harvey Siders points to the play on words which results when these labels are used to characterize Zappa's own development: "from bizarre to straight." We have already said (in the drum chapter) that the challenge of the seventies lies in combining the emotionality of rock with the sensitivity of jazz. That is precisely what is being done in the field of big-band music by Frank Zappa.

Big Bands Forever: The Seventies

Anyone who realizes how few convincing rock big-band records have appeared until now, and on the other hand takes into account the many great productions featuring the conventional big-band set-up released in growing numbers from the early seventies on, certainly cannot speak of the "end of big bands." Many outstanding leaders and arrangers have proven that the big band still has noteworthy pos-sibilities, even on today's music scene. Among these musicians are Don Ellis, Buddy Rich, Louis Bellson, Thad Jones-Mel Lewis, Oliver Nelson, Doc Severinsen, and—in Europe—Kenny Clarke-Francy Boland and Chris McGregor and his Brotherhood of Breath. In addition, there is a whole line of arrangers and band leaders who have been active for decades and have kept their music alive as times changed—among them Woody Herman, Count Basie, Maynard Ferguson. . . .

The scope of contemporary big-band music has become so broad because while on the one hand new possibilities are continually being discovered, on the other nearly all the possibilities that have been discovered in 40 years of big-band history have remained alive.

Don Ellis came out of the George Russell sextet of the early six-ties, and later studied Indian music with Hari Har Rao. He is espe-cially interested in developing new meters and rhythmic sequences. Other musicians, to be sure, used asymmetrical meters in jazz before Ellis—Thelonious Monk and Max Roach, then Dave Brubeck and Sonny Rollins, and as early as in the thirties, Benny Carter—but no-body went as far as he. Ellis says: "I reasoned that since it was possi-ble to play in a meter such as a 9, divided 2-2-2-3, it should then be possible to play in meters of even longer length, and this led to the development of such meters as 3-3-2-2-2-1-2-2-2 (19). To arrive at this particular divison of 19, I tried many different patterns, but this was the one that swung the most. The longest meter I have attempted to date is a piece in 85."

Some of Ellis' meters look like mathematical equations—for in-stance, the blues in 11 that Ellis plays as $\frac{3\frac{2}{3}}{4}$ with natural, swinging ease. Ellis once said, ironically, that if his orchestra had to play a traditional 4/4 beat, one would best explain it to the band as "5/4-1," otherwise it would be no fun.

On one of his records, "Tears of Joy," Ellis also incorporated a string quartet and a woodwind quintet in the big-band line-up. Through a novel technique of electronic amplification and adjustment —the Barcus-Berry Transducer System—it has become possible to give as much volume and power to the strings and woodwinds as to the brass and sax sections.

Buddy Rich, on the other hand, did not experiment at all. His big band "celebrated" his spectacular drum artistry effectively. Rich, the great maestro, figured so prominently at the center that hardly any of the young musicians in his band were able to play their way into prominence, except for saxophonist Pat LaBarbara. Rich's interest in his sidemen seemed rather limited. Basically, all Rich wanted from his musicians was that they be well drilled—like splendid machines.

An evening with the Rich Big Band was show business in the conventional sense, but so professionally and movingly presented that it reached even young audiences. The band's repertoire included evergreens, classic jazz themes (such as "Two Bass Hit") originals by arrangers including Bill Holman, Don Menza, and Don Sebesky, and contemporary tunes by The Doors, Paul Simon, Burt Bacharach, and others. Rich disbanded it in 1974.

Another drummer, *Louis Bellson,* occasionally also makes big-band recordings, but he does not appear so much as the star in the center, rather taking on a functional role in order to present musicianly, convincing arrangements (frequently his own) which combine the great big-band tradition with the contemporary rock atmosphere. This is done in similar fashion (but more along the lines of a versatile, clever studio big band that can play anything) by, among others, trumpeter and band leader *Doc Severinsen.*

In Europe, the *Clarke-Boland Big Band* has proven how alive the big-band tradition can be even when no concessions are made to the *Zeitgeist.* Under the co-leadership of drum patriarch Kenny Clarke and of Belgian arranger Francy Boland, some of the best-known American expatriates, among them trumpeters Benny Bailey, Art Farmer, and Idrees Sulieman; saxophonists Herb Geller and Sahib Shihab have united with European musicians of the caliber of Swedish trombonist Ake Persson, German trumpeter Manfred Schoof,

British sax men Ronnie Scott and Tony Coe. The band's second drummer is a British musician similar to the famous Clarke not only in playing, but also in name: Kenny Clare. He impressively supplements Clarke's musicianship and stylistic feeling with his professional dependability, occasionally also disguising a lack of stamina in Clarke, the grand old master.

For years, pianist Francy Boland's arrangements were evaluated as the "most traditional contemporary big-band arrangements" on the jazz scene. Especially characteristic of this are the albums "Sax No End" (with tenorists Johnny Griffin and Eddie "Lockjaw" Davis) and "Faces" (with musical portrait sketches of the band members). From the impact of a Japanese tour, on the occasion of the 1970 World Exposition in Osaka, Boland changed markedly. On the tour, he played with such modern musicians as German trombonist Albert Mangelsdorff, British saxophonist John Surman, and French violinist Jean Luc Ponty, and after some hesitation took up some of the cues of their music. A result is the 1971 recording by the Clarke-Boland Big Band with Stan Getz as guest soloist which truly lives up to its name: "Change of Scenes."

The musically most convincing of all more recent big bands is the *Thad Jones-Mel Lewis* Orchestra. As the Clarke-Boland Big Band has celebrated its greatest triumphs in London's Ronnie Scott Club, Thad Jones-Mel Lewis have for years presided over New York's "Village Vanguard" every Monday night. Without making compromises with the rock spirit of the times, the band still has managed to create an orchestral jazz which no one could deny the attribute "contemporary." Jazz discoveries of all periods—including the jazz of the sixties and the music of John Coltrane and the post-Coltrane era —merge in the arrangements, furnished mainly by trumpeter and co-leader Thad Jones, but also by other former and current band members, such as trombonists Garnett Brown and Bob Brookmeyer.

Members of this band have included the outstanding lead trumpeter Snooky Young; saxophonists Jerome Richardson, Joe Farrell, Eddie Daniels, Pepper Adams, and Billy Harper; pianist Roland Hanna; bassist Richard Davis—an elite of New York musicians! From time to time, depending on availability, there are changes in personnel, yet Jones and Lewis have for years succeeded in giving the band an easily identifiable sound without turning to tricks or gimmicks. Jones had his first major big-band experience with Count Basie during the mid-fifties. On his first combo recording, he was presented by Charles Mingus. Lewis came to the fore in the jazz world as Stan Kenton's drummer from 1954 to 1956.

Aside from these established big bands, a number of arrangers make an occasional orchestral jazz recording, and have in this way helped to shape the contemporary big-band scene. Among them are some who have been mentioned before as well—above all, *Oliver Nelson*. Nelson, who lives in Los Angeles, is best characterized by a list of his favorite musicians: Charlie Parker, John Coltrane, Gil Evans, George Russell.

Nelson learned the tricks of the big-band trade in bands that played mainly for black audiences—the Louis Jordan big band of 1950/51, the Erskine Hawkins orchestra of the fifties—and he fuses this background with an apparent openness to the free sounds of the sixties. The title of one of his best-known works, "The Blues and the Abstract Truth," signifies Nelson's position: the tension-field between the tradition of the blues and the truth of avant-garde abstractions. The big-band arrangements Nelson wrote at the 1971 Montreux Jazz Festival for Argentinian tenorist Gato Barbieri celebrate Barbieri's ecstatic tenor excursions on a level that calls to mind the concertos of Ellington. The Basie band never sounded more "modern" in recent years than on "Afrique," for which Nelson wrote the arrangements.

In Britain, South African pianist *Chris McGregor* has "applied" the Ellington tradition to free jazz in his "Brotherhood of Breath," to which he added, as a further element, Bantu and Zulu rhythms and melodies and motifs of his homeland. South African emigrants play alongside British musicians—certainly not with the usual studio precision, but precisely this friction of intonation and harmony within the "Brotherhood of Breath" has an Africanizing and intensifying effect. The Brotherhood is the kind of band that can convey the excitement of orchestral jazz to a young, rock-oriented audience especially well.

All in all, clearly a comeback of tradition can be found on the big-band scene. It is no longer free-jazz orchestras or rock big bands, but the conventional big-band instrumentation (four trumpets, four trombones, a five-piece saxophone section, with minor deviations, alterations, and additions) that today again is the focal point of big-band attention—20 or 25 years after the period when there first was talk of the "death" of the big bands. This element of the big-band tradition seems convincing also to musicians and listeners who consider themselves "contemporary." Virtually symbolic of this tendency is "Let My Children Hear Music," the record Charles Mingus made with a big band in 1971. Around the turn of the fifties, Mingus had been the great avant-gardist, helping to pave the way for everything that descended upon us in free jazz during the sixties. In the early seventies, Mingus appears as a mature classic summing up the jazz tradition, who finds his points of orientation in Charlie Parker and Lester Young, as one might in classical music with Beethoven or Bach. "Jazz is black classical music," says Mingus and points out that we would lose the music if we were to neglect its tradition: "Let my children hear music—for God's sake—we've heard enough noise. . . . I, myself, came to enjoy the players who didn't only just swing, who invented new rhythmic patterns, along with new melodic concepts. And those people are: Art Tatum, Bud Powell, Max Roach, Sonny Rollins, Lester Young, Dizzy Gillespie, and Charlie Parker, who is the greatest genius of all to me because he changed the whole era around. But there is no need to compare composers. If you like Beethoven, Bach or Brahms, that's okay. They were all pencil composers. I always wanted to be a spontaneous composer. . . ."

THE JAZZ COMBOS

The Jazz Combos

JAZZ IS initially a music of small ensembles. Jazz was a combo music long before the word "combo" existed. This word came into being when it became necessary to distinguish between big bands and small groups. Before that, any jazz band was automatically a combo, and if one did not know from hindsight what would evolve from the bands of Fletcher Henderson and Duke Ellington in the twenties, these ensembles, too, could be regarded as "combos."

Since jazz from the start has been an art of small ensembles, a history of combos must be written differently from a history of big bands. Since practically every jazz man has played in combos, such a history would turn into an endless listing of names. The required selective principle rests in the fact that a combo should be more than merely a group of musicians who have come together to play. By way of the Modern Jazz Quartet and John Lewis, "integration" has become a key term in jazz criticism. Here indeed is the key to our history of the combo in jazz. Integration—in terms of mathematics or music—means that everything belongs to a whole, that all elements are subordinate to one main idea. But integration also requires—as far as jazz is concerned—that what is integrated is genuine soloistic jazz expression. In this sense, we must exclude from our combo history not only combos in which some of the greatest solos of jazz history might have been played, but without significant connection between these solo efforts and their setting, but also combos in which this connection is present, but where the solo efforts do not reach the required level. Thus *Red Nichols,* for example, had a combo in the late twenties and early thirties (the famous Five Pennies) with integration that placed it far ahead of its time; other New York jazz combos of the day—such as trumpeter Phil Napoleon's *Original Memphis Five*—also had more "integration" than the leading ensembles of Chicago. Nonetheless, one recalls the Five Pennies or the Memphis Five rather gloomily, and collectors of vintage records seldom collect Red Nichols but often collect records from the same era *without* integration, but with significant solo efforts: records by, for instance, Bix Beiderbecke, Jimmie Noone, or Johnny Dodds.

In this sense, Dave Brubeck made a relevant statement about the combo situation: "The important thing about jazz right now is that it's keeping alive the feeling of the group getting together. Jazz, to make it, has got to be a group feeling. . . ." This describes what we have frequently referred to as the sociological situation of jazz—e.g., at the beginning of the section dealing with Swing style and in the chapter about the arrangement. Jazz is at once music of the individual and music of the collective. No other art has attained both in such extreme measure. In such simultaneity the sociologist may find philosophical, political, and historical aspects. With jazz, this simultaneity of the individual and the collective, of—if you will—freedom and necessity, has acquired musical aspects for the first time. Rarely is jazz seen so clearly as a legitimate artistic expression of our time as in this point. And since this is so, the combo history of jazz is almost something like a concentration of jazz history *per se.*

In the selective sense in which we wish to concentrate combo history, Jelly Roll Morton's *Red Hot Peppers* (1926 to 1930) and Louis Armstrong's second *Hot Five* with Earl Hines (1928) are the first significant jazz combos. Morton was the first to map out recordings from beginning to end and give them the stamp of a formative personality; Armstrong's Hot Five recordings achieved integration through the somnambulistic rapport between Louis and pianist Earl Hines.

Orrin Keepnews writes in the liner notes to a Morton album: "This is complex, intricate music. The musicians reputedly did not play from written scores but each number was preceded by perhaps a half-hour of studying the tunes, deciding on the placements of solos, memorizing the basic arrangements. It is the definitive answer to anyone who would claim that jazz is deficient in counterpoint or in depth of musical structure. It is a remarkable combination of improvisation and arrangement. . . . These are all talented musicians, but nevertheless, the voice that is heard here, the single, unified sound, is Morton's. This the mark of his greatness. . . ."

In the Hot Five with Hines (they consisted of six and sometimes even seven musicians) and in the Red Hot Peppers we see for the first time a coming together of elements which previously had only existed separately: the collective improvisation of the old New Orleans bands (and also of the first available recordings, those of the Original Dixieland Jazz Band in 1917) in which soloistic achievement, and the individuality of the improviser in general, had barely begun to develop; this soloistic achievement itself; and, lastly, the conscious or intuitive creation of form through an outstanding personality.

The Swing Combos

What the thirties brought was, compared to this, initially a step backwards. In 1935 Benny Goodman formed his *Goodman Trio*. It became the germ cell not only for all the other Goodman combos—the Quartet with Lionel Hampton and eventually the Sextets with Charlie Christian and Cootie Williams—but also for all the combos which developed as "bands within bands" in all the important large orchestras. Thus, Artie Shaw formed his *Gramercy Five* with himself on clarinet and first Billy Butterfield and then Roy Eldridge on trumpet. Tommy Dorsey, Bob Crosby, and Jimmy Dorsey formed Dixieland combos within their big bands: Tommy Dorsey his *Clambake Seven* with Pee Wee Erwin (trumpet), Bud Freeman (tenor sax), Dave Tough (drums), and others; Bob Crosby his *Bob Cats* with Matty Matlock (clarinet), Eddie Miller (tenor), Yank Lawson (trumpet), and the rhythm section mentioned in the big-band chapter. Later, toward the end of the forties, Jimmy Dorsey formed his *Original Dorseyland Jazz Band* wiith Ray Bauduc on drums. Chu Berry recruited his *Stompy Stevedores* primarily from the ranks of Cab Calloway's band, of which he was a member. Count Basie's band had its *Kansas City Six* and *Seven* and Woody Herman his *Woodchoppers*.

The most important of these "bands within the bands" originated in the *Duke Ellington* orchestra. Trumpeters Cootie Williams and Rex Stewart, clarinetist Barney Bigard, and altoist Johnny Hodges all made recordings in which the atmosphere of Ellington's music was, amazingly, projected into a small instrumental combination. The "Ellington spirit" served as the integrating factor. It was so strong that even some records made by Lionel Hampton with musicians drawn mainly from this band acquired a noticeable Ellington aura.

The opposite of the integration which permeates the recordings made by the Ellington musicians can be found in the recording groups put together by *Teddy Wilson* from 1935 on. In a sense, these groups should not be mentioned here, in view of our selective combo principles. Here solo follows solo, but precisely on this account it is amazing how often the musical climate creates its own unity—primarily when Billie Holiday and Lester Young are among the participants. In a record like "Easy Living" (1937) there is certainly nothing "integrated"—and yet, from first note to last we are in the unifying climate created by the tune, the lyrics, and the way in which Billie Holiday sings.

It is remarkable how the turning point in jazz evolution, which came toward the end of the thirties and beginning of the forties, not only relates to the harmonic, melodic, and rhythmic innovations of the bop musicians, but also to combo jazz. In 1938 bassist *John Kirby* formed an ensemble which in every respect made Swing music in the best sense of the term, yet was a combo in a sense which did not become the rule until the fifties. With Kirby—and with the King Cole Trio as well—begins a line which leads through the Art Tatum Trio and the Red Norvo Trio to all the characteristic combos of the fifties and sixties: the Gerry Mulligan Quartet, the Modern Jazz Quartet, the Jimmy Giuffre Trio, the Max Roach-Clifford Brown Quintet, the Miles Davis Quintet, the Horace Silver Quintet, Art Blakey's Jazz Messengers, the various Charles Mingus groups, the Ornette Coleman groups—and further on to Weather Report and John McLaughlin's Mahavishnu Orchestra. . . .

Kirby's "biggest little band in the land" created airy, complementary frameworks of sound within which trumpeter Charlie Shavers, clarinetist Buster Bailey, altoist Russell Procope, and pianist Billy Kyle improvised pretty and pleasing solos. The band had a clearly identifiable sound. It was the first ensemble to find success as a combo in the sense that the Gerry Mulligan Quartet or the Modern Jazz Quartet were to achieve it 15 years later.

Many of these successful later combos sprang up on the West Coast, and perhaps it is fitting that the combo which, alongside

Kirby, initiated this whole development also started there: the *King Cole Trio*. It is the first combo of the modern piano-trio type: not merely a pianist accompanied by a rhythm section, but three instruments constituting a single entity. The Nat "King" Cole Trio was formed in 1940, with Oscar Moore on guitar and Wesley Prince on bass. Later, Cole had guitarist Irving Ashby and bassist Johnny Miller. But in the course of the forties, the success of Cole the singer gradually began to overshadow the pianist, until Nat gave up his trio and became a singer of popular tunes—though still a singer whose jazz past made itself felt in almost everything he sang.

Bop and Cool

In the meantime, bop had arrived. The *Charlie Parker Quintet,* with Miles Davis on trumpet, set the standard for both the music itself and for the format of the combos who played this music. For the first time it was again as it had been in the old Dixieland jazz: music and structure belonged together. Then it had been the free counterpoint of trumpet, trombone, and clarinet over a two-beat rhythm; now it was trumpet and saxophone in unison over the new legato rhythm. This unity of music and structure remained obligatory for the combos of hard bop: *Art Blakey's Jazz Messengers*, the *Horace Silver Quintet,* the *Max Roach Quintet* (with trumpeter Clifford Brown and then with other musicians), and—above all—from the mid-fifties to the end of the sixties, the *Miles Davis Quintet* (and traces of this bebop structure can even be found in the "electric" Miles of the seventies). Primarily pianist Horace Silver strove to retain the basic bebop format while giving it structural variety. He did this through the individualistic construction of his themes. Thus, he might use two 12-bar blues phrases, follow them up with an 8-bar bridge taken from song form, and then repeat the blues phrase, thus combining blues and song form; or he might combine a 15-bar main theme with a 16-bar interlude—"even though it's not even, it sounds even," as Horace has said—and so on in many similarly conceived compositions. And it should be said clearly: If today's music, even rock, has become largely free of the schematic nature of the conventional, 32-bar song form, this is due in no small measure to Silver, who was the first to pave the way for this development. To be sure, there were unique forms deviating from conventions even in the early days of jazz—as in Jelly Roll Morton's music or in William Christopher Handy's (e.g., "St. Louis Blues")—but awareness of this had meanwhile been buried. Horace Silver unearthed it.

Seven years before the first Silver success in this field—around the turn of the forties—Lennie Tristano had already refined and abstracted the Parker format in the highest sense. He also had two horns, but they were both saxophones—Lee Konitz (alto) and Warne Marsh (tenor)—and to this he added a third horn-like line through Billy Bauer's guitar. In the *Lennie Tristano Sextette* could be found a highly mobile linearity, moving over highly differentiated harmonies. After bop had broadened the harmonic material, Lennie Tristano "widened" the line—from the conscious conviction that jazz musicians had been concerned with harmonic problems for years and that the time had come to apply harmonic discoveries to the melody. There were recordings—such as "Wow," on Capitol—with a vigor that only hard bop would return to the general jazz consciousness in the late fifties; but above all there was a thoughtful, inspiring coolness with something of the atmosphere of the medieval cloisters in which scholastic debates were held in the evening.

Even before Tristano, bop musicians had attempted to broaden the structure of the Parker Quintet—in terms of sound. Tadd Dameron, James Moody, and Charlie Ventura were primarily involved in this effort—Dameron in his recordings for Blue Note, for which he used such musicians as trumpeter Fats Navarro and tenorists Wardell Gray and Allen Eager; James Moody with his significant and much-too-neglected recording of "Cu-Ba" (also on Blue Note); and—most successfully—*Charlie Ventura* with his "Bop for the People" combo, in which vocalist Jackie Cain and pianist Roy Kral (later to become her husband) sang humorous, spirited vocal duets. All this culminated in the *Miles Davis Capitol Band*. In it, sound became definitively established as a structuring element. (In the Davis chapter, the ensemble is discussed in detail.)

What followed consists of manifold combinations and developments of these three elements: the harmonic, connected with the name of Charlie Parker; the element of sound, for which Miles Davis' Capitol Band created an ideal; and the element of integration, for which the John Kirby Band and the King Cole Trio had already broken ground.

On the West Coast, for example, *Shorty Rogers* with his "Giants" and *Gerry Mulligan* with his "Tentette" made recordings which further perfected the sound of the Davis Capitol Band, though sterilizing it a bit in the process. Later, Rogers reduced the Giants to the size of a quintet and created polished West Coast music within the Parker format—as did drummer *Shelly Manne*. Jimmy Giuffre played a role as clarinetist, saxophonist, and personality in the groups of both Rogers and Manne. Manne is one of the few West Coast musicians flexible enough to keep their musical concept alive by continually being able to re-orient themselves in the changing musical stream—right into the seventies. Today, with young musicians, he makes records that are partially rock-influenced, but retain the solid tradition of the excellent drummer and band leader Shelly Manne.

On the East Coast, *J. J. Johnson* and *Kai Winding* found an impressive solution. They joined their two trombones in a quintet, and thus on the one hand preserved the two-horn format of bop, and on the other discovered a structuring sound in the subtleties of differentiated trombone tones. This structure was so intriguingly simple that it was frequently copied. Winding himself did it—after the original combo disbanded—by replacing the two trombones with four. *Al Cohn* and *Zoot Sims* followed suit, combining two tenors—and on occasion, two clarinets—instead of trombones. *Phil Woods* and *Gene Quill* did something similar when they teamed up on alto saxophones. Tenormen *Eddie "Lockjaw" Davis* and *Johnny Griffin* projected the idea into the world of hard bop around the turn of the fifties. And in the early seventies, drummer *Elvin Jones* transplanted this "set-up" onto the post-Coltrane era, using the two sopranos of Dave Liebman and Steve Grossman.

High Points of Integration

At an earlier date—in the late forties—vibraphonist *Red Norvo* had formed a trio with guitarist Tal Farlow and bassist Charlie Mingus which made outstanding chamber jazz. In light, relaxed, transparent interplay, the lines of vibraphone, guitar, and bass flowed into, opposite, and around each other, and if Norvo—as a representative of the older jazz generation—didn't play quite as "modern" as Farlow and Mingus, the two-fold stylistic plateau thus created lent an added charm. The linear function Norvo had assigned to the bass of Mingus (later Red Mitchell) was adopted in *Gerry Mulligan's* successful Quartet from 1953 on. Gerry did away with the piano, let the changes be indicated by a single bass line which took on additional contrapuntal significance, and set the lines of his baritone sax and Chet Baker's trumpet above. Later, after Chet Baker (who became famous almost overnight through his playing in this quartet) had made himself independent, valve trombonist Bob Brookmeyer or trumpeters Jon Eardly and Art Farmer took his place. In a manner which can only be described as "busy," Mulligan played contrapuntal counter-melodies or riffs on his baritone behind the improvisations of the second horn in his quartet. So it became apparent that even the riff—one of the most rudimentary of jazz elements—could be used structurally in terms of modern combo integration. Of course, it also became apparent that such devices tended toward the cliché. Throughout the world, there suddenly appeared combos in which musicians sought to demonstrate their "modernity" by attempting to combine a baritone sax with another horn, a bass and a drum "à la Gerry." Mulligan, who is not only a great musician, but also a very farsighted man, enlarged his quartet to a sextet as soon as he saw the danger of formula growing into a cliché. Kai Winding and J. J. Johnson did likewise: they dissolved their two-trombone combo at the peak of its success. On the whole, it soon became increasingly clear that all combos using a sound as the main structural element of necessity had to be short-lived. The greater the initial surprise of the sound, the greater the danger of monotony once the surprise has evaporated.

The great exception to this short lifespan of "sound combos" was pianist John Lewis' *Modern Jazz Quartet,* with Milt Jackson, vibraphone; Percy Heath, bass; and first Kenny Clarke, then Connie Kay, drums. Founded in 1951, it is by far the longest-lived combo in jazz history. Lewis found much stimulation in the contrapuntal art of Johann Sebastian Bach. At the beginning, he often took over classical forms almost literally—above all in "Vendome," a precise and knowledgeable copy of a baroque invention—with the one difference that in the place of the "episodes" in the form of the invention are put improvisations by the Modern Jazz Quartet. Later, Lewis discovered contrapuntal possibilities more germane to jazz than to old music. As he said: "in the little piece entitled 'Versailles,' which also used a 'classical' form—the fugue—as a model, I don't feel that this has anything to do with the model, the best-known examples of which are Bach's. We have started to work on some new concepts of playing which give freer rein to the creativity of the improviser and yet produce an even stronger form. . . ." In those terms, Lewis has also worked on an incorporation of the percussion part into the linear and contrapuntal play of his quartet. His percussionist, Connie Kay, was equipped with a whole arsenal of auxiliary rhythm instruments: finger cymbals, triangles, small Chinese drum, etc. . . . And if drum instrumentation in general has become increasingly enlarged since the sixties, Connie Kay was among those who gave this direction its first impetus.

Characteristic of Lewis' thoroughly jazz-minded relationship to baroque music are these thoughts, expressed by him in connection with his suite, "Fontessa": " 'Fontessa' is a little suite inspired by the Renaissance Commedia dell' Arte. I had particularly in mind their plays which consisted of a very sketchy plot and in which the details —the lines, etc.—were improvised. . . ."

The MJQ—as Lewis' combo is abbreviated—has gone through a clearly perceivable development. During the sixties, there were hardly any Bach elements, but this was compensated for by a much more swinging jazz intensity. However, there is also a somewhat manneristic tendency toward light romantic music, stemming from a glorifying, imprecise view of the European tradition rooted in John Lewis' personality. This tendency may be the reason why many critics and listeners have complained about the sterile and static nature of the MJQ music. As imprecise in their approach to jazz as Lewis is in his attitude toward Europe are the critics who have said (and even written) that in the MJQ "the same thing is constantly being repeated in the same, bogged-down manner." In reality, no two MJQ recordings of even the same piece are alike. Lewis' "Django," for example, has gone through such a metamorphosis in various recordings currently available that even the character of the composition has changed. For the connoisseur, it is an illuminating experience to follow the development of the themes Lewis has repeatedly recorded from the fifties to the seventies. In general, there is a development toward greater intensity. The MJQ disbanded in 1974.

The MJQ had great influence. Even in the hard-bop combos with their Parker Quintet structure, one suddenly could detect echoes of John Lewis' will to form. Even *Oscar Peterson*, whose trio at first was a kind of modernized King Cole or Art Tatum Trio, has paid respect to the integration principle . . . until he lost first his guitarist

Herb Ellis (in 1959) and then bassist Ray Brown (in 1966), and actually has been furnishing only piano music—however outstanding—with rhythm accompaniment since the late sixties.

A similarly long development was experienced by the Dave Brubeck Quartet, formed in 1951 from the Brubeck Octet (1946) and the Brubeck Trio (1949). Brubeck had more "hits" than any other jazz musician. His first partner was Paul Desmond, a "poet of the alto saxophone," whose improvisations have been valued much more highly by critics than Brubeck's piano playing. When Desmond withdrew in the late sixties, Gerry Mulligan stepped into his place. Mulligan has always been an immensely swing-oriented, "busy" improviser, and it is obvious that through his participation the until then somewhat pastoral, cool Brubeck Quartet definitely became a more intense, "hotter" group.

Brubeck also developed toward greater intensity in terms of drummers, as shown by what we said about Joe Morello and Alan Dawson in the drum chapter. Meanwhile, Brubeck has taken to presenting his sons in a kind of "family band," which is pleasant but lacks the high standards of the quartets with Desmond or Mulligan. The dilemma of the group is that the sons are moving into different musical areas. So Dave seems to have only two alternatives, neither of which is satisfying: Either the group falls apart, or he forces his sons into a unity that makes the music sterile because they can't express themselves in their own ways. It's pleasant to observe how clarinetist Perry Robinson uses humor to overcome this dilemma.

From Hard Bop to Free

We have already mentioned hard-bop combos in connection with the Charlie Parker Quintet. It is apparent that an evolution toward greater integration took place here as well. Even the most vital hard-bop group, the Messengers—thrust forward by Art Blakey's wild percussion work—has always had a musical "integrator" in the sense of the function of John Lewis within the MJQ, if in hard-bop terms. With the Messengers, this man was first Horace Silver, then Benny Golson, Bobby Timmons, Wayne Shorter, Cedar Walton, etc.—and, in the early seventies, pianist George Cables.

Marvelous integration is also characteristic of the various groups Max Roach has led since his work with Clifford Brown and Sonny

Rollins in the mid-fifties—ensembles partially with full, rich three-part horn sounds, without piano; later with pianist Ron Matthews and trumpeter Freddie Hubbard; frequently also with Roach's then wife, Abbey Lincoln. Max's main work, "Freedom Now Suite," is exemplary not only for content but also as a composition for a small ensemble in a large form.

At the center of all these groups stands the Miles Davis Quintet, which has become a kind of backbone for the entire development since the mid-fifties. It has been said that Miles in this process has developed into *the* "star-maker". Here is a list of musicians who have emerged from his groups: saxophonists John Coltrane, Cannonball Adderley, Hank Mobley, Wayne Shorter, George Coleman, Sam Rivers, Dave Liebman, and Steve Grossman; bass clarinetist Bennie Maupin; pianists Red Garland, Bill Evans, Wynton Kelly, Herbie Hancock, Chick Corea, and Keith Jarrett; guitarist John McLaughlin; bassists Paul Chambers, Ron Carter, and Dave Holland; drummers Philly Joe Jones, Tony Williams, Jack DeJohnette, and Billy Cobham; and percussionist Airto Moreira—truly a list defying comparison! In the chapters about the seventies and Miles Davis himself, the role this great musician has played is depicted from different points of view.

From the point of view of our combo-selection principle, it is important to see that the concept of "modality," introduced by Miles and John Coltrane, creates a high degree of connection—and thus integration. The integration factor here is "the scale"—no longer many, continuously varying chord changes, but only a single one which (not only musically, but also in mood) holds the whole piece together.

John Coltrane transplanted this principle into free jazz—in a sense shown in the chapter about him (and elsewhere throughout the book). One of the most beautiful recordings of the "classical" Coltrane Quartet—with McCoy Tyner on piano and Elvin Jones on drums—is the famous "A Love Supreme," which combines spiritual fervor with formal completeness in a way heretofore unachieved in jazz. After that, with "Ascension," 'Trane' created the most burning and consuming free-jazz work in existence. Even in the face of all the ecstatic, unrestrained freedom of this recording, form and structure were achieved through a consistently applied alternation between collective and solo improvisation—the solo crystallizing from the collective improvisation, to again give birth to a new collective: a principle of form immediately adopted by a number of other free-jazz musicians.

Among those groups which paved the way for the new jazz, three are important: the Jimmy Giuffre Trios of the fifties, Charles Mingus, and George Russell. In the early fifties, *Jimmy Giuffre* recorded his "Tangents in Jazz" (Capitol), in which the drummer—as percussionist—is drawn into the melodic and structural development of the music to such an extent that a continuous beat is entirely dispensed with. In the trio organized by Giuffre in 1954 there was no drummer at all, and one may surmise that this outcome was near at hand: once the drums are used purely as melody instrument, there must surely be other instruments capable of serving this purpose better. In this trio, Giuffre used guitarist Jim Hall and bassist Ralph Pena. Giuffre went one step further when he joined with valve trombonist Bob Brookmeyer in a trio without a rhythm section—two horns plus guitar—and nevertheless succeeded in conveying swing through phrasing. *Charles Mingus,* with his grinding, urgent expressions and his principle of collective improvisation, has been discussed in the bass chapter and in the big-band section, where we also spoke of *George Russell.*

Ornette and After

Beyond that point stands *Ornette Coleman,* who with his 1959 quartet made the whole jazz world conscious of "freedom," yet from the start met the integration criteria of this section. Appearing at the New York club, the "Five Spot," Coleman and his trumpeter Don Cherry enraptured audiences night after night, for months. The many musicians always present in the audience were fascinated by the precision with which Ornette and Don entered in unison after their long, free sclo excursions—though it wasn't recognizable to the majority of even the specialists why they entered at this precise spot and not somewhere else. One of the musician-listeners said then: "You can't hear it, but there is no doubt: Ornette and his men know what they're doing. In a couple of years, everybody else will know it, too" Bassist Charlie Haden had an especially integrating effect at that time, with his totally free bass lines that dispensed with conventional harmonies, yet created connection and structure.

A few years later, Ornette did away with the second horn in his trio. It may certainly be surmised that he took on the roles of trumpeter and violinist—however much he was criticized in them—in addition to his alto work because he needed further sound colorations but nevertheless wanted to mold the music of his group as directly and immediately as possible. Only toward the end of the sixties did Coleman succeed in finding a congenial horn partner in tenor saxophonist Dewey Redman.

From Coleman and Coltrane spring all the free-jazz groups that emphasize collective experience of their music to an extent heretofore unknown. Dismayed by the isolation of the individual in modern society, these musicians feel that their improvisations unite them to a degree "as otherwise, among humans, only love can do" (Don Cherry). Cherry's piece "Complete Communion," realized first in Paris and then in New York, is symbolic of this total communication among the musicians.

Other groups that replaced the isolation of the individual expressing himself without restraint (which is where a music that knows no harmonic or formal ordering factors must necessarily lead), with much stronger and more intensely personal collective relationships were the *Archie Shepp Quintet* with trombonist Roswell Rudd; the *New York Art Quartet* with altoist John Tchicai (and also with Rudd); the *Albert Ayler Quintet* and many European groups: around Tchicai in Copenhagen; Jan Garbarek in Oslo; Tomasz Stanko and Michal Urbaniak in Warsaw; Albert Mangelsdorff, Manfred Schoof, Peter Brötzmann, and Gunter Hampel in Germany; Michel Portal in Paris; John Stevens, John Surman, Allan Skidmore, Paul Rutherford, Tony Oxley, and others in London. . . .

Special attention in this connection is merited by the various groups of Chicago avant-garde musicians surrounding pianist *Richard Abrams* and saxophonist *Joseph Jarman*. Appalled by the lack of interest in free music and by the political and social implications of this lack of interest on the part of the American public, Jarman went into exile in Paris in the late sixties, with three other members of the Chicago "AACM": saxophonist Roscoe Mitchell, trumpeter Lester Bowie, and bassist Malachi Favors. Only shortly before, they had lost their fifth man, the drummer Phil Wilson, to the Paul Butterfield Blues Band, a popular group on the rock scene. They were not able to find a suitable substitute. Thus the four began playing diverse percussion instruments themselves, in constant alternation: Bowie playing the bass drum and Roscoe, Jarman, and mainly Favors playing the entire range of manifold percussion instruments which became customary in the new jazz. In this way, the percussion parts—played alternately by musicians whose main instruments were trumpet, saxophone, and bass—were integrated completely in the melodic activity. Therein lies one ground-breaking contribution of this "Art Ensemble of Chicago" which has not yet been sufficiently recognized.

As far as I know, there has never been a jazz combo that had so many different instrumental colors at its disposal as the *Art Ensemble of Chicago*. On their European tours, the four musicians carried whole bus loads of instruments. Particularly versatile are Mitchell (who plays alto, soprano, tenor, and bass saxophone; clarinet, flute, piccolo, sirens, whistles, bells, steel drum, congas, gongs, cymbals, etc., etc.) and Jarman (whose instruments include sopranello; alto, soprano, and tenor sax; alto clarinet, oboe, flute, piano, harpsichord, guitar, marimba, accordion, vibraphone, and several dozen others). With this instrumentation, the four made a series of records in France, Germany, and Great Britain between 1968 and 1971.

The Seventies

In the early seventies, the combo situation is similar to that of the big bands. There are three mainstreams and various cross-connections between them:

1. The well-known combos of conventional jazz, among which the hard-bop groups occupy a special place.
2. The rock groups, among which the blues and blues-rock groups are of primary importance from the jazz standpoint.
3. The jazz-rock groups, with Miles Davis' electric jazz and all that has come from it, at the center.

Aside from this, there is a single traditional jazz group of international class: *The Worlds Greatest Jazz Band*, led by trumpeter Yank Lawson and bassist Bob Haggart. The members of this group somewhere between combo and big band—it usually consists of nine musicians—have included some of the big names in traditional jazz: trumpeter Billy Butterfield, soprano saxist and clarinetist Bob Wilber, tenorman Bud Freeman, trombonists Benny Morton and Vic Dickenson. . . . It is a band as well integrated as any modern group.

Among the conventional jazz groups in the seventies are many that have already been mentioned: Art Blakey's Jazz Messengers, and their even more soul-inspired counterpart in California, the *Jazz Crusaders* with Joe Sample (piano), Buster Williams (bass), and Wayne Henderson (trombone); the Dizzy Gillespie Quintet; the *Cannonball Adderley Quintet;* and the Oscar Peterson Trio (although, as previously mentioned, Peterson has during recent years preferred to appear as a soloist); as well as *Phil Woods' European Rhythm Machine,* based for several years in Europe.

Cannonball Adderley made a rather stereotyped, cliché-ridden kind of soul music during the sixties, but had several commercially successful hits in compositions of Joe Zawinul, his pianist of those years. When Zawinul left Cannonball to collaborate with Miles Davis and found Weather Report, pianist George Duke took his place. Duke brought new life into the Cannonball group, coupled with a more rock-oriented spirit; and the group kept that spirit even when Duke left to join Frank Zappa.

Altoist Phil Woods, as Leonard Feather has written, "inherited the Parker style and modified it to his own ends more successfully than almost any other altoman except (Cannonball) Adderley." In 1968, Woods left the U. S. with his wife and children—among them Charlie Parker's son—to live in Paris. Unlike most other jazz expatriates, he did not leave because of lack of work. On the contrary, Woods was a musician in great demand in the New York studios at that time. He left because he was disgusted by the breakdown of American morality and of the "American dream."

In Paris, Woods founded his European Rhythm Machine, which according to most critics was the best jazz combo based in Europe from 1969 to 1972 (when Woods returned to the U. S.); its changing personnel included Swiss drummer Daniel Humair and the two Britishers Gordon Beck (piano, electric piano) and Ron Matthewson (bass).

(The other groups mentioned above need not be dealt with in detail here, because they were discussed already, or because their orientation is apparent from the discussion of the musicians in the instrumental chapters. Some of these groups experienced a certain "electronization" in the early seventies.)

A high point in combo music of this type came in 1971, when American impressario George Wein (at the instigation of the Berlin Jazz Days) assembled the *Giants of Jazz* for his annual Newport festival tour—and true giants they were: Dizzy Gillespie (trumpet), Kai Winding (trombone), Sonny Stitt (alto), Thelonious Monk (piano), Al McKibbon (bass), and Art Blakey (drums)—musicians, in other words, who had played a formative role in modern jazz during the forties. Most of them had since been leading their own groups, and it required all of Wein's persuasive powers to prompt them to tour in an all-star ensemble. Since the accent in jazz has shifted to perfect ensemble integration, musicians no longer like all-star groups.

To the surprise even of the members themselves, more than a mere all-star band resulted. The six men constituted a well-integrated ensemble, and playing together proved so enjoyable that they have since repeatedly appeared at festivals in Europe and the U. S.

Blues, Blues-Rock, Rock

The rock groups mentioned as the second "mainstream" among contemporary combos would be unthinkable without the heritage of black blues. They are therefore ordered approximately according to the degree to which they have moved away from the blues. The integration principle, set forth at the beginning of this section as the *leitmotif*, had to be modified somewhat in the process. There is a form of "human integration" in rock that is extra-musical and yet has a direct effect on the music. In conventional jazz, it could happen that a group that led integration to its utmost refinement could be almost at the point of disintegration in terms of human relationships: The members of the Modern Jazz Quartet parted as soon as they had finished playing—almost without human communication outside of music. In rock, that would be impossible. To be sure rock is musically much less developed than jazz. But in place of musicianship there is a force and solidarity on the human level that not only substitutes for musical integration, but in fact creates it. The extra-musical is more important in rock than in jazz.

At the head of this second "mainstream" among contemporary combos stand the authentic black blues groups. We refer in this context to what we said in the blues chapter. Most of these groups—and their musicians—hail from Chicago: groups formed around *Muddy Waters, Howlin' Wolf, Buddy Guy, Junior Wells, Freddie King,* and —above all—*B. B. King.* This is where the white musicians who led the blues from decades of obscurity to immense popularity have their roots. First it happened in Great Britain, then in the U. S. Since the later sixties, it has thus become popular practice to team up old black blues masters with their young white emulators—in a kind of meeting of fathers and sons.

Among groups stemming directly from black blues are, in Britain, the various ensembles built around guitarist *Alexis Korner* and *John Mayall*, and *Cream;* in the U. S., the *Paul Butterfield Blues Band*, the *Electric Flag* with Mike Bloomfield, *Canned Heat, Blues Project,* the *Elvin Bishop Group, Taj Mahal, Edgar Winter,* the *Allman Brothers,* the *J. Geils Band,* and many others. Some of these groups existed only for a short while, while others have grown and changed over long time spans.

Justifiably, Alexis Korner is designated the "Father of the White Blues." From his school emerged as many musicians in the field of white blues and beyond as from the Miles Davis school in new jazz: Lonnie Donegan, Mick Jagger, Brian Jones (and other members of the Rolling Stones), Ginger Baker, Jack Bruce, Manfred Mann, John Mayall, Eric Burdon, Long John Baldry, Dick Heckstall-Smith, Graham Bond, Dave Holland, John Marshall, John Surman, and many other names that have become famous.

Since 1954, Korner has been leading the most diverse blues groups: first a duo with Cyril Davis; then his famous "Blues Incorporated" (1961 to 1967); and after that "Free at Last" and various other groups; occasionally also duos with Peter Thorup and Robert Plant (who went to "Led Zeppelin"); and finally, from 1969 to 1970, the not only blues- but also gospel-inspired "New Church."

The phenomenon of Korner rests in the fact that he, though not a truly outstanding musician, has worked as a catalyst with his personality, his sobriety, his knowledge, his integrity, and his enthusiasm in a wider area than probably any other European musician: from jazz via blues and rock to pop music, including even the free jazz of the sixties.

The most successful white blues musician to emerge from a Korner group is harmonica player, singer and guitarist *John Mayall*. He has carried on—and mannerized and made flat—what Korner paved the way for: the creation of a characteristic, white "London Blues" —a concept that seems rather paradoxical in view of the "blackness" everybody connects with the blues. It is a sensitive, reflective, alienated kind of music—replacing the realism of black blues with white romanticism—thoroughly different from black blues, but yet unthinkable without it.

Mayall, who meanwhile has moved to Los Angeles, has changed his groups almost every year, using British as well as American musicians. His two most important groups were his "Blues Breakers" (1967 to 1968), who went on a veritable "crusade" for awareness and acceptance of blues among the young and his 1972 group, which had in its ranks outstanding jazz musicians including trumpeter Blue Mitchell and saxophonists Charles Owens and Clifford Solomon. The fact that a man as successful in popular music as Mayall associated himself with definitely jazz affiliated musicians may be viewed as symptomatic of the "jazz boom".

Guitarist Eric Clapton played in Mayall's "Blues Breakers." When drummer Ginger Baker and bassist Jack Bruce (who had met in an Alexis Korner band), and Clapton joined forces, *Cream* was born. It became a "super group" that shattered most scales of success known until then. It was also the first white blues-rock group to which our musical integration principle can be applied. Contrary to many other successful white blues musicians, the three Cream members repeatedly emphasized that they would be nothing without their great black examples—without B. B. King, Muddy Waters, and Howlin' Wolf—and without the generation of black blues guitarists whose records Eric Clapton had learned from in his formative years.

Cream lasted just two years—1967/68. When the group disbanded, the rock world experienced a shock that can be felt to this day. The Cream "Farewell Concert" in the giant New York Madison Square Garden was sold out weeks in advance. It was one of the most important and most discussed concerts of the rock age—approximately on the level of Bob Dylan's first "electric" appearance in Newport in 1965, of Woodstock in 1969, and of George Harrison's Concert for Bangla Desh in 1971.

In retrospect, the break-up of Cream appears as the first ghostly handwriting on the wall bespeaking the great rock crisis that would arise two years later. For the first time, the rock world realized that it could not go on from one sensation to the next, from one monster hit to an even greater one, from success to success—always in hot pursuit. For the first time, it was realized that sometime this era had to come to an end. A few years later, it did.

In a book on jazz, we can't possibly list all the popular blues-rock-groups—to which, in a way, even the Rolling Stones belong. Guitarist *J. Geils* combines contemporary blues-rock with the rock 'n' roll of the fifties—inspired by musicians like Jerry Lee Lewis, Bill Haley, and others. In Magic Dick, Geils secured for his band an outstanding harmonica player of remarkable authenticity in the sense of the blues tradition.

The *Allman Brothers* had a special brilliance in the team and duo work of their two guitarists, Duane Allman and Dicky Betts. Following Duane's death in a motorcycle crash in 1971, the band has suffered a string of accidents, giving rise to the most fantastic speculations in the pop world, which is superstitiously inclined to begin with. One year after Duane's accident, the band's bassist, Berry Oakley, died in a motorcycle crash three blocks from the spot where Duane had lost his life. During the night when Duane died, Oakley had had a serious accident with his sportscar. Despite all this, the band has preserved its power and intensity. Duane was not replaced—and for the arching lines of his guitar improvisations, propelled to even greater heights through their own immanent ecstasy, there is no likely substitute.

One of the most successful of the blues-rock groups is *Canned Heat,* whose five members have taken refuge in Topanga Canyon near Los Angeles. Canned Heat was founded by Bob "The Bear" Hite and the late Alan Wilson—both for long years avid collectors of blues and jazz records. "The Bear" alone has tens of thousands of records. He really studied the blues "from A to Z" before attempting to perform it.

Captain Beefheart, introduced in the singer chapter, is an "Albert Ayler of rock." In his Magic Band, he does with rock what many free-jazz players did with conventional jazz: he expands into areas which to outsiders show signs of the chaotic; treats it frivolously, and is also not afraid to be accused of dilletantism. In some respects, he is related to Frank Zappa, whose band-members he occasionally uses, and who produced one of his finest records.

Other groups have perverted the blues to such an extent that it hardly remains recognizable or only its shallow outer trappings are retained. This sort of music has found success particularly among audiences in their early teens, as is the case with, for example, Led Zeppelin or Ten Years After. In many respects, the dissolution of Cream was a *Götterdämmerung* of white pop blues. Since then, the British scene has either vulgarized the blues heritage or dispensed with it altogether. Today, the blues tradition is more alive in American rock music. Indeed, since the end of Cream, the European groups that have moved far away from the blues have been the most interesting. Examples are Pink Floyd, Emerson, Lake & Palmer, King Crimson, and—above all—Soft Machine. In their musical and instrumental-technical level, these groups are on par with Blood, Sweat & Tears, Chicago, Chase, and similar groups on the American scene. If one keeps this in mind, it becomes apparent that regardless of all the internationalism and universality of the rock world, there is a thoroughly British element that links these groups, dissimilar as they may be. There is also an American element, on the other hand, which seems to reduce the corresponding groups in the U. S. to a common denominator. The American groups are almost always harder, more aggressive, more rousing, more swinging, while the British groups are more meditative, sensitive, contemplative, many-sided. Exceptions prove this rule.

Regrettably, *Pink Floyd* further commercialized its concept in the early seventies, and now sound like dozens of other rock groups. But their double album "Ummagumma" laid the foundations for a cosmic outer-space sound—that, in rock, had a similar function as Sun Ra and His Solar Arkestra in jazz. This cosmic sound of Pink Floyd had an immense influence on German rock groups, not always for the best.

But back to Britain. The fact that *Soft Machine* was named for William Burroughs' avant-garde novel illustrates the introversion of its members. For jazz fans, this group is too "rock"; for rock fans, it is too "jazzy." And yet, as early as the late fifties—long before Miles Davis' "Bitches Brew" of 1970—Soft Machine anticipated the "electric jazz" affiliated today with Miles Davis and the groups inspired by him.

Soft Machine went through changes, too, but it has always been the most "intellectual" of rock groups. Today, recordings from Soft Machine's early days sound comparably tame and poetic—pieces like "Hope for Happiness" or "Joy of a Toy" even reflect in their titles that this music was made in a relatively secure, sane world. But even then, Soft Machine was ahead of other rock groups in its intellectual demands. The more complex and complicated rock music became, the more complex and complicated Soft Machine became— always a jump ahead of all the other groups in the rock world.

The music of Soft Machine is full of monumental coldness, impressive, and demanding of respect as few other phenomena on the rock scene. But there are probably just a few listeners who feel that they love Soft Machine simply and unconditionally. This may be due to the almost unsurmountable tension between the extrovertedness of the rock scene and the human introvertedness of the musicians that make up Soft Machine.

Our survey of blues, blues-rock, and rock groups was made from the jazz point of view. It is therefore of necessity incomplete. Many groups have been left out: The Beatles, The Rolling Stones, The Who, the San Francisco groups (which have had an immense influence in the U. S.; most versatile among them is The Grateful Dead with guitarist Jerry Gracia, closest to jazz is Jefferson Airplane) and finally, the fascinating, American folklore-influenced phenomenon that is *Crosby, Stills, Nash & Young*: Four great rock artists; each with his own self-contained personality, came together for a short time, and then—as might have been anticipated— again went their own ways. None was ever stronger by himself than they were together. From the musical point of view, however, the title of one of their albums rings true: "Déjà vu." Seen before—we've had that already. Déjà vu:The title does honor to the musicians who chose it. What is singular about this group—and so many others like it—is contained in the extra-musical, the atmospheric, in the personalities and the aura of the players.

Electric Jazz

The integration of jazz and rock—long awaited, often prematurely announced during the sixties, yet never accomplished satisfactorily —is shaping the style of the seventies. This integration was for the first time fully reached on *Miles Davis'* "Bitches Brew" in 1970 (see chapter about the seventies). But it also had forerunners—as everything in music.

The most important forerunner, of course, was Miles' own music: his development from Charlie Parker in 1945, via the cool Capitol Band in the late forties to hard bop and to modality in the late fifties, and—beyond that—to that characteristic "Miles Davis jazz" which kept the jazz audience enraptured during the sixties. For many jazz followers who did not go along with free jazz in the strict sense, this "Miles Davis jazz" was almost the only source of joy on the jazz scene of the sixties, after Coltrane had switched to free jazz.

Another forerunner, as we said, was the *Soft Machine*—although it must be remembered that Miles Davis, and the American scene in general, did not really become aware of the significance of this group until after "Bitches Brew."

Lastly, *Jeremy & The Satyrs* and the *Gary Burton Quartet* with guitarist Larry Coryell (both 1967) were forerunners of the integration of jazz and rock. These groups were the first to give indications in this direction—including all the other elements: blues, gospel, country music. At the time, they seemed like a promise of a future dissolution of categories. But the public was still much too caught up in conventional categorization—jazz here, rock there. Jeremy & The Satyrs, led by flutist Jeremy Steig, stumbled from one crisis to another and soon had to disband. Steig has such high-tension sensitivity —not only as a musician, but also personally—that he still does not seem to have completely recovered from the crises that overtook this band. He has a fine reputation as a flutist in Europe, but has yet to be fully recognized in the U. S.

In contrast, the Burton Quartet did not undergo crises, but changes. Guitarist Larry Coryell was replaced by Jerry Hahn, drummer Bobby Moses by Roy Haynes. Only the collaboration between Burton and bassist Steve Swallow remained intact during all these years. Not only through the level of his music, but also through its characteristic combination of charm and cleverness, Burton has managed to sustain himself until his integration of jazz and rock no longer is perceived as the work of a maverick.

There were a number of other groups in this mold before "Bitches Brew," all but forgotten today, which should be mentioned for this very reason among the trailblazers of rock-jazz integration. At the time, this integration was a momentary aspect of avant-garde activity, and the lifespan of these groups was rather short. Among them are guitarist *Jerry Hahn's Brotherhood,* pianist Pete Robinson's *Contraband*, and most importantly, *Fourth Way,* the group co-led by violinist Michael White and pianist Mike Nock.

Meanwhile, "Bitches Brew" had appeared. Interestingly, the musicians who had participated in the making of this record were among the first to present, right away, their own works pointing beyond "Bitches Brew": Wayne Shorter, Joe Zawinul, Chick Corea, Dave

Holland, John McLaughlin. But other musicians who had played with Miles Davis before—such as drummer Tony Williams and pianist Herbie Hancock—or were to play with him just after—such as pianist Keith Jarrett—also took part in this new development. At any rate, they all came from Miles—at first! Meanwhile, the stream of this development became so wide that musicians the jazz fan associated with entirely different stylistic worlds also dived in—for instance, drummer *Shelly Manne,* who had come out of West Coast jazz in the fifties, with his contemporary electronic groups; or soul pianist *Les McCann;* or *Hampton Hawes,* who once transferred the blues-world of Charlie Parker to modern jazz piano so ideally. The fact that even a Hawes, who had withstood so many fashionable trends during the course of his career, produced a record in the "electric-jazz" mold in 1972 serves to indicate how important these sounds have become for jazz musicians of all styles.

But for the moment, let us stay with the musicians affiliated with Miles Davis. The first step was taken by *Wayne Shorter* with two albums, "Super Nova" and "Odyssey of Iska." Shorter is the only hornman (on tenor and soprano) on the record; with him are a vibraphonist doubling marimba, a guitarist, two bassists, and three percussionists. The "Odyssey of Iska" is the mythical journey of a black explorer—a Nigerian Ulysses—who becomes a symbol for the human soul. Shorter said about the album: "Perhaps you can relate the enclosed (music) to the journey of your own soul."

"Odyssey of Iska" is an impressive "tone poem" in jazz, calling to mind the Herbie Hancock tone poems mentioned in the piano chapter. And in general, since Hancock's "Maiden Voyage," there has been an increasing tendency toward compositions in larger forms, complete within themselves, toward suites and tone poems. This is reflected in the wide field of records and bands discussed in the big-band section, ranging from, for instance, Zappa's "Grand Wazoo" or Santana's "Caravanserai," to "Zawinul" (released around the same time as Shorter's tone poems): "Impressions of *Joe Zawinul's* days as a shepherd boy in Austria. . . . A tone poem reminiscent of his grandfather's funeral on a cold winter day in an Austrian mountain village. . . . Zawinul's first impressions of New York when he arrived here as a boy on a ship from France. . . ." Three horns (flute, trumpet, soprano sax) confront two bassists and three percussionists; and this ensemble joins with two electric pianos—Zawinul's and Herbie Hancock's. Miles Davis was enthusiastic: "In order to write this type of music, you have to be free inside of yourself and be Josef Zawinul with two beige kids, a black wife, two pianos, from Vienna, Cancer and 'Cliché-Free.' "

In the light of all this, it is understandable that great things were expected when Zawinul and Shorter founded the group "Weather Report" in 1971. But "Weather Report" turned out to be less than the sum of its parts. Each of the co-leaders had made his most beautiful record by himself—Wayne Shorter, "Odyssey of Iska;" Zawinul, "Zawinul." "Weather Report" at first did not work out physically. We have quoted Zawinul's statement that "in this band, either nobody plays solo, or we all play solo at the same time." Nevertheless, one of the effects of the "physical" gravity of sound is that when everybody solos at the same time, the listener feels that actually only one instrument is doing so— the horn of the group: Wayne Shorter.

Herbie Hancock had left Miles Davis before "Bitches Brew." In 1972, he created the record "Crossings" with a rich electronic instrumentation (electric piano, melotron, Moog synthesizer), into which three horns are interwoven: Benny Maupin (saxophone, alto flute, bass clarinet, piccolo), Eddie Henderson (trumpet), and Julian Priester (trombone). By electronic means, Hancock achieves sounds reminiscent of Gil Evans' big-band sounds. He was one of the first to use electronics as a structural element. "Quasar", the title of one of his pieces, is representative of the music: mystical, primordial cosmic explosions, in which time seems to be moving in retrograde, and beginning and end become one. In subsequent recordings, Hancock was able to reach large audiences with his electronic sounds.

Drummer *Tony Williams* had also left Miles Davis in the second half of the sixties to start a career in pop music. His "Lifetime" and his later group "Ego" were advanced jazz-oriented rock groups, whose integration problems Williams failed to solve—less for musical than psychological reasons. But in Tony Williams' "Lifetime," John McLaughlin gathered the tools he needed for his Mahavishnu Orchestra.

Not even Larry Young (alias Khalid Yasin) was able to realize the full potential of his organ artistry in Williams' "Lifetime." On the other hand, Williams, "Lifetime" and "Ego" illuminate particularly well the complexity of the musical and human mechanisms of such groups. It is truly a stroke of luck when such organisms produce great music—a string quartet has it easier.

Another ex-Miles Davis drummer, *Jack DeJohnette,* has a happier disposition. In his group, "Compost," five musicians from different worlds teamed up: DeJohnette himself came from Davis; the second drummer, Bobby Moses, had worked with Gary Burton and Roland Kirk; bassist Jack Gregg had lived in Nashville, the capital of country music; percussionist Jumma Santos learned his African rhythms at their point of origin—in Africa (he teaches enthnomusicology); and saxophonists-flutist Harold Vick has his roots in jazz, blues and gospel music.

"Compost" combined all these elements—in addition to sounds from Trinidad and the Caribbean—in such an entertaining, happy way that the listener is unaware of any of the problems the other groups mentioned in this context have had to cope with. No odysseys, no journeys through time and space, no quasars, no complex-laden egos!

Before he joined Miles Davis, DeJohnette played with Charles Lloyd. Pianist *Keith Jarrett* traveled the same route: from Lloyd via Davis to his own groups—groups, however, whose non-electronic character Jarrett emphatically emphasizes: "I play acoustic music." That is also characteristic: Anyone making music in the stylistic world of the seventies makes a point of it if his music is acoustic. The Jarrett trio, with bassist Charlie Haden and drummer Paul Motian, very likely is one of the best-balanced piano trios in jazz history. The group plays jazz chamber music, with a spiritual orientation related to Bartók's string quartets—yet it stays snugly within jazz. The Jarrett trio represents the most highly developed point to date of the formation known as "piano trio." The main goal of a piano trio is to reach a state where the accompanists not just accompany the pianist —a state in which they function as wholly integrated equal partners. The origin of this development was the King Cole Trio of 1939. Further way stations along this line (to recapitulate briefly) are the Art Tatum Trio of 1943 (with Slam Stewart, bass, and Tiny Grimes, guitar), the Ahmad Jamal Trio from 1952 on, and then—above all —the Bill Evans Trio, with varying personnel from 1959 to date.

Like Miles Davis' pianists, John Coltrane's man, McCoy Tyner, also leads an important group in the early seventies: the *McCoy Tyner Quartet*. "Sahara" is the title of one of the quartet's outstanding albums; here, too, the theme of the "Odyssey of the soul" appears. Tyner quotes the Arabian historian Ibn Khaldoun: "This desert is so long, it can take a lifetime to go from one end to the other, and a childhood to cross at its narrowest point." McCoy Tyner, with intensity as well as sensitivity, transforms Coltrane into the music of the seventies. That is no mean feat.

Jazz history can also be written from this point of view: What are the dominant themes, the spiritual horizons of the songs and compositions the musicians take up? In the old blues, it was the man's longing for the return of his woman, who had quit him. In Swing, it was fun and happiness. In bop, it was loneliness. On today's scene, it is the spiritual journey, the caravan, the Odyssey of the soul through time and space. The cosmos, the ocean, the desert are merely symbols for the infinity of one's own self.

When Wayne Shorter left Miles Davis' "Bitches Brew" group to make himself independent, Miles hired altoist-sopranoist *Gary Bartz* as the second horn man of the group. Bartz stayed just a short while, then founded his "Ntu Troop," "Ntu" as Gary's wife Maxine explains, is the common denominator of Bantu philosphy that unifies all things: time and space, living and dead, seen, and unseen forces. . . . The Ntu Troop then becomes the messenger of Unity. . . ." For Bartz, this unity encompasses—musically, politically, philosophically, ideologically—folk blues and the planets, the Viet Cong and the "Uhuru!" of Africa. "Harlem Bush Music" is what Bartz calls his albums, referring both to Harlem as a jungle and to the survival of the African jungle in contemporary Harlem, and to the fight for survival, here as well as there.

But even this does not exhaust the wealth of music and musicians traceable to Miles Davis at the turn of the sixties!

Chick Corea went along an especially far-reaching path. After leaving Davis, he formed the trio "Circle" with bassist Dave Holland and drummer Barry Altschul. Here, he abstracted his experiences with Davis (and before that with Herbie Mann, Stan Getz, and others) in terms of free jazz, at the same time romanticizing them. But this trio was only the preliminary stage for the Chick Corea Quintet, to which Brazilian percussionist Airto Moreira and his wife Flora Purim brought an additional color: sounds from Bahia Rio in the wide area between the rhythms of the West African Yorubas (who furnished the most important element in the development of Brazilian music) and the charm of modern bossa nova. "Return to Forever" by this Corea Quintet (which also included flutist Joe Farrell and bassist Stan Clarke) is one of the happiest, airiest products of the new jazz—not in the brawny, robust manner of DeJohnette's "Compost," but on a spiritual plane: "Here we are all together /

Free to have and do and be / What we see . . . . / What game shall we play today?"

Regrettably, Corea disbanded this group after an in equal parts triumphant and chaotic Japanese tour. Fittingly, considering the delicacy and transparency of his music, he has enjoyed his greatest success in Japan. His next group tended very much toward the first Mahavishnu Orchestra and in so doing lost much of the charm and ease which seem Corea's real strength. It became only too obvious: Corea wants to "make it" with the rock audience.

I should like to end this chapter with John McLaughlin though his first Mahavishnu Orchestra disbanded—or let us say "exploded" —while the American edition of this book was in preparation. The development doesn't stop. New horizons loom in the musics of Herbie Hancock, Billy Cobham, Keith Jarrett and others—and, of course, in McLaughlin's second Mahavishnu Orchestra.

McLaughlin, to me, symbolizes the complete integration of all the elements that have played a role in the development of today's music, and in such a way that from the old elements rises a new unity. In this unity, categories have ceased to be categorical. One still knows—at least the specialist does—where it all comes from, but it has become meaningless to speak of this music in terms of jazz and rock, of blues and Indian music, of the European tradition, of old and new folklore.

John McLaughlin meditates, and that lives in his music: "The Dance of Maya," "A Lotus on Irish Streams," "Meetings of the Spirit," "Vital Transformation." The power of this meditativeness demands loud music—immense volume that creates stillness by virtue of being so overpowering. Anyone who "is" in this loudness is truly alone—in a space, a cathedral of sounds that admits nothing but these sounds. For Mahavishnu McLaughlin, believing that meditation has anything to do with secluded "quietude" is a pious, romantic self-delusion. Mahavishnu—the name McLaughlin received from his Indian guru, Sri Chinmoy—is the name of an Indian god. It means "divine compassion, strength and justice." McLaughlin: "That's to me what the band and the music stand for." And in a different context: "You see that God is the Master Musician, the soul of music, the spirit of music. I'm just trying to reach Him by letting myself be His instrument. . . . I think of my music as an offering to God. . . ."

Three of the five musicians of the first Mahavishnu Orchestra were

Europeans: Englishman McLaughlin, Irish bassist Rick Laird, Czech keyboard man Jan Hammer. Drummer Billy Cobham is of Panamanian ancestry. This signifies the growing importance of the European scene, of which more in the next chapter. The open eclecticism of the Mahavishnu Orchestra is doubtless a European element. And yet, we Europeans should not overestimate the importance of Europe. At the jazz festival at the 1972 Olympics in Munich, where I first presented him in Europe, I spoke to McLaughlin in this vein. He answered: "Yes, you know, that might be important. But don't forget: it could happen only in New York." Comparing McLaughlin's earlier European recordings to his American records, one senses that he attained the power, the tremendous, stunning determination of his playing only in the U. S.

These are the two characteristic elements of his music: power and clarity. The power Mahavishnu John McLaughlin attained in confrontation with America. The clarity he attained through meditation. This conclusion finds support in his own words.

In the music of the Mahavishnu Orchestras, the elements of tradition are stronger than those of the avant-garde. It is an error to take this music to be avant-garde in the sense in which Ornette Coleman and John Coltrane, Albert Ayler and Cecil Taylor were avant-garde in the sixties. The Mahavishnu Orchestras—and the groups presented in this chapter in general—are avant-garde only inasmuch as embracing the tradition is the truly modern position at the present point of jazz development. In this sense—and in this sense only, because the musical conditions are quite different—the combo situation conforms with the state of affairs we arrived at at the conclusion of the big-band section (and many other chapters in the instrument section). That may be the reason why today's young people know so little about what took place during the earlier stages of jazz history. The jazz tradition is *here*—it is today and now.

EUROPEAN JAZZ TODAY

European Jazz Today

To BE SURE—there were Django Reinhardt and Stan Hasselgaard, the two great exceptions: the only Europeans to have a stylistic influence on American jazz. But outside of that, European jazz musicians have been spellbound by the great American players as long as jazz has existed. Thus, of necessity, they created a "second-hand" music. But in the latter half of the sixties, things began to change—at first, gradually and only recognizable by the careful observer, but soon more fundamentally and emphatically—in fact, so much so that the Japanese critics, the most perceptive on today's international jazz scene, now place European jazz on an equal level with American.

The first man who emphasized—as early as the late fifties—the importance of European jazz was pianist John Lewis. But Lewis loves counterpoint and fugue, German cathedrals and Italian Commedia del' Arte, and his wife is a classical pianist from Yugoslavia. What fascinated him in European jazz was what he had sought and found in Europe: the great tradition of European art. Of course, this tradition is also present in European jazz. But already then the question was posed whether romantic cantilenas or classical cadenzas or baroque fugatos can be valid criteria for jazz improvisation. These elements, applied to jazz, appear as naïve to the jazz connoisseur as it does to the European music lover when an American generously concedes: "He could really swing, your Johann Sebastian Bach!" The question is not whether it is true—within limits, it is. The question is whether it is relevant.

The path for an independent development of European jazz was cleared only when jazz in general freed itself from the rule of

403

the constant pulse, of conventional functional harmonies, of symmetrical periods and phrases. Once again, the stimulus came from America, from musicians such as Cecil Taylor, Ornette Coleman, Don Cherry, Sun Ra—who created "free playing" around the turn of the fifties. But this stimulus had an incomparably deeper and more lasting effect in Europe than in the U. S.; it seems to have fallen on especially fertile soil in the Old World—primarily because "atonality" (using the concept in its widest sense) is far more shocking to Americans than to Europeans. For quite some time, avant-garde concert music had been opening European ears to atonal music activity and —in contrast to the U. S.—had been fully integrated in concert hall and radio programs. What in the U. S. was realized by only a few connoisseurs was widely known among musically aware audiences in Europe: Meaningful and artistic music is possible also outside the realm of functional harmony handed down from romanticism.

The disintegration of functional harmonies opened the road to free, unchained collective improvisation. To be sure—this too first appeared in the U. S.: with Charles Mingus in the late fifties. And hearing the free intertwining of the horns in Mingus' music, critics in those days loved to point out that jazz had begun that way in New Orleans 50 years earlier—in the three-part counterpoint of the traditional collective. The only difference is that Dixieland was tied to functional harmony, while the free collective of new jazz is not.

This free collective has meanwhile become the virtual hallmark of the new European jazz.

Don't misunderstand: Today free collectives can be found everywhere in jazz, also—of course—in America. Famous examples are Ornette Coleman's "Free Jazz" and John Coltrane's "Ascension." The differences must always be taken with a grain of salt. With this in mind, we can state: American jazz has until today remained—primarily—a soloistic jazz, a jazz of "stars" and the individual; European jazz is—again primarily— a collective jazz in which the individual merges with the group.

If we recall the highlights of European jazz in recent years, we cannot help but think of collectives: *Mike Gibbs'*, *Mike Westbrook's* and *Chris McGregor's* ensembles of Britain's best jazzmen; the *London Jazz Composers Orchestra; Alexander von Schlippenbach's* "Globe Unity;" *John Tchicai's* "Cadentia Nova Danica;" *John Stevens'* "Spontaneous Music Ensemble;" *John Surman's* various recordings; *Peter Brötzmann's* work with Han Bennink and Fred van

Hove; the *Mangelsdorff Quartet;* the various *Jazz Workshops in Baden-Baden,* at the *Berlin Academy of Arts,* at different *French* and *Scandinavian* festivals. . . .

Consideration of the highlights in American jazz of the sixties still brings individuals to mind: Cecil Taylor, Pharaoh Sanders, Ornette Coleman, Albert Ayler; Miles Davis and the various musicians he made famous. . . .

Schlippenbach's "Globe Unity" holds a key position in this development. He was the first to create orchestral works complete within themselves in the spirit of the new jazz. No American had done that before him—not even Sun Ra. Indeed, the concept, "orchestral works complete within themselves created in the spirit of the new jazz," should be taken literally: it means orchestral works that meet all standards of "composed," formally structured European music, and still do not lack the entirely jazz-like intensity and ecstasy unreachable in the European tradition. Before, combinations of this sort always wound up as compromises, lacking either structural completeness or intensity.

No doubt, Schlippenbach created his solution by way of his specifically European attitude toward the collective and toward the European tradition. This attitude—as is so often the case in the history of revolutionary arts—also works in, and even through negation.

The term "collective," wherever it may be applied, has social, psychological, and political connotations. In music as well, it cannot be used without such implications. Students of sociology and politics in East and West, regardless of ideological convictions, agree that the growing population of our planet and the increasing demands of technology will cause restrictions of personal freedom. (Horkheimer: "The more justice, the less liberty.") Collectives will take the place of individuals. As we approach the end of the twentieth century, the contest between the freedom of the individual and the collective claims of society—a battle waged since the French Revolution in all fields—is being decided more and more clearly in favor of collectivism—while in the nineteenth century the balance was almost exclusively in favor of personal liberty.

In this sense, it may be argued that today's European jazz scene already anticipates and indicates in musical terms the sociological problems of tomorrow's society—artists have always been ahead of scientists, politicians, and "realists." The American scene, on the other hand, is still under the spell of the nineteenth-century glorification of liberty—and is certainly also shaped by the wider range of freedoms that is still given in American society.

It is characteristic of the collective spirit on the European jazz scene that its most brilliant representatives should be big-band-like ensembles. Many of the above-named groups are big bands, while nearly all of the American names mentioned have achieved their best performances in combos. The exception is Sun Ra, but this very exception proves the rule: the problem of collective discipline in his Solar Arkestra remains unsolved. Listen to its inaccurate and poorly intonated ensemble playing!

The extent to which the European scene tends toward collectivism and the American toward individual freedom is made evident, even ironically blatant, through the many Americans who are (or were) affiliated with the European scene: Don Cherry (see the trumpet and big-band chapters), Lester Bowie, Anthony Braxton, Alan Silva, George Russell, Joseph Jarman, Burton Greene, and others have all created convincing big-band realizations of their music in Europe. In the U. S., they have played (and still play) almost exclusively in combos.

Certainly, all this has economic reasons, too. But the economic conditions reflect the societal state of affairs. I believe that we can insist: Jazz is unthinkable without the tension between individualism and collectivism. Both aspects are omnipresent wherever jazz is played—in the U. S. as well as in Europe, or anywhere else. But within this tension-field, the European scene is more inclined toward collectivity, the American more toward individuality: that is one of the main features of the new European jazz.

There are others, too. The integration of jazz and rock achieved in Britain by musicians like *Keith Tippett* (with *Mark Charig* and *Elton Dean*), and groups like *Nucleus*, with *Ian Carr* (trumpet), *Chris Spedding* (electric guitar), and two musicians now part of Soft Machine, *Karl Jenkins* (baritone and electric piano) and *John Marshall* (drums)—this integration is essentially different from its American counterpart, being more distant from blues—in fact, bluesless—and relating more strongly to the European tradition. And in Scandinavian jazz today there is still a "coolness" that makes this element the actual timeless characteristic of the jazz of these countries, while it was merely typical of a certain stylistic era in the U. S.—the cool jazz of the fifties. The Poles have also enriched jazz with their own tradition—above all through the wonderful pianist, band leader, and jazz and film composer, the late *Krzystof Komeda,* whom film director Roman Polanski brought to Hollywood, and who not coincidentally has been called a "Chopin of modern jazz." Other Polish jazzmen are also brilliant in this aspect of a particular kind of Polish sensitivity: violinists *Michal Urbaniak* and *Zbigniew Seiffert,* trumpeter *Tomasz Stanko,* singer *Ursula Dudziak.* . . .

In Holland, *Willem Breuker* and his groups have produced a peculiar combination of jazz and the common ballad music of medieval times, in which Breuker uses free jazz in a similar way as Kurt Weill used twentieth-century European concert music in the twenties.

In electronics, too, there is something like an independent European road, where—consciously or not—much is brought to bear that has been achieved in the electronic studios of avant-garde concert music (in Cologne, for example, by Eimert and Stockhausen) since the mid-fifties. German pianist *Wolfgang Dauner* is an especially fitting example of this; others are Dutch keyboard man *Jasper van t'Hof* and his British colleague *Dave McRae.*

I cannot mention all the important names on the European scene. The history of European jazz has yet to be written, and a description of even Europe's contemporary jazz scene would fill an entire volume. Some of the most important Europeans—insofar as they have created their own styles—have been discussed elsewhere in the book —Terje Rypdal, Jean-Luc Ponty, Albert Mangelsdorff, Simeon Shterev, and others—but of necessity, this had to be a sampling.

Nevertheless, we have yet to discuss the most important point: rhythm. The new European drummers, whose exemplary poles can be designated by the names of Swiss drummer *Pierre Favre* and his Dutch colleague *Han Bennink,* have transcended the image of the conventional jazz drummer. They no longer derive their intensity only from the black tradition (that is much more difficult to assimilate in Europe than in the U. S.), but from all sources in the world that generate ecstasy and convey ritual power and trance—i.e., swing is only one of many sources! These musicians have widened the rhythmic base just as they widened their instrumental range—incorporating instruments from all over the world. This is something quite different from the element of European jazz that appealed to John Lewis in the fifties. What appeared respectable at the time because it included counterpoint, strict formalistic rules, and the textbook knowledge of conservatory professors, was—at best—a cautious start. Today's European jazz musician has at his command a musical palette with colors mixed from all the great musical cultures and folklore of the world. And he also—naturally—knows his Stockhausen and Ligeti better than any of his American colleagues. And he uses them with less inhibition and more skill than either American jazzmen or European concert musicians, because the former are as hidebound by the jazz tradition as the latter by the tradition of European concert music.

And so, the European jazzman has achieved a certain counterbalance to the still undeniable superiority of the American musician in terms of swing and ecstatic intensity—i.e., in terms of the black tradition. I do not want to be misunderstood: nothing becomes us Europeans less—especially in jazz—than nationalistic chauvinism. For a few years after John Coltrane's death—in 1968/69—more was indeed happening on the European scene than on the American. And immediately, a few critics in Europe—and also in Japan, by the way—spoke of the "end of American jazz" and said that "European jazz is now superior to American." All that is nonsense. There is no European Charlie Parker or John Coltrane, not even a European Freddie Hubbard or Keith Jarrett. Even the successful white American musicians—from Benny Goodman to Dave Brubeck—are typically American. It is hard to imagine that musical personalities could grow in Europe capable of measuring up to them.

Yet, what had been approaching for so many years finally did happen: the creative European jazzman has ceased to imitate Americans. He has stopped competing with them in the fields—mainly swing and the black tradition—where he will never be able to match them. But he has discovered his own realms, of which the vast majority of the American public as yet has no idea and which finally have put European jazz on its own two feet. This music deserves attention and encouragement, especially since it is in constant danger of falling between all the available chairs. British pianist Howard Riley hit the spot when he said: "The cry often goes up that this music is not jazz. Fine. But then it's obviously not straight music, because of its feeling and the emphasis on improvisation. The plain truth of the matter would seem to be that here is a genuinely new music with an identity of its own. . . . No one in the media seems prepared to give it an outlet. The rock/pop establishment can't make enough quick money out of it, the jazz establishment has trouble enough keeping its head above water. And the straight establishment seems loath to admit that anything outside their own tradition can be recognized as serious music."

DISCOGRAPHY

Discography

by

ACHIM HEBGEN

Revised for the American Edition by DAN MORGENSTERN

The discography is intended primarily for use in connection with this book. It represents a selection of the best recorded work available by jazz artists prominently mentioned in the text. Availability of records is, of course, the primary factor in the compilation of a discography designed for a practical purpose. The record market in the United States is in constant flux, and no one can predict how long a jazz album will remain in the active catalog. Discontinued albums, however, may be obtained at shops with large stock, or at specialist stores.

Aside from the section dealing with anthologies and collections, recordings are listed alphabetically by artist. The reader is also referred to recordings by other artists on which the performer in question can be heard.

ABBREVIATIONS

ac	acoustic
arr	arranger
as	alto saxophone
b	bass
bcl	bass clarinet
bs	baritone saxophone
cl	clarinet
co	cornet
comp	composer
d	drums

413

e	electric
fl	flute
g	guitar
ldr	orchestra leader
org	organ
p	piano
sax	saxophones
ss	soprano saxophone
synth	synthesizer
tb	trombone
tp	trumpet
ts	tenor saxophone
vib	vibraphone
viol	violin
voc	vocal

RECORD LABEL ABBREVIATIONS

At.	Atlantic
Blu.	Blue Note
Cad.	Cadet
Cap.	Capitol
Col.	Columbia
Cont.	Contemporary
Cou.	Counterpoint
Dec.	Decca
Del.	Delmark
Ent.	Enterprise
Fan.	Fantasy
Fly.	Flying Dutchman
FMP	Free Music Production (Germany)
GTJ	Good Time Jazz
JCOA	Jazz Composer's Orchestra Association
Lim.	Limelight
Main.	Mainstream
Merc.	Mercury
Mil.	Milestone
MJR	Master Jazz Recordings
Pac.	Pacific Jazz
Phi.	Philips
Prest.	Prestige
RCA	RCA Victor
Rep.	Reprise
Riv.	Riverside

Rou. Roulette
S-S Solid State
UA United Artists
Van. Vanguard

For imported records, the country of origin is indicated as follows:

germ. Germany
french France
engl. Great Britain
jap. Japan

Anthologies and Collections

THE SMITHSONIAN COLLECTION OF CLASSIC JAZZ: 1916-63, compiled and annotated by Martin Williams. Scott Joplin, Jelly Roll Morton, Robert Johnson, Bessie Smith, King Oliver, Louis Armstrong, Sidney Bechet, James P. Johnson, Earl Hines, Bix Beiderbecke, Frank Trumbauer, Fletcher Henderson, Hot Lips Page, Fats Waller, Meade Lux Lewis, Benny Goodman, Coleman Hawkins, Billie Holiday, Art Tatum, Ella Fitzgerald, Jimmie Lunceford, Gene Krupa, Roy Eldridge, Benny Carter, Lionel Hampton, Lester Young, Count Basie, Charlie Christian, Duke Ellington, Johnny Hodges, Cootie Williams, Ben Webster, Rex Stewart, Don Byas, Dizzy Gillespie, Charlie Parker, Max Roach, Miles Davis, Erroll Garner, Bud Powell, Sarah Vaughan, Lennie Tristano, Tadd Dameron, Dexter Gordon, Thelonious Monk, Milt Jackson, Fats Navarro, John Coltrane, Gil Evans, Sonny Rollins, MJQ, Charles Mingus, Clifford Brown, Cecil Taylor, Ornette Coleman, Don Cherry and Elvin Jones are among the many artists represented in this outstanding compilation—the best available, and likely to remain so for years to come. Smithsonian P6 11891 (6-LP Set)
THE SOUND OF NEW ORLEANS: 1917-1947, with Original Dixieland Jazz Band, Louis Armstrong, Luis Russell, Wingy Manone, Bunk Johnson, Jelly Roll Morton, King Oliver, Jimmie Noone, New Orleans Rhythm Kings, Sam Morgan, many others. Col. C3L 30 (3-LP set)
THE SOUND OF CHICAGO: 1923-1940, with King Oliver, Louis Armstrong, Al Wynn, Richard M. Jones, Carroll Dickerson, Eddie Condon, Red McKenzie, Bud Freeman, Jimmy Yancey, Earl Hines, Roy Eldridge, Horace Henderson, many others.
Col. C3L 32 (3-LP set)
THE SOUND OF HARLEM: 1920-1942, with Mamie Smith, Eubie Blake, James P. Johnson, Thomas Morris, Fess Williams, Bessie Smith, Fletcher Henderson, Ethel Waters, Victoria Spivey, Clara Smith, Fats Waller, Cab Calloway, Claude Hopkins, Chick Webb, Erskine Hawkins, Teddy Hill, Frankie Newton, Billie Holiday, Benny Carter, Jimmie Lunceford, many others. Col. C3L 33 (3-LP set)

A JAZZ PIANO ANTHOLOGY: From Ragtime To Free Jazz, 1921-71, with Eubie Blake, James P. Johnson, Fats Waller, Art Tatum, Teddy Wilson, Meade Lux Lewis, Thelonious Monk, Bud Powell, Erroll Garner, Horace Silver, Bill Evans, Cecil Taylor, many others.   Col. KG 32355 (2-LP set)

FROM SPIRITUALS TO SWING: concerts at Carnegie Hall 1938/39, with Benny Goodman Sextet, Count Basie Orchestra, Kansas City Six w. Lester Young and Charlie Christian, Sidney Bechet, Tommy Ladnier, James P. Johnson, many others.
                                    Van. 8523/4 (2-LP set)

THE GOSPEL SOUND Vol. 1: 1927-66, with Blind Willie Johnson, The Golden Gate Quartet, Mitchell's Christian Singers, Mahalia Jackson, The Staple Singers, Marion Williams, The Abyssinian Baptist Gospel Choir, others.   Col. KG 31086 (2-LP set)

THE GOSPEL SOUND Vol 2: 1929-66, as above plus Arizona Dranes, Dorothy Love Coates And The Original Gospel Harmonettes, The Pilgrim Travelers, Bessie Griffin, others. Col. KG 31595 (2-LP set)

THE STORY OF THE BLUES Vol. 1: 1928-68 (compiled by Paul Oliver) Blind Willie McTell, Blind Lemon Jefferson, Leadbelly, Bessie Smith, Bertha Chippie Hill, Robert Johnson, Brownie McGhee, Joe Williams, Big Bill Broonzy, Joe Turner, Otis Spann, Elmore James, Johnny Shines and many others.   Col. G 30008 (2-LP set)

THE STORY OF THE BLUES Vol. 2: 1928-68 (compiled by Paul Oliver) Little Hat Jones, Lonnie Johnson, J. B. Lenoir, Son House, Whistlin' Alex Moore, Cripple Clarence Lofton, Roosevelt Sykes, Maggie Jones, Clara Smith, Victoria Spivey, The Yas Yas Girl, Big Maybelle, Mississippi Mud Steppers, Otis Rush, Magic Sam, John Littlejohn and many others.   (germ.) CBS 66 232 (2-LP set)*

THE TENOR SAX: LESTER YOUNG, CHU BERRY & BEN WEBSTER: 1938-44. Young w. Kansas City Six (1938 edition w. Buck Clayton, Eddie Durham, Freddie Green, Walter Page, Jo Jones and 1944 edition w. Bill Coleman, Dickie Wells, Joe Bushkin, John Simmons, Jones); Berry w. Roy Eldridge, Clyde Hart, Danny Barker, Artie Shapiro, Sid Catlett (1938) and Hot Lips Page, Hart, Al Casey, Al Morgan, Harry Jaeger (1941); Webster w. Marlowe Morris, John Simmons, Sid Catlett (1944).   Atl. SD 2-307 (2-LP Set)

THE COMMODORE YEARS: EDDIE CONDON & BUD FREEMAN 1938-39. Bobby Hackett, Jack Teagarden, Pee Wee Russell, George Brunies, Jess Stacy, Dave Tough, George Wettling a.o.
                                    Atl. SD 2-309 (2-LP set)

TOOTIN' THROUGH THE ROOF, Vol. 1: JOE THOMAS/HOT LIPS PAGE/CHARLIE SHAVERS: 1945-46, w. Buddy De Franco, Hank Jones, Slam Stewart, Sid Catlett, Dave Tough a.o.
                                    Onyx ORI 209

TOOTIN' THROUGH THE ROOF, Vol. 2: LOUIS ARMSTRONG/ BOBBY HACKETT/BUCK CLAYTON: 1934-45, w. Armstrong's

* Not yet released in the U.S.

rare 1934 Paris recordings ft. Herman Chittison; Clayton w. Flip Phillips, Teddy Wilson, Slam Stewart, Danny Alvin; Hackett w. septet incl. George Wettling and Carl Kress.　　　　Onyx ORI 213
52ND STREET, Vol. 1: TONY SCOTT/SLAM STEWART/DON BYAS/SID CATLETT: 1945-46. Scott w. Dizzy Gillespie, Trummy Young, Ben Webster, Sarah Vaughan a.o.; Stewart w. Erroll Garner and Doc West; Byas w. Johnny Guarnieri, Al Hall and Sid Catlett; Catlett w. Coleman Hawkins, Tyree Glenn, Hilton Jefferson, Billy Taylor.　　　　Onyx ORI 203
THE PANASSIE SESSIONS: 1938-39, w. Tommy Ladnier, Sidney Bechet, Frankie Newton, Sidney DeParis, James P. Johnson, Pete Brown, Mezz Mezzrow, Cozy Cole, Zutty Singleton, Pops Foster, Teddy Bunn, Al Casey a.o.　　　　RCA LPV-542
VIOLIN SUMMIT: 1966, w. Stuff Smith, Stephane Grappelli, Svend Asmussen, Jean-Luc Ponty a.o.
　　　　(germ.) BASF-MPS 20 626 or Prest. 7631 (disc.)
NEW VIOLIN SUMMIT: 1971, w. Jean-Luc Ponty, Sugarcane Harris, Michal Urbaniak, Nipso Brantner a.o.
　　　　(germ.) BASF-MPS 21 285 (2-LP Set)
BADEN-BADEN FREE JAZZ MEETING: GETTIN' TO KNOW Y'ALL: 1969, various groups and big band incl. Lester Bowie, Joseph Jarman, Roscoe Mitchell, Albert Mangelsdorff, John Surman, Alan Skidmore, Willem Breuker, Terje Rypdal, Karin Krog a.m.o.
　　　　(germ.) BASF-MPS 20 728

Alphabetical Listings

JULIAN "CANNONBALL" ADDERLEY (as, ss)　　　　9/15/1928
Cannonball and Eight Giants: with Blue Mitchell, Bill Evans, Milt Jackson, Art Blakey, others.　　　　Mil 47001 (2-LP set)
Mercy, Mercy, Mercy: w. Nat Adderley, Joe Zawinul, Roy McCurdy, others.　　　　Cap. 2663
The Black Messiah: 1970, w. Nat Adderley, George Duke, Walter Booker, Roy McCurdy.　　　　Cap. SWBO 846 (2-LP set)
HENRY RED ALLEN (tp, voc)　　　　1/7/1908-4/17/1967
s.a. Fletcher Henderson, Jelly Roll Morton, Artie Shaw, Lionel Hampton, Billie Holiday
Henry Red Allen: with J. C. Higginbotham, others.　　　　RCA LPV-556
THE ALLMAN BROTHERS BAND
At Fillmore East: 1971, live, with Duane Allman, Greg Allman, Dicky Betts, Berry Oakley, others.　　　　Atl. SD 2-802 (2-LP set).
DUANE ALLMAN (g, bottleneck-g)　　　　1946-10/29/1971
s.a. Allman Brothers Band
An Anthology: 1967-71, with Wilson Pickett, Aretha Franklin, King Curtis, Eric Clapton and many others.
　　　　Capricorn 2 CP 0108 (2-LP set)

GENE 'JUG' AMMONS (ts)   4/14/1925-8/6/1974
s.a. Woody Herman
Jug & Dodo: 1962, with Dodo Marmarosa a.o.
Prest. 24021, (2-LP set)

LOUIS ARMSTRONG (tp, voc)   7/4/1900-7/6/1971
s.a. Bessie Smith, Fletcher Henderson, Ella Fitzgerald, King Oliver.
The Genius Of Louis Armstrong, Vol. 1: 1924-32, with Sidney Be-
chet; Hot Five and Hot Seven with Kid Ory, Johnny Dodds, Lil Har-
din; Earl Hines, Zutty Singleton; various Luis Russell big bands, others.
Col. G 30416 (2-LP set)
July 4, 1900-July 6, 1971: 1932-56, various big bands; All Stars w.
Bobby Hackett, Jack Teagarden, Vic Dickenson, Peanuts Hucko, Bar-
ney Bigard, Sid Catlett, others.   RCA VPM 6044 (2-LP set)
Rare Items: 1935-44, various big bands.   Dec. DL 9225
Satchmo At Symphony Hall: Boston, 1947, w. Jack Teagarden, Barney
Bigard, Dick Cary, Sid Catlett, others.   Dec. DXS 7195 (2-LP set)
Plays W. C. Handy: 1954, w. Trummy Young, Barney Bigard, others.
Col. CL 591

ART ENSEMBLE OF CHICAGO (also AACM)
s.a. Baden-Baden Free Jazz Meeting.
Les Stances A Sophie: 1970, w. Lester Bowie, Joseph Jarman, Roscoe
Mitchell, Malachi Favors.   Nessa N-4

ASSOCIATION P.C.
Rock Around the Cock: 1973, w. Joachim Kuhn, Toto Blanke, Siggi
Busch, Pierre Courbois, K. H. Wiberny.   BASF/MPS 21 763

ALBERT AYLER (ss, as, ts)   7/13/1936-11/5/1970
The Last Album: 1969, w. Bobby Few, Muhammad Ali, others.
Imp. AS/9208
Nuits De La Foundation Maeght, Vol. 2: 1970, w. Mary Maria, Call
Cobbs, Steve Tintweiss, Alan Blairman. (French) Shandar ST SR 10004

CHET BAKER (tp, voc)   12/23/1929
See Gerry Mulligan.

GATO BARBIERI (ts, fl)   11/28/1933
s.a. JCOA, Gary Burton, Charlie Haden, Oliver Nelson.
Under Fire: 1973, w. Lonnie Liston Smith, Stan Clarke, Airto Moreira, others.   Fly. FD 10156

GARY BARTZ (ss, as, p)   9/26/1940
s.a. Woody Shaw
Uhuru: Harlem Bush Music: 1970-71, NTU Troop w. Andy Bey,
Ron Carter, Nat Bettis, Harold White, others.   Mil. MSP 9032

COUNT BASIE (ldr., p)   8/21/1904
s.a. Lester Young, Charlie Christian, Benny Goodman, Billie Holiday,
'From Spirituals to Swing.'
The Best Of: 1937-39, w. Buck Clayton, Harry Edison, Lester Young,
Herschel Evans, Chu Berry, Benny Morton, Dickie Wells, Walter
Page, Jo Jones, Jimmy Rushing, others.   Dec. DXS 7170 (2-LP set)
Super Chief: 1936-42, various groups and big bands, musicians as
above, plus Teddy Wilson, Mildred Bailey, Buster Bailey, Don Byas,

Harry James a.m.o. Col. G 31224 (2-LP set)
Basie! 1957, arr. by Neal Hefti, w. Joe Newman, Thad Jones, 'Lock-
jaw' Davis, Frank Wess, others. Rou. ST 52003
(French) Rou. ST CVR 56012
Afrique: 1970, arr. by Oliver Nelson, w. 'Lockjaw' Davis, Eric Dixon,
Bob Plater, Hubert Laws, Nelson. Fly. ST FD 10138
SIDNEY BECHET (ss, cl) 5/14/1897-5/14/1959
s.a. Louis Armstrong, The Panassié Sessions, anthologies.
Jazz Classics, Vol. 1: 1939-46, w. Sidney De Paris, Vic Dickenson,
Max Kaminsky, Bunk Johnson, Art Hodes, Meade Lux Lewis, Pops
Foster, Sid Catlett, others. Blu. 81201
Ragtime Jazz: 1940, w. Muggsy Spanier, Carmen Mastren, Wellman
Braud. Olympic 7113
Sidney Bechet, Vol. 3: 1940-41, w. Rex Stewart, Earl Hines, Red
Allen, Charlie Shavers, Willie "The Lion" Smith, Sid Catlett a.m.o.
(French) RCA 741.069
CAPTAIN BEEFHEART (Don Van Vliet, voc. ss)
Lick My Decals Off, Baby: 1970 Straight ST 6420
BIX BEIDERBECKE (co, p) 10/3/1903-8/6/1931
Story, Vols. 1-3: 1927-29, w. big bands of Paul Whiteman, Frank
Trumbauer; Jimmy Dorsey, Eddie Lang, Pee Wee Russell, Adrian
Rollini a.m.o. Col. CL 844, 845, 846
HAN BENNINK (d, perc) 4/17/1943
s. Peter Brötzmann, Don Cherry
BUNNY BERIGAN (tp) 11/8/1908-6/2/1942
s.a. Benny Goodman, Tommy Dorsey
His Trumpet and His Orchestra, Vol. 1: 1937-39, w. Georgie Auld,
Buddy Rich, Ray Coniff, George Wettling, a.o. RCA LPV-581
CHU BERRY 9/3/1910-10/31/1941
s.a. Count Basie, anthologies, Lionel Hampton, Teddy Wilson, Fletcher
Henderson.
16 Cab Calloway Classics: 1939-41, w. Dizzy Gillespie, Cozy Cole,
Milt Hinton a.o. (French) CBS 62950
ART BLAKEY (d) 10/11/1919
s.a. Miles Davis, Giants Of Jazz, Charlie Parker, Thelonious Monk.
Orgy In Rhythm Vol. 1: 1957, w. Jo Jones, Art Taylor, Herbie Mann,
Ray Bryant, others. Blu. 81554
Moanin': 1958 Jazz Messengers w. Lee Morgan, Benny Golson, Bobby
Timmons, others. Blu. 84003
Buhaina's Delight: 1961 Jazz Messengers w. Freddie Hubbard, Wayne
Shorter, Curtis Fuller, others. Blu. 84104
CARLA BLEY (comp, p, org) 5/11/1938
s.a. Don Cherry
A Genuine Tong Funeral: s. Gary Burton.
Escalator Over The Hill: s. JCOA.
Liberation Music Orchestra: s. Charlie Haden.
PAUL BLEY (p, syn) 11/10/1932
Open To Love: 1972, p-solo. ECM 1023

BLOOD, SWEAT & TEARS
Two: 1969, w. David Clayton-Thomas, Dick Halligan, Fred Lipsius, Steve Katz, a.o.   Col. CS 9720
New Blood: 1972, w. Dave Bargeron, Lou Marini, Georg Wadenius a.o.   Col. KC 31780
PETER BRÖTZMANN (as, ts, bs, bass-sax)
s.a. Alexander von Schlippenbach.
Elements/Couscouss De La Mauresque/The End: 1971 w. Albert Mangelsdorff, Fred van Hove, Han Bennink.
     (Germ.) FMP ST 0030/0040/0050 (3-LP set, also available singly)
CLIFFORD BROWN (tp)   10/30/1930-6/26/1956
s.a. Sonny Rollins, J. J. Johnson
The Beginning and the End: 1952-56; first and last recordings.
                                                                     Col. KC 32284
MARION BROWN (as)   9/8/1935
s.a. John Coltrane
Afternoon Of A Georgia Faun: 1970, w. Anthony Braxton, Chick Corea, Jeanne Lee a.o.   ECM 1004
DAVE BRUBECK (p, comp)   12/6/1920
Brubeck On Campus: 1954-57, w. Paul Desmond, Norman Bates, Joe Morello, Joe Dodge.   Col. KG 31379 (2-LP set)
Brubeck In Amsterdam: 1962, w. Desmond, Gene Wright, Joe Morello.   Col. CS 9897
We're All Together Again For The First Time: 1972, w. Paul Desmond, Gerry Mulligan, Jack Six, Alan Dawson.   Atl. SD 1641
Truth Is Fallen: 1971, w. Cincinnati Symphony choir, rock group, etc.
                                                                     Atl. SD 1606
JACK BRUCE (b, voc)   5/15/1943
s. Cream, Tony Williams Lifetime, The Jazz Composer's Orchestra.
MILT BUCKNER (p, org)   7/10/1914
s.a. Lionel Hampton.
Play Chords: 1966, with Jimmy Woode, Jo Jones.   BASF/MPS 20 631
KENNY BURRELL (g)   7/3/1931
s.a. Jimmy Smith, Billie Holiday.
Guitar Forms: 1964, with Gil Evans Orch.   Verve V6-8612
GARY BURTON (vib, p)   7/23/1943
Duster!: 1968, w. Larry Coryell, Steve Swallow, Roy Haynes.
                                                                     RCA LSP 3835
A Genuine Tong Funeral: 1968, w. Larry Coryell, Steve Swallow, Steve Lacy, Gato Barbieri a.o.; comp. by Carla Bley.   RCA LSP 3988
Alone At Last: 1971 (vib-solo)   Atl. SD 1598
DON BYAS (ts)   10/21/1912-9/1/1972
s.a. Count Basie, Dizzy Gillespie.
Anthropology: 1963, w. Danish Rhythm section   Black Lion BL-160
BENNY CARTER (as, ts, cl, tp, arr, comp, ldr.)   8/8/1907
s.a. Django Reinhardt, Coleman Hawkins, Teddy Wilson, Lionel Hampton, Benny Goodman, Artie Shaw.

Further Definitions 1961: w. Coleman Hawkins, Phil Woods, Jo Jones a.o.   Impulse S-12
RON CARTER (b, cello)   5/4/1934
see Miles Davis, Gary Bartz, Eric Dolphy, Freddie Hubbard, Steve Kuhn, Hubert Laws.
RAY CHARLES (voc, p, as)   9/23/1932
s.a. Aretha Franklin
His All-Time Great Performances   ABC SD 731 (2-LP set)
Live: 1958-59, Newport Jazz Festival/Atlanta, with David Newman, Hank Crawford, others.   Atl. SD 2-503 (2-LP set)
DON CHERRY (pocket-tp, fl, voc)   11/18/1936
s.a. Ornette Coleman, The Jazz Composer's Orchestra, Albert Mangelsdorff, George Russell.
Eternal Rhythm: 1968, w. Albert Mangelsdorff, Sonny Sharrock, Karlhans Berger, Joachim Kühn, others.   BASF/MPS 20680
'MU' First Part: 1969, with Ed Blackwell.   (French) BYG 529301
Actions/Humus—The Life Exploring Force: 1971, with The New Eternal Rhythm Orchestra, w. Manfred Schoof, Albert Mangelsdorff, Peter Brötzmann, Gunter Hampel, Han Bennink, others (backed with 'Actions' comp. by K. Penderecki)   (Germ.) Phil. 6305153
Relativity Suite: 1973, The Jazz Composer's Orchestra w. Carlos Ward, Frank Lowe, Dewey Redman, Leroy Jenkins, Charlie Haden, Carla Bley, Ed Blackwell, others.   JCOA LP 1006
CHICAGO (TRANSIT AUTHORITY)
Chicago Transit Authority: 1969, w. James Pankow, Walter Parazaider, Terry Kath, others.   Col. GP 8 (2-LP set)
CHARLIE CHRISTIAN (g)   1919-3/2/1942
s.a. Benny Goodman, Lionel Hampton, Edmond Hall, 'From Spirituals To Swing'.
The Great C.C.: 1941, Minton's sessions, w. Thelonious Monk, Hot Lips Page, Kenny Clarke, others (rev. Dizzy Gillespie).   Cou. 554
Solo Flight: 1939-41, w. Benny Goodman, Lionel Hampton, Cootie Williams, Georgie Auld, Count Basie a.m.o.   Col. G 30779 (2-LP set)
KENNY CLARKE (d)   1/9/1914
s.a. Miles Davis, Ch. Parker, Modern Jazz Quartet, Ch. Christian, Dizzy Gillespie, Bud Powell.
KENNY CLARKE—FRANCY BOLAND BIG BAND
Ebullient—Roaring—Screaming: 1967, w. Benny Bailey, Derek Humble, Eddie 'Lockjaw' Davis, Johnny Griffin, a.o.   BASF/MPS 25102
ERIC CLAPTON (g, voc)   3/30/1945
s. Cream, John Mayall, Howlin' Wolf.
BUCK CLAYTON (tp)   11/12/1911
s. Count Basie, Benny Goodman, Earl Hines, Billie Holiday, Teddy Wilson.
BILLY COBHAM (d)
s.a. John McLaughlin, Dreams, Steve Kuhn.
Spectrum: 1973, w. Jimmy Owens, Jan Hammer, Joe Farrell, Ron Carter.   Atl. SD 7268

WAYNE COCHRAN & THE C. C. RIDERS: 1972, arr. by Charlie
Brent.   Epic ST E 30989
AL COHN (ts, arr)   11/24/1925
s.a. Woody Herman.
Body and Soul—Al Cohn and Zoot Sims: 1973, w. Jaki Byard, George
Duvivier, Mel Lewis.   Muse MR 5016
NAT KING COLE (p, voc)   3/17/1917-2/15/1965
From The Very Beginning: 1936-41, w. Oscar Moore, Wesley Prince,
Eddie Cole.   MCA 2-4020 (2-record set)
ORNETTE COLEMAN (as, ts, viol, p, comp)   3/19/1930
The Shape of Jazz To Come: 1959, w. Don Cherry, Charlie Haden,
Billy Higgins.   Atl. SD 1317
Free Jazz: 1960, double-quartet, w. Eric Dolphy, Cherry, Freddie Hub-
bard, Scott LaFaro, Haden, others.   Atl. SD 1364 (2-LP set)
Science Fiction: 1972, w. Cherry, Haden, Higgins, Dewey Redman,
Ed Blackwell, Bobby Bradford, Asha Puthli.   Col. KC 31061
Skies Of America: 1972, w. London Symphony Orch.   Col. KC 31562
ALICE COLTRANE (p, harp, org)   8/27/1937
s.a. John Coltrane
Universal Consciousness: 1971, w. string-quartet (John Blair, Leroy
Jenkins, others) arr. by Alice Coltrane/Ornette Coleman.
                                                 Imp. ST AS 9210
JOHN COLTRANE (ss, ts)   9/23/1926-7/17/1967
s.a. Miles Davis, Sonny Rollins.
John Coltrane: 1957-58 w. Red Garland, Paul Chambers, Art Taylor.
                                           Prest. 24003 (2-LP set)
My Favorite Things: 1960, w. McCoy Tyner, Jimmy Garrison, Elvin
Jones.   Atl. SD 1361
Impressions: 1961/63, w. Eric Dolphy, McCoy Tyner, Reggie Work-
man, Jimmy Garrison, Elvin Jones.   Imp. AS 42
A Love Supreme: 1964, quartet with McCoy Tyner, Jimmy Garrison,
Elvin Jones.   Imp. AS 77
Ascension: 1965, w. Freddie Hubbard, Dewey Johnson, Marion
Brown, John Tchicai, Pharaoh Sanders, Archie Shepp, McCoy Tyner,
Art Davis, Jimmy Garrison, Elvin Jones.   Imp. AS 95
Live At The Village Vanguard Again: 1966, w. Pharaoh Sanders, Alice
Coltrane, Jimmy Garrison, Rashied Ali.   Imp. ST AS 42
CHICK COREA (p, e-p)   6/12/1941
s.a. Miles Davis, Joe Farrell, Marion Brown, Richard Davis, Bobby
Hutcherson.
Piano Improvisations, Vol. 1: 1971 (p-solo).   ECM ST 1014
Return To Forever: 1972, w. Joe Farrell, Stan Clarke, Airto Moreira,
Flora Purim.   ECM ST 1022
LARRY CORYELL (g)   1943
s.a. Gary Burton, The Jazz Composer's Orchestra.
Offering: 1972, w. Steve Marcus, Mike Mandel, others.
                                                 Van. VSD 79 319

CREAM
Wheels Of Fire: 1968, w. Eric Clapton, Jack Bruce, Ginger Baker.
Atc. 2700 (2-LP set)
TADD DAMERON (p, arr, comp)   2/12/1917-3/8/1965
See Fats Navarro
MILES DAVIS (tp)   5/25/1926
s.a. Charlie Parker, Lee Konitz.
The Complete Birth Of The Cool: 1949-50, Capitol Orch. w. J. J.
Johnson, Kai Winding, Lee Konitz, Gerry Mulligan, Max Roach,
Kenny Clarke, o. arr. by Gil Evans, Johnny Carisi, John Lewis, Mulli-
gan.   Cap. M-11026
Tallest Trees: 1953-56, w. Thelonious Monk, Milt Jackson, Charles
Mingus, Sonny Rollins, John Coltrane, Horace Silver, Max Roach,
Art Blakey, Kenny Clarke, others.   Prest. 24012 (2-LP set)
Miles Davis: 1956, w. John Coltrane, Red Garland, Paul Chambers,
Philly Joe Jones.   Prest. 24001 (2-LP set)
Miles Ahead: 1957, w. Gil Evans (arr).   Col. CS 8633
Sketches Of Spain: 1959, w. Gil Evans (arr).   Col. CS 8271
Kind Of Blue: 1959, w. Coltrane, Cannonball Adderley, Bill Evans,
Wynton Kelly, others.   Col. CS 8163
Greatest Hits: 1956-61, w. Wayne Shorter, Coltrane, Hank Mobley,
Kelly, Chambers, Philly Joe Jones, Herbie Hancock, Ron Carter,
Tony Williams, Gil Evans, others.   Col. CS 9808
Filles De Kilimanjaro: 1969, w. Shorter, Hancock, Chick Corea, Ron
Carter, Dave Holland, Tony Williams.   Col. CS 9750
Bitches Brew: 1970, w. Shorter, Benny Maupin, John McLaughlin,
Corea, Joe Zawinul, Larry Young, Holland, Jack De Johnette, a.m.o.
Col. GP 26 (2-LP set)
RICHARD DAVIS (b)   4/15/1930
s.a. Thad Jones-Mel Lewis Big Band, Eric Dolphy, Tony Williams,
Freddie Hubbard, Roland Kirk, Pharaoh Sanders, Ben Webster.
The Philosophy Of The Spiritual: 1972, with Chick Corea, Sam
Brown a.o.   Cobblestone 9003
SIDNEY DE PARIS (tp)   5/30/1905-9/13/1967
s.a. The Panassié Sessions
De Paris Dixie: 1944-51, w. Vic Dickenson, Edmond Hall, James P.
Johnson, Jimmy Archey, Omer Simeon, Pops Foster, a.o.   Blu. B-6501
PAUL DESMOND (as)   11/25/1924
see Dave Brubeck
VIC DICKENSON (tb)   8/6/1906
See also Sidney Bechet, Sidney De Paris, Louis Armstrong.
Septet: 1953-54, w. Ruby Braff, Edmond Hall, Sir Charles Thomp-
son, Walter Page, Jo Jones, others.   Van. VRS 8520/1 (2-LP set)
JOHNNY DODDS (cl)   4/12/1892-8/8/1940
s.a. Louis Armstrong, King Oliver, Freddy Keppard.
Johnny Dodds: 1926-28, w. Honore Dutrey, Lil Armstrong, a.m.o.
RCA LPV-558

ERIC DOLPHY (as, bcl, fl, cl)   6/20/1928-6/29/1964
s.a. Ornette Coleman, John Coltrane, Charles Mingus, Chico Hamilton, Oliver Nelson, George Russell.
Eric Dolphy: 1960, w. Freddie Hubbard, Jaki Byard, Ron Carter, Roy Haynes.   Prest. 24008 (2-LP set)
Far Cry: 1960, w. Booker Little, Jaki Byard, Ron Carter, Roy Haynes.   Prest. 7747
Out To Lunch: 1964, w. Freddie Hubbard, Bobby Hutcherson, Richard Davis, Tony Williams.   Blu. ST 84163
TOMMY DORSEY (tb, ldr.)   11/19/1905-11/26/1956
This Is T.D.: 1936-44, big band w. Bunny Berigan, Max Kaminsky, Bud Freeman, Buddy DeFranco, Dave Tough, Buddy Rich and many others.   RCA VPM 6038 (2-LP set)
DREAMS
Dreams: 1970, w. Mike and Randy Brecker, Billy Cobham, others.
                                                       Col. 30225
JULIE DRISCOLL (voc, g)   6/8/1947
Streetnoise: 1969, w. Brian Auger And His Trinity.
                                          Atc. SD 2-701 (2-LP set)
GEORGE DUKE (keyboards)
see Cannonball Adderley, Frank Zappa, Jean-Luc Ponty.
ROY ELDRIDGE (tp, voc)   1/30/1911
s.a. Teddy Wilson, Fletcher Henderson, Billie Holiday, Gene Krupa.
The Nifty Cat: 1970, w. Benny Morton, Budd Johnson, Nat Pierce, Oliver Jackson, Tommy Bryant.   MJR MJF 8100
Arcadia Shuffle: 1939, w. Prince Robinson, Franz Jackson, Clyde Hart a.o.   Jazz Archives JA-14
DUKE ELLINGTON (p, comp, arr, ldr.)   4/29/1899-5/24/1974
s.a. Ella Fitzgerald
The Ellington Era, Vols. 1 & 2: 1927-40, w. Bubber Miley, Tricky Sam Nanton, Harry Carney, Johnny Hodges, Cootie Williams, Barney Bigard, Lawrence Brown, Ben Webster, Jimmy Blanton, a.m.o.
          Vol. 1: Col. C3 L27 (3-LP set); Vol. 2: Col. C3 L39 (3-LP set)
This Is Duke Ellington: 1927-45, as above, plus Rex Stewart, Ray Nance, Cat Anderson, Jimmy Hamilton, a.m.o.
                                          RCA VPM 6042 (2-LP set)
At His Very Best: 1927-46, as above; "Ko-Ko," "Black, Brown And Beige."   RCA LPM-1715
At Newport: 1956, live w. Paul Gonsalves, Anderson, Clark Terry, Nance, Quentin Jackson, Hodges, Hamilton, Carney, a.o.
                                                       Col. CS 8648
Money Jungle: 1962, trio with Charles Mingus, Max Roach.
                                                       S-S SS 18022
. . . And His Mother Called Him Bill: 1967 (in memory of Billy Strayhorn)   RCA LSP 3906
70th Birthday Concert: 1969, w. Hodges, Cootie Williams, Norris Turney, Harold Ashby, Rufus Jones, others.   S-S SS 19000 (2-LP set)
New Orleans Suite: 1970, as above.   Atl. SD 1580

DON ELLIS (tp, d, ldr.)   7/25/1934
s.a. Charles Mingus, George Russell, Maynard Ferguson.
At Fillmore: 1970, w. Glenn Stuart, Glenn Ferris, Sam Falzone, John
Klemmer, others.   Col. G 30243 (2-LP set)
Tears Of Joy: 1971, with amplified string-quartet, woodwind quartet;
Milcho Leviev, Sam Falzone, Fred Selden, Jim Sawyer, others.
                                                 Col. G 30927 (2-LP set)
BOOKER ERVIN (ts)   10/31/1930-8/31/1970
s.a. Charles Mingus
The Space Book: 1965, w. Jaki Byard, Richard Davis, Alan Dawson.
                                                      Prestige 7386
BILL EVANS (p, e-p)   8/16/1929
s.a. Miles Davis, Cannonball Adderley.
Undercurrent: 1959 (duo with Jim Hall).   S-S SS 18018
Live At The Village Vanguard: 1961, trio w. Scott La Faro, Paul Mo-
tian.   Riv. RS 3006
Conversations With Myself: 1963 (p-solo with overdub).
                                                       Verve V6-8526
At The Montreux Jazz Festival: 1968, trio with Eddie Gomez, Jack
De Johnette.   Verve V6-8762
Living Time: 1972, with George Russell (arr) and Orch.
                                                      Col. KC 31490
GIL EVANS (arr, p)   5/13/1912
s. a. Miles Davis, Kenny Burrell.
Out Of The Cool: 1960, w. Johnny Coles, Jimmy Knepper, Budd
Johnson, Ron Carter, Elvin Jones, others.   Imp. AS/4
Svengali: 1973, w. Marvin Peterson, Billy Harper, Ted Dunbar, How-
ard Johnson, Bruce Ditmas a.o.   Atl. SD 1643
ART FARMER (tp, fh)   8/21/1928
From Vienna With Art: 1970, w. Jimmy Heath.
                                        (Germ.) BASF/MPS ST 20741
Gentle Eyes: 1972, w. large orchestra.   Mainstream MRL 371
JOE FARRELL (ss, ts, fl)   8/21/1928
s.a. Chick Corea, Thad Jones, Mel Lewis Orchestra, Elvin Jones, May-
nard Ferguson.
Outback: 1971, w. Chick Corea, Buster Williams, Elvin Jones, Airto
Moreira.   CTI 6014
MAYNARD FERGUSON (tp, ldr.)   5/4/1928
s.a. Stan Kenton
A Message From Newport/Newport Suite: 1958-60, big bands w. Bill
Chase, Slide Hampton, Don Sebesky, Willie Maiden, Don Ellis, Joe
Farrell, Jaki Byard, Stu Martin, others.   Rou. RE-116 (2-LP set)
MF Horn 2: 1972, big band with English musicians.   Col. C 30466
CLARE FISCHER (p, org)   10/22/1928
Reclamation Act of 1972: (p-solo and trio).   Revelation 15
ELLA FITZGERALD (voc)   4/25/1918
s.a. Chick Webb, Benny Goodman
The Best of Ella, Vol. 1: 1938-55, with big bands of Chick Webb, Sy

Oliver, Benny Carter, others. Dec. DXS 7156 (2-LP set)
The Best Of E.F.: 1956-64, with big bands of Count Basie, Marty
Paich, Johnnie Spence; Paul Smith, Jim Hall, Lou Levy, Oscar Peterson, Herb Ellis, Barney Kessel, Louis Armstrong, others.
Verve V6-4063
Ella & Louis: 1956, with Armstrong, Peterson, Ray Brown, Ellis,
Buddy Rich. Verve V6-4003
At Duke's Place: 1965, w. Duke Ellington Orch. Verve V6-4070
ROBERTA FLACK (voc, p)
Quiet Fire: 1971, w. Joe Farrell, Hubert Laws, Chuck Rainey, Bernard Purdie, others. Atl. SD 1594
THE FLOCK
The Flock/Dinosaur Swamp: 1969-70, w. Jerry Goodman, Fred Glickstein, Rick Canoff, Tom Webb, others.
(Germ.) CBS S 67278 (2-LP set)
THE FOURTH WAY
The Sun And Moon Have Come Together: 1969, Michael White,
Mike Nock, Ron McClure, Eddie Marshall. Harvest SKOA-423
ARETHA FRANKLIN (voc, p) 1942
Greatest Hits. Atl. SD 8295
Live At Fillmore West: 1971, w. Ray Charles, King Curtis, Billy Preston, Pretty Purdie, others. Atl. SD 7205
Amazing Grace: 1972, w. James Cleveland & The Southern California
Community Choir. Atl. 2-906 (2-LP set)
BUD FREEMAN (ts) 4/13/1906
see Tommy Dorsey, Benny Goodman, The World's Greatest Jazz Band,
anthologies
JAN GARBAREK (ts, ss, bs, bass-sax, fl)
s.a. Terje Rypdal
Triptykon: 1972, trio with Arild Andersen, Edward Vesala.
ECM ST1029
ERROLL GARNER (p) 6/15/1921
Concert By The Sea: 1955, with Eddie Calhoun, Denzil Best.
Col. CS 9821
Feeling Is Believing: 1970, w. Jose Mangual, George Duvivier,
Charles Persip, others. Mer. ST 61308
STAN GETZ (ts) 2/2/1927
s.a. Woody Herman
At Storyville—Boston Vol. 2: 1951, w. Al Haig, Jimmy Rainey, a.o.
(French) Vogue CMDRO 9851
At The Opera House: 1957, live w. J. J. Johnson, Oscar Peterson,
Herb Ellis, Ray Brown, Connie Kay. Verve V6-8490
Focus: 1961, arr. and cond. by Eddie Sauter. Verve ST V6-8412
Dynasty: 1971, with Eddie Louiss, René Thomas, Bernard Lubat.
Verve ST V6-8802 (2-LP set)
GIANTS OF JAZZ
Giants Of Jazz: 1971: Dizzy Gillespie, Sonny Stitt, Kai Winding,
Thelonious Monk, Al McKibbon, Art Blakey.
Atl. ST SD 2-905 (2-LP set)

DIZZY GILLESPIE (tp, voc)   10/21/1917
s.a. Charlie Parker, Lionel Hampton, Giants Of Jazz, Chu Berry.
The Great D.G. 1941, Minton's Playhouse Sessions with Joe Guy,
Kenny Kersey, Nick Fenton, Kenny Clarke, Chu Berry, Don Byas,
others. (Reverse Ch. Christian, q.v.)   Cou. 554
In The Beginning: 1945-46, w. Charlie Parker, Al Haig, Sonny Stitt,
Milt Jackson, Kenny Clarke, Clyde Hart a.m.o.
                                      Prestige 24030 (2-LP set)
At The Salle Pleyel: Paris 1948, big band with Benny Bailey, Dave
Burns, John Lewis, Kenny Clarke, a.o.   Pres. 7818
Swing Low, Sweet Cadillac: 1967, quintet with James Moody, Mike
Longo, a.o.   Imp. AS/9149
'Reunion' Big Band: 1968, Berlin Jazz Festival, w. Jimmy Owens,
Curtis Fuller, James Moody, Sahib Shihab, Mike Longo, a.o.
                                      BASF/MPS ST 29682
Giants: 1972, w. Bobby Hackett, Mary Lou Williams, a.o.
                                      Perception ST 19
PAUL GONSALVES (ts)   7/12/1920-5/15/1974
see Duke Ellington
BENNY GOODMAN (cl, as, ldr.)   5/30/1909
s.a. Teddy Wilson, Charlie Christian, Billie Holiday, 'From Spiri-
tuals To Swing'.
This Is Benny Goodman: 1935-39, quartet and big band, w. Bunny
Berigan, Harry James, Ziggy Elman, Toots Mondello, Bud Freeman,
Vido Musso, Jess Stacy, Teddy Wilson, Dave Tough, Gene Krupa,
Lionel Hampton, a.m.o.   RCA VPM 6040 (2-LP set)
Carnegie Hall Concert: 16/1/1938, w. trio, quartet, big band; guests
Count Basie, Lester Young, Buck Clayton, Cootie Williams, Johnny
Hodges, a.o.   Col. OSL 160 (2-LP set)
The Small Groups: 1936-38, trio and quartet with Wilson, Krupa,
Hampton.   RCA LPV 521
DEXTER GORDON (ts)   2/27/1923
Go!: 1962, w. Sonny Clarke, Billy Higgins, Butch Warren
                                      Blu. ST 84112
A Day In Copenhagen: 1969, w. Dizzy Reece, Slide Hampton, a.o.
                                      BASF/MPS ST 20698
STEPHANE GRAPPELLI (viol, p)   1/26/1908
s.a. Django Reinhardt, Violin Summit
Venupelli Blues: 1969, w. Joe Venuti, Barney Kessel, others.
                                      (French) BYG 529122
WARDELL GRAY (ts)   1921-5/25/1955
Memorial Album: w. Dexter Gordon, many others.
                                      Pres. 7343 (2-LP set)
GERGE GRUNTZ (p, org, arr)   6/24/1932
Jazz Meets Arabia—Noon In Tunisia: 1967 w. Jean Luc-Ponty, Shahib
Shihab, Eberhard Weber, Daniel Humair + quartet of bedouins.
                        (Germ.) (BASF/MPS ST 20640
BOBBY HACKETT (co, tp)   1/31/1915
see Louis Armstrong, Dizzy Gillespie.

Bobby Hackett 4: 1973, w. Dave McKenna, a.o.
Hyannisport HR 1001
CHARLIE HADEN (b)   8/6/1937
s.a. Don Cherry, Ornette Coleman, Keith Jarrett, The Jazz Compos-
er's Orchestra, John McLaughlin.
Liberation Music Orchestra: 1969, arr. by Carla Bley, w. Gato Barbi-
eri, Don Cherry, Roswell Rudd, Howard Johnson, others.
Imp. AS/9183
EDMOND HALL (cl)   5/15/1901-2/12/1967
s.a. Louis Armstrong, Sidney De Paris, Vic Dickenson, Coleman Haw-
kins, Lionel Hampton.
Celestial Express: 1941-44, quartet w. Ch. Christian, Meade Lux Lewis,
Israel Crosby, All Stars w. Red Norvo, Teddy Wilson, others.
Blu. B-6505
JIM HALL (g)   12/4/1930
s.a. Bill Evans, Ella Fitzgerald, Chico Hamilton, Hampton Hawes, Lee
Konitz, Gerry Mulligan.
It's So Nice To Be With You: 1969 (trio)   BASF/MPS ST 20708
CHICO HAMILTON (d)   9/21/1921
Chico Hamilton: 1956-58, w. Buddy Collette, Jim Hall, Paul Horn,
Fred Katz, Eric Dolphy, others.   Pac. ST 20108
GUNTER HAMPEL (vib, bcl, fl p)
s.a. Don Cherry, Alexander von Schlippenbach.
Out Of New York: 1971, w. Jeanne Lee, Perry Robinson, Jack Gregg.
BASF/MPS ST 20900
Dances: 1970 (solo-LP)   Birth ST NJ 002
LIONEL HAMPTON (vib, p d, voc)   4/12/1913
s.a. Charlie Christian, Benny Goodman, "From Spirituals To Swing"
Best Records: Vols. 1 (1937-38); 2 (1938-39); 3 (1939-40), w. Chu
Berry, Charlie Christian, Coleman Hawkins, Benny Carter, Johnny
Hodges, Cootie Williams, Ziggy Elman, Jo Jones, Cozy Cole, Gene
Krupa a.m.o.   (French) RCA 730-640, 730/641, 731-048
Stardust/Just Jazz Concert: 1947, w. Charlie Shavers, Willie Smith,
Barney Kessel, Slam Stewart, a.o.   GNP Crescendo S 15
Newport Uproar!: 1967, big band with Milt Buckner, Illinois Jacquet,
Joe Newman, Alan Dawson, a.o.   RCA LSP-3891
HERBIE HANCOCK (keyboards)   4/12/1940
s.a. Miles Davis, Joe Henderson, Freddie Hubbard, Joe Zawinul.
Maiden Voyage: 1965, w. Freddie Hubbard, George Coleman, Ron
Carter, Tony Williams.   Blu. 84195
Sextant: 1973, w. Eddie Henderson, Benny Maupin, Julian Priester,
Buster Williams, Billy Hart, others.   Col. ST KC 32212
JOHN HANDY (as)   2/3/1933
see Charles Mingus
DON 'SUGAR CANE' HARRIS (viol, voc)   ·   6/18/1938
s.a. Frank Zappa, New Violin Summit
Got The Blues: 1971, Berlin Jazz Festival, w. Wolfgang Dauner,
Volker Kriegel, Terje Rypdal, Robert Wyatt, others. BASF/MPS 21283

STAN HASSELGARD (cl)   10/4/1922-11/23/1948
Jazz Classics, Vol. 4: 1947, w. Red Norvo, Barney Kessel, others.
                                                    Cap. M-11029
HAMPTON HAWES (p, e-p)   11/13/1928
All Night Session, Vol. 1: 1956, w. Jim Hall, a.o.   Cont. 7545
COLEMAN HAWKINS (ts)   11/21/1904-5/13/1969
s.a. Fletcher Henderson, Lionel Hampton, Django Reinhardt, Billie
Holiday.
Body And Soul: 1927-63, w. Fletcher Henderson Orchestra, Lionel
Hampton, Fats Navarro, Sonny Rollins, a.m.o.   RCA LPM 501
Classic Tenors: 1943, w. Eddie Heywood, Oscar Pettiford, Shelly
Manne, (Rev. Lester Young)   Fly. FD 10146
FLETCHER HENDERSON (p, arr, lead)   12/18/1898-12/29/1952
s.a. Louis Armstrong, Benny Goodman, Charlie Christian, 'From Spir-
ituals To Swing'.
First Impressions, Vol. 1: 1924-31, w. Louis Armstrong, Joe Smith,
Tommy Ladnier, Coleman Hawkins, Don Redman, Buster Bailey and
many others.   Dec. DL 79227
Swing's The Thing, Vol. 2: 1931-34, w. Henry Red Allen, Rex Stew-
art, Ben Webster, a.m.o.   Dec. DL 79228
Story: 1923-38, as above, plus Chu Berry, Roy Eldridge, Benny
Carter, Fats Waller a.m.o.   Col. C4L19 (4-LP set)
JOE HENDERSON (ts)   4/24/1937
s.a. Freddie Hubbard, Lee Konitz, Larry Young
Power To The People: 1969, w. Herbie Hancock, Mike Lawrence,
Ron Carter, Jack De Johnette   Mil. MSP 9024
JIMI HENDRIX (g, voc)   1942-9/18/1970
Electric Ladyland: 1968, w. Noel Riding, Mitch Mitchell.
                                          Rep. ST S 6307 (2-LP set)
WOODY HERMAN (cl, ss, as, voc)   5/16/1913
The Thundering Herds: 1944-48; arrs. by Ralph Burns, Neal Hef-
tin, Shorty Rodgers; w. Bill Harris, Sonny Berman, Flip Phillips, Red
Norvo, Stan Getz, Pete and Conte Candoli, Dave Tough, Chubby
Jackson, Don Lamond, a.o.   Col. C3L25 (3-LP set)
Early Autumn: 1948-50; w. Rodgers, Getz, Zoot Sims, Al Cohn,
Serge Chaloff, Red Rodney, Gene Ammons, Milt Jackson, Oscar Petti-
ford, a.m.o.   Cap. M-11034
Brand New: 1971; arr. by Alan Broadbent, w. Mike Bloomfield, a.m.o.
                                                       Fan. 8414
EARL HINES (p, ldr, voc)   12/28/1905
s.a. Louis Armstrong, Sidney Bechet
57 Varieties: 1928-33 (p-solos)   (French) CBS 63364
Grand Terrace Band: 1939-40, w. Walter Fuller, Budd Johnson, a.o.
                                                    RCA LPV-512
Fatha Blows Best: 1968, w. Buck Clayton, Budd Johnson, Bill Pem-
berton, Oliver Jackson.   Dec. 7504
The Quintessential Recording Session: 1970 (p-solo)
                                              Chiaroscuro CR 101

At Home: 1970 (p-solo)   Delmark DS 212
Quintessential Continued: 1973 (p-solo)   Chiaroscuro CR 120
ART HODES (p, ldr)   11/4/1904
s.a. Sidney Bechet
The Funky Piano of A.H.: 1944-45, w. Sandy Williams, Max Kaminsky, Mezz Mezzrow, Omer Simeon, a.o.   Blu. B-6502
JOHNNY HODGES (as, ss)   7/25/1906-5/11/1970
s.a. Duke Ellington, Lionel Hampton, Teddy Wilson, Benny Goodman, Gerry Mulligan.
Things Ain't What They Used To Be: 1940-41, w. Cootie Williams, Lawrence Brown, Harry Carney, Duke Ellington, Jimmy Blanton, Sonny Greer, Ray Nance (rev. Rex Stewart, q. v.)   RCA LPV-533
Back to Back/Side By Side: 1958-59, w. Ellington, Harry Edison, Roy Eldridge, Ben Webster, Jo Jones, a.o.   (Eng.) Verve (2-LP set)
BILLIE HOLIDAY (voc)   4/7/1915-7/17/1959
s.a. Teddy Wilson, Artie Shaw
The Golden Years, Vols. 1 & 2: 1933-42, w. Lester Young, Teddy Wilson, Buck Clayton, Roy Eldridge, Chu Berry, Ben Webster, Johnny Hodges, Buster Bailey, Red Allen, Hot Lips Page, Benny Morton, Dickie Wells, Jo Jones, Freddie Green, a.m.o.
                          Col. C3L21, C3L40 (3-LP sets)
Strange Fruit: 1939-44, w. Frankie Newton, Eddie Heywood, Sid Catlett, a.m.o.   Atlantic SD 1614
Lady In Satin: 1958, w. Ray Ellis Orch.   Col. CS 8048
JOHN LEE HOOKER
Live at Cafe Au Go-Go: 1966, w. Otis Spann, Muddy Waters, a.o.
                                        BluesWay BLS 6002
LIGHTNIN' HOPKINS (g, voc)   3/15/1912
In New York: 1960   Barnaby Z 30247
HOWLIN' WOLF (Chester Burnett) (voc, g, harm)
The London Sessions: 1971, w. Eric Clapton, Lafayette Leake, Steve Windwood, others.   Chess S 60008
FREDDIE HUBBARD (tp, fh)   4/7/1938
s.a. Art Blakey, Ornette Coleman, John Coltrane, Eric Dolphy, Herbie Hancock, Quincy Jones, Oliver Nelson.
The Hub Of Hubbard: 1969, w. Eddie Daniels, Roland Hanna, Richard Davis, Louis Hayes   BASF/MPS 20726
Red Clay: 1970, w. Joe Henderson, Herbie Hancock, Ron Carter, Lenny White   CTI 6001
BOBBY HUTCHERSON (vib)   1/27/1941
s.a. Eric Dolphy
Total Eclipse: 1966 w. Harold Land, Chick Corea, others. Blu. 84291
MAHALIA JACKSON   10/26/1911-1/27/72
see 'The Gospel Sound' Vol. 1 & 2 (anthologies)
MILT JACKSON (vib)   1/1/1923
see MJQ, Miles Davis, Sonny Rollins.
ILLINOIS JACQUET (ts)   10/31/1922
see Lionel Hampton

KEITH JARRETT (p, e-p, org, ss, steel-d) 5/8/1945
Facing You: 1971 (p-solo) ECM 1017
The Mourning Of A Star: 1971 (p-solo/trio) w. Charlie Haden, Paul Motian. Atl. SD 1596
Ruta + Daitya: 1972 (duo) with Jack De Johnette ECM 1021
THE JAZZ CRUSADERS (now The Crusaders)
Freedom Sound: w. Wayne Henderson, Wilton Felder, Joe Sample, a.o.
  Pac. ST PJ 27
THE JAZZ COMPOSER'S ORCHESTRA (JCOA)
The Jazz Composer's Orchestra: 1968, w. Cecil Taylor, Roswell Rudd, Pharaoh Sanders, Larry Coryell, a.o.; music composed by Mike Mantler. JCOA Records ST LP 1001/2 (2-LP set)
Escalator Over The Hill: 1968-71, "chronotransduction" by Carla Bley and Paul Haines; w. Gato Barbieri, Don Cherry, Charlie Haden, Roswell Rudd, John McLaughlin, Jack Bruce, Sheila Jordan, Jeanne Lee, Paul Motian a.m.o. JCOA 3LP-EOTH STEREO (3-LP set)
Liberation Music Orchestra: see Charlie Haden
Relativity Suite: see Don Cherry.
BUNK JOHNSON (co, tp) 12/27/1879-7/7/1949
s.a. Sidney Bechet
And His Superior Jazz Band: 1942, w. George Lewis, Jim Robinson, Walter Decou, others. GTJ M-12048
JAMES P. JOHNSON (p) 2/1/1891-11/17/1955
s.a. Sidney De Paris, Panassié Sessions
Father Of Stride Piano: 1923-39, p-solo, also group w. Henry Red Allen, J. C. Higginbotham, Gene Sedric, Sid Catlett, a.o.
  Col. CL 1780
J. J. JOHNSON (tb) 1/22/1924
s.a. Miles Davis, Stan Getz, Gene Krupa
J. J. Johnson: w. Kai Winding, Bill Evans, Paul Chambers, Roy Haynes.
  Imp. AS/1
The Eminent J.J.J.: 1953-54, w. Clifford Brown, Jimmy Heath, John Lewis, Kenny Clarke, others. Blu. 81505
ELVIN JONES (d) 9/9/1927
s.a. John Coltrane, Gil Evans, Joe Farrell, Roland Kirk, Albert Mangelsdorff.
Puttin' It Together: 1968, w. Jimmy Garrison, Joe Farrell.
  Blu. ST 84282
Merry-Go-Round: 1971, various groups w. Joe Farrell, Dave Liebmann, Steve Grossman, Pepper Adams, Frank Foster, Chick Corea, Jan Hammer, a.o. Blu. ST 84414
JO JONES (d) 7/10/1911
see Count Basie, Milt Buckner, Vic Dickenson.
QUINCY JONES (arr, comp, ldr., tp) 3/14/1933
Quincy Jones: 1961, big band w. Clark Terry, Thad Jones, Freddie Hubbard, Curtis Fuller, Phil Woods, Oliver Nelson, others.
  Imp. AS/11
Smackwater Jack: 1972, big band w. Hubert Laws, Freddie Hubbard,

Harry Lookofsky, a.o.   A&M 3037
THAD JONES (tp, fh)   3/28/1923
see Count Basie, Quincy Jones, Thad Jones-Mel Lewis Orchestra.
THAD JONES-MEL LEWIS ORCHESTRA
  Live At The Village Vanguard: 1967, w. Richard Williams, Bob
  Brookmeyer, Garnett Brown, Joe Farrell, Eddie Daniels, Pepper
  Adams, Roland Hanna, Richard Davis, a.o.   S-S 18016
  Monday Night: 1969, similar personnel.   S-S 18058
  Consummation: 1971, similar pers.   Blu. B ST 84346
JANIS JOPLIN (voc)   1943-10/5/1970
  Cheap Thrills: 1967, w. Big Brother & The Holding Company
                                                    Col. KC 32168
STAN KENTON (p, arr, ldr.)   2/19/1912
  The Kenton Era: 1940-54, w. Stan Getz, Kai Winding, Shelly Manne,
  Art Pepper, June Christy, Laurindo Almeida, Bud Shank, Maynard
  Ferguson, Lee Konitz, Bill Holman, Frank Rosolino, Bill Russo, Zoot
  Sims, a.m.o.   Creative World 1030 (4-LP set)
  Artistry In Jazz: 1946-65, similar personnel; Shorty Rodgers, Bill Per-
  kins, Jack Sheldon, a.m.o.   Cap. M-11072
  The Fabulous Alumni Of S.K.: 1945-56, w. Anita O'Day, Vido
  Musso, Art Pepper, Maynard Ferguson, June Christy, Lee Konitz,
  others.   Creative World 1028
  Live At Redland University: 1971, w. Quinn Davis, Richard Torres,
  Warren Gale, Dick Shearer, John Von Ohlen, a.o.
                                   Creative World ST 1015 (2-LP set)
FREDDIE KEPPARD (co)   2/15/1889-7/15/1933
  Freddie Keppard: 1924-26, various groups w. Jimmy Noone, Johnny
  Dodds, Jimmy Blythe, a.o.   (French) BYG 529075
BARNEY KESSEL (g)   10/17/1923
  see Stephane Grappelly, Lionel Hampton, Stan Hasselgard, Oscar Pe-
  terson, Ella Fitzgerald.
B. B. KING (g, voc)   9/16/1925
  Lucille: 1967, w. big band.   BluesWay BLS 6016
  Indianola Mississippi Seeds: 1970, w. big band, various groups, w.
  Leon Russell, Carole King, others.   ABC ABCS-713
ROLAND KIRK (manzello, strich, ts, fl)   8/7/1936
  s.a. Charles Mingus
  I Talk With The Spirits: 1964, w. Horace Parlan, Michael Fleming,
  Walter Perkins, a.o.   Lim. 86008
  Rip, Rig & Panic: 1965, w. Jaki Byard, Richard Davis, Elvin Jones.
                                                      Lim. 86027
  Blacknuss: 1972, various groups, w. Cornell Dupree, Bernard Purdie,
  a.o.   Atl. SD 1601
LEE KONITZ (as)   10/23/1927
  s.a. Miles Davis, Stan Kenton, Lennie Tristano, Albert Mangelsdorff,
  Gerry Mulligan.
  Ezz-thetic: 1951, w. Miles Davis, Billy Bauer, Max Roach, others.
                                                     Prest. 7827

The Lee Konitz Duets: 1967, w. Jim Hall, Joe Henderson, Karl Berger, Ray Nance, a.o. Mil. MSP 9013
ALEXIS KORNER (voc, g) 4/19/1928
Bootleg Him!: 1961-70, w. Ginger Baker, Jack Bruce, Alan Skidmore, John Surman, Peter Thorup, Robert Plant and many others.
(Germ.) Metro. DALP 2/3101 (2-LP set)
GENE KRUPA (d, ldr) 1/15/1909-10/16/1973
s.a. Benny Goodman, Lionel Hampton.
Gene Krupa, his Orchestra, and Anita O'Day: 1941-45, w. Roy Eldridge, Charlie Ventura, Don Fagerquist, Johnny Bothwell, a.m.o.
Col. KG 32663 (2-LP set)
STEVE KUHN (p) 3/24/1938
Steve Kuhn: 1971, arr. & cond. by Gary McFarland, w. Ron Carter, Billy Cobham, Airto, a.o. Buddah BDS 5098
TOMMY LADNIER (tp) 5/28/1900-6/4/1939
see *The Panassié Sessions*, Fletcher Henderson.
YUSEF LATEEF (ts, fl, bassoon, oboe, shenai) 1921
s.a. Cannonball Adderley, Les McCann.
Jazz Round The World: w. Richard Williams, Hugh Lawson, a.o.
Imp. AS/56
HUBERT LAWS (fl) 11/10/1939
s.a. Quincy Jones, Count Basie.
The Rite Of Spring: 1971, w. Bob James, Ron Carter, Jack De Johnette a.o. CTI 6012
GEORGE LEWIS (cl) 7/13/1900-12/31/1968
see Bunk Johnson.
JOHN LEWIS (p, arr) 5/3/1920
s. MJQ, Miles Davis, J. J. Johnson, Dizzy Gillespie.
ALBERT MANGELSDORFF (tb) 9/5/1928
s.a. Don Cherry, Peter Brötzmann.
And His Friends: 1967-69, duos w. Don Cherry, Elvin Jones, Karl Berger, Attila Zoller, Lee Konitz, Wolfgang Dauner.
(Germ.) BASF/MPS 20697
Never Let It End: 1970, with Heinz Sauer, Gunter Lenz, Ralf Hübner.
(Germ.) BASF/MPS 20733
Trombirds: 1973, tb-solo. (Germ.) BASF/MPS/21654
HERBIE MANN (fl) 4/16/1930
s.a. Art Blakey.
The Evolution Of Mann: 1962-68, various groups w. Bill Evans, Chick Corea, King Curtis, David Newman, Baden Powell a.o.
Atl. SD 2-300 (2-LP set)
LES McCANN (p, e-p, voc) 9/23/1935
Invitation To Openness: 1972, w. Yusef Lateef, David Spinozza, Pretty Purdie, Al Mouzon a.o. Atl. SD 1603
'BROTHER' JACK McDUFF (org) 9/17/1926
The Heating System: 1972. Cad. ST 60017 (2-LP set)
CHRIS McGREGOR (p, arr, ldr)
Brotherhood Of Breath: 1971, big band w. Dudu Pukwana, Mongezi

Feza, Alan Skidmore, John Surman, Mike Osborne, Harry Beckett
a.o.   (Engl.) RCA-NEON ST NE2
JOHN McLAUGHLIN (g)   1942
s.a. Miles Davis, Tony Williams, The Jazz Composer's Orchestra,
Wayne Shorter.
Devotion: 1969, quartet w. Larry Young (Khalid Yasin), Billy Rich,
Buddy Miles.   Douglas ST 4
My Goal's Beyond: 1971, octet w. Jerry Goodman, Dave Liebman,
Charlie Haden, Billy Cobham, others.   Douglas KC 30766
Birds Of Fire: 1972, The Mahavishnu Orchestra with Jerry Goodman,
Jan Hammer, Rick Laird, Billy Cobham.   Col. KC 31996
CARMEN McRAE (voc, p)   4/8/1922
The Great American Songbook: 1972, w. Jimmy Rowles, Joe Pass
a.o.   Atl. SD 2-904 (2-LP set)
JAY McSHANN (p, ldr)   1/12/1909
"New York-1200 Miles": 1941-43, big band feat. Charlie Parker.
                                                       Dec. 9236
CHARLES MINGUS (b, p, comp, ldr)   4/22/1922
s.a. Charlie Parker, Miles Davis, Oscar Pettiford.
Better Git It In Your Soul: 1959, w. John Handy, Booker, Ervin,
Benny Golson, Don Ellis, Horace Parlan, Roland Hanna, Dannie
Richmond, a.o.   Col. G-30561 (2-LP set)
Mingus Presents Mingus: 1960, w. Eric Dolphy, Ted Curson, Dannie
Richmond.   Barnaby Z 30561
Mingus At Monterey: 1964, w. Charles McPherson, John Handy, Jaki
Byard, Dannie Richmond a.m.o.   Fan. JWS-1/2 (2-LP set)
The Great Concert Of C.M.: Paris, 1964, w. Eric Dolphy, Johnny
Coles, Clifford Jordan, Jaki Byard, Dannie Richmond.
                                  Prest. PRST 3-4001 (3-LP set)
C.M. And Friends In Concert: 1972, orchestra w. Lonnie Hillyer,
Charles McPherson, Bobby Jones, Gerry Mulligan, Lee Konitz a.m.o.
                                  Col. KG 31614 (2-LP set)
THE MODERN JAZZ QUARTET (MJQ)
Modern Jazz Quartet: 1952-55, Milt Jackson, John Lewis, Percy
Heath, Kenny Clarke, Connie Kay   Prest. 24005 (2-LP set)
European Concert: 1960.   Atl. SD 2-603 (2-LP set)
Plastic Dreams: 1971.   Atl. SD 1589
THELONIOUS MONK (p)   10/10/1920
    s.a. Charlie Parker Miles Davis, Charlie Christian, Sonny Rollins,
Giants Of Jazz.
Solo Monk: p-solo.   Col. CS 9149
In Concert: 1959, w. Donald Byrd, Phil Woods, Charlie Rouse, Pep-
per Adams, a.o.   Riv. 673022
Thelonious Monk: 1952-54, various groups w. Art Blakey, Sonny Rol-
lins, Max Roach, Frank Foster, others.   Prest. 24006 (2-LP set)
JAMES MOODY (as, ts, fl, ss)   2/26/1925
s.a. Dizzy Gillespie

And The Brass Figures: 1965, w. Jimmy Owens, Kenny Barron, Mel Lewis a.o. Milestone MSP 9005

WES MONTGOMERY (g) 3/6/1925-1968
Movin' Wes: 1965, w. Clark Terry, Jimmy Cleveland, Urbie Green, Grady Tate, others. Verve ST V6-8610
While We're Young: 1960-61, w. Tommy Flanagan, Hank Jones a.o. Milestone 47003 (2-LP set)

JELLY ROLL MORTON (p, comp, ldr) 9/20/1885-7/10/1941
s.a. King Oliver.
Stomps And Joys: 1928-30, Red Hot Peppers w. Omer Simeon, Albert Nicholas, Wilbur De Paris, others. RCA LPV 508
The Immortal J.R.M.: 1923-25, p-solo and orchestra. Mil. MLP 2003
New Orleans Memories & Last Band Dates: 1939-40, w. Red Allen. Atl. SD-2-308 (2-LP set)

GERRY MULLIGAN (bs, p, arr, ldr) 4/6/1927
s.a. Miles Davis, Dave Brubeck, Charles Mingus.
Mulligan/Baker: 1951-53, original quartet w. Chet Baker, Carson Smith, Chico Hamilton; big band w. Allen Eager, George Wallington, others (Chet Baker, 1965) Prest. 24016 (2-LP set)
Walking Shoes: 1953, w. Baker, Bud Shank, a.o. (+ Stan Hasselgard) Cap. M-11029
Konitz Meets Mulligan: 1953, quintet w. Lee Konitz, Baker, a.o. Pac. Pj. 20142
Jazz History, Vol. 14: 1957-62, various big bands and combos, w. Bob Brookmeyer, Jim Hall, Johnny Hodges, Ben Webster a.m.o. (Germ.) Verve 2632014 (2-LP set)

FATS NAVARRO (tp) 9/24/1923-7/7/1950
s.a. Charlie Parker, Bud Powell.
Good Bait: 1948, Tadd Dameron Sextet w. Allen Eager, Kenny Clarke, others. Riv. RS 3019

OLIVER NELSON (as, ss, arr, lead) 6/4/1932
s.a. Count Basie, Quincy Jones, Leon Thomas.
Blues And The Abstract Truth: 1961, w. Eric Dolphy, Freddie Hubbard a.o. Imp. AS/5
Swiss Suite: Montreux Jazz Festival 1971, international big band w. Danny Moore, Charles Tolliver, Harry Beckett, Michal Urbaniak, Bosko Petrovic, Pretty Purdie, Na-Na, others; feat. Gato Barbieri, Eddie Cleanhead Vinson, Oliver Nelson. Fly. FD 10149

FRANKIE NEWTON (tp, arr, lead) 1/4/1906-3/11/1954
Swinging On 52nd Street: 1937-39, w. Pete Brown, Ed Hall, Buster Bailey, Ken Kersey a.o. Jazz Archives JA-9

ANITA O'DAY (voc) 12/18/1919
s.a. Gene Krupa, Stan Kenton.
In Berlin: Jazz Festival 1970, w. George Arvanitas Trio. BASF/MPS 20663

KING OLIVER (co) 5/11/1885-4/10/1938
The Immortal K.O.: 1923-24-28, w. Jelly Roll Morton; Creole Jazz

Band w. Louis Armstrong, Johnny Dodds, Honore Dutrey; Clarence
Williams Orchestra, a.o.   Mil. MLP 2006
West End Blues: 1923-28.   (French) CBS 63610
THE ORIGINAL DIXIELAND JAZZ BAND
    The O.D.J.B.: 1917-18.   RCA LPV-547
KID ORY (tb)   12/25/1886-1/23/1973
s.a. Louis Armstrong.
Tailgate: 1944, w. Mutt Carey, Omer Simeon, Buster Wilson, a.o.
    GTJ L-12022
ORAN 'HOT LIPS' PAGE (tp, voc)   12/7/1908-11/9/1954
s.a. Spirituals to Swing, Billie Holiday, Tootin' Through the Roof.
After Hours in Harlem: 1940-41, jam sessions at Minton's, etc., w.
Rudy Williams, Joe Guy, Tiny Grimes, Donald Lambert a.o.
    Onyx ORI 207
CHARLIE PARKER (as)   9/28/1920-3/12/1955
s.a. Jay McShann, Dizzy Gillespie.
Bird Symbols: 1946-47, septet w. Miles Davis, Lucky Thompson; quartet w. Erroll Garner; quintet w. Miles Davis, Max Roach, a.o.
    (French) Musidisc CV 982
Charlie Parker: 1948, quintet w. Miles Davis, Duke Jordan, Tommy
Potter, Max Roach, Red Rodney, Roy Haynes.
    Prest. 24009 (2-LP set)
Bird & Diz: 1950, quintet w. Dizzy Gillespie, Thelonious Monk, Buddy
Rich, a.o.   Verve V6-8006
The Greatest Jazz Concert Ever: Massey Hall, 1953, w. Dizzy Gillespie, Bud Powell, Charles Mingus, Max Roach (+ Bud Powell Trio).
    Prest. 24024 (2-LP set)
OSCAR PETERSON (p)   8/15/1925
s.a. Ella Fitzgerald, Stan Getz.
Action: trio w. Ray Brown, Ed Thigpen.   BASF/MPS 20668
My Favorite Instrument: p-solo.   BASF/MPS 20671
OSCAR PETTIFORD (b, cello)   9/30/1922-9/8/1960
s.a. Coleman Hawkins, Duke Ellington, Woody Herman, Bud Powell.
My Little Cello: 1953-59, sextet/trio w. Julius Watkins, Charles Mingus, a.o.   Fan. 86010
JEAN-LUC PONTY (viol)   9/29/1942
s.a. Violin Summit, New Violin Summit, Frank Zappa, George Gruntz.
Sunday Walk: 1967, quartet w. Wolfgang Dauner, Niels Henning
Orsted Pedersen, Daniel Humair.   BASF/MPS 20645
The Jean Luc Ponty Experience: 1970, quartet, w. George Duke, a.o.
    Pac. 20168
Plays The Music Of Frank Zappa: 1970, w. Frank Zappa, George
Duke, Buell Neidlinger, Ian Underwood.   Pac. 20172
BADEN POWELL (g)   8/6/1936
s.a. Herbie Mann.
Images On Guitar: 1971.   BASF/MPS 29057
BUD POWELL (p)   9/27/1924-8/1/1966
s.a. Charlie Parker, Cootie Williams.

The Amazing B.P. Vols. 1 & 2: 1949-53, w. Fats Navarro, Sonny Rollins, Roy Haynes, Max Roach, a.o.   Blu. 81503/81504
SUN RA (keyboards)
The Heliocentric Worlds Of Sun Ra, Vol. 2: 1965, Arkestra, w. Marshall Allen, Pat Patrick, John Gilmore, a.m.o.   ESP S 1017
It's After The End Of The World: 1970, live, Intergalactic Research Arkestra, personnel as above plus Danny Davis, Danny Thompson, Alan Silva, June Tyson a.m.o.   BASF/MPS 20748
OTIS REDDING (voc)   1941-1967
The Best Of O.R.: w. Booker T. And The MG's, a.o.
                                         Atl. SD 2-801 (2-LP set)
DJANGO REINHARDT (g)   1/23/1910-5/16/1953
And The American Jazz Giants: 1935-37, w. Benny Carter, Coleman Hawkins, Bill Coleman, a.o.   Prest. 7633
BUDDY RICH (d)   6/30/1917
s.a. Bunny Berigan, Tommy Dorsey, Ella Fitzgerald, Charlie Parker.
Rich In London: Live At Ronnie Scott's 1972, w. Pat LaBarbera, Bruce Paulson, Jeff Stout, a.o.   RCA LSP 4666
TERRY RILEY (comp, keyboards, ss)   1935
In C: 1964.   Col. MS 7178
A Rainbow In Curved Air: 1971.   Col. MS 7315
MAX ROACH (d)   1/10/1925
s.a. Miles Davis, Thelonious Monk, Lee Konitz, Charlie Parker, Bud Powell, Sonny Rollins.
Jazz In 3/4 Time: 1957, quintet w. Kenny Dorham, Sonny Rollins, a.o.   (Jap.) Merc. 8002
It's Time: 1961-62, w. Abbey Lincoln, Richard Williams, Julian Priester, a.o. + choir.   Imp. AS/16
SONNY ROLLINS (ts, ss)   9/7/1929
s.a. Miles Davis, Coleman Hawkins, Thelonious Monk, Bud Powell, Max Roach.
Sonny Rollins: 1951-56, w. Max Roach, Theolonious Monk, John Coltrane, Red Garland, Philly Joe Jones, Clifford Brown, Kenny Dorham, Art Blakey, Modern Jazz Quartet, a.o.   Prest. 24004 (2-LP set)
Next Album: 1972, w. George Cables, Bob Cranshaw, Jack Dc Johnette, a.o.   Mil. MSP 9042
ROSWELL RUDD (tb)
s. Archie Shepp, The Jazz Composer's Orchestra.
JIMMY RUSHING (voc)   8/26/1903-6/8/1972
s.a. Count Basie.
The You And Me That Used To Be: 1971, w. Ray Nance, Zoot Sims, Al Cohn, Budd Johnson, Mel Lewis, a.o.   RCA LSP-4566
GEORGE RUSSELL (p, comp, arr, ldr)   6/23/1923
s.a. Bill Evans.
123456extet: 1961, sextet w. Eric Dolphy, Don Ellis, Dave Baker, a.o.
                                              Riv. ST 3043
At Beethoven Hall, Vol. 1 & 2: 1965, w. Don Cherry, Bertil Loevgren, Al Heath, a.o.   (Germ.) BASF/MPS 20608/9

PEE WEE RUSSELL (cl) 3/27/1906-2/15/1969
Ask Me Now: 1965, w. Marshall Brown, a.o. Imp. AS-96
TERJE RYPDAL (g, comp) 1947
s.a. Baden-Baden Free Jazz Meeting.
Terje Rypdal: 1971, w. Jan Garbarek, Bobo Stenson, Jon Christensen,
a.o. ECM 1016
PHARAOH SANDERS (ts, ss) 10/13/1940
s.a. John Coltrane, The Jazz Composer's Orchestra.
Karma: 1969, w. Leon Thomas, James Spaulding, Julius Watkins,
Lonnie Smith, Richard Davis, Reggie Workman, a.o. Imp. AS-9181
SANTANA (leader: Carlos Santana)
Caravanserai: 1972, w. J. C. Areas, J. M. Lewis, Armando Peraza,
Mike Shrieve, Hadley Caliman, a.o. Col. KC 31610
ALEXANDER VON SCHLIPPENBACH (p, comp)
Globe Unity: 1966, orchestra, w. Manford Schoof, Peter Brötzmann,
Willem Breuker, Gunter Hampel, Karlhans Berger, a.o.
(Germ.) BASF/MPS ST 20630
ARTIE SHAW (cl, ldr) 5/23/1910
This Is A.S.: 1938-41, w. Red Allen, Benny Carter, George Auld,
Buddy Rich, Billie Holiday, Tony Pastor a.m.o.
RCA VPM-6039 (2-LP set)
WOODY SHAW (tp) 1945
s.a. Larry Young, Joe Zawinul.
Blackstone Legacy: 1970, w. Gary Bartz, Bennie Maupin, George Ca-
bles, Ron Carter, Lenny White. Cont. 7627 (2-LP set)
ARCHIE SHEPP (ts, ss) 5/24/1937
s.a. John Coltrane.
Live At The Donaueschingen Music Festival: 1967, w. Roswell Rudd,
Grachan Moncur, Jimmy Garrison, Beaver Harris. BASF/MPS 20651
Attica Blues: 1972, w. orchestra, singers, etc. Imp. AS-9222
WAYNE SHORTER (ts, ss) 8/25/1933
s.a. Art Blakey, Miles Davis, Weather Report, Joe Zawinul.
Super Nova: 1969, w. John McLaughlin, Sonny Sharrock, Miroslav
Vitous, Jack De Johnette, Chick Corea, a.o. Blu. 84332
Odyssey Of Iska: 1970, w. Dave Friedman, Ron Carter, Cecil McBee,
Billy Hart, Al Mouzon, a.o. Blu. 84363
HORACE SILVER (p) 9/2/1928
s.a. Miles Davis.
The Best Of H.S.: 1954-62, w. Kenny Dorham, Hank Mobley, Don-
ald Byrd, Blue Mitchell, Junior Cook, a.o. Blu. 84325
NINA SIMONE (voc, p) 2/21/1932
The Best Of Nina Simone. RCA LSP-4374
ZOOT SIMS (ts, ss) 10/29/1925
see Al Cohn, Woody Herman.
BESSIE SMITH (voc) 4/15/1894-9/26/1937
The World's Greatest Blues Singer: 1923/1930-33.
Col. GP 33 (2-LP set)
Any Woman's Blues: 1923-24/1929-30. Col. G 30126 (2-LP set)

The Empress: 1924-25/1927-28. Col. G 30818 (2-LP set)
Empty Bed Blues: 1924-1928. Col. G 30450 (2-LP set)
Nobody's Blues But Mine: 1925-27. Col. G 31093 (2-LP set)
(These five volumes contain Bessie Smith's recorded legacy.)
JIMMY SMITH (org, voc) 12/8/1925
Greatest Hits Vol. 1: 1956-62, w. Lou Donaldson, Kenny Burrell,
Stanley Turrentine, a.o. Blu. 83135/6 (2-LP set)
STUFF SMITH (viol) 8/14/1909-9/25/1967
see Violin Summit.
WILLIE 'THE LION' SMITH (p, voc) 11/23/1897-4/18/1973
Music On My Mind: 1966. BASF/MPS 20628
SOFT MACHINE
Third: 1970, w. Mike Ratledge, Elton Dean, Hugh Hopper, Robert
Wyatt, others. Col. G 30339 (2-LP set)
MUGGSY SPANIER (co) 11/9/1906-2/12/1967
s.a. Sidney Bechet
The Great 16: 1939, w. George Brunies, Rod Cless, Joe Bushkin a.o.
RCA LPM-1295
JEREMY STEIG (fl) 9/23/1942
Legwork: 1970, w. Sam Brown, Eddie Gomez, Don Alias.
S-S SS 18068
REX STEWART (co) 2/22/1907-9/7/1967
s.a. Duke Ellington, Fletcher Henderson.
Things Ain't What They Used To Be: 1940-41, w. Lawrence Brown,
Ben Webster, Harry Carney, Duke Ellington, Jimmy Blanton, Sonny
Greer (Rev. Johnny Hodges). RCA LPV-533
SONNY STITT (as, ts) 2/2/1924
s.a. Giants Of Jazz.
Tune-Up!: 1972, w. Barry Harris, Sam Jones, Alan Dawson.
Cobblestone 9013
JOHN SURMAN (ss, bs)
see 'The Trio,' Chris McGregor.
ART TATUM (p) 10/13/1910-11/5/1956
God Is In The House: 1940-41, private recordings. Onyx ORI 205
Solo Piano: 1949. Cap. M-11028
The Essential A.T.: 1953-56, p-solo/quartet w. Ben Webster.
Verve V6-8433
CECIL TAYLOR (p) 3/15/1933
Unit Structures: 1966 w. Jimmy Lyons, Ken McIntyre, Alan Silva,
Andrew Cyrille a.o. Blu. ST 84237
Nuits De La Fondation Maeght: 1969, w. Jimmy Lyons, Sam Rivers,
Andrew Cyrille. (French) Shandar ST 10011
Air: 1960, w. Archie Shepp, Buell Neidlinger, Dennis Charles.
Barnaby Z 30562
CLARK TERRY (tp, voc) 12/14/1920
s.a. Duke Ellington
Gingerbread Men: 1966, w. Bob Brookmeyer, Hank Jones, Bob Cranshaw, Dave Bailey. Mainstream S/6086

JACK TEAGARDEN (tb, voc)   8/20/1905-1/15/1964
s.a. Louis Armstrong, anthologies.
Jack Teagarden: 1928-57, w. Eddie Condon, Benny Goodman a.m.o.
                                                  RCA LPV-528
LEON THOMAS (voc)   10/4/1937
s.a. Pharaoh Sanders
In Berlin: Jazz Festival 1970, w. Oliver Nelson, Arthur Sterling, Gun-
ter Lenz a.o.   Fly. 10142
LUCKY THOMPSON (ts, ss)   6/16/1924
Goodbye Yesterday!: 1972, w. Cedar Walton, Larry Ridley, Billy Hig-
gins.   Groove Merchant GM 508
RALPH TOWNER (g, p)
Trios/Solos: 1973, w. Glen Moore, others.   ECM 1025
LENNIE TRISTANO (p)   3/19/1919
Crosscurrents: 1949, w. Lee Konitz, Warne Marsh, Billy Bauer, others.
                                                  Cap. M-11060
THE TRIO
The Trio: 1970, John Surman, Barre Philips, Stu Martin.
                                   (Engl.) Dawn DNLS 3006 (2-LP set)
McCOY TYNER (p)   12/11/1938
s.a. John Coltrane.
Sahara: 1972, w. Sonny Fortune, Calvin Hill, Al Mouzon.
                                                  Mil. MSP 9036
SARAH VAUGHAN (voc)   3/27/1924
1955: w. Clifford Brown, Roy Haynes, Paul Quinichette, a.o.
                                                  Trip TLP-5501
A Time In My Life: 1971, w. big band, arr. and cond. by Ernie Wilk-
ins.   Main MRL-340
JOE VENUTI (viol)   9/1/1899
s.a. Stephane Grappelly.
. . . The Daddy Of The Violin: 1973, w. Lou Stein a.o.
                                   (Germ.) BASF-MPS 2120885-0
FATS WALLER (p, org, voc)   5/21/1904-12/15/1943
s.a. Fletcher Henderson.
Valentine Stomp: 1929-36, solo, combo and big band; w. Herman Au-
trey, Gene Sedric, Al Casey. a.o.   RCA LPV-525
Smashing Thirds: 1929-37, p-solo and como w. Autrey, Sedric, Casey,
Slick Jones a.o.   RCA-LPV-550
DINAH WASHINGTON (voc)   8/29/1924-12/14/1964
Dinah Jams: 1954-55   Trip 5002
WEATHER REPORT
Sweetnighter: 1973, w. Wayne Shorter, Joe Zawinul, Miroslav Vitous,
Eric Gravatt.   Col. KC 32210
BEN WEBSTER (ts)   2/27/1909-9/20-/1973
s.a. Duke Ellington, Fletcher Henderson, Lionel Hampton, Teddy Wil-
son, Gerry Mulligan, Billie Holiday, Rex Stewart, Art Tatum.
See You At The Fair: 1964, w. Roger Kellaway, Richard Davis, a.o.
                                                  Imp. AS/65

At Work In Europe: 1969, w. Kenny Drew, a.o.

Prestige P-24031 (2-LP set)

COOTIE WILLIAMS (tp) 7/24/1908

s.a. Duke Ellington, Charlie Christian, Lionel Hampton, Teddy Wilson.
Sextet and Orchestra: 1944, w. Bud Powell, Lockjaw Davis, Cleanhead Vinson a.o. Phoenix LP-1

MARY LOU WILLIAMS (p, arr) 5/8/1910

s.a. Dizzy Gillespie.
Black Christ Of The Andes: 1963, w. Budd Johnson, Grant Green,
The George Gordon Singers, a.o. (Germ.) BASF/MPS ST 20611
From The Heart: 1971 (solo) Chiaroscuro CR 103

TONY WILLIAMS (d) 12/12/1945

s.a. Miles Davis, Eric Dolphy, Herbie Hancock.
Life Time: 1964, w. Sam Rivers, Bobby Hutcherson, Herbie Hancock,
Richard Davis, Gary Peacock. Blu. 84180
Turn It Over: 1970, w. John McLaughlin, Jack Bruce, Khalid Yasin
(Larry Young). Pol. 244021
Ego: 1971, w. Ted Dunbar, Ron Carter, Khalid Yasin, Don Alias, a.o.
Pol. 244065

TEDDY WILSON (p) 11/24/1912

s.a. Edmond Hall, Benny Goodman, Billie Holiday.
And His All Stars: 1935-40, w. Billie Holiday, Roy Eldridge, Ben
Webster, Johnny Hodges, Buster Bailey, Chu Berry, Harry Carney,
Benny Goodman, Buck Clayton, Lester Young, Cootie Williams, a.m.o.
Columbia K631617 (2-LP set)

KAI WINDING (tb) 5/18/1922

see Miles Davis, J. J. Johnson, Stan Kenton, Giants Of Jazz.

PHIL WOODS (as) 11/2/1931

s.a. Quincy Jones, Thelonius Monk.
At The Frankfurt Jazz Festival: 1970, 'European Rhythm Machine'
with Gordon Beck, Henri Texier, Daniel Humair. Embryo SD 530

THE WORLD'S GREATEST JAZZ BAND

What's New: 1971, w. Yank Lawson, Bob Haggart, Billy Butterfield,
Bob Wilber, Bud Freeman, Gus Johnson, Vic Dickenson, Ralph Sut-
ton, Lou McGarrity. Atl. SD 1582

LARRY YOUNG (Khalid Yasin) (org) 10/7/1940

s.a. John McLaughlin, Miles Davis, Tony Williams.
Unity: w. Woody Shaw, Joe Henderson, Elvin Jones. Blue. 84221

LESTER YOUNG (ts, cl) 8/27/1909-3/15/1959

s.a. Count Basie, Benny Goodman, Billie Holiday, Teddy Wilson, an-
thologies.
Classic Tenors: 1943, w. Bill Coleman, Dickie Wells, others. (Rev.
Coleman Hawkins) Fly. FD 10146
Young Lester Young: 1936-39, w. Count Basie, Buck Clayton, Jo
Jones, a.m.o. (French) CBS 65384

FRANK ZAPPA (g, comp, arr) 12/21/1940

s.a. Jean-Luc Ponty
Hot Rats: 1969, w. Sugarcane Harris, Jean-Luc Ponty, Ian Underwood,

Paul Humphrey, a.o.   Bizarre ST 6356
The Grand Wazoo: 1972, 18-piece orchestra w. George Duke, Don
Preston, Sal Marquez, Bill Byers, Ernie Watts, Ansley Dunbar a.o.
                                                    Reprise ST MS 2093
JOE ZAWINUL (keyboards)   7/7/1932
s.a. Weather Report, Cannonball Adderley, Miles Davis.
Zawinul: 1971, w. Herbie Hancock, Woody Shaw, Miroslav Vitous,
Wayne Shorter, Earl Turbington, Joe Chambers, a.o.   Atl. SD 1579
ATTILA ZOLLER   6/13/1927
s.a. Albert Mangelsdorff.
A Path Through Haze: 1971, Masahiko Sato and Attila Zoller.
                                            (Germ.) BASF/MPS 21282

INDEX

Index

445